DUSE

WILLIAM WEAVER

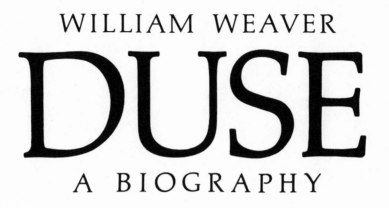

DUSE

A BIOGRAPHY

HARCOURT BRACE JOVANOVICH, PUBLISHERS
San Diego   New York   London

Requests for permission to make copies of any part of the work
should be mailed to: Permissions, Harcourt Brace Jovanovich, Publishers,
Orlando, FL 32887.

Library of Congress Cataloging in Publication Data
Weaver, William, 1923–
    Duse, a biography.

    Bibliography: p.
    Includes index.
    1. Duse, Eleonora, 1858–1924. 2. Actors — Italy —
Biography. I. Title.
PN2688.D8W4   1984   792'.028'0924 [B]   84-4600
ISBN 0-15-126690-5

Printed in the United States of America
First American Edition
A B C D E

CONTENTS

The illustrations appear between pages 160 and 193

for Harriett and John Weaver

Preface

Eleonora Duse was not even a name to me when, a number of years ago, I dropped into the Museum of Modern Art in New York to kill an afternoon in the film theatre. They were showing a program of silent movies made by once-famous stage artists. It began, as I recall, with Minnie Maddern Fiske in some costume piece. As the actress jerked and lurched about the screen, the audience began to laugh, not at the humor of the story, but at the interpreter's ludicrous antics. Then came Sarah Bernhardt, and the laughter continued. I am ashamed to say that, cruel as it was, I joined in it, even when the poor, aged, crippled actress was seen to fall, like a tree, straight forward onto a pile of cushions conveniently arranged in front of the throne (she was playing Queen Elizabeth, I believe).

Then the words *Cenere* and Eleonora Duse flashed on the screen; and the audience—including me—settled back to continue the sadistic enjoyment. But no laughter came. Even in the first scenes, when the artist—playing a young girl—kept her face hidden, there was an alert silence in the auditorium, an expectation. Then, as the same girl twenty years later, Duse revealed her crown of white hair, her worn features, and her quiet dignity; without a voice, with little assistance from others, she began to work her spell. I remember how deeply I was impressed by a single gesture: in one scene, Rosalia—Duse's character—had to leave the house; she snatched a shawl and flung it over her head with the natural movement of a peasant woman who had been putting on shawls for a lifetime, as her mother and grand-mother had worn them in lifetimes before hers. The movement was not only natural; it possessed the subtle grace and economy of certain simple, handsome objects of unsophisticated elegance.

There were defects in *Cenere*; and if we had not been subjugated by Duse's authority, we might have laughed again at the exaggerated grimaces and flailing arms of her leading man or at the too-obvious cardboard of some of the sets. But Duse's interpretation, and the authenticity of the outdoor scenes, made any cynicism impossible.

When I came out of the Museum into the New York dusk, I was still pondering the experience I had just had. Beyond the film, even beyond Duse's interpretation, I sensed the presence of a great and haunting personality, a compelling, extraordinary woman. She had been dead for decades by then. A whole generation—my generation—had grown up not knowing her. But, unaware, in succumbing to her charm, posthumously, I was simply following the example of the thousands of admirers of earlier generations who had seen and heard and worshiped her.

Not long after that, I went to Italy to study. There I felt her as a continuing presence, an ideal, a criterion. She was commemorated in almost every Italian city by a Via Duse or a Teatro Duse. There were a number of books about her, and as my grasp of the language tightened, I read many of them. I met theatre people who remembered her and spoke of her; one of my first Italian friends was named Eleonora, her grandfather, Ermete Zacconi, had on two occasions been Duse's leading man. The Italian theatre of the past—unlike Italian music and Italian literature—did not have a large gallery of heroes: Goldoni, Alfieri, Pirandello, among playwrights; Adelaide Ristori, Tommaso Salvini among players. Duse was a heroine apart.

When, in those student days in Rome, I started going to the theatre, I saw the rule to which Duse was the exception. To a great extent the repertory I saw in the early postwar years resembled the repertory of the turn of the century, Duse's heyday. I saw, for example, Marco Praga's domestic bourgeois drama, *La porta chiusa*, the last play in which Duse appeared; and even then, in 1924, she considered it hopelessly dated. I saw plays by Dumas *père* and Dumas *fils*, by Sardou, along with an assortment of translated French sentimental confections, involving blind girls and adultery and bankruptcy.

There was always one big star, Zacconi or Ruggero Ruggeri or one of the Gramatica sisters, usually surrounded by actors who were mediocre or worse. This was an unfortunate Italian tradition, from which Duse herself was not always exempt. Traditional, too, was the presence of the prompter (often audible, since rehearsals tended to be few and a company's repertory would be large). The star's appearance would inspire a welcoming applause, at which the star would step completely out of his or her part and respond with bows or "thank yous," unvoiced but easily lip-read, or even a blown kiss. Favorite scenes—a Hamlet monologue, for example—would bring cries of *bis*; and the star would graciously consent to an encore. I once heard a beloved actor recite "To be or not to be" three times, as I had heard Tito

Schipa twice repeat "Una furtiva lacrima" in *L'elisir d'amore*. And in a performance of Pirandello's *Così è se vi pare*, the actress playing the mysterious Signora, having made her exit to tumultuous approbation, actually backed onto the stage and repeated the exit.

In those immediate postwar years, there were, to be sure, new forces at work in the Italian theatre, notably men like Giorgio Strehler and Luchino Visconti. And I remember Visconti talking to me about Duse, whom he had seen as a young man. He remembered the first time: it was a performance of *The Lady from the Sea*, in Milan, in 1921. The thing that impressed Visconti, already then a theatre-goer if not yet a director, was Duse's entrance, or rather her failure to make an entrance. She was suddenly there, on stage, before you could realize how she had got there: a little, white-haired old lady, who seemed at first totally insignificant, but who seized the attention, the imagination of the public, and held it.

I was told about those last Ibsen performances by another person who had seen them, the sister of the actor Tullio Carminati, a member of Duse's troupe. Though very young, Signorina Carminati was already used to going to the theatre, and the prospect of seeing the legendary Duse had made her feverishly excited. Duse appeared and spoke her first lines. "I was dreadfully disappointed," the lady told me years later, "and I asked myself: when is she going to begin to *act*?" As the play continued, the dejected girl realized that Duse was, indeed, acting, as no one in the Italian theatre had acted before.

Duse's spell was not confined to the stage, to the actress. The private Duse could be equally compelling. The story of her life is rich in episodes of friendships forged at first sight. Succumbing to her, people of every age or station would drop everything and follow her, as they would a pied piper or a prophet. A chance encounter with a young soldier in a bookshop shaped the man's life; inspecting a house with a view to renting it, she saw a young widow's grief and, with affectionate concern, revived the woman and created a bond that continued till Duse's death. On the endless, exhausting tours which comprised much of her life, she always had some companion, part daughter, part secretary, part slave (for Duse could be a demanding, even tyrannical friend); and from the countless hotel rooms where she spent the majority of her days, she kept the lines of this network of affections under control, with frequent, scrawled letters, with telegrams and messages, flowers, presents.

Her biographers, her friends, insist that even if she had never stepped onto a stage, had never won celebrity, she would still have been an exceptional person. And she was an exceptional friend. From the accounts of her life, a complex, elusive figure emerges. Her interests were vast; she was insatiably curious about people, places, things, ideas. Each friend found her different, according to his own nature. With the literary Boito, she was literary; with the imaginative user of words, D'Annunzio, she was D'Annunzian; with the religious Edouard Schneider, she was a mystic; with the pragmatist Giovanni Papini, she was pragmatic. To her many young women friends, she was a mother; to the soldiers she wrote to during the war, she was a patriot. In these associations, Duse was not simply a mirror, reflecting the ideas of others; she was a contributor, a critic. And these were not roles; these were all genuine Duses, who, together, made up the extraordinary woman and her extraordinary life.

It was not extraordinary from the beginning. She was no Mozart, stretching his fingers for the keyboard before his eyes could look down on it. Like dozens of other Italian actors of her time, she was born poor and born to act, since it was the family trade. She could have remained poor and obscure until her death, playing tear-jerkers and scary melodramas in cold, cramped theatres in provincial towns.

Books began the process of her liberation. She read, she observed, she thought. She grew slowly as an actress; and as her genius was recognized, she could affect the theatre in which she had grown. Where did the genius come from? What made her the supreme artist and woman? No biographer can answer these questions. He can only set forth the facts, present the evidence. Duse herself holds the only key to the mystery of her personality. Insofar as possible, I have let her—and those who saw her and knew her—tell the story.

W.W.
Monte San Savino

Part One
1858–1894

1
The beginning of the road

The legends about Eleonora Duse begin with her birth. Several biographies say that she was born on a train, bound for Vigevano. The story is appropriate for this artist who spent most of her life traveling, for whom trains and hotels and ocean liners were often home for weeks and months on end. But as Camillo Antona Traversi, one of her very first biographers, pointed out, there were no trains to Vigevano in 1858. So much for that legend.

Reality is emblematic enough. She was born—as she was to die—in a hotel room, in the Albergo Cannon d'oro in Vigevano. For the Duse family, itinerant actors, this was better accommodation than they usually had and was probably an extravagance due to the Signora's pregnancy. As a rule, the little troupe had to make do with the humblest of rented rooms, whatever lodging they could afford. Actually, there is doubt that they could have afforded the train fare, even if there had been a train; some of Eleonora's earliest memories were of the jolting *carrozzone*, the wagon that carried actors and baggage, or of walking from one town to the next, clinging to her mother's hand.

The Cannon d'oro was only a short walk from Vigevano's cathedral, the imposing sixteenth-century Duomo of Sant'Ambrogio, which dominates the harmonious Renaissance square, justly the pride of the city. In the parish office, the ledgers for 1858 are still preserved, and the future actress's birth is duly recorded there. She was born at 2 a.m. on 3 October and baptized two days later, given the names Eleonora Giulia Amalia. Her father is described as a "dramatic artist," Vincenzo Duse (he was usually called Alessandro, however); and her mother Angelica Cappelletto (Duse) is misleadingly listed as "of private means." The infant's uncle, Enrico Duse, also an actor in the company, was godfather.

And immediately there is another legend. It was the custom then, in Northern Italy, to carry an infant from home to church for baptism in a little, coffin-like glass case. Some families had their own; others rented or borrowed one. Again Eleonora's early biographers tell how, as her father was leading the little family procession to the Duomo, carrying the baby in such a case, a troop of Austrian soldiers, assuming that the case housed a precious relic, came to attention and saluted. On returning to the hotel, after the sacrament had been administered, Alessandro said to his wife: "Our daughter will grow up to be somebody important, she has already received military honors."

The story is pretty, but impossible: there were no Austrian troops in Vigevano in 1858, as the town was part of the Kingdom of Sardinia and thus independent of the Austrian dominion that governed nearby Milan.

Alessandro Duse had become an actor through inheritance, as was the custom in the Italian theatre of the last century. His father, Luigi Duse, had for a time been one of the most popular and highly paid actors of his day. Born into a family of prosperous merchants in the town of Chioggia, near Venice, Luigi was meant to go into business himself. But acting, first a hobby, grew into a passion. Unwisely, his father sent him to Padua, to gain practical experience and get over his artistic notions; instead, young Luigi joined a successful company of actors and embarked on his career.

Soon he had his own theatre in Padua, the Teatro Duse. At the outset, he shone in tragic roles; then he began to specialize in Venetian comedy, both in dialect and in Italian. He played Goldoni, and interpreted the popular role of Ludro in the comedies of his contemporary Francesco Augusto Bon. He invented his own stock character (or *maschera*), the humorous Giacometto. One of the most widely performed serious dramas of the day was Casimir Delavigne's *Louis XI*; Luigi Duse invented a dialect parody, *Gigi Undese*, and triumphed. He was considered, in the field of comedy, the equal of the great Gustavo Modena in tragedy.

But success creates enemies. In the turbulent year of 1848, the year of Daniele Manin's short-lived Venetian republic, Luigi Duse was in Padua; and in his absence, his rivals at home spread rumors asserting he was disloyal to the Venetian cause. When he returned to Venice, as the theatres reopened, audiences were hostile. Embittered and impoverished, he soon retired, the Teatro Duse passed into other hands (and was renamed Teatro Garibaldi) and on 25 January 1854 he died.

His talent skipped a generation. His four sons inherited a profession, but that was about all they inherited. None of them had a brilliant career, and the rich merchant branch of the family had long since severed ties with the less respectable acting clan. Even before Luigi Duse's death, his children were on the stage. But as his fortunes ebbed, so did theirs. Alessandro and Enrico joined forces, forming one of the numerous, down-at-heel wandering companies that toured the smaller towns, played brief seasons, never arrived at such important stands as Milan or Venice or Padua, but ventured—out of necessity— as far afield as the Lombard plain, the Tuscan Alps, the Istrian peninsula.

The expression "strolling players" is misleading. It summons up, erroneously, a happy image of jolly vagabonds, companions of the open road, genial improvisers, the Crummles family in Dickens or Huck Finn's companions the Duke and the Dauphin. Reality, in the Italy of the mid-nineteenth century, was far less amusing. Most of the time, traveling players led lives of brutal poverty, homelessness, and humiliation. In his memoirs, Ermete Zacconi, Eleonora Duse's contemporary and future leading man, tells how, when he came to a town with his actor-father, the local children would call him the *fiol del sciarlatan* (literally, the "son of the charlatan"), mocking him and even beating him up. Often these ostracized "children of art" were denied schooling, and several of Italy's most famous actors grew up in near-illiteracy.

Angelica Cappelletto Duse, Eleonora's mother, may well have been illiterate herself, nothing unusual for a girl of poor family in those days; she was of peasant stock, skilled in domestic arts, of delicate constitution and sensitive spirit. When he met her, Alessandro had already begun his wandering life. Many years later, he wrote in a diary an account of that meeting. The diary is now lost, but his granddaughter, Eleonora's daughter Enrichetta, read it, and wrote down what she recalled from it. "As he was walking along the road one day, some earth, rubbish, and geranium leaves fell on him. He raised his eyes and saw that a girl was tending her flower-box, where she grew geraniums and carnations. They gazed at each other, and he took to walking along that same road every day, passing under that same window. And one day he decided to climb the many stairs and speak to her. Angelica was the twenty-first child of the Cappelletti [*sic*] family, and when a young man came to ask for her hand, the father consented, although he may not have been pleased that she wanted to marry a poor actor."

For that matter, Angelica was also poor. Still, the change from her stable home to her husband's roving life must have come as a shock. According to Enrichetta's recollection of her grandfather's diary, "She was extremely clever with her pretty hands and was an unsurpassed mender, a great asset in such a poor family. She taught her daughter that being poor and wearing old clothes did not matter, and that neat-ness and cleanliness were what was absolutely necessary, that all tears could be mended, that she was, however, never to spot her things (with grease or candle-wax, etc.). She even had an enchanting way of winding up wool into a ball—a way she also taught my mother, who could make it up into a neat ball, prettily 'dimpled' on top and bottom and beautifully wound into lines—a perfect pattern of crisscross.''

Angelica, apparently with some reluctance, took up her husband's profession. Another actress in the family meant one less share of the meager proceeds to be given to an outsider. And so Angelica became, as required, Francesca da Rimini or Mary Stuart or Pia de' Tolomei, playing opposite her husband or brother-in-law.

The performances would have continued, out of economic necessity, almost to the moment of her daughter's birth, to be resumed shortly thereafter. Angelica had little time to play with her child. Eleonora was often left alone, and she quickly learned to deal with solitude. Years later, in a letter to the writer Giovanni Papini, she said: "This way I have of talking, whether, as now, with my pencil, running on and on, or in my thoughts, is for me another inheritance bequeathed to me long ago by my Mother, who, poor dear, saw heaven only knows what magic gifts in me. . . . She was delighted when she saw how self-sufficient I was as a child, and how I used to talk to the chair, or to other objects close at hand, which for me, in their silence, contained a great enchantment—and they seemed to listen patiently to me, who demanded no answer."

Enrichetta, recording some of her mother's childhood reminiscences, wrote, "Her childhood was hard indeed, and when she talked to me about it, she used to say, that she wished no child to suffer as she had, but that it had been a wonderful school. She never went to any school, her father taught her to read and write, her mother loved her and taught her other things, and as soon as she could read well, she bought as many books as she could afford, a thing she kept up until she died."

During Eleonora's childhood, her parents managed every now and then to spend some time in Chioggia; and there the little girl learned to love the sea, the Venetian lagoon, the soft dialect. In later life she often spiced her letters and her speech with an occasional dialect word or turn of phrase. When she was depressed, she spoke of *smara*, a Venetian form of *Weltschmerz*. And, thinking back beyond the family merchants, she liked to say she came of seafaring folk.

These holidays were few. More often, the Duse company was on the road. They "had to travel about from town to town," Enrichetta recalled, and "many a time it meant walking. My mother told me how in 1866, she walked miles and miles, holding her mother's hand and holding on to her skirt. They were trying to leave the war zone, for wherever war came, the theatres were closed, and they could not work, and being workless, they often suffered hunger."

As a rule, they tried to reach a big town at fair time or on market-day, when the streets were full, and the country people would briefly leave their farms and their chores for a taste of urban life. Having sold their chickens or produce, they would have, exceptionally, some cash in their pockets and might be in a mood to spend a modest sum on a theatrical performance.

What would they see for their pennies? A company like Alessandro Duse's would have to have a large repertory, ranging from farce to tragedy, with a generous supply of popular melodramas. A typical favorite, for example, was Daubigny's *Les Deux Sergents*, in which two friends are unjustly sentenced to death but saved at the last minute by a nobleman in disguise, who also rights several other wrongs and unites a pair of lovers. Though many of the plays most frequently done were adaptations from the French, there were also some Italian works in the genre, like Paolo Giacometti's *La morte civile*, first performed in 1861. This story, of an escaped convict, believed dead, who kills himself to save the happiness of his innocent daughter, has lasted well into the TV era.

The standard repertory of the mid-nineteenth century would also include some imitations of beloved opera librettos. The spoken theatre, in fact, was the ugly stepsister of the more fashionable and glamorous lyric theatre. Even in the large cities, the opera house nightly attracted the cultivated, socially distinguished public, while the "prose" theatre (as it is called, even when the plays are in verse) played on bad nights or off seasons or in humbler houses.

Actors would also commission adaptations of familiar novels, those of Alexandre Dumas *père* or Eugène Suë, for example, or even of exotic works like *Uncle Tom's Cabin*. It was in just such an adaptation that Eleonora made her debut, in Chioggia, aged four, playing the part of Cosette in *Les Misérables*. At least, this is what most of her biographers say. But one, a mysterious C. Bullo, who seems to have been close to the Duse family, claims that her first appearance was in Trento (Trient, it would have been then), at the age of five, in a drama entitled *Corleone*. Duse herself, however, used to tell of playing Cosette and of how, to make her cry, someone in the wings took a switch to her legs before pushing her on stage. Thus she learned, early and without metaphor, that in order to entertain the public, the actor had to suffer.

A poster of the Nobile Teatro, Zara, announcing the spring season of 1863 of the company headed by Duse's uncle Enrico and Giuseppe Lagunaz, lists the five-year-old Eleonora among the actresses, along with her mother and eight others. Though her name may be there partly to swell the ranks and make the modest troupe look more impressive, she was without doubt appearing regularly on the stage by this time. When she was twelve, her mother fell ill, and Eleonora had to step into the part of Francesca da Rimini in the Silvio Pellico tragedy and that of Pia de' Tolomei in the tragedy by Carlo Marenco, dating from the 1830s. In Victor Hugo's *Angelo, tyran de Padoue* Eleonora alternated as Catarina and La Tisbe.

Alessandro Duse taught his daughter to read and write; he probably also taught her to act, in a rudimentary way. Acting was hardly considered an art at that time. If anything, it was a science, a technique; and there were standard manuals of instruction, in which the aspiring actor was told how to express this or that emotion, much as an infantryman is taught how to assemble the parts of his rifle. Widely read texts were Antonio Morrochesi's *Lezioni di declamazione e d'arte teatrale* (1832) and Alamanno Morelli's *Prontuario delle pose sceniche* (1854). The latter, a handbook of "stage poses," gives a notion of what acting of the time must have looked like. And this was probably the sort of acting that the child Eleonora saw in the family performances.

According to Morelli, *love* should be portrayed with the "head hanging somewhat towards the side of the heart; mouth slightly opened and held in a sweet smile; respiration long and subdued, broken at times by sudden sighs; a staring gaze; hands slowly joined; one arm grasped by the other person's; head resting on the other's bosom, in turn; cheek warmed by cheek; lips pressed to lips; smiling, sighing, and constantly gazing." The actor had to move about more, if he wanted to show *fury*; he was instructed to "rise, put hat on, jam it down on the head, fling it on the ground, pick it up, tear it to pieces; walk in great, awkward strides, now straight, now obliquely; hands in the hair; pull down waistcoat, button it up, unbutton it, tear it. Pause briefly, first here, then there. Strike the fist hard on the furniture; overturn chairs; break vases, dishes; strike the nape with the fist. Slam doors shut; sit down hard. Stamp the foot, wheel around, spring up again."

Acting, in short, was exterior, melodramatic, operatic. Morelli's *Prontuario* was a codification of the gestures and stage-business used by most actors and actresses, illustrious and obscure. The stagnant repertory, combined with these standardized movements, meant that a performance was a ritual. For that matter, there were few rehearsals, sometimes none at all; nor were the players expected to be word-perfect in their lines. The presence of the prompter allowed a nightly change of bill and meant also that even a child, like Eleonora, could assume a leading part on short notice. The audience accepted the prompter's voice, as it accepted the familiar costumes: the same toga would see service one night in a classical tragedy, say Alfieri's *Virginia*, and the next night in a Biblical story, like the same author's masterpiece *Saül*.

Actors played many *parts*, but they tended to stick to one *role*, a recognized, codified type. Thus an actress might be categorized as a *madre nobile*, as an actor might be the *servo sciocco*; and from play to play, she would always be a noble mother, and he, a foolish servant. And authors, usually writing for a specific cast in a repertory company, would take care to exploit the talents of the "first lover" or the comic *brillante*, as a composer would write an aria for a particularly gifted tenor or adjust his notes to the faults and virtues of a soprano.

In this world of faded velvets, threadbare canvas, rhetorical declamation and rigid movements, Eleonora grew up and took her first steps as a performer. Luigi Rasi, who in later years was a member of her company, described her acting in her adolescence as "singular, though a kind of listlessness dominated her, which showed she was bored, virtually disgusted with life. Her eye, at times, seemed to become lost in space, vague, without focus; at other times, on the contrary, she looked squarely ahead and upwards, as if expecting something from on high, something she could not clearly distinguish, but whose arrival she anticipated."

Rasi's words have the ring of romantic hindsight (when he wrote them, Duse was world-famous); but there was, indeed, a crucial event in Eleonora's career, which came to dispel that listlessness. She was fourteen; her uncle Enrico had left the family troupe; Eleonora and her father had remained with the actor Giuseppe Lagunaz in a company that now included the fairly well-known actress Celestina Paladini. It was summer, and the company was passing through Verona. Eleonora was to play Juliet, a girl of her own age, in Juliet's own city.

This performance remained in Duse's memory all her life, and she described it, on various occasions, to her friends. In 1897, she told the story to Count Giuseppe Primoli, who was preparing a long article about her for the *Revue de Paris*. Later, she repeated the story to Gabriele D'Annunzio, at the height of their love; and he used it for one of the most effective chapters of his novel *Il fuoco*, in which the protagonist, La Foscarina, is avowedly a portrait of Duse. Unfortunately, there is no documented contemporary description of that performance of *Romeo and Juliet*. Italian newspapers of a century or more ago, especially in a provincial town like Verona, seldom had drama critics. At most, the local paper would list the titles of the plays currently to be seen, sometimes announcing the arrival or departure of a company or underlining a major event, such as the appearance of Ernesto Rossi, a famous star who visited Verona at this same period with his successful *Hamlet*.

Rossi's Hamlet (and his Othello and Lear) aside, Shakespeare was still a far-from-popular author in Italian theatres. And though Duse's biographers (and, apparently, Duse herself) always insisted that the Juliet she played was Shakespeare's, it is also possible that the work performed was a *Giulietta e Romeo* by the Veronese Giuseppe Daldò, printer and autodidact, whose drama was a local favorite and was given, in that summer of 1873, by the Coltellini–Vernier company, as it was given also by other troupes.

Relying on Duse's recollection, Primoli, a quarter-century afterwards, set the scene: "A holiday, a hot afternoon. Four o'clock tolled from the Verona spire. The arena steps are filled with men in shirt-sleeves and women with red kerchiefs on their heads: four *centesimi* a seat!"

The little company was playing in the Anfiteatro, the vast Roman arena in the very heart of the city. But it was not on a great stage of the sort created in the present century for the sumptuous, internationally celebrated opera productions. In a part of the arena, a makeshift wooden construction had been set up (the local paper complained frequently about its indecent shabbiness) for "popular" theatre. The grand companies, like Ernesto Rossi's, played indoors, in the Teatro Ristori or the Filarmonico; the poorer companies, usually with a repertory of farces and melodramas, appeared in the arena from late April until autumn, weather permitting. In April the performances began at 5 in the afternoon. As spring turned to summer and the days lengthened, curtain time became slightly later. These arena-theatres existed also in other cities; where the ancient Romans had failed to provide an amphitheatre, the city fathers constructed a modern one for cheap, daytime performances of plays, or for circuses and other shows (embalmed whales were a characteristic attraction).

Not all the audience was in shirtsleeves and kerchiefs. There were *poltrone*, proper seats downstairs. But the middle-class spectators ran some risks. Just at the time when Duse was to play Juliet, the Verona paper, *L'arena*, published a denunciation of the "plebeian rascals" who threw paper darts with nails and stones from the cheap seats—the Roman steps—down on the more fashionable public.

But Duse saw and remembered none of that. As Primoli said, repeating her account, "The Veronese have turned out in a crowd: besides the feverish anticipation of theatrical emotion, these good people feel pride in imagining they are going to witness a kind of national drama, local history, the most poetic legend their city has ever illustrated.

"A shaft of sunlight illuminates the scene and casts on the daybreak of the drama that Italian radiance that the poet, with his miraculous intuition, has felt. There she is: she is Juliet in person! All her meager savings she has spent to buy some roses, some pale, delicately hued roses, flesh-colored with a pink heart. How could she play Juliet without roses in her hand? For her those roses are a talisman, a charm. . . .

"Romeo appears. Their eyes meet, and the roses tremble in Juliet's hands. One rose escapes from the bouquet and falls at her feet. . . ."

In her later career, Duse tended more and more to avoid unnecessary props or frills, to banish fussy stage business; but she retained a passion for flowers, especially roses, and whenever the text permitted, she liked to have them on stage. She was devoted to flowers offstage as well, and in one of the happiest times of her life, when she lived in the house she called La Porziuncola, the garden was filled with roses.

The performance was rapturously received, but it was not the applause that mattered to the adolescent Eleonora. She had heard it before (as she had also heard whistles and booing). When she later described the performance to her friends, she told them how she had received, in the course of it, a revelation: *la grazia* was the word she used. A kind of divine grace had descended on her; and for the first time—after almost a decade of acting—she realized what the creation of a character could be. "She had become Juliet," Primoli wrote; "she had received her revelation." Acting, now, was no longer just the family trade. It was—or it could be—an art, an ideal, something to which she could devote her life.

Tragedy on the stage was a merchandise she had often delivered, probably with that listlessness of which her colleagues complained. But she was to know tragedy also in her personal life. In the course of their travels, Angelica Duse became seriously ill, too ill to go on acting. In Ancona, she was confined to the hospital; and for a while her husband and daughter divided their time between the paupers' ward and the stage. Then the company had to move on; Angelica was left behind.

The troupe was back in Verona, and one night, 15 September 1875, at the end of the second act of the performance, Eleonora was handed a telegram, announcing Angelica's death. Of course, she finished the performance, postponing her grief until after the final curtain. She had no money to buy proper mourning, the weeds that would have been customary in Italy then. All she could do was sew a little fold of black crape to the bodice of her one dress. Some of her fellow-actresses made unkind comments, accusing her of lack of feeling. Their own insensitivity drove the already solitary girl still deeper into her solitude. Though later, in her years of fame, she was prodigal in her help to other actors and actresses in distress, she was never a *bonne collègue*; she always shunned the traditional mateyness of the stage family and chose most of her friends outside the profession.

After Angelica Duse's death, Eleonora and her father left the Lagunaz company and joined the Benincasa troupe, an even less distinguished organization. But then they moved on—with Eleonora in the role of "seconda donna"—to the company of Icilio Brunetti and Luigi Pezzana. For Eleonora, in some respects, this position was a step up. Pezzana, then in his sixties, was not only a popular actor; he was also a man of some culture (he had studied at the University of Padua) and of vast and various experience. In his long career, he had worked with many leading artists, including Adelaide Ristori, who was looked on as a national glory.

But Pezzana was vain and obstinate, and he came up against the obstinacy of his obscure but determined young actress. Fond of applause, he was willing to debase his style and repertory to seduce the public. Duse had her own ideas, so there were frequent disagreements. In the course of one of them, Pezzana is reported to have said, "Why do you insist on being an actress anyway? Can't you realize it's not for you? Choose another profession!"

Duse kept silent; but as soon as she could, she moved on to other companies, not always improving her position. Pezzana was not alone in his negative estimate of her qualities. In Trieste, in the company of Ettore Dondini and Adolfo Drago, again as seconda donna, she was such a failure that the audience rejected her outright, and she was temporarily relieved of her duties. This was a very low point in a story that, until this moment, had had few high points.

2
Seconda donna

As members of the respected Ciotti, Belli-Blanes company, Eleonora and her father arrived in Naples towards the end of 1878. At that time, the city was the largest in Italy, with a population of about half a million. Until the arrival of Garibaldi in 1860, it had been a world capital, the seat of the Kingdom of the Two Sicilies and, for centuries, popular with foreign visitors. Travelers to Naples would take apartments for the mild winter season there, pay leisurely visits to Pompeii, Herculaneum, Capri, and—the more adventurous—to Sicily. To reassure these guests from abroad there were Scottish physicians, an American dentist, Swiss-run hotels, and a branch of the London and Westminster Bank.

Though demoted from its world-capital status and depressed by the unsympathetic and uninformed administration of the new national government in Rome, Naples still maintained its gaiety, its cosmopolitan tone, its cultivated society. It was also—and had been for centuries—a theatre-loving city. The aristocracy patronized the opera at the San Carlo, but they also sponsored the legitimate theatre. Dialect comedy, a tradition that still flourishes today, was popular with the poorer, local public; the great Neapolitan comic actors, Antonio Petito and the rising young Eduardo Scarpetta, attracted also more sophisticated audiences.

The Ciotti, Belli-Blanes company was playing at the Teatro dei Fiorentini, the city's leading legitimate theatre, described by *Murray's Guide* (1873) as "very popular"; it was also considerably run-down.

As in the smaller cities, the company had a sizable repertory in Naples, so that the bill could be changed every night, and only the more successful offerings were repeated. The two actor-managers and their leading lady, Giulia Gritti, had an eye out for newer works, and one of the plays they put on in Naples was Emile Augier's *Les Four-chambault*, fresh from its success (on 8 April 1878) at the Comédie Française in Paris. Despite its novelty, this Naples presentation was not the play's Italian premiere; another company, the Paolo Ferrari-Pietroboni troupe, had already translated and played it. But exclusive rights were practically unknown, and often rival companies would present the same play on the same night.

Les Fourchambault is a play about money, false bourgeois morality, and true innocence. The heroine, Maria—or Maia, as she is called—was created by Sophie Croizette in Paris. She is a waif-like, exotic creature, a sort of poor relation in a vulgar, nouveau-riche family. She is not the absolute protagonist of the play, which has other meaty parts (the great Coquelin created one); but she is the moral focus of the story, and the solving of her situation is the pivot around which the elaborate plot revolves. In Naples, la Gritti was naturally given the part. In the best theatrical tradition, however, she fell ill; and Eleonora, the seconda donna, took over.

In the audience that evening was the actor Giovanni Emanuel, only thirty-one years old but already well established. Duse's performance made a deep impression on him, perhaps because of its unusual restraint (and, it must be said, Maia might have been written for the elusive Eleonora). Emanuel too was considered a "modern" actor, regarded with suspicion by many of his older colleagues.

At that time, the Teatro dei Fiorentini was changing hands. It had been bought by the Principe Don Baldassare Caracciolo di Santobuono, and his Principessa was taking over the direction. In *L'omnibus* for 7 January 1879, a news item read: "At the Fiorentini, for the Lenten season, there will be many changes. The Principessa owner will form a company with la Pezzana, who will be joined by Emanuel . . . The whole theatre will be restored; the stairways will be made of marble; the gilt decorations will be redone; the seats will be made wider (unbearable as they are now)." The author of the article then went on to advise the new management firmly against the use of gas light ("a constant danger with heat and stink").

Another writer records that, under the new management, the Fiorentini became "a genuine, most elegant meeting-place for society. The second-tier box—letter A—of the Duchessa di Casteldisangro, daughter-in-law of the Principe di Santobuono, was a little salon."

Emanuel, after seeing Eleonora in *Les Fourchambault*, recommended her to the Principessa; and so, on 24 January 1879, when the prospectus of the company was published in *L'omnibus*, both Duses were included in the company, which numbered fourteen women and sixteen men. The repertory promised fifty-nine new productions, with works by Sardou, Meilhac, Legouvé, Augier, Pailleron, and the Italians Marenco, Torelli, Ferrari, among others. The prima donna was Giacinta Pezzana (no relation to Eleonora's previous manager, the hostile Luigi), who was to be a catalyst in the creation of "la Duse."

On 15 March 1879, the Principessa gave a big party in the restored theatre for its subscribers, with ices and dancing and gate-crashers. The following night came the grand opening: *La Dame aux camélias*, by Alexandre Dumas *fils*. The anonymous reviewer of *L'omnibus* had favorable words for Giacinta Pezzana, found Emanuel miscast, and made no mention of the others.

Meanwhile, the Belli-Blanes company and la Gritti had moved to the Teatro Sannazaro, a new house inaugurated in 1875; and there was open, fierce rivalry between the two troupes. The critic of *L'omnibus*—perhaps because the Principessa, disregarding his advice, had installed gas illumination at the Fiorentini—sided, more or less covertly, with the opposition. Sometimes, as was the custom, the two companies competed with the same play. One of these was *Hamlet*, which drew a huge audience to the Fiorentini (the theatre had been suffering a series of near-empty houses).

On 5 April 1879, the national theatrical paper, *L'arte drammatica*, reported: "Eleonora Duse was as ideal as a vision, courtly as a princess, sweet as a maiden, beautiful as Ophelia. She was Ophelia!" In the fourth act, after her final scene, she was called out five times. A few weeks later, she played Elettra in the *Oreste* of Alfieri, and the critic of the *Corriere del mattino* (probably Federigo Verdinois) wrote: "Signorina Duse was applauded. To win applause, to win attention, with la Pezzana, Emanuel, Maieroni, veteran and strong artists, cannot have been easy. But she succeeded, thanks to the great love she brings to her art, her . . . intelligence, her spontaneous, candid but effective feeling."

Another critic of the same performance said that on Duse's appearance "a wave of poetry uplifted the mediocre acting of her companions." The adjective "mediocre" applied to the rest of the company seems surprising, especially considering the presence of Giacinta Pezzana. This artist was widely admired for her impeccable diction and her beautiful voice, as well as for her patriotism (she was a devout Mazzinian). Undisciplined but generous, she was never in the strict sense Duse's teacher, but she was surely a stimulus; and her self-confidence, her disregard for convention, may also have influenced the shy, lonely younger actress.

In Italy the legitimate theatre was culturally retarded, lagging behind other branches of literature; but there was already some debate, in the latter part of the century, about realism, or more specifically, about naturalism. The name of Emile Zola was frequently seen in print. Literary news from France traveled fast; French works were translated promptly (the *Corriere del mattino* was running, at that time, a serialization of Zola's *Le Ventre de Paris*). And so when Zola's 1867 novel *Thérèse Raquin* was dramatized and staged in Paris in 1873, though it was not a success, an Italian version was immediately prepared by the Turin critic Vittorio Bersezio. In 1879 it was still a novelty for Naples, and when it was announced by the company at the Fiorentini, expectation was high.

During rehearsals—for, unlike the itinerant troupes of Eleonora's childhood, this serious company of Pezzana and Emanuel *did* rehearse—she seemed subdued, excessively understated, as if intimidated by the presence of Pezzana in the powerful part of the mother-in-law. But on opening night, 26 July, Duse blazed forth. Giuseppe Primoli—a friend of Zola and later to become a friend of Duse—had gone to Naples for the occasion. In his 1897 article, already quoted, he recalled: "In the great scene between the two women, Eleonora, overwhelmed by her passion, dared raise her head and confront the other: she felt then that la Pezzana was staring at her with her lioness's eyes, apparently feeling more pleasure than envy. . . . Zola would have been pleased. Looking each other in the eye, foaming at the mouth, they were sublime."

A Neapolitan critic, Edoardo Boutet, wrote: "The triumph of that evening cannot be forgotten. I see her in her short, black dress, leaning against the window, with an absent air, living in falsehood, guilt, crime, alarm, terror, disgust, hatred. . . . In the last act, when love has turned into fierce hatred, and the paralytic mother smiles mercilessly at the torment of the guilty couple—we trembled, a shudder ran through our body, and with our spirit subdued we had not even the courage to applaud. The old doorman of the Teatro de' Fiorentini that evening said to me: 'Signurì, chesta è essa!' [Sir, she is it!]"

The *Corriere del mattino* was less uncritical and said: "The sweet nature of the actress does not allow her, as it should, that vulgar note that is often dominant in Thérèse's character. So the acting, while it never lacks truth, surely loses effectiveness." Still, at the end of the article, the critic referred to Duse as a rising star.

As Naples was a city of theatres, so it was a city of newspapers. And among these the *Corriere del mattino* was the newest and the most enterprising. Its founder and editor was the thirty-eight-year-old Martino Cafiero, who collected around him a whole group of lively young writers. Besides Verdinois, who wrote about theatre and translated from several languages, Cafiero encouraged the future playwright Roberto Bracco, and, at the time of Duse's appearances in Naples, a young telegraph operator named Matilde Serao, already a budding writer and a future leader of Neapolitan—and Italian—journalism and cultural life, who became Duse's lifelong friend.

Cafiero was a passionate theatre-goer and, what is more, a *tombeur de femmes*, a stage-door Johnny. Somehow he met Eleonora, and the encounter was fatal. By all accounts, Cafiero was a man of taste, elegant, polyglot (he also translated from the French), a man of the world. He wrote and published in his paper sophisticated stories, in a vein later mined with genius by Gabriele D'Annunzio, of society ladies abandoned by their lovers. He was at home in the fashionable yachting-clubs along the sea-front, ready to fight a duel—as he did with a member of Parliament—if the social code required it; and ready, also in the best Neapolitan style, to pursue a young actress, even if she were not the conventional, voluptuous beauty then in vogue.

So he pursued and won Eleonora. She had lived her whole life in the theatre, notorious—and not without reason—for its relaxed morality; and yet, going her solitary way, she had preserved an unusual innocence. On the stage, and in the books she devoured constantly, she learned about adultery, murder, immorality of every description; and she was often called upon to play sinners, even criminals. But in the real world, of which she knew surprisingly little, she was remarkably unsophisticated.

It is easy to imagine the Naples—the world—that the brilliant Cafiero revealed to her, in that seductive late summer and autumn of 1879: carriage rides along the Riviera di Chiaja past the Aquarium and the Villa Pignatelli, instructive visits to the rich museum, ices at the Gran Caffè del Palazzo ("handsomely fitted up," Murray says). And, no doubt, there were visits to the offices of the newspaper, virtually a literary club, where the contributors gathered in the evening to discuss the cultural and political events of the day, and perhaps the juiciest morsels of Neapolitan gossip. All her life, Eleonora had loved, almost worshiped books; now she was actually meeting writers, forming intellectual friendships, as she would continue to do always.

Meanwhile Eleonora's career took another turn. At the end of the financially unsuccessful first season of the Principessa di Santobuono's management at the Fiorentini, the mercurial Emanuel quit the company. Out of loyalty, Eleonora also resigned (and her father, now little more than an appendage, obviously did the same).

Giacinta Pezzana had already announced that, for the coming season, she would be joining the company of Cesare Rossi. The Duses were then engaged by Rossi as well. Father and daughter were to receive an annual 7,250 lire, an average salary. The actor Claudio Leigheb and his wife Teresa, both well established, were paid 12,000, while the leading man, Flavio Andò, received half that. The young character actor Tebaldo Checchi, who had also been in the Emanuel company, was given 4,600.

Rossi had made an offer to the city authorities of Turin, to take over the historic Teatro Carignano, municipal property. In addition to an annual rent of 3,000 lire, Rossi had to guarantee that he would bring a first-rate company and a select repertory. His was not the only bid: another impresario had offered even more, but was rejected because he planned a season of operetta and popular drama. The city was concerned for the decorum of the Carignano, the lovely eighteenth-century house where, a century earlier, Alfieri had made his debut as a dramatist.

The Duses had to leave Naples. At the station Eleonora was expecting Cafiero to come and see her off; he failed to appear. Nor, in the weeks that followed, did he come north to join her. Her entreaties were increasingly desperate, because she had discovered she was pregnant. Finally, he agreed to meet her in Rome; and she made the long journey there from Turin. Their meeting, in a hotel room, shocked and revolted her. It is not clear exactly what happened (he may have proposed an abortion), but it is certain that he refused to marry her. He may also have wanted to exploit her physical presence and the hotel room.

In any case, she rushed from the hotel and wandered the streets until she could take the train—third class, as always—and return to Turin. Commendatore Rossi, a kindly and experienced man, granted her the necessary leave. Some writers have implied that Rossi himself took a more than comradely interest in Eleonora, but she always denied this; and their surviving correspondence lends no support to the charge.

Marina di Pisa was a simple fishing village on the Tuscan coast, which was then quite different from the string of seaside resorts it is today. Eleonora is said to have gone there to await the birth of the child conceived in Naples. When the child, a boy, was born, he was frail and apparently survived only a few days. There is no record of his birth, baptism, death, or burial in the archives of Marina di Pisa or of the Pisa Archbishopric. Even the boy's name is unknown. Matilde Serao was with Eleonora during the ordeal. When the child was buried, Eleonora took the train back to Turin, to work.

3
Prima donna

Turin, at the beginning of the 1880s, had a population of about 240,000; in other words, it was less than half the size of Naples. But it was different also for other reasons. Like Naples, it had once been an important capital; but the rulers of the Kingdom of Sardinia, the House of Savoy, had been more bigoted even than the Bourbons of Naples, and less pleasure-loving. They had scant interest in the arts; and the Torinesi had a reputation for being conservative, narrow-minded, and, worse, indifferent to the theatre. A writer of the period said: "All these people, since the puppeteers and jugglers were removed from Piazza Castello and Piazza San Carlo, no longer frequent public places. . . . In the evening they remain decently in the bosom of the family, and so divide their time among home, work and church, considering themselves fortunate to be able to follow all the novenas, the tridua, the Forty Hours. . . . If conversation turns to the theatre, everything begins and ends with the Compagnia Reale, *et tantum sufficit.*"

The Compagnia Reale Sarda, a government-subsidized repertory company, had existed in Turin between 1821 and 1852 and had boasted the presence of such famous actresses as Carlotta Marchionni first, and Adelaide Ristori later. But, in fact, it was no more than another dramatic troupe—somewhat timid in its repertory—until, after its support was withdrawn and it disbanded, it became another bit of local lore, like the risottos that Prime Minister Cavour ate at the Ristorante Cambio.

Duse appeared at the Carignano on the Rossi company's opening night, 28 March 1880, in a secondary part in *Marianna* by Paolo Ferrari. Then she seems to have been absent for about a month (this was probably the time of the child's birth and death). By 22 April she was back, playing the role of Bona in *Il conte rosso*, a new verse drama by the thirty-two-year-old Piedmontese writer, Giuseppe Giacosa. The premiere coincided with the 4th National Exposition of Fine Arts, a grand event; and the drama—about a Savoy monarch—was festively received, except by the author, who wrote to his friend Arrigo Boito, three days after the opening: "Between ourselves, it was acted barbarously, so that it wasn't even worth hearing to the end." And he called the Rossi company a "pack of dogs." Soon both Giacosa and Boito were to be important figures in Eleonora's life.

After six performances, while the Exposition was still bringing crowds to Turin, Rossi presented another work by a living Italian, *La sposa di Menecle*, by the left-wing member of Parliament Felice Cavallotti, an ex-*Garibaldino*. Again Eleonora appeared and was well received, though her acting was dutiful, without spark. Still, her position in the company was about to improve.

On 12 December 1880, Alessandro Duse wrote to his brother Enrico: "I must tell you that I am staying on with Rossi for the coming year and that my daughter will change her role [i.e., to prima donna], but the pay will be the same as last year. This will serve to launch her career. Now for Eleonora a new fate is in store; with that Neapolitan rogue it's all over. She seems, however, to want to marry. When I know something definite, I'll send you word. When you write me it's best not to refer to you know what, because Eleonora believes I have told you nothing; otherwise she would take it badly. I too am awaiting the happy outcome, so the poor girl will not remain alone in this *dog* of a world. . . . My daughter nearly died; she can thank her guardian angel. She is recovering, and I hope (though she is very run down) that she can preserve her health. . . ."

Though Rossi's repertory, despite his obligation to the city authorities, was not particularly interesting or noble, Eleonora seemed to regain an interest in her work, as she regained her health. On 4 February 1881, for her "serata d'onore" (a customary special performance to honor a company star, who received all or a large part of the box office receipts) she played a comedy by Romolo Monti, *Il cavallo di Troia*, and two other short pieces, and was rewarded with flowers and cheers. A week later, she starred in *Divorçons*, by Victorien Sardou and Emile de Najac, a brand-new importation from Paris. *La gazzetta piemontese* wrote: "Signorina Duse revealed herself to be an enchanting artist."

A week later, Giacinta Pezzana's "serata" was a flop. In this case Pezzana had chosen a risky work, *La Princesse de Bagdad* by Dumas *fils*, which had been a failure at its Paris premiere, only a few weeks before. On the night of Pezzana's attempt, her rival Adelaide Tessero appeared in the same play at the Teatro Gerbino in Turin. She was received just as coldly. Pezzana had already decided to leave the Rossi company, complaining of the "vulgarity" of the audience; and the audience paid her back. On 1 March, Rossi and company left Turin—without Giacinta Pezzana—and Duse soon changed her role, to "prima donna".

After the Parisian failure of his play, Dumas *fils* appealed to his friend Count Giuseppe Primoli in Rome. Half-French (his mother was a Bonaparte), half-Italian, "Gégé" Primoli served as a kind of liaison officer between French and Italian culture. His Roman palazzo (now the Napoleonic Museum and the Fondazione Primoli) played host to visiting French artists, who met their Italian colleagues there. Evidently, despite the fiasco in Paris, Dumas was hoping his friend could give the play a push in Italy. "Croizette [who had played the protagonist] was absolutely admirable," the dramatist wrote; "I believe you must find in some beautiful and impassioned Italian girl the equivalent of our Parisienne, since the role particularly requires nature and temperament."

In May, when the Rossi company was in Rome, Duse persuaded Rossi to let her essay the part in which Pezzana had come to grief. The result—as Primoli immediately wrote Dumas—was a complete triumph. "It had been presented to us over a month ago by some mediocre players, so a young actress yesterday imposed it on the most recalcitrant audience and forced them to bow before your work and applaud with enthusiasm your boldest strokes."

Primoli was particularly impressed with Duse's performance in the last scene: "As for the denouement, she was such a lioness and such a mother that her fury and sobs prevented the public from being astonished, even for a moment, by the unexpected change of heart; and imitating the example of Comte de Hun, they would have fallen at Lionnette's feet in a body. She emphasized her three words 'I swear it!' with such authentic feeling that even the most suspicious and least loving husband could not fail to be taken in; and, in addition, her final reiteration of her solemn oath was accompanied by a gesture that—although not specified in the printed text—greatly enhanced the effect, for it must have been in your mind. In rising, she took her child, whom she placed between herself and Jean, who was still uncertain; and looking her husband straight in the face she swore on the head of her child."

Soon Primoli and Duse were friends, and through him, the actress came to be a prized interpreter of Dumas.

Also in May, from Rome, Alessandro Duse wrote a newsy letter to his brother, in which he boasted, "My daughter is marching on the road of artistic glory, but it is a path strewn also with thorns, and where women beginning in the art all have an uncle or a cousin who sets them up in a luxury that is certainly none too *pure*." Since Enrico usually wrote asking for money, Alessandro thought it wise to hedge his boasts: "I conclude by saying that my daughter has many debts to pay, if God gives her health, and that she has no money, and I less than she. Rossi gives me the same pay as last year. . . . So you see, our condition for the present is not too rich. Prima donna! Together with another prima donna—she is la Paladini, wife of Andò, the leading man—who, not doing a thing, makes them pay her very handsomely. That's luck for you! And if my daughter had not got ahead in her art through her talent she would have been *crushed*. If she has gained a position she owes it only to her merit. . . . You know what I pay for lodging in Rome: 150 lire a month! . . . Rossi is not doing good business here in Rome, though there is much applause. . . . I must add that, since she has reached her majority, my daughter is already independent. She is the prima donna, receives her pay, spends, keeps accounts, runs the house, buys . . . in short, I no longer command."

The result of this was that, in the future, Enrico wrote his begging letters directly to his niece.

In Alessandro's earlier letter, the references to Eleonora's thoughts of marriage were probably inspired by the persistent courtship of another member of the company, Tebaldo Checchi (his real surname was Marchetti). He had also been a member of the Naples troupe, and had known Eleonora during the time of her unhappy love-affair with Cafiero. Though he was not a star, Tebaldo was a respected artist; he even occasionally wrote little pieces that were acted on benefit nights. Luigi Rasi summed up his gifts in these terms: "A leading character actor, notable for his correct diction and aristocratic bearing, his uncommon intelligence and culture." At thirty-seven, Tebaldo had just about reached the peak of his career: without any aspirations to being a leading man, he had a solid position, lived carefully, saved money. He was devoted to Eleonora, appreciated her talent; and to her—disillusioned, tormented by debts and ill-health—he must have seemed a welcome port in the storm; they became lovers and soon married.

As Tebaldo recalled this period a few years later in a letter to a friend: "When la Duse was engaged by Rossi and joined our company, I was promptly led to feel affection for her, seeing her so alone, so sad, with an impossible father, fighting poverty." Tebaldo's disapproval of Alessandro may have been prompted by the old man's incapacity as an actor and breadwinner; for the rest, he sounds like a sweet and loving father, and Eleonora was devoted to him.

"I paid her court," Tebaldo's letter continues, "and fell seriously in love, for the first time in my life. I proposed marriage to her, and she accepted with enthusiasm. I paid all her debts, bought her a lady's wardrobe, and began that constant, assiduous, unremitting work with her that was meant to bring her, as it did, quickly to the position she now occupies. I fought against all the difficulties, even against death, from which I wrested her fully three times. I made her life easy, serene. She had to concern herself only with her art; all the troubles, all the headaches were for me. What can humanly be done to make a woman happy, I did; and I did it with love."

Tebaldo's claim to have made Eleonora into the great actress she became may have some justification: she was quick to learn from anyone who could teach her, and especially from fellow-actors. But he was not her only teacher, then or later. Matilde Serao—who came from Naples to Florence to be a witness at Eleonora's wedding, on 7 September 1881—was another; and so was Count Primoli, with whom a friendship was already developing. In Eleonora's subsequent visits to Rome over the next few years, the Count and his fashionable circle were to form the core of the actress's large following of admirers.

On 4 November 1881, the *Gazzetta piemontese* announced that the Rossi troupe—its official title was Compagnia della Città di Torino—was back at the Carignano, where it had opened the previous evening with a double bill of works by Edouard Pailleron (*Le Monde où l'on s'amuse*) and Carlo Goldoni (*Le gelosie di Lindoro*), both starring the new prima donna, who was warmly welcomed and was applauded even more enthusiastically on 5 November, when she performed *La Princesse de Bagdad*. She was "truly splendid," the *Gazzetta* said.

"The great Rossi has a large deficit," Alessandro Duse wrote to his brother, "but since he has a *reserve*, he is holding on, waiting for good times. He is a shrewd speculator, but in Turin his star has waned (this is between ourselves). Eleonora is well. I showed her your letter, but now she is taken up by her husband and the heir to the throne, who will not keep us waiting much longer. Today is her benefit [one word illegible], and many boxes are sold. She works, toils, and if her health assists her, she will have a fine career. The Role [prima donna], so debated, so envied, she has; her hostile rivals have been routed, or are at her feet. . . . She triumphs, but through artistic worth, not other means. Signor Tebaldo Checchi loves her very much and devotes himself entirely to her, providing her with every luxury for the stage. . . . Next year we are again with Rossi, then the contract will have to be renewed, on fairer terms . . . or else . . . Here in Turin we have every sort of entertainment, and all the theatres are well attended except ours. Let us hope for some new production that may have a success."

The new production, that month, was Achille Torelli's *Scrollina*, a bitter-sweet comedy which had had its premiere, in Bologna, only a few months previously. Though her pregnancy was far advanced, Eleonora played the title role, and won the public's admiration, even if she did not raise the fortunes of the company. She continued acting— on 21 December she participated in Tebaldo's "serata"—until a fortnight before the birth of the heir.

Who proved to be the heiress. On 7 January 1882, Enrichetta was born. Some years later, Theobaldo (as he signed himself by then) recalled the event in a letter to her: "It is half past two in the morning, the very moment when you came into the world, in a lovely, bright room in the Casa delle Colonne at 15 Via Oporto, in Turin. I was the first to hold you in my arms, and I covered you with kisses, weeping, as you screamed and wriggled."

Outside the little family, Tebaldo's life was not easy. Envious members of the troupe accused him, openly or in hints, of marrying out of interest, hitching his wagon to a star (the very star against whom they had advised him before the marriage). Matilde Serao, who was on his side, recalled afterwards: "How much vituperation, in whispers, of Tebaldo Checchi because of his marriage. In whispers: *brute of a speculator*! Aloud: *husband of the leading lady*! He knew and saw everything, and shrugged and laughed them off. Yes, he was the husband of the leading lady; but he was also the watchful guard of this most elect creature, defending her against all mortal annoyance."

Tebaldo could not defend her, however, against the annoyance of her colleagues who, after slandering him behind his back, went to Eleonora with the same insinuations: that he was exploiting her or—for her more irritating—that it was his influence with the newspapers that was making her career.

After Enrichetta's birth, Eleonora was gravely ill—this is one of the bouts with death that Tebaldo mentions—and it was some weeks before she could return to the stage. Meanwhile, the baby was taken to the village of Leinì, a short distance from Turin, and left with a peasant wet-nurse and her family, who would care for her while Eleonora regained her health and resumed work.

While she was still resting, an extraordinary theatrical event took place. Sarah Bernhardt, on a European tour, decided to give a few performances in Turin, and Cesare Rossi ceded the Teatro Carignano to her. At the age of thirty-seven, Sarah was an international star, with all the allure of a great diva. Her arrival—complete with entourage of admirers and pets—brought a gust of new, exotic life to the old theatre. The leading lady's dressing room, which Eleonora had vacated, was filled with Sarah's belongings and soon became an elegant salon. In spite of raised prices, the theatre was packed; the audiences included many writers and artists, as well as members of the royal family and the local aristocracy.

On opening night, 25 February 1882, she played *La Dame aux camélias*. During the first act, there was a trivial accident: a paper door was torn; and when Sarah came out for her calls, she angrily ripped away another piece of it. This only endeared her further to the public, who gave her an ovation. Cesare Rossi gave her a gold-and-silver lyre, studded with gems.

Her repertory included *Le Sphinx* by Octave Feuillet, *Adrienne Lecouvreur* by Eugène Scribe and Ernest Legouvé, and *Frou-frou* by Henri Meilhac and Ludovic Halévy. Sarah herself apart, the company was judged mediocre or worse; but Eleonora did not miss a performance, ill as she yet was. And when Sarah had gone, Eleonora recalled later, "As a great ship leaves behind it—how do you say it? a wake?—yes, a wake—for a long time the atmosphere of the old theatre remained what she had brought to it. Only she was spoken of in the city, the salons, the theatre. One woman had done that! And, as a reaction, I felt liberated, I felt I had the right to do what I wanted, something other than what was imposed on me. . . . I went every evening to hear her and to weep!"

Sarah's tour was being managed by the colorful Dutch impresario José Schurmann. While all other eyes were on the stage, he took time to study the Carignano audience. In it, he wrote later, he noted "a dark young girl, her hair badly coiffed, the purest Italian type, not beautiful but with an extremely mobile face, which, in the grip of an emotion, almost became beautiful." He enquired about her and learned that she was considered very ambitious, "but with that physique, I do not believe she will ever have a success in the theatre."

To Schurmann, to any theatre professional, and even to laymen, there would have seemed to be an abyss between the glamorous, flamboyant Sarah and the reserved, apparently insignificant Eleonora; and indeed there was. But the older actress's achievement had inspired the younger. When Sarah went off again, with her lion cub and her young Greek husband, Eleonora's determination was reinforced. She is quoted as having said: "Here is a woman who uplifts the profession, who induces the crowd to a respect for the beautiful, leads it to bow before art."

Sarah's last performance—*Frou-frou*—took place on 25 February. On the 26th the Rossi company was back in the Carignano, and the following evening Eleonora appeared, in *Divorçons*, after over two months' absence. "The greeting," according to the *Gazetta*, "was long, warm, heartfelt, and must have shown the lovely artist once again how much friendship and affection the Turin public feels for her." For the rest of the season, she appeared in her familiar parts; then the company set off on tour in early April.

Her health was still uncertain, and for a part of that summer of 1882, she went to the seaside—curiously, despite its sad memories, to Marina di Pisa—and rested. There she was visited by the drama critic Antonio Fiacchi, who interviewed her for the journal *Il piccolo Faust*. After receiving reassurances about her health, he discussed acting with her. Though her great international celebrity still lay in the future, she was already consciously forging her individual, controversial style.

"A part of the public does not yet accept me as I wish to be accepted," the young prima donna declared, "because I do things in my own way: I mean, in the way I feel them. It is established that in certain situations the voice must be raised, one must carry on outrageously; and I, on the contrary, when I must express violent passion, when my spirit is gripped by pleasure or sorrow, often fall mute, and on stage I speak softly, barely murmuring. . . . Then certain people say I have no expression, that I do not feel, do not suffer. . . . Ah, but . . . they will come."

At the end of that summer Rossi's company was in Rome, at the Teatro Valle; and Eleonora was already beginning the task of renewing her repertory (and invading Sarah's more boldly). On 28 October, she wrote to the impresario-editor Ernesto Somigli, in Florence: "I have played 7 *Odettes*, 4 *Frou-frous*, 2 *Dames aux Camélias*, 2 *Fernandes*, 3 *Scrollinas*, and, as of today, 6 *Femmes de Claude*."

Of these heroines, only one—Scrollina—was Italian. The part of Marguerite Gautier in *La Dame aux camélias* was new for Eleonora, a brave choice, since the work was already familiar to Italian audiences through the interpretation of a number of stars. Apart from Sarah herself (whose Italian appearances had been few at that time), the part had been played by the frail Clementina Cazzola (who died of consumption in real life), and by the passionate Fanny Sadowsky (who, in Naples, kissed her Armand so realistically that she was fined for immorality). But Duse, as she said, interpreted the heroine in her own way. Luigi Pirandello, who saw her in the play early in her career, wrote that anyone who had the good fortune to see her, "still young, but already at the peak of her art, playing the part of Marguerite in *La Dame aux camélias*, will never forget the romantic spell, the secret sweetness, and the overwhelming passion that she was capable of expressing in that part."

During the 1882 season in Rome, she was also preparing another Dumas part, which represented a different sort of challenge: Lydie, in *Une Visite de noces*. This one-act play, first given in October 1871, was famous for the interpretation of its creator, Aimée Desclée, whose brief and tragic life—she had died in 1874 at the age of thirty-seven—had made her a legend. In Italy, Fanny Sadowsky had triumphed in the part, and though Sarah Bernhardt had not played it there, the Italians knew of her success as Lydie.

Eleonora studied the part all summer, making copious annotations on her script. She was already—as she was to remain—her own director. The trickiest line was a single word—or ejaculation—"Pouah," with which Lydie expresses her disgust with her now-married lover, who has proposed a resumption of their relations. In the margin of the text, beside the crucial word, Duse wrote: "stand erect, summon to the spirit all the words spoken, feel again all the torments of the love that is dead, reflect, realize that *he* never loved her in return: sum up all this in a single exclamation: puah!"

The Dumas piece had not been a success in Paris, even with the beloved Desclée, but Duse brought the Roman audience to its feet; and the echo of her triumph reached Turin. When the Rossi company returned there, for the opening night Eleonora chose *Frou-frou*—last seen at the Carignano with Sarah—as a test. One critic spoke of the "great and very rapid road that Duse had covered in recent months" and recognized that the Meilhac–Halévy vehicle was the most difficult interpretation she had yet faced. But her next work, *La Femme de Claude* by Dumas *fils*—again the Turin audience was seeing a familiar play but with Duse for the first time—was an even greater success. It was given six performances (a high number at that time), followed by Duse in another French favorite, Sardou's *Odette*, which had originally starred Réjane. Finally, on 10 January 1883, Turin saw Duse as Marguerite Gautier. Every big scene was wildly applauded: Eleonora had invaded Sarah's terrain and, for the moment, she had conquered.

During that winter in Turin, Eleonora saw something of the playwright Giuseppe Giacosa. As a young girl, she had acted in a play of his in Trieste, and she had also been in the cast of *Il conte rosso* at the Carignano in 1880, though the author had paid little attention to her. At thirty-six Giacosa was already a well-known man of letters and an important figure in the cultural world of Turin; his literary friendships, however, extended much farther, and he was in close touch with Boito, with Antonio Fogazzaro, and—since his excellent French made him virtually bilingual—with French authors, among them Zola.

For Duse's "serata" on 19 January 1883, the Rossi company was presenting a little one-act verse play of Giacosa's, *Il filo* (The Thread), in which the actors pretend to be marionettes. The play's success—Duse and the author had three calls, and the *Gazzetta* spoke of the work's "grace and cleverness"—obviously encouraged both Rossi and Giacosa to continue the collaboration. During the company's spring tour, they gave another Giacosa work, *La zampa del gatto* (The Cat's Paw), at the Arena Nazionale in Florence.

From there, on 12 April 1883, Giacosa wrote to his mother: "I couldn't have conceived or hoped for a huger, more triumphant success. An enormous theatre, packed with people, and more people in the foyer, the corridors, in the street . . . When the work began to go well, I abandoned the dressing room and stood in the wings to eavesdrop, though I couldn't see anything, and Yorick and Barbera [two critics] and others later told me that la Duse in particular had been marvelous. . . . At the end there was a yell of voices and a storm of applause to make the theatre shake. When I was called out on stage, I saw her limp as a rag."

In his pleasure, another report says, the staid Giacosa waltzed Duse around the stage after the curtain came down.

In Rome, later that year, the play was again a success. In the city for a meeting of the government's Musical and Dramatic Commission (Boito was also a member), Giacosa was able to attend the exciting first night. He also had another verse-play ready, *La sirena*, and supervised the rehearsals. At first they did not go well, as he reported to his mother on 20 October 1883 that "La Duse acts in a remarkable way, but the others, and especially Diotti (Marco), are really distressing. At this morning's rehearsal, when they came to the scene for the two of them, she was so upset by the actor's inadequacy that she made a nervous scene and quit, saying she had had enough, she didn't feel like going on, and then covering me with vituperation because I had wanted the play cast like this. I'm quite pleased she is interested in the work, but this morning . . . I finished by saying I was quite prepared to withdraw the piece and leave. She apologized lavishly and promised that tomorrow she would display exemplary patience. Poor woman! I know she is irritated at the sight of the poor young man's clumsiness, and her irritation stems chiefly from her fear of losing her impetus since the other lacks any at all."

One of the people Giacosa came to know in Rome was Count Primoli, "a very cultivated man"—he wrote in the same letter—"simple, shy, full of affection, and a bit of an ascetic." Giacosa also referred to Primoli's stimulating conversation.

The more taciturn Giovanni Verga had also come up to Rome, from Catania, for his friend's opening. Seven years Giacosa's senior, Verga had recently abandoned the overheated, romantic strain of his early fiction and had produced his first volumes of stark Sicilian stories, *Vita dei campi* (1880) and *Novelle rusticane* (1883), as well as his masterly novel *I Malavoglia* (1881). He, too, was a friend of Primoli (from whom he occasionally borrowed money), and a part of the new intellectual Rome, the "Roma bizantina," so called after the new, polemical weekly paper, *Cronaca bizantina.*

Rome had been Italy's capital for just over a decade, but it was already a different city from the closed, provincial bigoted Rome of the Popes. The national Parliament brought leading figures from all over the country, and writers also came, as, in an earlier generation, they would have gone to Florence or Milan. Gabriele D'Annunzio, barely twenty, was already publishing, turning women's heads, and shocking his elders. Eleonora's friend Matilde Serao had left Naples and settled in the capital, and had just brought out a novel with the significant title *La conquista di Roma.* It was reviewed (unfavorably) by another brilliant young journalist, Edoardo Scarfoglio, a friend of D'Annunzio and Serao's future husband and partner.

Primoli met Matilde in the summer of 1883, and they became friends at first sight. She was younger than he, but richer in practical experience; she gave him encouragement and advice about his attempt to write a novel (never completed); and Primoli gave her considerable help by arranging French reviews and providing a translator for her fiction.

In his journal for 1 October 1883, Primoli wrote: "I have written little these past few days, because these journals which constitute the distraction of my infirmarian's life [Primoli's father was mortally ill] have been replaced by a more living distraction. A young and already great actress, the true interpreter of the plays of Dumas, has come to give some performances in Rome. She has made me return to the theatre, where I hadn't been for twenty months."

And the following day's entry reads: "Received a letter from Dumas, who promises me a part for la Duse. He is in the process of writing a 'very strange play,' he tells me."

Giacosa's play, which opened on 22 October 1883, was a fiasco. Two days later he described the performance to his mother: "Icy silence from the beginning to the end, except one round of applause for la Duse, who, aware of the tempest, acted marvelously. The others were two genuine dogs, two mastiffs, two newfoundlands, who tore my poor verses to shreds and ruined my beautiful work."

The playwright's numerous Roman friends, the city's literary society, rallied around him; and his play received some encouraging reviews. But Duse, also being reviewed, emerged as the star: "As artist, as interpreter, she is a miracle of naturalness," Guido Biagi, editor of *Capitan Fracassa*, wrote in his paper; "she does not shout, does not sob, does not sing. She speaks naturally, without raising the tone of her voice; and she unfolds the sentences of her speech without listening to herself. She can be elegant without affectation, she can be beautiful without recourse to the secrets of cosmetics: she has only to show the public her intelligent face, her large, deep black eyes, her diaphanous Andalusian profile."

The company left Rome at the end of the month. On the evening of 31 October 1883, Primoli wrote in his diary: "Morning at the Diva's. Went to fetch her with a carriage to accompany her to the station, where Verga, Giacosa, Cecconi, Vassallo, De Angelis, d'Arcais, etc. and la Serao were waiting for her. Walked home with Verga and la Serao. In the evening accompanied Verga to the station." It is curious that, in all these diary entries, Tebaldo is never mentioned; he was, truly, becoming "the husband of the prima donna," and he apparently did not share her interest in literary men.

A few days later, Verga wrote to Primoli from Milan, thanking him for his interest in the dramatization Verga had made of his own short story *Cavalleria rusticana*, with which he was hoping to begin a theatre career and, at the same time, earn a bit more than the meager income provided by his fiction. On Verga's behalf, Primoli was discussing the play with a Roman company, but, as the letter makes clear, Verga had already offered *Cavalleria rusticana* also to Cesare Rossi for Turin.

Rossi was not enthusiastic, and even Verga's friends were skeptical about the play's possibilities. It was submitted to a kind of advisory committee, consisting of Boito, the publisher Emilio Treves (who was not an admirer of Verga's stories anyway), the Francophile writer Luigi

Gualdo, and Eugenio Torelli-Viollier, founder and editor of the *Corriere della sera* and sometime drama critic.

It was an unlikely group to judge a brief, bleak drama of Sicilian peasant life; and only Torelli-Viollier, a Neapolitan, was optimistic. But he failed to transmit his enthusiasm to Rossi; and even Duse's initial faith in the play was shaken. As Giacosa wrote to Verga, "Duse is of course influenced by her actor-manager and she, too, now predicts failure."

The main problem was the expense: Rossi's notorious reluctance to spend money was a real obstacle. "Duse's views I don't take seriously," Giacosa went on. "She has tremendous ability and, as an actress, she is indeed courageous; but she is extremely shy about judging anything before it is performed and, moreover, is frightened that by encouraging you she may assume responsibility towards Rossi and eventually be blamed."

Giacosa's attitude towards Duse was always ambivalent (as she came to realize), and though they were to see a great deal of each other, for professional and private reasons, over the next few years, they never developed a real, reciprocal trust. When Primoli formed one of his characteristic, secret, hopeless crushes on the actress, Giacosa wrote him from Turin on 21 November 1883, "I am convinced that if you had continued your intimacy with her, and if you had delved deeper into passion, you would one day have found her arid and ungrateful, and you would have suffered very much; though I am also convinced that so far she has felt a sincere fondness for you."

Primoli's loves were never serious, but Giacosa took everything seriously, and in the same letter he analyzed the young Eleonora's character: "I see her very little and I discuss only art and theatre with her. I find her sulky, and I see the prima donna emerging and growing, to the detriment of the woman, whom I so liked. Basically, I feel a great compassion for this excitable, morbid creature, full of intelligence, aristocratic and elegant, and forced by her profession to become vulgar and to suffer at such vulgarity and display it, boasting of it, for fear of our commiseration. I do not believe she is good. I mean: I do not believe her capable of doing something good, of refraining from something bad out of pure goodness. I do not believe her capable of an enduring feeling, but I believe that for the short time she is under the sway of a feeling she is capable of great sacrifices and great heroism. She is an egoist who loves suffering."

The prim, conventional Giacosa was surely wrong about Eleonora's goodness, her stability of feeling; but his analysis of her character has some insights and concludes: "Most of all, she is full of pride, and more than pride, the senses dominate her in a frightful way."

Verga came back to Turin and again discussed the play with Giacosa and with Flavio Andò, the thirty-two-year-old Sicilian actor who would play Turiddu. In the course of the discussion, it became clear that money was Rossi's chief objection. Verga went to him and agreed not only to waive his author's royalties but also to supply the costumes.

Verga took Duse's measurements (hip to foot 100 cm.; waist 58–59 cm.; sleeves 36–37 cm.) and sent them to his brother Mario, who lived in Vizzini, the town where *Cavalleria* is set. Mario's wife, Lidda, was so enormous that she required a resident dressmaker, who was immediately put to work on the costumes. Santuzza's was thus described: "white mantellina, spencer of yellow and chocolate striped muslin, with flower pattern. Turquoise-colored skirt. Cotton kerchief across the bosom, colored cotton kerchief for the head—the two kerchiefs to be of contrasting colors."

To judge by accounts in the press, Duse had been enjoying a brilliant season, which, after opening with *Fédora*, had included *Une Visite de noces, La Dame aux camélias, La Femme de Claude*, and—on her "serata"—yet another Sarah war-horse, *Adrienne Lecouvreur*. Two of her performances were graced by the living monument Adelaide Ristori, now the Marchesa Capranica del Grillo, who applauded very visibly.

Meanwhile, Giacosa continued writing to Primoli, about the Turin theatre and about Duse. On New Year's Day 1884, he reported: "She acts in spurts, sometimes divinely, sometimes wildly, more often badly than well. I see her rarely, but we are good friends again, and when I come onto the stage she gives me a thousand sincere welcomes. Poor thing! those who surround her are worth so little that her deference doesn't flatter me. In any case, I take her as she comes, and this is best. Her husband becomes more of a cretin every day, and more and more envelops her in a corrupt, vulgar atmosphere. This distresses me because, removed from these deleterious influences, that woman could elevate herself greatly and would deserve to succeed in doing so."

On 13 January, in the *Gazzetta piemontese*, Giacosa wrote a preparatory article about *Cavalleria rusticana*, which was to open the following night: "Verga's newness does not consist of doing *more*, but rather in doing *less*, and certainly in doing it all in a completely new way. . . . Whatever may be in store, I feel that tomorrow's date will not only be an important one for Verga, but a date to remember for all of us."

Torelli-Viollier reported the event in the *Corriere della sera* of 15 January: "The Carignano last night was absolutely packed. Every single seat was occupied; by 7.45 you could not move downstairs. There were many students present." The students, and the rest of the audience, saw first a one-act "scherzo" entitled *La società dei tredici,* then Verga's play. "From the moment the curtain rose, the public followed the play with rapt attention up to the scene of the dialogue [between Santuzza and Turiddu], during which applause began to explode. From then on, roaring applause marked every scene. The fall of the curtain provoked a tremendous ovation. The public called for the author, shouting 'Viva Verga!'"

Having no faith in the outcome, Verga had gone to see an operetta in another theatre. Boito—to his later dismay—had also assumed the piece would fail and had prudently remained in Milan. Receiving news of the success, he sent Verga an abashed telegram.

For the second performance, the next night, Verga was in the house; and Duse—overcoming his profound shyness—drew him onto the stage, with Rossi's help. This was the only curtain-call of Verga's life, and he agreed to it largely because Duse had accused him of "not condescending" to appear with the actors.

In his distrust of the play, Rossi had passed what would have been his part—Alfio, the husband—to Tebaldo Checchi. Andò was Turiddu, while Rossi appeared as an old peasant, a walk-on.

Verga was delighted with his leading lady. From Turin, on 24 January, he wrote to Primoli: "I would so much have liked you to be here [Primoli's father had finally died on 30 December], to see what an artist that Duse is and how she took my work to heart."

In theory, this outstanding success of a first play by one of Italy's most interesting and gifted writers should have been a turning-point not only for Verga, but also for Duse and for the Italian theatre, still dominated by translations from the French or by Italian imitations of French dramas. After the success of *Cavalleria* there were other *verismo* plays: Verga's friend Luigi Capuana wrote *Giacinta* a few years later, but Duse turned it down. Verga himself wrote other plays, and some of them were performed, the most successful being *La lupa,* written in the early 1890s. But Duse's tastes did not coincide with the harsh realism of this literary movement, and neither did the tastes of the Italian public. Sardou and Dumas remained the favorites.

At the end of February, after a number of repeats of *Cavalleria* and an immensely successful "serata" featuring *Une Visite de noces* and *La Femme de Claude,* Duse and the company set off on a brief tour: Trieste,

Padua, Milan. From Trieste on 4 March Eleonora wrote to Gégé Primoli offering some constructive criticism of a play sent her by a friend of his, then continuing "You know something, O Gégé? For *months* now I haven't talked. This seems a *phrase*, but still, my beautiful evenings in Rome haven't returned. In Turin, I had a court—not of intimates—around me; and in Trieste I know nobody—and I mean nobody—because I leave stage acquaintances at the stage door . . . and at home, I am more or less alone. . . . You know something else? I had a *fiasco*—really *enormous*—the other evening in the *Dame aux camélias*. A month of successes—and of emotions given and received by these good irredentists—were not enough to save me. . . . In fact, I'll send you the papers, which speak about it, as you will see, without *mercy*."

The tone of the letter suggests that the fiasco troubled her very slightly, but her boredom is evident. Having had a taste, in Rome, of urban, sophisticated intellectual life, Eleonora was not content now with only her work and the company of Tebaldo (who probably was not the "cretin" that Giacosa considered him, but was surely no intellectual).

But then, in May, when the company reached Milan, things improved. On the 11th there was *Cavalleria rusticana*, which got off to a bad start (the audience silenced its few members who applauded Duse's entrance), but ended in an ovation. Now Eleonora was the ruling diva of Milan as she already had become of Rome and Turin. The triumph continued as she was seen in the rest of her repertory, especially when she played Marguerite Gautier, the very part that had been so badly received in Trieste.

She chose *La Dame aux camélias* for her "serata," and after the performance a banquet was given in her honor at Cova's, the fashionable literary restaurant near La Scala. There, amid the gilt and the mirrors, in the rooms where every important figure in the city was to be seen (even Verdi dropped in occasionally when he was in Milan), a special table was arranged for Duse. The guests included Milan's mayor, Gaetano Negri, an enthusiastic patron of the arts, and naturally Verga, and Luigi Gualdo. Cesare Rossi and Flavio Andò were there, but, oddly enough, Tebaldo Checchi seems to have been absent. Torelli-Viollier and the critic Giovanni Pozza represented the press.

Duse sat next to the mayor. To her right sat the composer and writer Arrigo Boito: his position at the table confirms his position in Milanese life. Bosom friend of Giacosa, friendly also with Verga and Primoli, Boito somehow had failed to meet Duse before, though he had seen her act and admired her. In the course of the evening, he asked for a signed photograph. She sent it a short time later; and on 25 May, three days after the Rossi company had left Milan for Turin, where she was opening that night in Sardou's *Fédora*, Boito mailed her a little note of thanks, addressed to Signora Eleonora Duse Checchi. "That's the very portrait I wanted. I thank you for having guessed and for remembering to send it to me. You have left, and the thread is broken [perhaps a reference to Giacosa's play *Il filo*], and we have all fallen to the ground, Verga, Gualdo, and I, our noses on the floor. Now, after thirty-six hours of catalepsy, the arm resumes its movements and my hand turns over this card which is dedicated to you, and here I am forced to write that you are good and kind. Arrigo Boito."

There is a P.S. "You are not obliged to answer. Be well and happy. Cordial greetings to Cav. Checchi."

But Duse did answer, on 31 May.

Politely . . . very politely . . . you have closed the door on me, saying: there's no need to reply—don't come back . . .—Obviously, this is reasonable—but it is more kind to allow me to think and to write—that today is the *last day of May* . . . And I feel the wish to greet it—and also to greet you——

Besides—in addition—I have a *little present* to ask of you—(ah! Prima Donnas!!). The present is this: I need to fill a corner of my room—Don't be frightened, because the cost of the object is not high! You will send me (ah! how good of you!) a child's little face—or else a picture of a lovely woman—or—an old woman—or—a maiden's profile—or the portrait of someone illustrious—or the view of a green landscape—or the photograph of a campanile of Padua [Boito's birthplace]—or even of the Duomo of Milan—in other words—a white card—with drawn—or painted—photographed—on it, something that *speaks*.

I'm not asking for a precious object, or an inscription or an autograph—most precious—on it. At most you will put a date—if you have one—one of those dates one is fond of—that are written on the wall of the private room—in the corner of the desk—on the sand of a favorite path—something of the sort, in other words . . .

Boito's answer was that he could find nothing suitably fragile, but, as a stop-gap, from a French calendar he tore off the page of the "defunct month of May" and sent it with a little quatrain, playing on the word *mai* (May in French, but "never" in Italian).

This was the half-playful beginning of what, a few years later, was to develop into an important, crucial love, affecting both their lives and leaving—especially in Eleonora—a memory that, in later years, assumed an ideal, haloed quality. In speaking of Boito, towards the end of his life, she always referred to him as "il Santo."

In 1884, when Boito met Duse at the Ristorante Cova, he was forty-two years old and famous. Even while still a student at the Milan conservatory, in his teens, he had achieved a certain local notoriety for his cosmopolitan, avant-garde musical and literary tastes, for his precocity not only as a composer but also as a poet and critic. In 1862, barely twenty, he had collaborated with Verdi in Paris, supplying the text for the *Hymn of the Nations* (*Inno delle nazioni*), one of Verdi's rare pieces of occasional music. Soon Boito's polemical articles, his espousal of the cause of foreign music, his translation of Wagner, and his open scorn for what was old and traditional, all aroused Verdi's resentment, and the two men were long estranged. In 1868 Boito's ambitious opera *Mefistofele* had been an epoch-making failure at La Scala, but then—much revised and toned down—it had succeeded completely at the Comunale of Bologna in 1875 and, in 1881, at La Scala itself. With maturity and with success, Boito revised his attitudes, grew more and more conservative. He was regularly sought out for musical juries and government commissions; he was the friend and adviser of ministers. By all accounts he was a charming companion, courtly, absent-minded, curious. A confirmed bachelor, for some time he had been carrying on a discreet affair with a married woman (so discreet that even today only her first name, or nickname—Fanny—is known); her family situation and her chronic ill-health relieved him of any pressing duties towards her.

That summer of 1884 Eleonora was supposed to prepare a new play by Giacosa, *Resa a discrezione* (Unconditional Surrender), and Boito was planning to go to Turin for the opening. But on 13 July Giacosa wrote to his friend, the novelist Antonio Fogazzaro, that she had fallen ill at the first rehearsal. "I fear her illness is grave: Professor Bozzolo even calls it tuberculosis, but hopes to cure her; in any case he ordered her a stay in the mountains, at medium altitude, and, three hours from Parella [Giacosa's home], I found her a discreet little house in a delightful position."

The place, Brosso, was Duse's introduction to the Piedmontese mountains, to which she was to return often. She spent several weeks there with Tebaldo and, at least part of the time, another member of the Rossi troupe, the comedian Zolis. To the journalist Arturo Fiacchi, she wrote: "from this altitude, modest and yet considerable, from this perfume—the pure, I would say *immaculate* smell of the mountain—, from this green that reposes the eye irritated by the city's gaslight, from this air that renews the weary lungs . . . I feel myself reborn, good, without pretension, with few clothes, with little *money*, with many ideas."

With Giacosa and Verga, Boito paid a visit to the house, recorded in a pencil sketch with an annotation by Tebaldo. Before and after this meeting, Boito also sent Eleonora some more of his elegant, intricate little poems, with their word-games and their light irony.

But now Eleonora was thinking about her work. For some time Dumas *fils* had been working on a new play, which—it seemed understood—was meant for her. But some doubt concerning her priority (which, of course, had no legal basis) had been expressed in the Italian papers. From Intra, on Lake Maggiore, where she was still resting (the Rossi company was having a two-month break), she wrote to Primoli on 14 September 1884: "My good Gégé—I ask you a favor—a real favor—You are sensitive and kind and will understand me. You knew me in the *so-called* . . . happy . . . period of my life, but I don't believe I was able to conceal my self, even in that *so-called* happiness. On the stage—if you haven't already understood—it was never *success* that I sought—but *refuge* in art . . .—

"I have told you this—not out of a *mania* to utter confidences—but because I would like you to descend into the *real truth* of me—and not into what appears. When you are convinced that *I don't love the theatre*—but—I adore—only *art*—then with greater trust you can grant me the favor I am asking of you——and it is: to write to M. Dumas—to assure him I have nothing to do with—the silly—absurd—indelicate—inopportune—and *inopportuning* gossip of all the Italian papers! . . . I have never spoken of the new work of Dumas—and I have never answered the newspapers that have questioned me . . . When you, my good friend, passed by Turin—you were the one who spoke to me of it—I didn't dare question you about it. When you wrote me, giving me some hope—I didn't even answer you what I felt—and I never dared send a line to Dumas. . . ."

The tempest died down. On 11 October Dumas wrote to Primoli, "I hope the play will be finished when you receive this letter. It is in four acts rather than three, and I believe the woman's part is well within Duse's range. Give me her news."

Duse was already back at work. The Rossi company had reopened at the Carignano on 1 October with *Fédora*. "The excellent artist, her health completely recovered, was the object of admiration and applause throughout the evening," the *Gazzetta* reported. In addition to resuming her usual repertory she was rehearsing another new Giacosa play, *L'Onorevole Ercole Mallardi*, written specially for her. Though, in Giacosa's opinion, Duse was splendid and the whole interpretation was "perfect," the play failed. It was given only two performances, then *Fédora* was resumed. On 29 October, Rossi's "serata," the company ended its season, and with it Rossi ended his management of the Carignano. The troupe set off for Rome.

There, at the Teatro Valle, they opened with *Fédora* in the first week of November, the expected success. Eleonora was still not entirely well, and towards the middle of the month, Tebaldo was aghast when he read in the newspapers that Martino Cafiero was mortally ill of cholera in Naples. He said to Matilde Serao at one point: "If Cafiero dies tonight, tomorrow I will go out of Rome . . . I want to free her of my presence for a day at least, so that she can give way to her grief without restraint . . . You go to her, be with her."

And Matilde went. Mixed though they may have been, Eleonora's feelings for Cafiero were deep and enduring, as her close friends were aware, and Primoli wrote in his diary on 20 November, "From the paper I learned of Martino Cafiero's death, which made me grieve for Eleonora, who loved him."

January 1885 was a busy month. First, the company began to rehearse one of its most ambitious undertakings: Sardou's *Théodora*, a brand-new superspectacle, which had just had its premiere in Paris at the Théâtre de la Porte-Saint-Martin with Sarah Bernhardt in the title role. Duse was to play the Byzantine empress, with an immense cast, a hundred supers, a chorus and orchestra. Because of the amplitude of the production, they rehearsed at the Teatro Costanzi, the opera house.

But at the beginning of that month, something even more important for Eleonora occurred. On 4 January, Primoli wrote to Dumas:

> Last night la Duse came to my house and I read her *Denise*! I was sorry you were not here, for the different emotions she felt would have amused, interested, moved you. You can understand how her heart beat. The first act charmed her, transporting her into that milieu of honest folk; but she was waiting for her part. The second act interested her, but . . . she was still waiting. She said nothing, but I realized what was going on inside her: a great admiration for the play, regret at seeing that Denise stayed in the wings. . . . She [Denise] did not appear. She [Duse] dreamed, in turn, of playing Madame de Thauzette, then Marthe; she came close to wanting to

play André. Half the third act goes by: no Denise! . . . She didn't know if she should laugh or cry over the fine role that was eluding her . . .

But then comes the confession scene, the one on which the play turns—one of the most beautiful you have written—and I was sure of the effect. She remained breathless, her color changed, tears fell from her staring eyes and rolled down her cheeks . . . At the details, so realistic, of the little dead child, she stood up suddenly, biting her handkerchief; and she had to listen to the end of the reading behind the protection of a screen.

She understood then the purity of Denise's character, who goes through the play chaste, proud, sweet, silent. Behind her impassive mask one must sense the secret that gnaws at her until, in the end, it escapes her. She never laughs, but doesn't cry either. She sings sometimes, but her notes are so sad that, if her eyes remain dry, she makes those who hear her weep. . . .

As he was writing this letter, Primoli received a hasty note from Duse, delivered by hand. He copied it into his own letter to Dumas, as a P.S.

"Gégé—good friend—

"As I had last evening, when I left you— I still have the perfume and melody of *Denise*—in my ear and in my heart. I see that form—turning—turning—vague—undefined—full of sorrow—and full of hope—I don't know!

"Yesterday evening when you went away—I dashed off a few lines for *Dumas*—which—this morning I do not dare—and do not want—to reread——it isn't a letter——it isn't a thank-you.

"When I am calmer, I will write both. Meanwhile—since, in us women the *first impression* must always be calculated—you send, with a letter of your own, this page I am sending you. . . .

"Thank you, good friend!—The atmosphere of *Denise*—how it purifies!—"

The emotion of listening to *Denise*, and perhaps the lingering sorrow after Cafiero's death, contributed to the illness that suddenly struck Eleonora down. Once again, her life seemed threatened. On 9 January, Primoli sent the news to Dumas:

"Confident, she was living with her eyes fixed on the part she already saw as hers. . . . Yesterday she came close to passing into the next world, and it still is not sure she will remain in this one. She had said farewell to those around her, not without pangs. Her eyelids were lowered, and she raised them by an effort of will, fearing to close them for the last time . . . She did not want to die; she wanted to be Denise first! . . .

"The doctors entered and left, discouraged. One of them even had the cynicism to say he would come back to sign the death-certificate. Crazed, she heard him, found the strength again to send him away, and fell back, shattered. . . .

"If she gets up again, I fear they will force her to act, to act until she falls . . . In a few days she will be on the boards again, unless she is enclosed in four boards, which is still possible. She asked me for Denise's confession, to keep her company when she is able to open her eyes once more. . . ."

In February she was back, as Primoli predicted, treading the boards; and on 14 March 1885, at the Teatro Valle, came the world premiere of *Denise*. It had a mixed reception, and Duse was exhausted, not only by the preparations for the play but because rehearsals had resumed for *Théodora*, which opened later that month.

Primoli reported to Dumas: "*Théodora* has been the final blow for her. After the premiere they had to cut an act; after the second night, they suspended the play altogether. . . . She took to her bed and got up only to leave for South America."

The Rossi company sailed at the beginning of April for Montevideo to undertake an extended South American tour. But before leaving Rome, Duse insisted on giving *Denise* once more and—according to Primoli—it triumphed. But Dumas also read the Italian papers, which were less encouraging. He taxed Primoli with concealing the truth, and Gégé answered: "*Denise* was given ten times [again an exaggeration surely], which is the equivalent of a hundred performances in Paris."

Primoli also described Duse's performance in greater detail: "If a reproach can be ventured concerning her interpretation . . . , it is that she has identified herself too much with her [Denise]. She is no longer Denise: she is herself. In the famous confession scene, it was her own child that she wept over, and her prolonged sobs, her tears that she couldn't stop, might finally have wearied the audience if it had not been gripped. Each evening she inspired unanimous applause with the *no* she replied to André when he asked her if she still loved Fernand: it was the *pouah* of [*Une*] *Visite*. . . ."

4
South America

For Italian actor-managers and for Italian opera singers, South America in the latter half of the nineteenth century and the first decades of the twentieth was a frontier. For some, it was also an El Dorado. A tour there could spell quick, considerable gains; but it was unpredictable, adventurous and, on occasion, disastrous. In the major cities—Buenos Aires, São Paulo, Rio de Janeiro—there was a large emigrant population, eager to hear the operas—and the divas—of home and to attend plays in their native language. But this audience was capricious, and though Duse was by now undeniably a star in Italy, she was totally unknown outside the country.

There were ways to boost one's welcome, and—probably incited by the publicity-wise Tebaldo—Eleonora took the necessary steps. Before leaving Rome, she sought the blessing of the great Adelaide Ristori. Only recently retired (her official final performance was at the Thalia Theatre in New York on 12 May 1885) la Ristori had been a pioneer in touring both Americas and even Australia. Eleonora paid a duty call on the actress at the Palazzo Capranica in Rome, and was given a signed photograph, along with valuable letters of introduction. One, at Duse's request, was to Dom Pedro II, Emperor of Brazil and great patron of the arts.

The Rossi company was to sail from Genoa on the Italian ship *Umberto I*. First they stopped briefly in Turin, where Giacosa had hoped to see Eleonora; but through Checchi's clumsiness (or deliberate rudeness) Giacosa learned of her presence only as she was about to take the train to Genoa. He complained in a letter to Primoli, and it was a while before the always shaky friendship between author and actress was reestablished.

The first stop on the tour was Montevideo, where they arrived at the end of April after a voyage of twenty-six days. This was the longest journey Eleonora had ever made, the first of many crossings. An opera company was also on board, and one night the two troupes gave an "accademia" for the benefit of the Italian hospital of Montevideo. Their arrival was hailed by a huge crowd, and their opening—1 May 1885, with *Fédora*—was sold out. Duse at first had to combat a certain coldness in the audience (attributed to the excess of publicity), but she soon won them over, even though admission prices had been raised.

A Montevideo correspondent of the *Gazzetta piemontese*, writing about the Rossi–Duse performances at the Teatro Cibils, described the local theatres in general: "Half the stalls have armchairs and the other half straight chairs. To occupy these seats you have to pay an extra scudo-and-a-half for the armchairs and one scudo for the straight chairs besides the scudo for admission, so to attend the performance you have to spend at least two scudos, unless you prefer the 'Paradiso,' where admission is a half-scudo. The boxes cost eight scudos per evening. The Paradiso is unusual in that it is reserved for men only and, as in Europe, it is the top tier of the theatre, whereas the tier just below it is the 'cazuela,' or the Paradiso of the ladies."

The weather was cold and rainy, but audiences still came. The popularity of the company meant that prying reporters sought interviews, and at a certain point Eleonora was obliged to write a letter to the *Bandiera italiana*, a local Italian-language paper, defending her privacy: "I believe it is pointless to give you dates and details about my life as an actress, and I feel it is indelicate, indeed coarse, to dig out my life as a woman. If the latter has shaped the former, why ask one the secrets of the other?"

In mid-June the company moved from Montevideo to Rio de Janeiro, and there a real-life tragedy occurred. Arturo Diotti, the young actor who had played opposite Eleonora in Giacosa's *La sirena* (and had been severely criticized by the author), fell gravely ill on 25 June and died on the morning of the 28th. As Rossi wrote, on 12 July: "Some say he was stricken with yellow fever, others not. What's sure is that Diotti committed some excesses, eating and drinking a great deal on board a ship, where some friends had invited him. Most of all, he stuffed himself with fruit."

On 28 August, also from Rio, Duse wrote Matilde Serao a slightly different account:

I had to achieve a success, and I achieved it . . . I didn't believe I had so much strength! . . . While poor Diotti was ill (he fought that cursed disease for five days), we went on—without him (how one is *replaced*, eh? Ah, how sad!) The first night: *Fédora*. The theatre jammed—and a complete *fiasco* for your little Nennella [the Neapolitan diminutive was Serao's name for Eleonora] . . . A huge,

huge theatre . . . I felt weak and tiny . . . my voice—it seemed to me impossible that it could reach the back of the house . . . I would have had to say: *I love you, O Loris* as I might have said: *get out of here.* . . . A constant, constant irritating murmur . . . in the stalls and boxes to the end of the play. . . . I changed in a hurry and, in even more of a hurry, went home. I closed myself in my room; and what sadness . . . what emptiness that evening! The next day's papers gave no *exact* judgment—they declared only that I had a *certain something* that had impressed them. . . . The next day . . . *Denise*, second performance. The theatre—that parade-ground—almost empty. . . . This time, a bit of attention. My poor *Denise*, simple, without *toilette*, without being a princess, nothing in common with that feverish *Fédora*, commanded attention. Well, in the first act and in the second, I wept, and made them weep. . . . The boat was beginning to move a little . . . yes, slowly. But my daze caused by that theatre, its vastness, started to pass . . . It's also true that the part of Fernando that evening was taken by Cottin, instead of Diotti, still sick . . . That sick man made me forget the details of acting. It seemed to me that in order to be able to act, I had to close my heart and head against the present, calling up only the past . . . But then, the life of a poor young man was involved, so good, who had never done me any harm, never done any to anyone in his life . . . then, there . . . before those footlights, hateful and blessed, I said: "Madonna, show us your grace and save that poor boy—do it—don't fail us—save him—and damn me as an artist . . ."

Two days later it was all over, and we . . . we, left in battle, went on without him . . . and your little Nennella conquered . . . conquered . . . My third performance was *Fernande* . . . Never, as that evening, have I felt I had a heart—I had blood—had intelligence—had *will*. I acted—well—nobly. To you I confess it—you are good—you are noble—You do not *make fun* of those who uplift the soul and the intellect . . . *You have never said to me that life is vulgar.* You have only—sadly—agreed with me that life is heavy.

A few days before this letter, Eleonora wrote another, to the "illustrious and good" Adelaide Ristori, a letter of open adoration and of thanks. "His Majesty received me on my arrival—which would not have been granted me except for your letter. That letter . . . gave me *breath* . . . to answer, just barely, the questions of His Majesty . . . (it's hard for me to speak with a sovereign!) Fortunately. His Majesty spoke much of you. . . . Your letter then sustained me also in the battle of the

first days—when, with the success of the public, I had also to obtain
. . . the approval, the encouragement of His Majesty. . . ."

Dom Pedro attended the theatre, invited Duse to his box, showed
her every courtesy, and wrote—on 20 August—also to la Ristori,
speaking of Duse's "remarkable talent" and her success.

Diotti's death, the initial coldness of the Rio audience, problems of
protocol, were not the only concerns that made life heavy for Eleonora
during those weeks. The letter to Matilde, with its complaint of someone who tells her life is *vulgar*, gives a clue. The tension between
Eleonora and Tebaldo had been increasing for some time, and before
the tour ended, their marriage was to end. On 27 August (the day
before Eleonora wrote Matilde), Tebaldo wrote a revealing and precau-
tionary letter to Marchese Francesco d'Arcais, editor and critic of
L'opinione in Rome, a senior figure in the city's intellectual milieu. He
had been a friend both to Eleonora and to her husband, and obviously
Tebaldo—knowing how fast gossip could travel, even despite
oceans—was afraid that rumors had reached him.

"Dear Marchese, since bad news flies with frightful speed, I would
bet that even before you receive this letter of mine, you will hear some
talk. But I don't want you to puzzle your head, and I will speak frankly,
once and for all. On 1 December, our whole company—minus two
people—will embark for Italy, for Rome. One of the two who will not
see his country again is poor Diotti . . . the other one who, for the
present, is not returning to Italy and is remaining in Buenos Aires is
me. . . .

"You will be amazed by this, and the first question you will ask
yourself will be: now why is Checchi taking such a step, leaving a
position, a wife and a daughter? . . . Marchese, do not judge me by
appearances, and do not believe I am perverse or cynical. No . . . to
you I can speak openly, from the heart, and say what I could not say to
others."

Then Tebaldo related the story of his courtship and the slander of
some of his colleagues. "If you keep on slandering, something will
stick, they say, and so it did . . . All the old gossip, all the new, the
poison subtly administered by those vipers' tongues has achieved
something. For a while now I had realized that Leonora was no longer
the same with me, but I attributed this to her ill-health, her nerves; and
frankly, I never thought that the maliciousness of that scum had managed to make any impression on her. When we arrived in America, at
Montevideo, as I spoke of the journalists and the visits I wanted to pay
them [Tebaldo, like other actresses' husbands, served as press-agent],

she made a gesture of impatience and came out with these words: Oh, leave the journalists alone, and let me earn their support and the audience's; otherwise, here too they'll say you're the one who gets people to applaud me and you contrive my success! I was dumbfounded at these words and especially by the irritation of their tone; but it was a warning for me, and I began to observe her.

"I did not visit the journalists, who then naturally said very little about the opening. I brought the matter up with her again, pointing out how wrong she was to neglect such things."

Apparently Tebaldo's reminder only irritated her further, and when some reporters came to call she received them crossly. The letter continues: "Then I called on those gentlemen, delivered the letters I had; I was introduced at the Club Oriental. In short, I made acquaintances, contacts, friendships. . . . I entered Uruguayan society, I was welcomed, well received, fêted. Things changed: the papers began to sing hymns of praise, the ladies began to come to our house. The usual life of receptions, visits, dinners, etc., began."

Again, Tebaldo did not fail to point out his success to Eleonora, who took offense, then "sprang up and said: 'You think perhaps that I couldn't do the same, without you? I am an individual who can manage on her own.' . . ."

Tebaldo suggested separation and, after some days of silence between them, he brought up the subject again, proposing that he remain with the company till the end of the tour, to avoid scandal. After that, he would stay behind. "There, my dear Marchese, is the sad story," his letter goes on to say. "From that day to this we have been as we decided three months ago: not another word has been exchanged between us. Only she is very happy and has never been in such good health as today; she is lively and merry.—Obviously—and you see I speak without second meanings and with an open heart—obviously, I repeat, I was blind and lived in the blissful illusion that this woman felt, if not love, at least friendship for me, gratitude if nothing else, for having saved her three times from death. But nothing of the sort . . . it's clear she lived with me unwillingly. . . . I do not believe Eleonora is at all wicked, but only spoiled by the false friends who painted me to her in grim colors, and by the few who, exalting her, commiserated with her for being chained to a vulgar creature like me for the rest of her life.—Add to this the intoxication of constant success, the unhealthy reading of the lives of Rachel, la Desclée, Bernhardt, and so on—the example of the corrupt society we live in—my perhaps boring character, with my constant preaching, my weakness in the face of her whims, and perhaps my love, more a lover's than a husband's. . . .

"She, poor thing, is not to blame: it is her restless character that never allows her to find repose in anything. To live, she always needs something new and bizarre, some emotion; and I with my tranquil good health could give her none of this. With me, except for her art, life was flat, monotonous, solid bourgeois. . . ."

For all his protestations of openness, Tebaldo was keeping something back. In one cryptic sentence he hinted: "without wanting to be a prophet, I forsee that things will not go smoothly for her, unfortunately. At the beginning, all is fine, because of the novelty of the thing—but then?"

The "novelty" which Tebaldo could not bring himself to reveal was a blazing love-affair between Eleonora and her leading man, Flavio Andò. This sudden passion was strange, since actor and actress had known each other for several years; and it must have begun after their arrival in South America, because in one of his letters Rossi suggests that, on board the *Umberto I*, Andò was carrying on with a ballerina. In any event, the "novelty" soon wore off; the affair was over within the space of a few weeks. And although Eleonora continued to respect Andò as an actor, she retained very little esteem for him as a man. "He was handsome," she is supposed to have said, years later, "but stupid."

From South America, Rossi sent an announcement to the Italian press: because of popular demand, the company's stay in South America would be prolonged and they would arrive in Rome only for the Carnival season of 1886. And on 26 September 1885, the *Gazzetta piemontese* announced, having had further news from South America, that with the conclusion of the current 1885–86 season, Eleonora Duse would leave the Rossi troupe and form a company of her own.

Until the time of their departure, in November, she went on accumulating successes. Tebaldo, as he had decided, stayed behind in Buenos Aires. A few years later, Michele Puccini—younger brother of Giacomo—saw him there and reported to his brother: "One person who has a good position here is Tebaldo Checchi, the *pe'orone* [cuckold] of la Duse, or rather the pimp, as he is called here. He is employed at the Foreign Ministry and is very friendly with Sommariva, critic of the *Patria*." In 1890, after a political upheaval in Argentina, Tebaldo was named Argentine consul at Newhaven and Newport, in the south of England. He remained in Britain for many years, then left it during the First World War, and died in Lisbon in 1918. His contacts with Eleonora in later life were few; she remained uncharacteristically bitter towards him and transmitted her bitterness to their daughter Enrichetta, who grew up virtually fatherless.

On arriving in Rome, Eleonora found—further reason for bitterness—that stories about her separation (and about Andò) had preceded her and had even found their way into the press. To one paper, *Capitan Fracassa*, she wrote a reply, meant for publication.

One who has come back—begs you—to accept in your paper a few words which she feels obliged and entitled to send you.

One who has come back has read an article of yours, in which she wishes—simply—to correct the errors about some *private* matters concerning her *home*.

I do not know whether, outside my art, my humble person deserves such lively attention. I do not know if an artist, a woman—alone, helpless—is obliged to speak of her private life, of her misfortunes, her sorrows, herself—in a newspaper . . .—I do not know if all this can interest the press and its readers . . . but . . . in the emotion of the return, so much desired, I feel the need—woman though I am—to look around and to answer for what I can and must answer.

Your article—certainly without any evil intention on your part—but obviously because of inexact information—virtually offends. A delicate and difficult question, more difficult and delicate than any other for a woman: because it is a question of interest.

From experience I know that figures are boring; but as a *simple correction* of your way of expounding things, I am forced, despite myself, to declare that today, as I write you, today, when I have finally come back to my country—a little tired, but serene—today, returning from a long and sad journey, from a theatrical venture that was profitable—for the management—today, after some years of working, I return with a considerable amount of debts, which precludes any possible suspicion that there was squandered for me any personal fortune, *which never existed in my family or my husband's*.

And I can prove it.

I declare this—without rancor, for that matter—because it is surely not an *inheritance* that I regret not having found in my path.

What could embitter is—as you rightly say—a man, *young and healthy, far from his country, searching for work*; but *for me*, at this moment, there is comfort in the knowledge that I can honor my husband's signature, united to mine as guarantee, with patience and work and courage—honor all my debts, even though I am alone, even though far from him.

Art—and determination—will help me. That art . . . which was—always—in every grave moment—the protection, the sweetness, the refuge, the smile of my life . . .

On this first tour Eleonora had learned that crowded houses, huge box-office receipts, ovations do not necessarily spell large earnings. It was a lesson, however, that did not always serve her in good stead; on the countless tours she was soon to start making, in Europe and the Americas, she too would sometimes return with more debts than savings.

But now, even with her debts, she was consoled by the thought that she was able to support her father. Over a year before her departure, he had happily retired and was living in Venice. From there, on 17 February 1886, he wrote to his brother Enrico, who was still on the road as an actor. "At last I see your handwriting!! after a long silence! Whereas you must be aware that for two years my residence has been Venice. But the pen weighs on your hand, though I know you have written my daughter Eleonora, even if she is always traveling about. But you were right, for she is generous and kind, as I cannot be, since I receive my daily bread from her—You must know that she is now in Rome and was attacked by a serious illness, which now is past. You must also know that my very dear son-in-law stayed in America, leaving her the heavy task of respecting the obligations he had assumed before leaving. . . . During Lent I hope to embrace my dear daughter again! This is for me a dear and happy moment, longed for amid all the fears and uncertainties I have gone through. . . ."

A few weeks later, the Rossi company—and Eleonora—were in Venice, and Alessandro had the joy of witnessing, from the house, his daughter's success. "The last performance was her benefit," he reported to Enrico later, "the theatre very crowded, many flowers and poems offered her. If she could have performed more often, she would have profited more, but in all of Lent she acted only fifteen evenings, always to a full house. The other evenings, the house was unfortunately almost empty. She is in partnership with Rossi, but next year that is dissolved. I believe that after Trieste, she will take two months off. For that matter she is better now, and if her health assists her, she will be able to satisfy everyone and everything."

The Trieste season, which ended on 3 June, was a success for Eleonora, but not a happy time. Summing up the results, the anonymous chronicler of the Teatro Verdi wrote in his ledger, "The forthcoming separation of la Duse from C. Rossi produced some ill-humor in the company, hence scarce inclination to rehearse the old plays and even less the new, because la Duse, being indisposed and under medical care, had orders from the physician not to tire herself."

Still, on her "serata," 1 June, when she played Dumas's *Denise*, the Verdi was filled, and—the chronicler reports—she received "ten bouquets, a cushion [of flowers], star, fan. This last, with two bouquets, was from the management of the theatre." Trieste had made amends.

5
Arrigo

"This evening the company of Cesare Rossi gives its final performance. At Lent it is dissolving: la Duse becomes an actress-manager. Cesare Rossi is taking a year's rest, then he will return as actor-manager." Thus the *Corriere di Roma* reported the closing night of the troupe, 19 December 1886. The drama critic of the year-old newspaper, run by Matilde Serao and her husband Edoardo Scarfoglio, was the Neapolitan Edoardo Boutet, a protégé of Cafiero's. In summing up the Rossi-Duse season, Boutet said, "Frankly, I am glad this company is breaking up. Little by little, imperceptibly, it had become one of those curious companies for which Salvini and Ernesto Rossi set the bad example. . . . The performances of the Rossi company were of two kinds: those with Duse and those without Duse. When Duse was not performing, the negligence, the limpness, the error of the staging affected everything and reached the interpretation. When Duse acted, there was an enormous gap between her and the other actors; but something different could be observed: a certain improvement, from the furniture to the ensemble, to the revelation of the characters. The obvious difference does not lie in the great talent of Duse and the lesser talent of the others: it lies in the want of direction."

Though in later years, Duse expressed—and proved—her gratitude to Rossi for the important contribution he had made to the shaping of her career, their last months together were not harmonious. For that matter, their characters were bound to be incompatible: unlike Duse, Rossi was a penny-pincher. And he was also conventional in his choice of repertory. He not only opposed *Cavalleria rusticana*, which then proved a huge hit; but he also flatly refused to consider Giacosa's *Tristi amori*, arguably the author's best play, which—after another company had failed in it—Duse presented triumphantly in her first season under her own management.

What, exactly, did being a manager mean, in the Italy of the late nineteenth century? In Duse's case, it meant that she chose the repertory, the troupe, cast the plays, supervised the *mise-en-scène*. Moreover, she was financially responsible for everything: she signed the contracts with the owners of the various theatres, collected the takings, and paid the actors. If for some reason performances had to be canceled, the troupe still had to be paid. And since, increasingly, her own ill-health required such cancellations, she was frequently in financial difficulties, even though she played to capacity audiences at high prices. For the day-to-day running of the company, she had an *amministratore*, a manager; but he was an employee (sometimes he would also be a bit-player), and she often treated him as one.

Her new company was called the Compagnia della Città di Roma, and associated with her was Flavio Andò, who had also left Rossi. Though Duse did not have a high opinion of his intelligence, Andò was an asset. Handsome, elegant, he was not only a popular, versatile actor but also skilled and intuitive as a director and could assume responsibility for the staging of the repertory.

Except for *Tristi amori*, a work in Giacosa's new, Ibsenesque vein, that repertory at first was not particularly adventurous. Duse and Andò were seen in *Fédora*, *Denise*, *Divorçons*, and other familiar plays by Sardou and Dumas. Duse revived Goldoni's *Pamela nubile*, one of the Venetian writer's less frequently-played comedies, and had a personal success. But her intellectual restlessness, her constant desire to extend her range as an actress, would soon lead her to explore new authors, new areas of the drama. Ahead of her lay Ibsen, Maeterlinck, D'Annunzio, and—briefly—Shakespeare. She was to return to him, not in the part of Juliet that had revealed her art to her, but in the character of a less limpid, more demanding heroine: Cleopatra. She came to the play through Arrigo Boito, who was to influence the rest of her life.

After their brief meeting in 1884 and their exchange of playful, half-flirtatious, but innocent letters, Eleonora and Boito had apparently had no further direct communication, though, since they had many friends in common—chiefly Giacosa and Primoli—they must have known about each other's activities. Eleonora's successes, for that matter, were reported constantly in the newspapers; and Boito, having provided the libretto for Verdi's *Otello* (premiere at La Scala, 5 February 1887), was a cultural hero.

Eleonora was now twenty-eight, and though she was nationally famous she was still at the outset of her career. At forty-five, Arrigo was at the peak of his. At the end of January 1887, a few days before the *Otello* opening, as Milan was already filling with foreign critics, composers, dignitaries, celebrities, when not a ticket was to be had at any price, Giacosa told Boito that, if a ticket were to become free, Duse would like to attend, though she was too shy to ask the librettist himself. Whether she did go to the first *Otello* or not is unknown. But on 11 February, six days after the clamorous event, the Verdis and Boito were in a box at the Teatro Manzoni, where Duse was playing Goldoni's *Pamela*.

Years later, Eleonora wrote Arrigo from St Petersburg:

"Do you remember, one of the first evenings?

"Verdi was in the box, with you—Goldoni was on the boards. You came to see me in the interval . . . we smiled . . . no more—

"You had some flowers in your buttonhole—and as you left, ten fingers entwined, one with the other."

On 20 February 1888, Boito also recalled the beginning: "For a year we have lived in a dream! Exactly one year: not an hour more, not an hour less." And so we know, almost to the minute, when Eleonora and Arrigo became lovers.

Their correspondence, most of which seems to have survived, has been published; it fills a thick volume of almost a thousand pages. Love letters are seldom enjoyable reading (except for their recipients), but these are particularly tiresome, surprisingly so since both writers were people of exceptional intelligence. Still, as they were frequently separated, the letters often give an almost daily record of their relationship, over long periods. Their relationship: not their lives. Boito does occasionally refer to *Falstaff* (the libretto for Verdi was begun in 1889, and the opera was first performed in 1893) and, more often, he mentions his own *Nerone*, the opera he worked on—or pretended to work on—for most of his life and left in a muddle at his death. Duse rarely talks about her repertory, and almost never about the day-to-day life of the theatre, which was, after all, *her* life.

Mostly, they write about their feelings; and they discuss plans, arrange meetings, which frequently failed to come off. Duse's first letters are brief, ecstatic, breathless, somewhat like the telegrams she had a lifelong passion for sending. None of these early notes is dated.

"Arrigo—Come—

"Come at once.

"The blessed room, where you live, I already blessed yesterday—

"You come here—

"If I came to you, I would be late, and I have only minutes.

"Come.

"At once."

And another one goes:

"At one—to the study.

"I will come—

"Tonight, at my place, it is impossible because I have a dinner.

"At one—to the study.

"—See the door is unlocked—I will come."

Meticulous, precise, Boito was a creature of habit. He never married, and lived in the same building—but in his own apartment—with his brother Camillo, a distinguished architect, and Camillo's wife. Boito's rooms, his study and bedroom, were on the ground floor, opening off the courtyard of the building, a large, modern palazzo at 1 Via Principe Amedeo. In her letters, Eleonora often refers to the details of the rooms and their furnishings.

The first weeks were impassioned, dazed. In their private world (the affair was, and remained, a jealously guarded secret), they invented dozens of baby-names for each other: Eleonora was Bumba, Zozzoletta, Bimbuscola, or—in more serious moments—Lenor; Arrigo was Bumbo, Bombi, Ozzoli, Zozzi. The kittenish tone encouraged them also to write of themselves in the third person, in a vocabulary that included made-up words, dialect expressions, private jokes. Boito's letters, for the most part, are written in his tidy, regular hand; he had a phobia about breaking up a word at the end of a line so would enlarge or reduce his writing to make sure that each line ended with a completed word. Duse's letters splash and sprawl, words run down margins, take up most of a page. Sometimes she would write their two names—Lenor and Arrigo—superimposed, a graphic emblem of their love.

Inevitably, after the first weeks, they were separated. Lenor went off with the Compagnia della Città di Roma; Arrigo spent much of that month of April 1887 at the Hotel Eden in Nervi, where he was supervising the French and English translations of *Otello*, corresponding with Verdi, who was still in his winter residence in nearby Genoa. From time to time, however, Arrigo managed to steal away and join Lenor. In early summer, June and July, she was in Sicily; and the lovers met in Palermo, traveled to Reggio Calabria together, then back to Messina.

In August Lenor had some time free; and they stayed for a while in a remote mountain locality, San Giovanni Bianco, north of Bergamo. The little town, at the confluence of two rivers, is delightfully picturesque, a town of bridges and sudden, broad views; and for the lovers it was a magic holiday. Boito communicated to Eleonora his passion for Dante. "You remember the Canto of Faith?" he wrote later.

"We read it on the other side of the river. When we reached the last terzina, I couldn't go on, and I broke off, saying: 'It's too beautiful!'— Our little house stood out, white against the hill, like the page of a white book."

In the little house they also read Shakespeare; and it was there that the idea of Boito's translating *Antony and Cleopatra* for Duse was born. Evidently he actually began work on the translation, because a short time afterwards, when he had left, Eleonora wrote him that she would copy it out.

He stayed in the little white house only a week; then he had to go to Milan and Switzerland. Lenor stayed on for a while, but felt lost without him. On 19 August she wrote:

"1st Day—ARRIGO—LOVE—ZOZZOLI—Arrigo! It's the first day—and the first hours are painful

"But we will recover!—

"Arrigo—Arrigo! Arrigo!

"—All! All!

"Lenor: calls Arrigo."

In the same envelope, on a separate slip of paper, there is a mis-spelled note in a childish hand from the five-year-old Enrichetta: "Dear Signor Boito, you left and I was unable to say goodbye. I say goodbye very much and are you well? When will we see each other again?" It is signed: Nerichetta (the child also had a pet name, naturally); and with a P.S.: "Mamma sends greetings."

That night, or rather at two the next morning, Lenor wrote again: "How empty your room is . . . The bed unmade. . . .

"I know—I know—It was necessary—It had to be done. . . . You have . . . *your work* waiting for you. . . .

"But the one who stays behind! who finds each object still warm— who cannot regain the heavy sleep of two hours before, who remembers the chair in the same place, and the cigarette with the tiny, imperceptible mark of the little tooth,—ahi ahi. . . ."

At four a.m. she added another page, and then a P.S. after dinner. She wrote him again on the 22nd and then on the 24th and 25th. The little house, without him, had become unbearable, even though his letters arrived promptly and regularly. She left on the 25th, stopping in Bergamo, where she had heard they were doing his *Mefistofele*. But she got there on the night the theatre was dark. She pressed on to Genoa, where her company was to assemble for the coming season. But in spite of all the concerns connected with her organization, she main-tained her resolve and worked on their Shakespeare project. On

14 September she wrote: "It's 3—I had sat down at the desk to continue copying out the other parts in *Cleop.*"

On 16 September the company opened with *Fédora*, and on coming back to her rented apartment Lenor wrote Arrigo, at half-past midnight, "The premiere went well!—Arrigo! . . . what an effort it is to resume the road! God, how I had forgotten all that—and how I am in the midst of it again!— . . .

"This evening, as I was working, and as I forced out the words, I said to myself—'a year and a half still!'—"

Though Boito had written a play himself (in collaboration with his friend Emilio Praga) and was a regular theatre-goer, he often expressed a contempt for the theatrical world, for the falsity of the stage—the legitimate stage, that is, not the opera house. And he transmitted this contempt to Lenor, not only encouraging her to break away from her familiar, worn repertory of Dumas and Sardou, but even suggesting she should give up acting altogether. His translation of *Antony and Cleopatra* was thus intended both as an ennoblement of her art and as a step towards her abandonment of it. Chronically unable to save money, Duse had put nothing aside from her already substantial earnings. Now, with Boito's moral support, she was planning to work only another two seasons, saving enough to take care of herself and Enrichetta. After that: retirement—and Arrigo.

Concluding this long letter, she wrote: "Arrigo!—Blessed be your work!—If mine does not hold up, between the ideal and the real—too bad . . . Blessed be yours! Last night, I had *unlearned* everything—everything, how base a thing the *theatre* is, when it doesn't rise to the highest circle!—"

And the letter is signed "Venezia," because the dream of retirement—and of living with Boito and Enrichetta, now about to be bundled off to boarding-school—was set in Venice. There, in Boito's phrase, the "three heads at one window" would be able to look out at the lagoon, whose color—Eleonora said—was reflected in Arrigo's gray-green eyes.

But *Cleopatra* was still in the distant future. Meanwhile, Duse continued with her familiar parts, struggling against bouts of ill health and the uncomfortable theatre in Genoa. At the beginning of October, Arrigo paid her a quick, twenty-four-hour visit, then went on to Cernobbio on Lake Como, where he always spent a month in the autumn, visiting his old friend, the Milanese aristocrat Donna Vittoria Cima. Lenor's letters—sometimes two in a single day—followed him there.

At the end of October, the company went from Genoa to Turin, where they opened on 1 November at the Teatro Gerbino with an old play, *Amore senza stima* by Paolo Ferrari. The Turin public, which felt a kind of proprietary affection for Duse, welcomed her back—she had been absent from the city for several seasons—with "one of those loud, cordial, endless ovations [as the *Gazzetta* reported] reserved for great art."

The season at the Gerbino went on for almost two months and was successful, but it was a period of difficulties and concerns for Eleonora. In addition to the continued separation from Arrigo, there was also the question of Enrichetta. She was now approaching her sixth birthday and her mother had found a boarding-school just outside Turin, an exclusive and costly *collegio* (the down payment was a thousand lire, an enormous sum); and in November the child was taken there, the first in a long series of schools and *pensionnats* which would house her in Italy, Germany, France, and finally England, which became her home.

She suffered, and Duse suffered too. (In later years, when Enrichetta had grown up, her mother frequently wrote self-justifying letters, explaining the necessity of their separation.) Lenor's letters to Arrigo tell of the child's unhappiness and are, perhaps, also hinted references to the imagined future of the three of them together, a family, after Duse's equally imaginary retirement in the space of a couple of seasons.

The future with Boito may have included a notion of marriage, for also at this time Eleonora wrote to Florence for a copy of her marriage certificate. "In two or three days' time I'll set in motion the business I must attend to," she wrote to Boito on 1 November, referring to the process of legal separation, to be handled by the prominent lawyer Nasi. Eventually, when Tebaldo threatened to claim Enrichetta, the idea had to be dropped.

Professionally, Eleonora was also frustrated. After the warm welcome, and despite a good press, she felt that the audience had turned fractious. After one of his brief visits, Boito tried to console her: "The *Torinesi* this time seemed to me very provincial and petty bourgeois and stupid. If that's how they are, it's a misfortune for Turin, not for you. Their judgment will not influence that of the other cities that still do not know the beautiful play [*Francillon* by Dumas *fils*] . . . Rome will make it up to you."

In Turin, Eleonora saw a good deal of Boito's closest friend, Giacosa, the big, paternal, rather strait-laced "Pin." The free-spirited actress also observed what seemed to her the crushing, oppressive effect of family life on the writer. In a letter of 11 November she trained her acute eye—and her unconventional pen—on an evening at the Giacosas', for Arrigo's benefit:

"There were two lamps burning in his study, which is also the living room . . . (but *people* should not enter where work is done—*that* should be a private room, protected from people . . . like the *other*, the room of *love*)—

"Well—There was the mamma of his Wife—Maria—and two relations, two young men—And then—Pin, there in the middle, who tore his brain to shreds to entertain them—

"I can't repeat the *conversation* (!) for you (Pin talked all the time), nor can I give you a little portrait of the *characters*—but I admired our big friend so much, so very much—and I was so fond of him!—

"When I see you—I'll explain better—But—one more word—If you can facilitate it somehow, make it easier for Giacosa to move to Milan. Do it! do it!"

The following autumn, at least partially through Boito's now considerable influence, Giacosa was indeed able to move from the stultifying atmosphere of Turin to the more stimulating Milan (though, of course, he brought his family, including his widowed mother, along with him). Eleonora would not have approved.

"Giacosa needs a DENSE life," she wrote Arrigo. "They squeeze him, they shred him—They interrogate him—To interrogate talent!!! The poor man tells everything, of his heart and of his art.

"He hasn't a book that *they* don't leaf through—He hasn't an article, that *they* don't read in advance—he hasn't an ideal that isn't laid open before them—

"All that fertility, that *reproducing himself* EVERY DAY . . . is harmful—"

Eleonora's horrified description of Giacosa's domestic life, which—by all other accounts—was totally happy and serene, is an indication of her own restless, independent nature, her passion for privacy, her protectiveness towards her art. In this—though neither of them would have admitted it—she and Boito were alike; and so the dream of "three heads at one window" was just that: a dream that, for temperamental more than material reasons, could never conceivably be realized.

During Duse's first weeks in Turin, Boito was at Cernobbio, visiting Donna Vittoria Cima; but then he was in Milan, only a few hours away. He and Lenor could have seen each other often, constantly. Eleonora was working, but Boito was his own master, without fixed hours. In their letters, they speak always of his work ("I believe in it!" she wrote); but Arrigo spent little time at his desk, over his music-paper. Much of his day was spent doing minute, endless research on early-Christian Rome, for his millstone-magnum-opus, *Nerone*. And, when asked, he was always ready to serve on a committee or a board, to act as consultant. He was a chronic procrastinator, who, as he once confessed to Verdi, could work better for others than for himself. At the same time, he had spells of dejection, self-doubt, of a kind that the more vital Lenor could not have understood.

The two of them wrote and wrote about meeting, but they actually saw each other surprisingly little. This was the "anno vissuto nel sogno," the year lived in a dream. And to the reader of their letters today, it does seem a dream, that year; there is an abstract, almost artificial quality about their declarations.

In her letters to Arrigo, Duse rarely speaks of other actors; but while she was playing at the Gerbino in Turin, Ernesto Rossi (no relation of her old colleague Cesare) was giving a season of Shakespeare at the Carignano. On one of his free evenings, he came to her opening in *Francillon* and visibly led the applause. At sixty he was internationally celebrated and an Italian pride; he had toured all of Europe, and both Americas, to universal admiration. But by now he was tired, fat, bordering on the ridiculous. Lenor returned his visit and saw him in *Lear* and *Hamlet*; she was aghast. "A tooth-puller," she called him, to Arrigo; and after his Hamlet she said: "A horror as an actor, a charlatan as a man."

Still, those inadequate performances prodded her, fed the flames of another dream shared with Arrigo. "I WANT to play Shakespeare—! My head is full of visions and dreams—I didn't sleep all night!"

Then, after complaining about Rossi's Lear: "O beautiful soul of Shakespeare, how they ruin you! No! No! Truth—Truth!—and ideal, and poetry . . . there: there is so much stuff that makes one live! He so ennobled the human race!—"

And the letter ends: "I wish I were a man . . . I would like to have your strength: you'd see whether in Egypt I'll have a heart!—I'd like to be a man—I would tell you how one loves—"

But before she could face Shakespeare, she was to perform another of her acts of professional courage. At the end of the previous March, Giacosa's *Tristi amori* had been a disastrous failure at the Teatro Valle in Rome. Convinced of this work's value, Pin showed it to Duse and asked her to risk it. At first, she seemed to be staging it more out of kindness than conviction. As she wrote to Arrigo: "I will give *Tristi amori* in Turin—I won't argue the matter with you—I know I will please Pin—and I'm doing it—He is hoping for a success. . . . Perhaps this pleases you too—and I'm doing it—Am I doing the right thing? . . . Yes, yes . . . when I consider it, it seems to me that it will stand up in the theatre."

Later, in rehearsal, she began to have doubts. On 24 November, less than a week before opening night, she told Arrigo, "Pin's play doesn't have the ingredients of success.—Believe me!—The more I see it on stage, the more I find it without interest." Four days later, she was still not completely convinced. "Yesterday rehearsals went well, and Pin said he could feel the thrill of success—God will it!—Yesterday, for a moment, I also felt it, but, loving Pin, I realize I'm not a good judge. . . . Pin told me you will come with Gualdo. . . ."

Eleonora's lack of confidence in *Tristi amori* seems odd in view of her determination to present it. Partly she was doing it to please Arrigo, but—despite her misgivings—she must have realized the originality of Pin's new work, closer to Ibsen than to his own previous dramas.

Arrigo came to Turin, stayed at the Hotel Trombetta, attended the premiere, and kept vigil with Pin afterwards. The next day, 1 December, Eleonora had to get up early and take Enrichetta to her new school. At 1 p.m. Boito was at her apartment; he then stayed in Turin four or five days—for him, a long visit.

This time the play was a hit. Even the stuffy Turin public accepted this bitter story of adultery and sacrifice. The drama—a wife who renounces her lover to stay with her child and her husband in chaste, cold resignation—was not far removed, as far as the plot went, from the triangles of Augier and Dumas *fils*. But the familiar setting, in a provincial Piedmontese town, and the persuasive details (in the midst of a crisis, the wife has to go over the household accounts with the maid) were something new. In the *Corriere della sera* Giovanni Pozza, who had come from Milan for the premiere, wrote that it was "a solemn artistic event, such as the Italian theatre had not celebrated for some time. The Gerbino was packed, the audience crammed the stalls, the side aisles. Not one more person could have found a place downstairs or in the galleries, filled with a young crowd of students. Expectation was great. The importance of the innovating force of the theatre was known. . . . The public was swept away, from the very first scenes on. Success was immediate. At the end of the first act victory was decreed. Then there was a crescendo of admiration, of applause."

Again, as in the case of Verga's *Cavalleria rusticana*, this success should have been a turning-point for the Italian bourgeois theatre. But somehow it was not. Giacosa's next play, written in French for Bernhardt, was *La Dame de Challant*, another of his medieval verse dramas, a would-be star turn. After his move to Milan, he wrote some more plays (including *Come le foglie*, arguably his best, again in a bourgeois setting); but he devoted much of his time to other literary activities, including collaboration in the writing of librettos for Puccini. These—*La Bohème*, *Tosca*, *Madama Butterfly*—are what have made his name familiar to later generations.

The reception of *Tristi amori* should have marked a new direction in Duse's career, too. A Turin critic, Giuseppe Depanis, wrote: "I do not know Signora Duse personally, nor in the past have I burned that copious incense that threatened to suffocate her; but after her interpretation of the character of Emma, I can only think of the enormous progress dramatic art would make in a short time if la Duse's artistic criteria—criteria, mind you, not personal mannerisms—were to find many followers. In *Tristi amori*, Signora Duse proved, better than in other works, that she is a great artist. Here there are no scenes written for effect, no tirades, no display of fine sentiments or ostentation of wicked passions . . . instead, a sobriety of speech and movement unusual in her. A glance, a gesture, a silence—and the state of her soul appears to the public in its true light."

These last words could have described Duse's portrayals of the great Ibsen heroines: but Nora, Rebecca, Hedda, and Ellida were still in her future. After a few performances of *Tristi amori*, for her "serata" it was back to Dumas and *Denise*, and perhaps to a different style of acting, closer to the grand gestures of Sarah. It is interesting to compare Depanis's description of her Emma in *Tristi amori*, a watered-down *Doll's House*, with Primoli's description of her in *La Princesse de Bagdad*, quoted above in Chapter Three (p. 31).

Just before Christmas the company left Turin for Rome, where she was to play for over a month at the Teatro Valle. After the shabby Gerbino, the Roman house with its white hall and gold decorations seemed sumptuous; and the toilettes in the boxes, the audience of aristocracy, diplomats, statesmen, and artists, created a welcome air of elegance. In Rome, she found old friends, like Gégé Primoli, and old enemies: the critics (at least, she considered them enemies). Matilde Serao seemed to her to be trapped, diminished by the marriage to Scarfoglio (which, for that matter, did not last long). Primoli, Matilde, and especially Scarfoglio were all friends of Gabriele D'Annunzio, then twenty-four years old. He had been in Rome about five years, and was already recognized as a brilliant poet and a clever journalist. He wrote a much-followed society column and, of course, attended the theatre. According to some biographers, Eleonora met him in this period. It is quite likely, but, if she did, he did not make the impression that he would make some years later, when they met again, in Venice.

Her free hours were still filled with thoughts of Arrigo. Their correspondence continued, an almost daily exchange of letters (and reading them now, one can only envy the speed and reliability of the Italian postal services a century ago). Her letters are impetuous, sometimes silly, sometimes heart-baring, vivid. His, equally silly at times, are more sober, more cautious.

In October, following his long-standing custom, Boito spent some weeks at the villa of Donna Vittoria Cima. In December, again following his regular habits, he spent a period in Nervi, where the climate, milder than Milan's, would presumably foster his work. He occasionally made a brief visit to Milan, and from there, on 30 December, he wrote to Lenor:

"*Creatura!*—For almost a year I have lived only with my heart. Now I must shift the burning centre of life from the heart to the brain. I must work *continuously*; this word, our last night in Turin, I said almost in tears, and it was not for fear of the toil that I love and that exalts me: it was because I felt in that *continuously* the jab of a new sacrifice. *To work continuously* means having to forget for almost all waking hours, and every day, the sweet thought of us. It means being separated also in our spirit, to be separated by work far more than by distance. But this courage is necessary. I must work towards a life compared to which the one I have lived is only a shadow, and this life is *ours.*—I feel sad and strong. You are strong and happy. Courage! Stand erect! Let the soul uplift your body. Pride is your health.—Go, good creature, to the toilsome *festa* of every evening, go before the mob; it is I who thrust you and tell you to be beautiful and lofty. Honor is with you.—

"Peace is not far off—Work. . . ."

From Nervi then, Boito also wrote about Enrichetta's part in their future: "She will be your companion, ours.—We will save her from the fatal heritage [i.e. the theatre] that is perpetuated in your race, that condemns you to live only for others—No, the happy child will not be cast body and soul into that sad game of Pretence of life. Life is sacred, its rights are divine, they will not be taken from the girl. Even if she were to have the radiance of your mind and wanted to rise to where you are, we will prevent it with all our strength. . . ."

But while he was expressing this scorn of the theatre, of Lenor's profession, her art, Boito was also thinking of the Shakespeare tragedy he had translated for her. On 22 January 1888, he wrote her a long letter about the costumes for *Antony and Cleopatra*. He also proposed extensive cuts in the text, including the whole first part of the last act. In this way, he argued, her character would not be eclipsed.

In mid-February Eleonora was in Florence. On the 20th, Boito wrote to her from Nervi. It was the anniversary of their first night of love, and this is the letter in which he said they had lived for exactly one year in a dream.

A few days later, on 29 February, after reading an interview with her in a newspaper, he wrote in more severe terms:

"And another thing I wanted to say to you. How shall I put it? Do not fall in love with tears. I call you *poor* because this word is a caress, but remember what riches you have in your life. Art smiles upon you and, with it, good luck: your child is good, wise, sensible; she is beautiful and calls to you and soon you will see her. There is one who has accepted the strong sorrow of loving you. So do not abuse weeping.

"I read, not without embarrassment, that you wept copiously in front of a certain Gabardi, an interviewer. . . . A friend showed me, laughing, that vulgar piece of commercial prose where you are described in the clumsiest, most grotesque manner imaginable, running about the room, jumping up from the sofa, thrashing about in a paroxysm of emotion, unburdening yourself in endless confidences. . . .

"I have said these words to you so that you will not fall into a similar trap a second time. . . . You do not need those journalists. . . ."

The letter was hard on Eleonora, who even at this fairly early point in her career, was shy of interviews and standoffish with journalists; with the passing years, her shyness became part of the legend (and, inevitably, was condemned by some writers as a pose). Boito's letter must have offended her. Her answer does not survive, but his next letter, apologizing, suggests its tone: "Ass that I was last night! I wanted you different from what you are, different from the way I want you. It would be the same as killing you. Weep your tears, poor and good creature; weep them as long as you want. If the source is plentiful, it is more blessed by God and man. . . . And be silent or speak, as you like, with me and with others: I will kiss both your silence and your words! But cling hard, that I may feel your weight; when I seem not to feel it any more, all reason for living disappears.—Pass, untainted, through the corruption that your strange destiny collects around you.—I know who you are. . . ."

In that early spring, Lenor wanted to make a quick dash from Florence to Nervi, to see Arrigo; but he put her off, insisting the exertion would be too much for her. Actually, the days proposed by Lenor coincided with the end of the Verdis' stay in their Genoa winter residence, and Arrigo spent the time with them. Like Boito's other friends—except Giacosa—the old composer and his wife were unaware of the relationship between Boito and Duse.

Their meetings were almost always fleeting and had to be planned with the care of major strategical moves. It was usually Boito who, timetable in hand, worked out the arrangements. His letter of 8 March 1888 is typical:

Now pay attention. You, on a day of your choice (you will advise me by letter three days before), go to the station. Give a porter enough for him to buy you a ticket for Chiavari. You leave at eight in the morning. You arrive at Chiavari at 58 minutes after midday. I am already there, ready, having been waiting for you for a quarter of an hour. I will have been there a quarter of an hour if my train (which belongs to the tortoise variety) is not too late. If my train is late (it is a so-called *local train*), you will enquire at the station, and then you will wait, without moving, a few minutes; but it would be strange for it to be that late.

Then we go to the hotel to eat. Then we take a carriage and off! into the spring sun. (But you must provide yourself with a *lap-robe* and cover yourself well.) Then when we see a lovely spot we get out of the carriage and off! on foot, on the grass. Nothing will be visible but the sea and He who made it.—Then we return to the hotel and stay there, we dine alone, evening comes, night comes.—Then dawn comes. Our eighteen hours will be ended but we will have lived them with *our life*.—At six in the morning we will leave again. I accompany you to Sestri Levante, then we separate. I will go back on foot to Chiavari, where I will find the train that takes me home. But there is one bad thing, just one: think about it carefully. For your return you will have to travel in an *omnibus* train, which takes eight hours to reach Florence. However, those very slow trains have one great advantage: very few people take them and one is almost always alone in a compartment and comfortable.

You would be back in Florence at 2.15 in the afternoon, after having lunched in Pisa.—Waiting for the through train would not be advisable: you would reach Florence at 7.26 in the evening.— . . . In all the other places where the through train stops there are people who know me. The place I am suggesting is one that curious people have ignored. . . .

All this meticulous planning went for nothing; Lenor stayed in Florence. Later in the spring, when the company had moved to Venice, Boito had to be in Bologna for a while, at the great Esposizione di Musica (he was on the committee). As usual, he sent her all the possible train-times, and added: "I am staying in a ground-floor room of the annex of the Hotel d'Italia, a very free room, which has two exits, where nobody ever goes by; it seems made for us two. The room is three steps from an entrance to the building, without a sign of a doorman or attendant; the entrance is on a deserted street. Three steps, unseen by anyone, and you are in Zozzoli's room; the building entrance remains open till nine at night, even later."

In Venice Lenor saw her friend Matilde Acton, the Austrian-born widow of one of the Neapolitan Actons. With her, Eleonora devoted her free time to studying French. She was soon proficient in the language and, with time, she actually preferred it to Italian for conversation and correspondence. Arrigo joined her in Venice. It was, after all, the city of the dream, their imagined future together. But for the more immediate future, for the approaching summer, Boito was already making elaborate plans for another secret holiday in the mountains above Ivrea in Piedmont. Giacosa had found for them an abandoned convent, San Giuseppe, near Chiaverano. There the eighteenth-century hermitage looked down on the romantic Lake Sirio, in a bowl of wooded peaks.

There was an impediment, however: Lenor's lungs had been giving her trouble, and the doctors insisted that, when her season ended, she should go to Roncegno, in the Dolomites, to take the famous waters. Instead of reaching San Giuseppe—and Arrigo—on 1 July, as planned, she got there almost two weeks later, to stay till the end of August. Arrigo went there first. In the train on his way to Ivrea, he read the paper and received a shock. As he wrote her on 5 July: "Yesterday (on trains, out of idleness one devours newspapers) I read some news you had concealed from me. If you knew what a mistake you are making when you exclude me from your serious confidences and your resolutions, you would not do it.

"You know me, and you know I have never prevented you from any step in your career, never. It is hard for me to be told in the shameless jargon of the newspaper what you could say to me in all simplicity if you did not have that invincible horror of the courageous word that goes straight to the point, however painful it may be.

"The printed news said that you leave on 1 August for Germany and then for America."

The news was erroneous. From Roncegno, Lenor came to the old convent at San Giuseppe and stayed there for six weeks. She was not going to Germany, and almost five years would go by before her first visit to the United States.

At the beginning of September, however, she had to resume her work; and at the same time, she got down to the serious preparations for her production of *Antony and Cleopatra*. Boito stayed on at San Giuseppe for a while, to work; but on at least two occasions he was able to slip away for brief meetings with Lenor, in Pisa and then in Milan.

In her letters, she now spoke more about her work: that is, about *Cleop*, as she called it. Boito, in return, sent her instructions for the staging: "The two pickaninnies must remain. Don't worry about the way they'll walk. Children, on stage, are always winning, so long as they don't speak. If they walk awkwardly they'll be even more cute. But you must find some tiny, skinny ones, and when they are well costumed and well dyed black, with their kinky wigs, they will become two cherubs of local color, invaluable for the first impression. They will enter with Ant. and Cleop. and go out with Ant. and Cleop. The first scene is very brief."

After many other suggestions and elucidations, he ended the letter: "So you are there, you live in the immense tragedy! Lucky you! I never doubted. You know.—From the days of the white house I saw you, hour by hour, take possession of the masterpiece, reconstruct it. Yes, yes. Throw away all those costume sketches. *Tragic* lines and hues are what is needed, not something for a *choreographic action*. The character of Charmian is so easy to play that you can rehearse it yourself and experience it, then decide on your own from reality. . . ."

Two days later, on 3 November, he wrote again: "I like seeing you hard at work in the Shakespearean arsenal.—Do it your way, always in your own way; you will overcome all resistance. The idiots are heavy and inert masses, but with a good shove they can be made to roll where one wants.—You live now in the loftiest intellectual environment that exists in art, in a healthy and exquisite exaltation of activity. . . ."

Finally, on 22 November 1888, Shakespeare's *Antony and Cleopatra* opened at the Teatro Manzoni in Milan. This was not the tragedy's first Italian production, but the work was still little known, far less popular than *Hamlet* or *Macbeth*; and so this premiere was doubly a gala event. Boito—who had not allowed his name to appear on the playbills as translator—remained at San Giuseppe, where Lenor had promised to telegraph him the news of the outcome. The outcome was not good.

Duse, of course, was applauded; but in general the public was cold, and the adaptation was condemned.

As his letters, already quoted, suggest, Boito had allowed himself many liberties. There were not only sizable cuts, but also transpositions of lines, rearrangements. Since Boito's English was scant (if it existed at all), he based his work on the French translation of François-Victor Hugo, son of the poet, whose versions of Shakespeare have been described as "bourgeois" and "unpoetic." But it was not just the prosaic tone of Boito's text that caused the near-failure. In his effort to create a vehicle for Lenor, and in his low opinion of the rest of her company, he drastically reduced the importance of Antony and played down the smaller roles as well.

Though Shakespeare had entered the regular Italian repertory only a few decades earlier, the critics now had firm ideas about him and they were able to examine Boito's work with clarity and insight. In the Milanese paper *Il caffè* for 23/24 November, the drama critic wrote:

"Another disappointment. . . . The drama performed last night is only a pale reflection of the great page of history dramatized and brought to life, the tragedy by Shakespeare. . . . Scenes were cut that are absolutely necessary to explain the logical succession of events, characters who have a serious value both in themselves and in the drama are distorted. The great battle of Actium that constitutes the pivot of all the action is not sufficiently prominent. . . ."

On the other hand, the critic praised Duse for her courage in making this effort, "rather than reviving one of the works in which she would have a sure and easy triumph."

Some of the reviews suggest not only that Eleonora had won the enmity of certain critics but also that, as the Egyptian queen, she had temporarily abandoned the "Duse style," even forcing her usually soft, harmonious voice and subtle gestures.

The critic of *Il secolo* on 23/24 November wrote: "We are not among the fanatics of Signora Duse when she acts in a play, because we believe it is a caricature of the truth to turn your back on the audience when you speak, to indulge in unpleasantly wild gestures, to make the voice strident; and neurotic contortions may win all the applause you like as long as the fad lasts, but fads pass when they have no bases in sound art. It is certainly remarkable that Signora Duse, having been denied by nature a number of artistic gifts, has through study been able to force herself on the public and make it applaud her deservedly in many parts. But tragedy and drama of strong passions, like Shakespeare's *Antony and Cleopatra* . . . , are absolutely unsuited to her. She has neither the figure nor the voice for great characters. To achieve such a level she is forced to exaggerate with her voice, accenting the first syllable of every word and, abandoning the rest, to shout, to make efforts that become painful to those who see and hear her, when those who hear her are not already in the grip of preconceptions.

"The majority of the audience . . . applauded with great warmth, but we, who remember true and great artists, starting with the Maestra Ristori, confess that we were sadly struck by the immense gap."

Other papers were even more hostile. One described Duse's Cleopatra as "*La Femme de Claude* in Egyptian dress." The staging was generally praised, especially the costumes designed by Alfredo Edel, the twenty-nine-year-old artist who had also created the costumes for Verdi's *Otello* earlier that year.

Duse's morning-after telegram to Boito seems to be lost, but his letter to her, written on 23 November from San Giuseppe, indicates that she gave him at least a hint of the truth: ". . . That work, so brief, so stripped of all the shapeless but powerful exuberance of the text, seemed to me at the last moment something unworthy, a calumny of Shakespeare, a betrayal of Lenor.—And I had cruel thoughts against myself, I felt the guilt for the failure was mine, all mine, and that you, poor creature, tired, ill, in anguish, had to bear alone this blow which was brutal and which came to you from me! And I kept repeating: Forgive me, don't hate me! I was consoled by the idea that everyone would understand the fault was mine. And I thought they would laugh at the man who would not have his name on the poster and had remained hidden in the country. And I told myself it served me right. I deserve worse. And the fault really is mine if the success was unable to achieve its lofty climax in the last act.—The cause lies in the inept brevity of the adaptation. The public wants the right proportion, and is robbed if not given it, and comes out vexed and irritated. If, at the end, they did not disapprove, it is out of respect for you personally, for your name and your determination. I am convinced. And you must forgive me. . . ."

He suggested making further changes and offered to come to Milan; but Lenor—to his dismay—wrote him a short, rather curt note, asking him not to come: she was tired. And she was already packing to move on to Florence. Offended, Arrigo returned the note to her; but then he wrote again the next day, asking her forgiveness. These little quarrels-by-mail were a regular feature of their correspondence.

Temporarily, Duse dropped *Cleop* to revive the never-failing standby, *La Dame aux camélias*. By the beginning of December, she was installed in her Florentine lodgings, in Piazza Santa Maria Novella; and Arrigo's letters followed her there, sometimes apologetic, always encouraging. Verdi had seen her Cleopatra and was moved by it. "Verdi is all-wise," Arrigo wrote her, "and knows your worth as I do . . . Let that give you strength."

In Florence the public was eagerly awaiting the now notorious *Cleopatra* production. The critic of *La nazione*, Giulio Piccini (who signed himself "Jarro"), wrote a long, erudite article, which appeared over two days. After rambling on about Byron and Heine, quoting Pascal, referring to Guido Reni and Corneille, he praised Duse's unparalleled gifts, but said: "It must be admitted that the interpretation has not been sufficiently studied by the actress, even though she has studied it a great deal." And he complained about her "whining tone, which generates monotony," and her long, unnatural pauses. The theatre was very crowded, Jarro reported, but the reception was a bit cold. Duse rested for several days, then returned with Sardou's *Odette*, followed by his *Fernande* and Dumas's *Denise*. In these old warhorses, Jarro found her unrivaled.

From Florence to Naples. There Arrigo wrote her: "This time the battle of Shakespeare must be won. IT IS NECESSARY." His next letter indicates the outcome of the Neapolitan performance—"poor Shakespeare!"

But the failure of *Cleop* in Naples was not Eleonora's greatest worry there. In February, after a brief trip to Sicily, she came back to the city and fell ill, a gynecological ailment that involved painful treatment, cauterization, and left her weak, unable to work most of the time. In the month of February she gave only four performances; in March, one. And she had to go on paying the troupe while they were perforce idle. This was to become a recurrent situation as her career proceeded and her health—or her nerves—became less and less reliable. Because of her illness and her depression, she discouraged Arrigo from coming to see her. So, over the following months their correspondence assumed a feverish tone, filled with uncertainty, impatience, and long medical bulletins. At one point, her physician, the eminent Ottavio Morisani, mentioned the possibility of a hysterectomy, and Lenor wrote Arrigo in horror: "I would no longer be a woman. . . . I would revolt myself—I would feel I was one of those wretches who *feel* and don't *express*— . . ."

The operation was not necessary after all, and slowly Lenor regained her health. But the strain of those long weeks, months, of inactivity and separation had its effect also on the relationship with Boito. The two went on writing to each other, daily—sometimes more than one letter a day—but a forced tone creeps into some of the letters. There were more of their long-distance quarrels, an occasional flare-up of nerves over a trifle, a misunderstanding, a supposed reticence. Arrigo would accuse Lenor of telling less than the whole truth about her health or her plans. Lenor would write "crazy" letters, then send off long postscripts begging forgiveness.

In mid-June she was finally able to resume work, and she gave some long-postponed performances in Naples. In mid-July Arrigo joined her for two days; and after he had left, she walked to the station that same evening, "to follow the same street you had followed." And she ended that letter in an explosion of love: "Arrigo, Arrigo Arrigo! Ammmmore amore! so much, all all all all—so much much much all all! . . ."

Three days later, on 19 July 1889, Eleonora opened the newspaper and read of the appalling suicide of her young friend Matilde Acton, who had drowned herself in the Tegernsee. At once she wrote to Arrigo: "Arrigo—my little Acton! my little Acton!—Perhaps it's not true—she had such courage! she was so brave in the face of grief! My poor Acton. . . . Someone withdrew his protection of her——and she had had so much hope—she had so much courage. Arrigo! . . ."

Finally, on the evening of 23 July, she left Naples after a stay of nearly seven months. A few days later she was at San Giuseppe with Arrigo, where she remained almost three weeks. In spite of her long illness and the still-painful loss of Matilde, this must have been a happy holiday for Lenor. Temporarily giving up any pretence of working on *Nerone*, Boito was again working for Verdi: *Falstaff* was coming into existence, and both Boito and Verdi were excited about it. Boito had promised to take the first two acts of the libretto to Verdi in October, to the Villa Sant'Agata, after the usual autumn visit to Donna Vittoria Cima on Lake Como.

Eleonora was also eager to get back to work. From San Giuseppe she went first to Genoa, to collect Enrichetta and take her to Naples, where Lenor had to follow a brief cure under the supervision of Dr Morisani. She was nervous, impatient, and Enrichetta had to be entertained. "I do my best to amuse her—but there are times——. . . I feel exhausted——and then—and then . . . —Mind you! I *swear* I love that child . . . but I have moments . . . —when she does not suffice at all!"

At other moments, she praised the child's goodness, worried about Enrichetta's health as much as her own. But the important thing was that the cure seemed effective: "I CAN WORK!" she wrote. And in September she was back in Milan, and Enrichetta was back in boarding-school, happy to return. Arrigo was only a short distance away at Como, but he was as if sealed off by his aristocratic friends, the circle from which Lenor was excluded. On 27 September she wrote to him: "Signora Opp. [Oppenheim, a German friend, resident in Rome] yesterday wanted to take me to see the cathedral of Como. I felt tired and spent half the day in bed. . . .—If I had come to Como, how could I have resisted defying Donna Vittoria and PEEKING AT YOU from outside the gates?

"I didn't do it—

"I would never do it!!—I feel I would suffer too much!"

On 4 October, in Milan, she tried *Cleopatra* again, forbidding Arrigo to come to the performance. He left Como then on the 5th, and the two of them were together (or, at least, they were in the same city at the same time) until Lenor left for Naples once more around the middle of the month, and then on to Sicily. From Palermo, on 25 October, she wrote that her health was good, she was resuming work that night; and then there was a veiled, faintly bitter reference to Donna Vittoria, or perhaps even to Arrigo's mysterious friend, Fanny: "There are those in the world who can live at your side!—That is the true gift!—that is the true grace—."

Actually Fanny's health was deteriorating, but Boito had an even more painful concern. His closest friend, since their schooldays together, had been the brilliant conductor Franco Faccio—Boito was one of those men who seemed to feel more secure in male friendships than in his rapport with women—and now Faccio was ill. At this time he was showing the first, disturbing signs of the mental illness that was soon to develop into unmistakable insanity and lead to his death in 1891. In his worry and grief, Boito had to look after Faccio's affairs. Still, he managed to get away and meet Lenor in Naples—after the usual discussion of timetables and discreet hotels—and say goodbye to her before she set out again, for Egypt.

There she made her first foreign tour as her own manager. This was the modest beginning of her international career, the wide-ranging nomad life that was to be her existence for many years to come. In essence—except for one long interval—she was on tour until her death.

6
Egypt and Russia

The South American tour with Cesare Rossi had really been a continuation of the Italian years on the road, familiar since Duse's childhood. To Egypt she came not only as an absolute star but, more important, as her own manager, as founder and artistic director of the Compagnia drammatica della Città di Roma. The practical arrangements for the tour had been made by the impresario Sante Boni, a native of Leghorn, now resident in Egypt like so many other Italian entrepreneurs in the reign of the Khedive Tewfik, who—under British protection—was continuing the process of modernization begun by his energetic, controversial father Ismail Pasha.

Duse reached Alexandria on 17 December 1889 after a stormy crossing, which delayed her arrival twenty-four hours. But Boni's arrangements proved inadequate, and the first impressions were disappointing. "Difficulties have arisen," she wrote to Arrigo on New Year's Day. "And the management itself, here in Alexandria, achieved no concrete results. In the end I will barely clear expenses—no more and no less—so the anguish of the journey and the separation have been futile!—

"So it goes! We can almost never *work*, for one reason or another. And on the working evenings we have only an average Italian take—exactly—and so, since we are *abroad*, it just suffices—"

Egypt itself did not appeal to her at first. "A hateful country," she wrote, "a hateful place to work. An audience made up of seven varieties, each more vulgar than the other! The French colony, which is the largest in the country, is hostile and doesn't come. The climate, the hotel life—nothing of what I see is made for me! Alexandria is nothing but a *Bazaar*—dirty and wretched!—with stupefied people who smoke from morning to night—*dazed* by the sun—asleep—huddled up—"

But the Italian papers told a happier story. On 20 January 1890, the *Gazzetta Piemontese* carried the headline: "The triumphs of la Duse in Egypt," described the great ovations at her serata, the baskets of flowers, presents of Oriental fabrics, and "an oil painting by the distinguished painter Signor Lecchi," as well as a solid gold visiting card with an inscription from the Circolo Italiano of Alexandria. This was accompanied by a vellum scroll on which a member of the Circolo had written a sonnet. Some doves were set free in the gallery. Frightened by the applause, they took refuge on stage.

A few days later Duse left Alexandria for Cairo, and already her mood was improving. Now she began to find Egypt stimulating, and in Cairo she opened, appropriately, with *Antony and Cleopatra* (she had given it also in Alexandria, with unusual success). Then influenza struck; she had to cancel performances. In mid-February she went back to Alexandria, embarking directly for Marseilles, where she would take the train to Barcelona, her next stand.

Shortly after leaving North Africa, she wrote to Gégé Primoli: "I spent forty days in Egypt. . . . In old Europe there is nothing to equal it!"

During the Egyptian stay, she had had Italian papers sent to her (a habit that was to remain with her always on her future tours) and had tried to keep abreast of the news from home. The 1890s, for Italy, were a time of fierce, even bloody social strife; so the news was generally bad. She also remained curious about literary events. And, in the same letter to Primoli, she wrote that she was "no longer up on what has come out in Italy. I've read *La Bête humaine*. . . . Let me know what D'Annunzio is doing. In the *Tribuna* I read some extracts from *L'invin-cibile*—it seems to me a variation on *Il piacere*—That is a book. If you happen to see D'Annunzio, ask him if he has thought about writing *Salamandra*—Will you?"

Though the letter is not dated, it can only be from this period, and the curious question about D'Annunzio—and the indication that she followed his work closely—suggests that they did, indeed, meet in Rome, and that the meeting may have left a deeper mark than her biographers have generally believed.

The tormented correspondence with Boito went on. He had planned to meet her boat, but her plans kept changing. On 9 March, having delivered the third act of the *Falstaff* libretto, he wrote to Verdi: "Now, Maestro, again in the name of Shakespeare, give Art and our country another, totally new victory." And on the wave of this enthusiasm, he wrote to Lenor the next day, suggesting they meet in Marseilles between her Barcelona performances and her Madrid engagement at Easter.

Lenor's reply was written in a moment of recurrent malaise (her periodic disturbances were particularly painful and debilitating, and in her correspondence with Boito there are frequent references to them); it was an ironic refusal. She was too tired to dash about, their roads were mismatched, theirs was not a "happy" love. Boito's letter in return was dignified, patient, but depressed. After another chilly exchange, they made peace, and finally Arrigo went to visit her in Barcelona.

But tragedy was lying in wait for him. From Milan on 10 April he wrote:

"Lenor—if you knew what grief and what horror I live in you would spare me your cruel words and your suspicions. [These were in a now-lost letter.]

"My sick friend [Faccio] has come back, in worse shape. There is no more hope. It is frightening to see him. I spend my days, all my hours, at his side. . . . Be good to me, if you can. I have given you everything."

On 14 April, Lenor answered from Madrid: "Arrigo! Poor Arrigo! I've had your letter since yesterday, and I wanted to write you at once, and I couldn't, and I'm still haunted by your letter.

"Poor Arrigo! I understand so well your sorrow for your poor friend! When one *loves*, truly loves a friend, it is the best part of ourselves that lives in him!

"And then, the illness of that poor man is so terrible. It's better to die—yes—and that poor friend of yours perhaps no longer realizes that the *decisive minute* is still in his hand.

"In the space of less than a year, there, a friend whom you love—and for me the complete loss of another person [Matilde] that I loved so much!

"Yes! Let us hold each other tight! what a *dangerous* thing life is!—

"I don't know how to write you, Arrigo! but I put my arms around your neck. I beg you: calm and courage—and you will need them, more than ever. . . ."

A week later she wrote to him about business: Egypt had not turned out so badly after all, and with the earnings from there and from Spain she had paid numerous debts. But now she had to think of the future: "I believe I'll end up saying yes to Russia. I must." This somewhat casual line referred to a long tour that was to keep her away from Italy, and from him, for most of the next year. He wrote back immediately: "For two years, Lenor, our life has become sad and hard, and next year promises only sorrow.—Russia, America . . . What a chill in the soul!

"There! Courage.—

"Let us look closer at hand. April is dying—In four days it will be no more. We will count two months. In a month we will count the weeks."

He was counting the months and weeks until their next holiday together in the mountains: it was a game he had invented in the beginning, ticking off the days, to make time pass more easily. But now the game had grown automatic, weary. In the summer they met again— after the usual flurry of telegrams and study of timetables—for some weeks at San Giuseppe, interrupted while Lenor went to the nearby village of Graglia for a water cure. Towards the end of August Lenor had to return to Barcelona to resume her season there, and a few days later Boito went off to Lake Como and Donna Vittoria Cima.

On 14 October Lenor was back in Turin at the Teatro Gerbino, and Arrigo came to see her there. In Turin, too, she met the twenty-eight-year-old dramatist Marco Praga, son of Emilio Praga, an old friend of Arrigo's in his Bohemian youth. Emilio had died young (at thirty-six, in 1875), largely of alcoholism. Marco, left to support his widowed mother, became a bookkeeper until his writing could free him from such drudgery. In the fall of 1890, when he met Duse, he was already the author of one successful play, *Le vergini*; and he had a new drama in manuscript. Overcoming his painful shyness, he sent it to Duse, whom he had once met briefly through Flavio Andò.

Five days later he received a hastily scrawled letter from Turin: "I've read it. We must talk. Come. I'll expect you."

Praga took the next train, went to the Gerbino, and found Duse rehearsing. She asked him to come and see her the following evening at ten, when she would be free. Praga later recalled the meeting: "At nine I was walking up and down the Via di San Francesco di Paola. On the stroke of ten I went up. She had ennobled the large, rented sitting room, made it more beautiful and bizarre, covering the rearranged furniture with old fabrics, many flowers in many vases, many books on the tables, many cushions everywhere."

Without any formalities, Duse said bluntly: "Sit down there and read. Can you see?" Praga read the first act, without raising his eyes from his manuscript. When he did look up, she said simply: "Very well. Rest five minutes, then read act two."

Duse also approved of the second act, but when it came to the third she obviously had reservations, confirming the author's own doubts. After the reading, they talked for hours. Or rather, as Praga recalled, it was she who talked, "almost the whole time, and not always about my play: about art, about other plays, actors, mutual friends, Giacosa,

Boito, Verga, with that refinement and nobility that were always Eleonora Duse's, with that wit and vitality that were so hers, too, at that time, in the days and the good hours of gaiety . . ."

After a sleepless night, Praga went to a stationer's, bought a supply of paper, came back to his little hotel, and at the top of a clean page wrote "Act III, scene 1."

"I wrote, wrote, wrote, for three hours steadily, without standing up, without moving. Ah, what a strange thing! I was writing under dictation! It was Eleonora Duse who dictated! She, the night before, had told me nothing of the third act she wanted, nor how the scenes should proceed, nor what I should make my characters say. Nothing. And yet, now, it was Eleonora Duse who dictated."

Finally Praga reread what he had done, changed a few words, wrapped up the package of paper, and left it with Duse's concierge. That night he went to the Gerbino, thinking to say goodbye to Andò, expecting that Duse would write him later about the play. "When the dear and great woman saw me, huddled in a corner of the stage, my heart pounding too hard for me to dare approach her, she came to me, holding out her beautiful hands: 'I've read it. It's fine. In a week we go into rehearsal.'"

Praga followed the rehearsals, he said, with joy: "My poor prose, spoken like that, as la Duse spoke it, and as she made her actors speak, and she commented on it and explained it, and illustrated it to train her colleagues, to give them the right tones, the right gestures, the necessary movements."

The season at the Gerbino had gone well; even *Cleop* had been warmly received. Then, on 11 November 1890, the company presented Praga's *La moglie ideale* (The Ideal Wife), again the far-from-original triangle situation, but with a daring twist (the adulterous situation is considered "ideal") and a convincing Milanese setting. The success was immediate and wholehearted, and after the final curtain, Duse had to push the timid Praga on to the stage by himself. He bowed to the ovations, then—once he was again in the wings—he fainted. "Duse was supreme," the newspaper said the next day; "one touch less and there would have been a lack of passion; one touch more and the woman would have become contemptible, vulgar, unbelievable."

In the Italian theatre of that time, a new work, once it had been accepted for production, was mounted quickly. The audience was hungry for something fresh, and actor-managers were expected to vary their repertory. Duse, more than others, was eager to find new works, new authors. While she was repeating *La moglie ideale* (there were nine more performances before the company left at the end of November), she was already rehearsing another novelty, *Tutto per tutto* (All for All), by Edoardo Calandra, which opened on 26 November, Duse's serata. Calandra was a painter, illustrator of Giacosa, Verga and others, as well as being a novelist of some talent. His plays were the least successful of his various activities, and in fact *Tutto per tutto* was not a success, except for Duse, who dropped the play after a second performance.

The previous June when Duse was still in Spain, Arrigo had written to her about a conversation he had had with Luigi Gualdo, a more cosmopolitan member of the Boito–Giacosa clan. He lived in Paris much of the time (some of his novels were written in French), and was always informed on current cultural trends. "Your name cropped up in the conversation," Arrigo reported; "we talked of Ibsen, an old Norwegian pharmacist who has taken to distilling rhubarb for the theatre: such clumsiness. It's not possible that you like him. Now they are pretending to enjoy him in Paris."

But Lenor *did* like him. She had already read his works in French translations, and her taste—especially in drama—was forging ahead of Arrigo's more conventional likes and dislikes. On 9 February 1891, at the Teatro Filodrammatici in Milan, Duse presented *A Doll's House*. This was the first Ibsen play ever given in Italy; and for her it was the beginning of a passion for the Ibsen repertory that was to remain with her all her life.

In Italy, as in other European countries for that matter, Ibsen was still a controversial figure. Boito's dismissal of him is characteristic of the older generation's attitude. But Duse's courageous venture soon heartened other leading Italian actors; within the year Ermete Novelli had staged *Little Eyolf*, and even timid Cesare Rossi, the following year, put on *The Pillars of Society*.

From Milan, Duse and company went to Rome, their last Italian engagement before leaving on the bold Russian tour. On 8 March Lenor wrote to Arrigo:

"*I must leave*. The last working evening is *Friday 13* (fingers crossed) and on the 14th I leave, and—traveling with the *menagerie*, I do not pass through Milan. Nothing, I leave from here at 3, straight for Munich and Berlin. I arrive in Berlin on the morning of the 16th, and I'll make a stop there for a day, then leave the day after. I've agreed to travel with the others because by myself it's too much of a strain—and because between Rome and Petersburg I may well need to open my suitcase— and then one of those rogues will open it for me—. . .

"Love! pay no attention to the *dry* tone of my words. I smell already the *odor of the railway*, the confusion—cruel—of the last moments, an *exacerbation* of the sensations of exterior things, which I want to allay— Woe is me if I should feel anguish too much.

"No——no——love——no—I don't want to see you.

"It's better this way. I have everything ON TOP OF me—even the trifle of worrying whether a *shoe* might hurt me. And I drag after me an inert *mass, embarrassing* as the *ignorance* I have to pull through the straining of my lungs. . . .

"I don't need to kiss you, to revive love—no . . . no—the anguish is deeper down—and *doesn't come from the lips!*"

At about this same time she wrote Arrigo another letter, of which the first page—with the date—is missing. In it she complains of her *vita a strappi*, her life in fits and starts. And she adds:

"That other bore la Oppenheim brought me one morning *your* (of *your* CIRCLE) Velleda Ferretti.

"Well!—I didn't much like her—if I were to see her again I'd be bored, and if I were to see much of her, in the end I would hate her as I hate everything that surrounds you. . . ."

Duse's words were prophetic. She was, indeed, to see much more of Velleda, and the dislike remained. Boito had known Velleda since her childhood (she was five years younger than Duse); eventually she was to take Lenor's place in his life and remain close to him—or rather, at a comfortable, faithful distance—until he died.

In Rome, too, Duse saw another old friend, the Russian émigré painter Alexander Volkov or Wolkoff (who signed his works Roussoff). He had been one of the forces behind her forthcoming Russian tour, and he introduced her now to a whole circle of Italianized Russians, who added their encouragement to his.

The Compagnia drammatica della Città di Roma was not the first Italian troupe to visit Russia. Ristori had been there, of course; and, less than a decade earlier, Tommaso Salvini had also taken a company there with success. But it was still an adventure, a long and tiring journey. At the Russian border, they were held up by Customs. There, the Italians encountered another traveling company of actors, from Vienna, who were accompanied by the young Austrian critic Hermann Bahr. His first sight of Duse was of a "dark, stooped, veiled lady, who was guarding her luggage." Her face was wan, slack, empty. A member of the Austrian company, Jenny Gross, saw Duse's evident dismay and came to sit with her, trying to comfort her over the barrier of language.

The Austrian troupe was headed by the famous Joseph Kainz, Duse's exact contemporary, the former protégé of Ludwig of Bavaria; it also included the equally popular Friedrich Mitterwurzer and the young soubrette Lotte Witt.

The Lenten season in Petersburg was unusually brilliant that year: Tamagno was singing at the Opera, the Austrians were to appear at the imperial Alexandrinsky Teatr, Lucien Guitry and Mlle Menthe were at the Mikhailovsky, and—fresh from its Parisian triumphs—the Ciniselli circus was also drawing large audiences.

At the Maly Teatr the Italians decided to open with *La Dame aux camélias*, an unfortunate choice since this very play was being given by Menthe and Guitry, naturally in the original French, which was a second (if not first) language for the aristocratic audience. Memories of Bernhardt, who had toured Russia with the play, were also still fresh.

That opening night the audience was scant at the Maly and, no doubt, initially alienated by the incomprehensible language spoken by the cast. But the reports indicate that by the end of the evening the spectators were in ecstasies. Among them, fortunately, was an important critic, Alexey Suvorin, of the conservative paper *Novoye Vremya*. After the performance he went to the paper's offices and wrote an article, which said: "La Duse is truly a remarkable artist. She does not command Sarah Bernhardt's gift for advertising, but she surpasses her in talent, in extraordinary rightness of tone. . . . She does not gesticulate, does not declaim, does not invent scenic effects, but creates characters, *lives* them with a simplicity never seen before on the stage."

That night, or very soon afterwards, some of the Austrians were also in the audience. They, too, were overwhelmed. "Kainz ran, shouted, cheered, waved his hat, as people do when a monarch passes by," Bahr later recalled. "Little Lotte was in floods of tears and wanted to give up acting, saying she felt unworthy and ashamed. When we got back from the theatre and told our friends, they thought we were drunk or crazy. We were stammering ecstatically, waving our arms like lunatics—we must have made ourselves look pretty absurd."

Duse's company had a repertory of sixteen plays. On the second night they did *Antony and Cleopatra*, and—thanks to Suvorin's article and word-of-mouth enthusiasm—the house was sold out. And the rest of the run, also sold out, was prolonged beyond the originally scheduled closing until 20 April.

At midnight of 16 March, when the curtain had just gone down on the first performance of *Antony and Cleopatra*, one member of the audience was inspired to return to his room and write a letter. He was

Anton Chekhov, thirty-one years old, already the author of numerous stories and of two plays, which had been performed without much impact. He had only recently returned from a series of journeys, first to Sakhalin, then to Western Europe. That night he wrote to his sister: "I have just seen the Italian actress Duse in Shakespeare's Cleopatra. I do not know Italian, but she acted so well that I felt I was understanding every word. What a marvelous actress! Never before have I seen anything like it. I looked at this Duse and I felt sadness, because we must educate our sensibilities and our tastes through wooden actresses like X— and the others who resemble her, and that we consider great because we have seen no better. As I was watching la Duse, I realized why we are bored in the Russian theatre. . . ."

In *Novoye Vremya*, Suvorin continued to praise her, notably in an article entitled "Simplicity on the stage." There he wrote: "everything she does is her own. She has had only one school: *life*; she has formed herself through the observation of life, through the understanding of life. The simplicity of this Italian woman is the fruit of extreme complexity. It is simplicity achieved through the *penetration of the whole*. . . ."

News of her success traveled back not only to Italy but, thanks to an article by Hermann Bahr in the *Frankfurter Zeitung*, also to the German-speaking countries.

In early May the Duse company opened in Moscow, at the Korshch Teatr. The rivalry between Russia's two capitals meant that Duse, the new toast of Petersburg, had to face a curious, large, but not friendly public. Again, after some silent tension at the beginning of the play, she won the audience. The young writer Vyacheslav Ivanov—later a famous philosopher and refugee professor in Italy until his death in 1949—wrote in *Russkie Vedomosti*: "In the face of such great creation any difference in the temperament and aesthetic notions of the spectators disappears: all are as one person, carried away by the magical power of the artist."

It was a stifling spring, and yet the Korshch was packed every night, rivaling even the French Exposition, which featured the sensational novelty of electric light and illuminated fountains.

Before the Italians left Moscow on 22 May for a month's tour in the south—Kharkov, Kiev, Odessa—Ivanov wrote another, more reflective, but no less admiring article. Like so many critics, in retrospect he tried to grasp the secret of Duse's originality: "The essential, dominant aspect of Eleonora Duse's interpretations is the femininity of the characters she creates. It is not abstract, conventional, but enchanting in all the attributes of a woman who lives and suffers in reality. . . . In the performance of her parts there is nothing of what is called acting. During the whole play, the spectator will never observe a theatrical pose or an invented, contrived effect. . . . From the author Madame Duse takes only the main theme; all the other inventions of the author's imagination are, for her, only external bonds in the game of the artist. And under this exterior, a life of *her own* throbs and feels, filled, idealized, and penetrated by a creative idealization."

In Ivanov's opinion, the reality of Duse's interpretation made the intelligent spectator see the conventionality and banality of the French dramas in her repertory. Already Duse was being associated particularly with tragic or pathetic parts; but Ivanov acutely examined her less and less exploited comic gifts. "One is particularly impressed by the elegance and poetry of her performance of light, comic moments of the drama. These moments are inevitable in the plan of writers like Dumas, Sardou, Meilhac; and they must always precede the genuine dramatic moment. The authors try to amuse the public first, then surprise it with melodramatic terrors. Madame Duse performs these introductory scenes, as if *en passant*, not forgetting even for a moment that the chief interest of the character is in her dramatic nature."

Then Ivanov described Duse in a genuinely comic part, Goldoni's pert Mirandolina, the protagonist of *La locandiera*, a favorite part of hers (her love for the Venetian Goldoni was no doubt inherited from her grandfather Luigi, a Goldoni specialist). "The heroine has to amuse her suitor with every possible means, even keeping him 'company in drinking wine. With her usual tact and elegance, the artist played this part in all its comic moments, and in the end there emerged a deeply artistic genre painting, such as can be found only in a country steeped in innate style and beauty."

That summer, on her way back from Russia, Eleonora spent some weeks in Germany, partly for the purpose of finding a *Pensionat* where she could place Enrichetta. At nine, the child was going through a shy, nervous stage. "At every new face she sees, another recoiling. Tears and sulks, and it takes all kind of efforts to make her reasonable. So far I have always used sweetness and kind words—but her *contrariness* is such that perhaps a bit of harshness would be necessary. But I haven't the capacity—for the present."

On 2 August, in Bayreuth, Duse attended a performance of *Parsifal*. (Later, under D'Annunzio's influence she was to become a Wagnerite, again differing from Boito.) From there, she planned a trip to Naples to see Dr Morisani, because she had suffered a flare-up of her chronic ailment; and at the beginning of September she had to resume work. So clearly there could be no holiday at San Giuseppe that year.

Boito would hardly have been up to it. On 21 July, in the insane asylum of Monza (where his father, also insane, was confined), Franco Faccio died, not of his inherited syphilis but of "erysipelas of the head." Boito's great consolation that summer was the thought of Verdi hard at work, setting the *Falstaff* libretto to music and occasionally calling on Boito for some revisions.

As several Russian reviews indicate, the Duse–Bernhardt antithesis was becoming established in the public mind; and Duse did little to discourage it. In fact, by constantly taking up Sarah's repertory (though she could hardly have avoided it), she seemed to be inviting comparisons. Now, in that autumn of 1891, she was rehearsing Pin Giacosa's latest play, which had been commissioned by Bernhardt and written in French. On 4 October, the home-loving Pin was in Le Havre, to sail with Sarah for America, where his *La Dame de Challant* was to have its premiere. For this commission—and thinking, no doubt, more of Sarah than of Eleonora—Giacosa had abandoned the neo-Ibsen vein of *Tristi amori* to return to the historical superspectacle, the sort of vehicle that Ristori had favored a generation or more previously and that was also a Bernhardt specialty. Somewhat breathlessly, Pin followed the lively Sarah on her U.S. tour (and afterwards published an amusing travel-book about it).

When he left Turin for France, rehearsals of the play's Italian translation (by the author, naturally) were well advanced. "Are you leaving with your mind at ease?" he was asked by an interviewer. And he answered: "Completely. I have seen eight rehearsals and am truly content. Signora Duse is very great and very effective in it. Andò directs the rehearsals conscientiously and with love and acts the part of Gaiazzo with suitable warmth and assurance. I am content with all the others."

On 14 October *La Signora di Challant* opened at the Carignano. (Six weeks would go by before the New York premiere of the French original, much revised at Sarah's insistence.) For this important event critics came to Turin from all over Italy; and tickets were to be had only at scalper's prices, even though this was the very beginning of the season and many theatre-goers would still be in the country.

The event was important, but also controversial. In a series of lectures and interviews during the preceding months, as he gave readings of his play in several Italian cities, Giacosa had attacked the Italian theatre and audiences for not supporting Italian dramatists and had suggested that he had been virtually forced to write his new play for a foreign star. These interviews had irritated Eleonora, and also the critics. Still she had spared no effort to guarantee a success.

It was an expensive production, designed by Edoardo Calandra, the painter–dramatist whose play Duse had unsuccessfully presented the previous season. Calandra's work was supervised by the Portuguese–Italian architect, Giacosa's friend Francesco d'Andrade, who was an expert on the Middle Ages and responsible for the mock medieval castle which still stands in the Valentino park in Turin, a major influence on late nineteenth-century Italian taste with its love of fake Dugento.

But despite the elegance—which was even criticized as distracting—the play was not well received. Tepid applause. Hedging, if not outright hostile reviews. Duse did not stay to brood. By 8 November she was already back in Russia, first at the Korshch Teatr in Moscow, where she added *A Doll's House* to her Russian repertory and thus introduced Ibsen—an Italianized Ibsen—to the Russian audience, as she had to the Italian. At the end of the month she moved north, back to the Maly in Petersburg.

While she was there, on 11 January, Alessandro died in Venice. Four days earlier he had written to his brother in Sardinia, thanking him for his New Year's greeting and adding: "Unfortunately in this month we have been visited by influenza, which is spreading without fear or favor, bringing the usual consequences. Venice is full of it. . . . My daughter is in Petersburg, and I am always worried about her also because of the climate which is so dangerous. Enough. Pray God that He accompany her and remain benevolent towards her. I pass my days calmly and pray God for the welfare of my daughter."

Eleonora received the news at the Maly, during a performance of *A Doll's House*. She finished the performance, but canceled the next two. Three days afterwards, when she was back at work, again in *A Doll's House*, she reached the scene in Act I where Krogstad questions Nora closely about her father's death. This was one of the rare times in Duse's career when her emotion nearly overcame her, and she had a hard time keeping her tears under control. Finally, in the concluding scene, she regained her mastery and brilliantly portrayed Nora's defiant rebirth.

In Moscow, the next stop, Duse presented Marco Praga's *L'innamorata*, which she had given its world premiere at the Carignano in Turin on 15 October (the night after the premiere of *La Signora di*

Challant). It had failed in Turin, and it failed in Moscow, but the audience at the Paradis Teatr admired the actress's ability to shine in a weak vehicle. Among Duse's Moscow admirers was a young girl, M.A. Krestovskaya, later to become a well-known actress herself. Her memoir of Duse—whom she came to know well—has remained unpublished, though Duse's friend and biographer Olga Signorelli has translated and printed passages from it. The sensitive girl first saw Duse in *La Dame aux camélias*, and the immediate impression was: "How insignificant she is . . . The voice is nothing special either." But then, as the play continued, she—and the rest of the public—felt the magic. "After the third act, Nikulina was sobbing, her nose buried in Fedotova's bosom [these were two famous actresses at the time]."

Duse's bows, at the end of the performance, were also special: "she came out always pale, tired, and sad. She did not reply with a smile or a kiss of the hand, or any other gesture. She remained grave, still, and only as she went off, she bowed."

7
Berlin and New York

The year 1892, in Vienna, was an exciting time for the theatre. Bahr's critical essays on drama, on naturalism, on Ibsen, and on Duse were stimulating a circle of young writers, including Arthur Schnitzler, whose *Anatol* had been produced in 1890, and Hugo von Hofmann-sthal, who—though still in his teens—had also begun to write for the theatre and about it. One of Bahr's readers was a young, aspiring impresario named Täncer. He had scant funds, but plenty of daring; and on the basis of the enthusiastic report from Russia, he invited Duse and her company to Vienna.

Also in 1892 there was an officially sponsored International Theatre Festival, to which companies had been invited from all over Europe. Italy was to be represented by the Venetian dialect troupe of Giacinto Gallina, the Goldoniana, and by an operatic company formed by the publisher Edoardo Sonzogno, who planned to introduce his stable of new composers, the "young school" headed by Pietro Mascagni and Umberto Giordano. Duse had not been invited to the Festival, and at first she did not answer the less attractive invitation from Täncer. He wrote a second time, and negotiations continued for about a year. In his opinion, Duse was a bit afraid of the city of the Burgtheater, which—recently installed in its grand new house—was more eminent than ever. It was a fear other foreign artists shared, though, in the old house, both Ernesto Rossi and Tommaso Salvini had played with success.

In any event, Duse made her debut in a much less distinguished house, the Carl-Theater, on the other side of the Danube, near the Prater. There, on the evening of 20 February 1892, she opened as Marguerite Gautier to a half empty house.

It was the familiar story: bewilderment at first, then hesitant applause, then ovations. The next day there were magnificent reviews, and as an observer recalled: "All Vienna was talking about la Duse. The next evening, an enormous crowd surrounded the Carl-Theater, a crowd that could have filled it at least nine times."

She gave only four performances: after *La Dame aux camélias*, she was seen in *Fédora* on 23 February, *A Doll's House* on the 25th, and *La Dame aux camélias* again on the 27th. When Täncer accompanied her to the train for Trieste, the fiacre drivers recognized her and applauded her enthusiastically.

As in other countries, Ibsen was the standard borne by the younger generation, the rallying-cry; and Duse's performance of *A Doll's House* was as significant in Vienna as it had been in Milan and in Russia. She repeated the play when she returned to Vienna and the Carl-Theater in mid-May, adding also *Cleop* to her Viennese repertory.

Her young admirer Hofmannsthal wrote a long article on her first appearances, entitled "Legend of a Vienna Week," in which he asked the rhetorical question, "She plays Sardou and Dumas with Ibsen's psychology; how will she play Ibsen himself?" And then he answered:

"In *A Doll's House*, la Duse apparently seeks to play nothing but the story of an obscure woman's soul; and what she gives us is the mighty symbolism of a social and ethical indictment.

"She plays only what is individual; we experience what is universal. This is how the actor in the passion play, of whom we read in the old chronicle, must have played Our Lord Jesus Christ: as a tortured, helpless man, 'and yet everyone felt that the Son of God was concealed within.'

"She plays the gaiety that is not happiness, and with a light laugh she plays all the arid darkness behind the laugh; she plays the state of not-wanting-to-think and the state of not-being-able-to-help-thinking; she plays the squirrel and the lark. . . ."

Although no letters between Boito and Duse survive from the year 1892 and, with one exception, from 1893 (written on the night of 31 December), it can be assumed that the end of their love, or at least of their passion, dates from this period. There was not yet a dramatic, explicit separation—that would come later—but rather a gradual drifting apart, an estrangement. They apparently did not go to San Giuseppe that summer. Duse was in Venice, and Boito stayed in Milan, concerned with the preparations for *Falstaff* (which was to open in the following season), and of course working on his opera, *Nerone*.

On 9 August 1892, Boito wrote to Verdi, who was urging him to get on with *Nerone*:

"I promise you, in my great devotion to you, that I will bend every effort to finish the work in time for it to be staged the year after *Falstaff*. I will make every effort, I promise you. A promise to you is valid, I know. It is said. [This expression, *È detta*, was a favorite promise, a repeated love-slogan in his and Lenor's letters to each other].

"If I succeed, I shall owe you this immense benefaction. Your letter was like a strong handclasp that has pulled me to my feet again; it reached me at a very sad moment of my existence. Between men no more need be said."

What was the "very sad" moment? The separation from Lenor? Perhaps, but it seems—as Boito's biographer Piero Nardi surmised—that the perennially ill Fanny was now on the point of death, or had actually died.

In any event, these were the years when Duse was laying the foundation of her international fame. As she pursued it, or was driven by it, she spent less and less time in Italy, more and more on trains and ocean liners, in the abstract world of dressing rooms and hotels. She was also discovering a wider cultural world, as writers—not just critics, but poets and dramatists—became her fans. After Chekhov in Russia and Hofmannsthal in Vienna, she would be admired by Shaw and Rolland, Claudel and Willa Cather. Seen in this new, expanding perspective, the little Milanese circle of Boito and Giacosa and Praga— whatever her personal feelings for them remained—can only have seemed diminished, provincial.

Evidence of her position in the German-speaking world is the little volume (134 pages), *Führer durch das Gastspiel der Eleonora Duse*, brought out by the publisher Alfred H. Fried, with an essay by Bahr and a "portrait of the tragedienne." For her non-Italian-speaking public, the book provided scene-by-scene synopses of Duse's repertory, which, as the index indicates, included *Divorçons, Adrienne Lecouvreur, Antony and Cleopatra, Tristi amori, Fédora, La moglie ideale, La Dame aux camélias, Fernande, A Doll's House, La locandiera, Francillon, La Femme de Claude*, Marco Praga's *Le vergini*, and *Frou-frou*. In Vienna, when she came back there at the end of October 1892, she also played *Cavalleria rusticana*. (The Viennese now knew Mascagni's opera well.)

Joseph Kainz and Jenny Gross, who had seen Duse in Russia, pressed Oskar Blumenthal, founder (in 1888) and manager of the Lessing Theater in Berlin, to invite her there. She quickly added to her repertory the brand-new play *Heimat* (called *Magda* in Italian translation) by the thirty-five-year-old Hermann Sudermann, an Ibsen admirer. Sudermann was in the audience on Duse's first night in the work and, the next day, he wrote to his wife: "To describe her art is something I am incapable of doing. Imagine our ideal Magda and add thousands and thousands of surprises and revelations."

Again, Duse became the idol of intellectuals. Sudermann's contemporary and rival Gerhart Hauptmann came to several performances and hailed her as "the greatest artist" and "first interpreter of that psychological art that is now making its inevitable progress in the world."

Sudermann and Duse became friends. On the eve of the opening of *Heimat*, she wrote to the author: "Your *Magda* [the heroine of the play is a successful actress] has worked ten years, has she? . . . The undersigned has been working for twenty years. The difference is enormous, if you bear in mind that she is a woman, a woman who—unlike *Magda*—is counting the days till she can leave the theatre. *Magda* had seventeen years of 'home life.' The undersigned, nothing of that. At 14 they put long skirts on her and said: 'You must act.' . . ."

Many years later, in 1908, Duse gave a whole season of Ibsen plays in Berlin; interviewed on that occasion, she said that it had been in Berlin that she finally understood Ibsen. "I understood him," she declared, "for the first time, through German authors."

After the success at the Lessing Theater, the Viennese impresario Täncer was able to persuade Duse to go to North America at last. Tours in the United States had been proposed to her several times—as the references to possible departures in the correspondence with Boito indicate—but she had always been reluctant. The South American circuit was a known quantity, but, while Salvini, Ristori, and of course Bernhardt had toured the States, foreign companies were still something of a rarity and they ventured there at a risk.

Täncer now arranged a collaboration with two New York impresarios, Carl and Theodor Rosenfeld; and shortly after the New Year, 1893, Duse sailed on the *Aller* for New York. The crossing was terrible, and at first the city—already a metropolis of a million and a half inhabitants—horrified her. To the art historian Corrado Ricci, a friend of Boito's, she wrote: "When I set foot in America, after a stormy and painful crossing and saw the great city—nothing but railroads, automobiles, and business, nothing but spectacular buildings, colossal billboards, noise, and hubbub, without a single glimmer of art or repose for the eye or the soul—I thought of entrusting myself again to the stormy sea and coming straight back to Italy. I did stay, once I had overcome my first impulse; but I was continually filled with a deep and inexplicable melancholy."

She had arranged to land furtively, a week ahead of the rest of the troupe, thus frustrating the Rosenfeld brothers, who had planned to greet her with a tugboat full of reporters and photographers. Foiled, the impresarios then did their best to stir up interest in the unknown actress by sending as much information as they could to the newspapers. Much of it was hearsay or falsehood, as is clear in the article of the Sunday *New York Times*, 22 January 1893, four days after Duse's arrival and the night before her opening. Giving her age as twenty-six (she was thirty-four), the article declared that it could not "fairly be said that her fame has crossed the Atlantic, though she is now here in person. . . . It is asserted in her behalf that she has broken away from the conventional forms of Italian acting and is 'natural' above everything else. We shall all like her if that is true."

But they did not all like her. Accustomed to histrionic divas, prima donnas eager for publicity, the reporters did their best to invade Duse's privacy and were firmly rebuffed. She issued a statement that "she came here not to speak but to act," and when one enterprising newsman from the New York *Herald* followed her into the elevator of the Murray Hill Hotel, she said to him (according to the *Dramatic Mirror*): "Sir, I do not know you, neither do I wish to know you. I wish to be left alone." The intruder must have understood Italian or French, because Duse spoke no English and never learned the language.

She had arrived in New York with a valuable letter of introduction to Helena Gilder, sister of Mrs Arthur Bronson, longtime American resident of Venice and one of Duse's Venetian circle of friends. Helena Gilder's husband was Richard Watson Gilder, an influential man of letters and editor of *The Century Magazine*; and the Gilder home, at 55 Clinton Place (now East 8th Street) was a gathering-place for New York artists and interesting visitors to the city. In addition to writers, the Gilders also knew such important figures as the painter John La-Farge and the sculptor Augustus Saint-Gaudens.

The moment Duse arrived, Helena Gilder called on her, found she was not in, but left an invitation to a party at Clinton Place. She received this reply, which like the whole of their correspondence was written in French:

"I deeply regret having missed your visit. I thank you—and I am most grateful to Mrs Bronson and dear Mademoiselle Edith [Mrs Bronson's daughter, later Contessa Rucellai].

"But, much as I appreciate your kind invitation, I am not able to take advantage of it, as I *never* go out 'dans le monde.' It would give me the greatest pleasure, however, to see you and know you, and if you wish to come to see me, please write me a line telling me at what hour and on what day I may expect you. I will remain at the hotel to receive you at any time you name."

Mrs Gilder promptly called on Duse, and the two became friends practically at first sight. As with all her friends, Duse made use of Mrs Gilder in many ways, as interpreter, buffer, confidante, adviser. Soon Duse began visiting Clinton Place, and the Gilder home, with its comfort and taste, was a refuge from the confusion and, sometimes, the hostility of New York.

She opened at the Fifth Avenue Theater (28th and Broadway) on 23 January in *La Dame aux camélias*, her preferred opening vehicle. The play had already been seen in New York, in French with Bernhardt and in English with Modjeska, Matilda Heron, and Clara Morris. As always, she surprised the audience, right at the start, by not making an entrance, as the other stars had done in the part. She simply appeared, in a white dress, almost unnoticed among the guests, "not a woman of the world, but a girl in thought and feeling."

The shock of this new approach to an old part was reflected in the mixed reviews: the United States was not ready for her—or, indeed, for all of her repertory. Several writers expressed disapproval of the immoral play, and the next offerings—mostly her Dumas and Sardou warhorses, along with the *Cavalleria-Locandiera* double bill—were also criticized for the same reason. The unfamiliar language of the troupe also put some people off.

On 24 January, the *Times* said: "Signora Duse could only seem to be voluble rather than eloquent in many of those long speeches that cannot be conveyed well from the conversational French of Dumas to the Italian language. Her speech was of the sharp and *staccato*, where we had been used to the soft, melodious running together of French syllables. . . .

"She is an actress of original ideas, who is evidently not hopelessly bound to the cast-iron traditions of the Italian stage, though her mannered gesticulation would probably seem more effective, because more appropriate, in conventional tragedy than in prose drama of every-day life."

Then the critic went on to describe her: "She is slightly above the medium height, and seems to be somewhat more than 33 years old. Her figure is slender and she dresses richly and with good taste. . . . She has a typical Italian face, broad, with rather prominent cheekbones, deep-set expressive eyes, a jaw that is almost square, a large mouth, and handsome teeth. . . . She would not be called handsome, except perhaps by a homesick Italian living against his will in this ungrateful climate, but everyone who sees her will soon come to feel the fascinating influence of her presence."

There were many homesick Italians in the theatre, a presence that was remarked in all the newspapers and inspired a condescending editorial (on 25 January) in the *Sun*: "The large audience present at the opening performance of Eleonora Duse on Monday evening affords striking evidence of the growth of the Italian population of New York both in numbers and prosperity. The many Italians in the more expensive seats of the theatre showed by their attire and bearing that they are people of wealth, taste, and refinement, and in the upper galleries were an enthusiastic multitude of their countrymen who were able to pay the considerable prices charged for admission."

But the editorialist went on to describe the majority of New York's Italians as "humble people, very many of whom are immigrants who have been here only a short time and who are remarkable among the many races making up our population for their self-denying frugality."

Several writers complimented the Italian women in the audience for either refraining from wearing the then fashionable large hats (so destructive of sight-lines) or else removing them before the curtain rose.

Though the *Daily Tribune* of 24 January observed that "The time has long passed when any foreigner could 'astonish the natives' in this capital," there were signs of Duse's becoming a cult, a fad, especially among the snobbish audience and among intellectuals. The *Century*, of course, devoted much space to her, with a favorable but sober review by its drama critic, J. Ranken Towse, and there were also long and enthusiastic articles in the *Critic* and in *Harper's Weekly*, whose reviewer said they had been "privileged to witness the birth of a new dramatic star."

The new star—already the toast of Petersburg, Moscow, Vienna, and Berlin, not to mention Italy—was still the victim of philistine articles of the very sort she tried to avoid by refusing interviews. The *Herald*, whose man she had rebuffed in the hotel elevator, ran a long piece on 12 February entitled "Eleonora Duse without artificial glamour":

"Madame Eleonora Duse, now playing in Italian repertoire at the Fifth Avenue Theater, is as incomprehensible to most theatre goers as the Greek play, but she has become the fashion, and society is gazing at her through its lorgnette and claims to perceive transcendental genius, psychological power and magnetic force in large quantities.

"Then society glances covertly at its libretto to ascertain where it was at and looks up and says:— 'How weirdly terrible! What palpitant genius in her voice! What regal majesty in her gesture! How altogether lovely!'

"Then they gather up their belongings and steal silently away to the Vaudeville Club and listen to 'Daddy Won't Buy Me a Bow-wow' as a sort of refresher. . . ."

The anonymous reporter also indulges in some ethnic prejudice, suggesting that you have to take an Italian organ-grinder to the theatre with you to tell you what the play's about. And he goes on to criticize Duse's appearance, voice, and especially her carriage: "She walks with that peculiar hip movement of the Italian women that one can see any day in Mulberry Street, a natural awkwardness that is the inheritance of many generations of burden bearing women."

Even the unfriendly witness melted a bit, however, in describing Duse on stage: "Madame Duse has hair black as night, glossy and straight and piled loosely upon her head. . . . Her mouth is large when she smiles, displaying white, even teeth; but when her lips are closed there is a drawn, puckered look, which seems to have become a habit, as it only leaves the actress' face when it wears a pleased expression. Then she looks almost pretty, but in another moment she will have contorted all semblance of beauty from her features in some new emotions. But Madame Duse's most wonderful possessions are her arms and hands with which she points her speeches in a way which defies all accepted laws of grace or gesticulation."

He calls her clothes "plain almost to ugliness" (a complaint that probably did not disturb her, since she never cared much for chic), and concludes: "A 'chappie' waiting at the stage door, or a dude or a bird and a cold bottle are things not dreamt of in her philosophy. She would wither a 'chappie' with a look and a dude would shrivel up like a spider on a red hot shovel if she shook her gory locks at him . . . however maudlin she may become over a vivification of character, 'psychological grasp,' and 'dramatic assimilation,' the genius of Duse, as portrayed in her Italian repertoire, is as far from the conception of the box office as Mulberry 'Bend' is from Murray Hill."

If the articles in the American newspapers on Duse afford few insights into her work, they give a telling picture of the state of the press in the United States at the time; and the provincialism, the xenophobia, and the continued demand for interviews obviously upset her. She called on Helena Gilder to help her draft a statement that they hoped would explain her need for privacy. The letter, drafted on 55 Clinton Place stationery, is in Helena's hand, but the words are Eleonora's.

"I love freedom as though I were myself an American," Duse said. "But I am the slave of the public, which pays to see me, I am the slave of my engagements, I am the slave of the author who has written the play, I am especially the slave of my temperament which does not allow me, alas, simply to 'play' my parts but, much against my will, forces me to suffer with the beings I am forced to represent. That is why, dear Madame [the note was addressed to one woman journalist, to be read by all her colleagues], when I come home I have only one wish in my heart, that is to forget everything with the remotest connection to my work. You can easily understand then that interviews with journalists cannot contribute to providing me with that oblivion.

"That is why, though I bow before the rights and privileges of the press, I beg journalists not to insist on asking me for interviews. . . . I have a distinct dislike for advertising. . . ."

Duse became specially fond of the Gilders' little daughter, Francesca, and would stop by the house in her parents' absence to play with her. To amuse the child, Duse would pretend to sleep; and Francesca, before she knew Duse's name, referred to her illustrious babysitter as "the lady who snores."

Coming home one day, Helena Gilder found a scribbled note from Duse, who had dropped by the house. On a sheet of the Gilders' writing-paper Duse had written:

"I owe you   11. D. [dollars]
"(I don't know what for)
"Expenditure for the entrails of my watch   20—D.
"To buy some scraps of happiness . . .
          "Let's say — — — —   5 dollars
"Blue or green cretonne for two windows
          "and a table —   3.00
          "(ruin)"

During this stay in New York, the Gilders arranged for a cast of Duse's hand to be made. They consulted Saint Gaudens, who—aware of the actress's now notorious shyness—did not come in person, but sent an able assistant, who made the cast while Duse held little Francesca with her free hand and did some of her inimitable snoring.

A few days later, Duse wrote "chère Madame Gilder" that she had a little "ennui" for her. "I have promised *my hand* (in plaster) to two of my friends. . . . Is it possible for the same artist (!) who cast my hand at your house to make (!) another 2—for me."

The papers followed Duse's New York performances closely. After *La Dame aux camélias* she gave two Sardou plays—*Fédora* and *Fernande*—both of which had already been seen in the city. The reviewers differed in their appraisal of the scenery, but all admired the supporting cast, especially Flavio Andò. Even the inimical *Herald* had good words for the company, and said, of *Fédora*: "Not only does Madame Duse herself offer a wonderful illustration and give a wonderful lesson of what great things may be achieved by simple means, but the stage management of the company that surrounds her affords a lesson in perfection of detail and ease."

Bernhardt was notorious for engaging mediocre players and caring little for "stage management" (or direction) beyond the details of her own part. Duse, too, tended to choose the members of her troupe less for their brilliance than for their docility; but this quality could be useful in itself, for she gave much thought to the whole effect. Even in the days with Cesare Rossi, she worried about the *concerto*, the "concerting" of the action, and wrote to Primoli asking him to get information from Dumas about the staging of his plays.

The *Cavalleria-Locandiera* double-bill was a particular success. The *Times* wrote: "A more nearly perfect theatrical performance . . . has rarely been seen in this country. In pictorial and dramatic effect it far surpassed any previous effort of Signora Duse and her Company, and while this star, who has already shown herself to be an actress of extraordinary skill and power, was not always in the center of the picture, the interest was steadily sustained."

The Goldoni work also gave New Yorkers an opportunity to see Duse in comedy, a welcome relief from her French dramas, which then resumed with *La Femme de Claude*. While the press grew steadily warmer in its estimation of the star's genius, her choice of vehicles came in for further, severe reproof.

After one performance (*La Dame aux camélias*) in Philadelphia, she made the long journey to Chicago at the end of March.

The city was celebrating the four hundredth anniversary of the discovery of America with the World's Columbian Exposition, an immense fair which was running for six months and attracting hordes of tourists. Duse was unimpressed. A first letter to the Gilders consists mostly of the words "je crève"—I die—written in big letters. She was suffering, she informed them, from "Nostalgilder."

A subsequent letter, headed simply Sunday (probably 2 April 1893), reports: "Your Chicago is awful—with or without the Exposition buildings—with the buildings it is even more horrible! I obeyed you and asked Monsieur *Howland* to accompany me. On returning from this excursion, having seen so many *horrors*, I said as much to the gentleman. Monsieur *Howland* found me lacking in *amiability*; yes, it's true—but—'what a beautiful *sunset* we and the Gilders saw in New

Jorch'—that was my reply—as for the Exposition buildings—they are *horrible*. That is the *truth!*"

Still she made another engagement with the long-suffering Mr Howland to be taken again to the Exposition. As a rule, when her health and the climate permitted, Duse was a good, dutiful (if critical) tourist.

Chicago did not take to her any more than she did to it. The raised prices for her performances (because she played only three or four times a week) caused resentment, which was reflected in the local press. As usual there were some silly articles, including one entitled "Duse doesn't like crinoline" which told how she had ordered ten dresses from a Chicago dressmaker, worn two of them, then returned them all with a note: "Your crinolines wobble too much. I can't control them. Take them all out and use the softest silk you can get for the lining." The story sounds apocryphal, though the sentiments coincide with Duse's taste for soft, flowing garments, independent of current styles, the sort of dresses that Fortuny and Worth would soon be making for her.

In Chicago, again, reviews were mixed, but the serious critics hailed Duse as a major actress. In any case, she was a curiosity; and one paper complained about the stagehands, visibly peering around the scenery or through partially opened stage doors to watch her perform.

She finally escaped from Chicago on 8 April to Boston, where she had been urging the Gilders to join her ("bankrupt yourselves—life is so short"), and apparently they did pay her a visit there. She gave only four performances, as she was plagued by illness, and again prices were doubled. Still the performances were sold out, and the papers were full of praise.

There were, as always, dissenting voices. One critic quoted, with approval, a lady in the *Cavalleria* audience: "Is that all? Why I can see such things at the North End [the Italian neighborhood]." And, as in New York, her gesticulation was considered excessive; it must be remembered that to Anglo-Saxons, and Bostonians in particular, *all* Italians—not just actors—use their hands excessively in conversation. After two extra performances, Duse's first North American tour came to an end.

For her, it had been financially advantageous, even if the experience had not been satisfying. America remained an alien country, despite the friendships she had formed there. For the Americans who saw her, she, too, was alien (the word "mysterious" recurs in many articles about her); but she had already left her mark. Even the rest of the company had impressed, as the *Dramatic Mirror* wrote: "Managers of stock companies would do well to observe and profit by Duse's company's stage managment. . . . It departs from archaic stage conventions."

By "stage management" the critic meant direction or production, the *concerto* to which Duse paid such attention. Her rehearsals were usually patchy, often involving only one or two members of the troupe at a time, as she polished the duets, the trios, more concerned with matters of tone than with entrances and exits and bits of business. The *Dramatic Mirror* concluded that her staging "represents the highest developments of the stage manager's art that New York has seen." Many American actresses—including Helen Modjeska—went to see and study her.

On 22 April, Duse sailed for Europe. From the ship she sent a final note to the Gilders:

"Faith—
friendship.
courage
affection!—
au revoir—"

Her next communication with them was a telegram, again of thanks, from London, where she was engaged to appear at the Lyric Theatre from 11 May to 8 July. But the American trip and the crossing had left her tired and ill, and she postponed the opening for a week.

In London, too, the theatre was in a state of ferment. At the Lyceum, Ellen Terry and Henry Irving were still enthroned, monarchs of the elegant, respectable, aristocratic and upper-middle-class public. But only a few months before Duse's arrival in the city, Bernard Shaw had seen a play of his—*Widowers' Houses*—performed for the first time; and from the pages of *The World*, as drama critic, he poured out his unconventional, revolutionary ideas. With his friend William Archer, critic, playwright, and translator of Ibsen, Shaw was leading the battle for Ibsen's works in England and, in general, for a new theatre. Duse, he found, was an excellent weapon to be employed in the battle; and—two years later—his long, perceptive article on her in *The Saturday Review* served more than one purpose.

In her weariness, she again thought of leaving the stage, at least temporarily. At the same time she could not help thinking of the theatre, of its problems, its associations. Evidently, at about this time, she heard that her old mentor Cesare Rossi was in difficulties; and when he wrote to her for her opinion of a couple of actors, she seized the occasion to offer him a tactful hand. On 12 May, from the Savoy Hotel, she wrote:

"Dear, dear Cesarone! I've owed you an answer for three days—and I haven't found five minutes' peace to sit down at a desk.

"The *first performance* I had to give, the newness of the city, a thousand things occupied me morning and evening; and yesterday, when I was free, without the necessity of performing that night, I took the *first train* I could find, to escape from the city into the country.

"If I don't live *outside* the theatre, I am unable to act, dear Rossi!—So, yesterday, I *'promenaded myself'* beneath some great trees, thinking of the persons I love. *You know* well that among these is *Cesare Rossi*. . . .

"And so, I write to you, not only to answer your letter, but to assure you once more of my complete affection.

"You believe me, don't you?—"

She may have asked this question because she recalled some of their differences in the past and the not entirely friendly aspects of their final separation. Then she analyzed the Grassi couple, the actor and actress Rossi wanted information about.

"*Excellent elements. Ignorant as moles, both of them*; but, like *true children of actors*, steeped in the idea of *duty*. And so, within their power, they perform precisely and with good will. I cannot say whether *he* (the husband) could take on a role of 'leading character actor' in a company like yours where you *'work'*—for it doesn't seem to me he has all the aptitudes for a leading character actor—

"I see him, instead, in a role of the *'Saint-Gaudens'* sort, absolutely excellent. [Saint-Gaudens is a minor part in *La Dame aux camélias*.]

"As for her (the wife), she is . . . an *animal*! and it's not worth discussing her.

"In other words, do as you think best, dear Rossi, you who have a good nose (!) [a somewhat unkind reference to Rossi's prominent feature]."

After a reference to her "boring and *limited*" repertory (which made it impossible for her to judge the Grassis' ability in a broader range), she went on to make Rossi a proposal:

You know that next year I am resting—and if my health does not . . . *'reflower'* as that stupid *Marguerite Gautier* says, I will never manage a company again—

But . . . what *matters* to me, dear Rossi, is to show you, privately and publicly, how devoted and grateful I am to you.

—But how to do it?

I had then thought to give myself a *present* of such a pleasure and, for this, to dedicate an *evening*, in a capital city, such as Rome for example, during the next year, *an evening in your honor*—in which you would allow me to take part.

Perhaps, the public would approve and would *share* this wish of mine to pay you homage, and with the help of the public, the evening would be dedicated to you, to whom I owe my first boost.

So, if you agree, dear Cesarone, during the rest of this year, according to the 'tour' you have, we could set a performance for next year—provided, that is, you *believe that my participation can be and deserves to be* taken into consideration, provided you feel, as I do, the *real pleasure of our joining forces again* for an evening, in memory of our years of shared work, and in consecration of an *affection* that *cannot be shown through any other medium.*

If you agree, I will be very pleased, and we could 'mount' the thing with spiritual pleasure and with a useful result for you.—I hope, finally, *if the idea pleases you*, you will answer me, and we will talk more of it. . . .

Afraid, apparently, of ruffling his feathers through what might be misinterpreted as condescension on her part, she added a postscript: "*Understand*, I beg you, Rossi, that it is not *presumption*, my offering myself like this. Perhaps the thing may not interest the public, but it would be so dear to me, to *return to the ranks* under the old banner, for an evening."

On 14 June, after acknowledging receipt of his "good" letter, she wrote again, saying that her work had never been "so painful for me as now—because really my health is not so good at this moment. I will write you later from the country at length, from *Switzerland*, where I plan to take refuge at the beginning of July, and . . . I hope to be able to make a dash, if only for a day, to visit you wherever you will be. There—we will speak with peace and confidence of what (if I live) we can do in the future."

8
'It's over'

At the end of the summer she was in Venice. Sometime earlier that year she had found a kind of home, her first real, independent apartment, a suite of rooms on the top floor of the Palazzo Barbaro (not the grand Palazzo Barbaro where Henry James stayed, near the Campo Santo Stefano, but the smaller one, on the opposite side of the Grand Canal), between San Vio and the Catecumeni. Her landlord was her old friend the painter Wolkoff, who lived in the rest of the building with his English wife and their children.

Narrow and high, the little Palazzo Barbaro-Wolkoff is an unassuming sixteenth-century construction next to the contemporary, but more impressive Palazzo Dario and a stone's throw from the unfinished Palazzo Venier dei Leoni, in recent decades the home of Peggy Guggenheim and now the seat of her famous collection. There, in the autumn of 1893, Duse began settling in. And on 13 November she again wrote to Cesare Rossi, who was also in the city:

"Send me a line by the bearer and tell me *at what hour tomorrow* you are free, and I will expect you at my house, since I do not feel well enough to go out.

"The same gondolier will come for you tomorrow with his gondola—because the entrance to my house is not easy to find, being in a little *calle*, and the door . . . this is the *only time* I will regret not having a *Triumphal Arch* for you to pass through . . . like a Cesare [Caesar]. . . ."

When they met and talked, Duse suggested to Rossi that she assume the management of his company, with himself as one of the actors, for a return visit to London the following spring and for another brief season there in the autumn. Meanwhile she left Venice for five performances at the Carl-Theater in Vienna between 20 and 28 November, then on to Berlin.

There, on New Year's Eve, she wrote a letter to Boito headed "Last night of 93. *First* of 1894":

"And if it is the last date of the year I write—so be it. I regret little of it.

"Another 32 days, and it's all over. [She refers to the breaking up of her troupe.]

"—I had to gather my bread—and I did, and she who will live on after me [Enrichetta] will find bread and a humble house—

"They thought I would lose my way—No—but it is a wretched thing: we can help one another so little in this world—

"By oneself, and for oneself—there's a law for you!

"But it's over! and tonight I need to *yell* that I have worked—and it's over!

"From 1886 [actually from 1862] till today I've worked. Who helped me? No one. . . .

"One who has lived in PRISON, he, yes, he can understand me. One who has lived in darkness, under ground, without the oblivion of the dead. . . . He who has lived bound hand and foot, biting the gag and without screaming—he can understand, yes, if tonight I yell, it's over, it's over. And off, to the end of the world, in 32 days' time! . . ."

On 4 January 1894, she sent a signed contract to Rossi from Dresden; and on 12 January she wrote a more affectionate letter to Boito:

"Blessings on Arrigo—Nothing but blessings. You need not tell me to forgive.

"I never meant to make any reproach—never thought it—never—I shouted: it's over. . . ."

On the last day of January the German tour ended, after seven performances in Munich. At the last of these, the Regent of Bavaria invited Duse to his box and gave her a laurel crown. The company was dissolved and presented their manager-star with an emotional written farewell.

By 5 February Duse was in Milan, and from the Hotel Cavour she sent Arrigo a note:

"Here—near the familiar house—the old life catches me up again. I feel life and death gripping me again.

"Last night—I tapped at the window. How could I come back, how could I still live, and not do it?

"But *the two* were no longer there—Only the door was lighted . . .

"And now—I am leaving again . . . I couldn't live here an hour longer!"

But she added an enigmatic postscript: "If I live, perhaps—. . . ."

After the dissolving of her troupe she had dreamed of going off to "the end of the world." As it turned out, she went to Egypt that

February, seeking a warm climate and some rest. And she had hoped the Gilders would join her there, but they could not, and she was—as she wrote them, repeating the word six times—"désespérée."

On her way to Egypt on the ship, she wrote Boito a letter, mailed from Port Said, repeating the hint in the postscript of her earlier letter: "Arrigo? Is it still possible? Does Arrigo think so? . . .

"Are we not deceiving ourselves? Will we never deceive ourselves again? Could this tail-end of life that remains be for us? . . ."

But already the longed-for rest seemed to recede. Again in a P.S. she said: "In 4 weeks I'll be back in Italy—Arrigo must not be amazed if again—for a short while—I agree to a few weeks of work. It will be necessary to do it. . . .

"It is beneath your hand that I had desired to die—in a house that would be ours—that was remote and in peacefulness—and in the most complete humility—. . . ."

But even in Cairo she had to think of business. From there, on 20 February, she wrote to Cesare Rossi, with the repertory chosen by Görlitz, the London manager: "Dame aux camélias, Fédora, Cavalleria and Locandiera, Casa paterna [Heimat], and either Odette or Frou-frou."

Duse urged Rossi to prepare these plays with his company because "in London there is no prompter, and in general they don't allow one abroad. And that is right. So apart from La Dame aux camélias, which is in my own, special translation, the rest of the repertory will be with your scripts. . . ."

In April she was in Florence for some quick rehearsals of La Dame aux camélias with Rossi; and she wrote a hasty note to Boito, who was in Paris with Verdi for the premiere of Falstaff in French, at the Opéra-comique (18 April 1894). In Paris, too, was their old friend Luigi Gualdo, known as "gilet bianco" because of his elegant white waistcoats. Now the dapper Gualdo had been stricken by paralysis, and in her distress Lenor wrote Arrigo about the possibility of their taking in their friend. "It's a mad dream," she wrote, "Gualdo—Arrigo—Lenor—and we would keep him with us. It's absurd, I know! (But I need to think to keep from thinking)—. . .

"With us—in a place Lenor knows [San Giuseppe perhaps?]—where there is peace—where the days have 24 hours—where the dawn is seen—and then day comes—and evening—and night. All the hours necessary to life, like all the veins necessary to our body—"

Boito was still in Paris when Duse got there, after a short time in Venice. She stopped over in the French capital for only a few days before proceeding to London, but she wrote to Arrigo twice. It was not easy to see him, since he had to spend much of his time with his publisher Ricordi and with Camille Du Locle, his collaborator on the French translation of *Otello*, which was to be staged at the Opéra in the autumn.

One of her letters sounds like the enamoured Lenor of the early days: ". . . Madness, madness, madness! Venez—venez—Venez—venez—venez—Venez—La vie est courte! . . . Je meurs—je meurs—Je vis—je vis, je vis!"

They did manage to see each other, and the encounter apparently had a calming effect on Lenor, who sent Arrigo a note before setting off for London: "Be serene—I am. . . ."

Her next letter, from the Savoy, sounded ominously sensible: "Lenor has thought, and not knowing how to write the *entire* letter she would like to be able to write, she has nevertheless decided this: *not to see each other in London.* It is a dangerous thing at this moment. Arrigo will go back to the *well-known house* without 'passing by' London."

But then she went on to suggest a meeting in June. "In Paris, *disappearing from the world* for a few days, the two could meet and think about the summer, talk it over and work out a refuge which by letter they would be unable to do—."

Her chief worry at the moment (and the thing that made a meeting "dangerous") was the presence of Tebaldo in London. Referring to him as "Rocambole," she said he was probably seeking documentation, evidence with which to contest her suit for a legal separation. Thus he would gain control over Enrichetta.

Lenor wrote to Arrigo frequently. The London season was not going brilliantly; her troupe—or rather Rossi's, and Rossi himself—were coming in for criticism, though her own performances were praised. On the night of 7 May she began a long letter, which—after sleepless hours—she continued at eight the next morning:

"The so-called 'work' resumed yesterday evening seemed to me, more than ever, the most phenomenal absurdity, the meanness of my life, and of human life in general. How offensive it is to the soul to ape life. And I see around me, among those trees of papier-mâché, padded with green canvas, people who cling—to the chimera of chimeras. . . .

"What rabble! After making up their eyes, powdering their cheeks, they open their hands and mouths wide, and they think they are translating life. . . ."

Three nights later she wrote him about themselves, asking herself if the two of them had really been open and straightforward.

1894

Having loved each other near or far, regaining each other, promising each other love is nothing—it is nothing, or rather it is a dangerous thing, and also unworthy, if we do not love each other *better* than in the past.—Teach me! I will teach you!

I felt the hurt you caused me! You will make me repeat the hurt I caused you! . . .

We have already deceived ourselves so much. We have also lied, hiding or attenuating *such truths* as we were unable to face, that we would not be able, perhaps, to face even today.

Ah! after so many years, what use is life then?—Look! Even in art (and it is a small thing, comparatively) we have not dared say everything. Absurd!—From that enormous, phenomenal, absurd fiasco of the work of *Shakespeare* we have not dared, you and I, facing each other (one in the other's arms), to pick up the pieces; and we kept *silent* about it, we, *afraid* to speak of it—a childish, absurd, and sad thing, which is nothing in itself, but which *says so much*, just the simple fact.

I am telling the truth, when I declare to myself that I would like to *live* still by this love, but to live still requires pride and humility on both sides. Truth, truth is needed, the only aid! The aid that protects the dream, the ideal, the *reality* of these two lives, that want to be fused—. . . .

Lenor was talking about his reserve, his life separated from hers, and from her, with its forbidden areas. *"That path,"* she wrote, "I will not retrace, never again, never again—Your love means, today, for me, your *protection*—what was missing—then!"

She pondered the meaning of their hasty encounter in Paris. "I felt the flame, but little enduring joy, and little sweetness. I felt there was still a *world* between us!—And you also felt it."

She would now prefer to suffer "at a distance rather than near. At a distance, making a *dream* of this past—a complete dream in the spirit, which *uplifts* my life. But suffer it *beneath my lips*, remaining silent? No."

Again Duse was being prophetic. In after years her love of Boito was transmuted into a dream, a state of the spirit, in which he became the "saint," and a remote, spiritual figure, a guide but not a lover. Finally, in the long letter from London, there was a veiled reference to Fanny (Lenor, in spite of her protestation, still could not break certain silences): "My life is worth that of another woman. But you have never thought, or feared that *I* could die of it. And so you forced me to leave you—and so you could lose me again—I could go off—without suf-

112

fering from it—now—if I were to hope no more!—Let us not do it!! What's the use of having lived so much, in that case?"

Arrigo's answer must have been satisfactory, because Lenor went on writing in a vein closer to their old style, counting the days till they could meet. At the same time she was preparing to defend herself against "Rocambole," who now threatened to take Enrichetta to South America, though Duse believed the threats were only a pretext to extort money from her. Since the money she had put aside was meant as a nest-egg for the child, Duse was ready to defend that, too.

In the midst of these personal concerns, she continued performing; and on 18 May she and the company journeyed to Windsor Castle. Queen Victoria wrote that night in her Journal: "Besides us of the family, the Duchess of Atholl, Lord and Lady Salisbury, Mr Gorchen, Lord Hawkesbury, and Sir H. Ponsonby dined. At quarter to ten we all went to the white drawing-room, where a little stage had been set up, and the celebrated Italian actress, Signora Duse, acted in a piece called *La Locandiera*. She is nice-looking, with a most attractive voice and way of speaking, and her acting is admirable. She was presented to me afterwards." Originally Duse had wanted to give *La Dame aux camélias*, but the Queen's daughter thought it might be unsuitable for Her Majesty.

In London Duse met a friend, an old Italian painter, who told her D'Annunzio had published a new novel, *Il trionfo della morte*. Referring to him as "the poet we love," she wrote to Arrigo: "The *title* is so beautiful!!—Perhaps all life is the *Triumph of the end?*—"

It is unlikely that Boito loved D'Annunzio much, as a poet or as a man. To the older, staid writer, so reserved, so wary of scandal, the shocking youth—D'Annunzio was barely thirty-one—can only have been antipathetic. But Lenor could not repress her interest. In a later letter, on 26 May, she mentioned D'Annunzio again. "Did you receive the telegram that asked you to send me the book by that other (young) wizard [the old wizard was Verdi]—that devil Saint *Gabriele* and *D'Annunzio?*—And what a beautiful name he has. . . ."

At times the letters take on a nostalgic note, the tone of the remote dream. "What paradise, then!—" she wrote on 4 June. "What blissful blindness!—I was just then emerging from a tormented youth—the first hours of peace in my life I received from you, in those days—."

At last they arranged a rendezvous, worked out as usual to the hour. She would arrive in Paris on the morning of 15 June and would go to the Hôtel Continental. Arrigo would be at the Bristol. At nine that evening they would meet in Place Vendôme, at the door of the Grand

Hôtel. "From there," she wrote, "we will go and eat somewhere, so Lenor will tell you the number of the room she will have, without the necessity of your asking the Hotel clerks."

Before leaving London she went to see *Falstaff* and found, somewhat to her own surprise, that it was "melancholy", and she read *Il trionfo della morte* which Arrigo had obediently sent her.

"That *infernal*—divine *D'Annunzio*? That book—I've finished it—Ahi! ahi! ahi!!!—Each of us women . . . poor things—believes that it was *she* who found the words—That *infernal* D'Annunzio knows them all too!

"But where you will feel the most profound contempt for me is in this: that you say—(ahi!)—that *he* 'is *perfect*', No!—I don't want you to acknowledge in that book a soul, alive!—I would prefer to die *in a corner* rather than love such a soul. All the great *demonstration* of courage, all the great virtue of *bearing life* . . . all the enormous, anguished sacrifice that is living is destroyed by that book.

"No! no! no!

"*Feel contempt*, but neither *Falstaff* nor *D'Annunzio*—I mean . . . no, D'Annunzio, I detest him, but I adore him—. . . ."

Arrigo and Lenor did meet in Paris, and Enrichetta was also there. Boito had come to conclude the arrangements for the premiere of *Otello*. The two do not seem to have gone to San Giuseppe or to another refuge that summer. They met in Milan in July, but later that same month Lenor was in Switzerland, where she wrote to Cesare Rossi about business matters.

The London season had left a bitter taste. First, there was a question of billing: to many people, including impresarios and critics, it was not clear whether Duse was in Rossi's company or Rossi in Duse's. More important, and much more delicate, there was the problem of Rossi himself. The English press had been hard on him, and for the next tour Duse had carefully selected a repertory in which he would not be needed. She tried to be as tactful as possible about it: "I am very pleased that the limited repertory offers you the opportunity of remaining peacefully in Italy to rest. . . ."

After Berne, she went to Tegernsee to visit her old friend—and friend of Matilde Acton—Countess Sophie Drechsel, who acted as a kind of foster-mother to Enrichetta. The child was presumably there with her mother, too.

Then, in September, Duse was in Venice for a good month, and she answered a letter from Rossi. After repeating the same tactful compliments, she had to be more frank:

"Here is our situation. Monsieur Görlitz, the London impresario, refuses to pay me a large sum he had promised to pay me on the last day of August; and he intends to bring a lawsuit rather than pay. He bases his refusal on the inadequacy of the *troupe*. Should I bring a lawsuit against him? I have never sued, and I never will. I prefer TO SPIT on that money owed me, but you must understand, however, that this neither amuses nor encourages me—the more so because, on your part, with your letter you prove to me how hard it is to understand one another. I tried to safeguard *your* interests and *your* dignity. . . .

"To drag you hither and yon with a *troupe* already so compromised, at your age, and with your glorious past, seems to me immensely embarrassing, saddening, and indelicate. . . ."

Rossi was on tour with the same unhappy company, and Duse followed him with telegrams to Piacenza and Ravenna, where she went in late October to collect her actors from him. The telegrams indicate the repertory for the forthcoming season: *Heimat, Locandiera, Cavalleria,* and *La Dame aux camélias*; there would have been parts for Rossi in all of these plays.

When this tour ended, her relations with Rossi ended as well. The old Commendatore continued trouping until on 1 November 1898, in Bari, he died, the night before he was to open in Goldoni's *Un curioso accidente*. The company opened without him, playing instead Feydeau's *Hôtel du libre échange*. With Teresa Mariani and Ermete Zacconi, two other distinguished artists who had been helped by Rossi, Duse gave two special performances in his honor, both of works by Goldoni.

From Ravenna in that October of 1894, as she was collecting her company again, Lenor wrote to Arrigo. The letter indicates that she had asked him either to return her letters or to accept his letters to her, so that the correspondence could be destroyed. "I hope to come back to Italy in two months, and then I *must* speak to you. I will tell you then, how and why I wanted to destroy every trace of me, asking (giving) you our letters." Attached to this letter, as Boito saved it, there is a telegram sent from Venice on 14 October: "On your return to Milan destroy nothing—first must speak—. . . ."

The letters were never destroyed. Indeed, more were added to those already written. Boito kept them, hers and his own (which she did return to him at some point), neatly wrapped in a package which, on his death, passed to his literary executor, Giacosa's son-in-law Luigi Albertini. Their existence remained a secret until 1942 when Boito's biographer Nardi was allowed to use them; they were not published until 1979, under the auspices of the Fondazione Cini in Venice, to which they had been donated by Albertini's children.

Why, in October 1894, did Lenor want to destroy every trace of herself, of "the two," in Arrigo's life? From then on she stopped saving his letters to her, too. The question has no ready answer, though there may be some significance in the fact that, during that same autumn, she again met Gabriele D'Annunzio. Their meeting initiated the association, the love affair, the partnership, that for almost a decade was to dominate her life and her career, marking both forever.

Part Two
1894–1904

9
'Nothing but genius'

"I have worked for years and years—all my youth," Duse wrote to Gégé Primoli, in an undated letter, probably in 1894, "and now I want a great repose. I have earned enough to live on; and I am satisfied with that. I possess the greatest wealth: which consists of not wishing for any. I have fixed myself up a little house on the top floor of an old palazzo, in Venice, under the eaves, with a great Gothic window, which overlooks the whole city. The autumn is calm, the air pure, and I have such peace in my spirit."

Below Eleonora, on the other floors of the lovely palazzo, the Wolkoff family lived in comfortable, sociable style, receiving an international array of friends and visitors. Their rooms contained a tasteful and eclectic collection of rare pictures, sculptures, and *objets d'art*. The painter had also collected an extensive library of books on art. Duse furnished her rooms with her characteristic simplicity: many rugs, precious fabrics, a few pieces of antique furniture. The stairway leading up to her apartment was hung with scarlet cloth. While her broad front window looked down on the Grand Canal, the back windows of the house were over a typical lush, jungle-like Venetian garden, concealed by walls; beyond it, the Giudecca; and still farther on, the open water of the lagoon.

In Milan, looking into Arrigo's gray-green eyes, Eleonora had recalled that lagoon; now, seeing it from her windows, she may have recalled Arrigo, but she also had many distractions at hand. Proust's only Venetian visit was still a few years in the future, but this was already the city of Marcel and of *Albertine disparue*, where, "as we should have done in Paris on the boulevards, in the Champs-Elysées, in the Bois, in any wide and fashionable avenue, we passed the most elegant women in the hazy evening light, almost all foreigners, who, languidly reclining against the cushions of their floating carriages, followed one another in procession, stopped in front of a palace where they had a friend to call on, sent to inquire whether she was at home, and while, as they waited for the answer, they prepared to leave a card just in case, as they would have done at the door of the Hôtel de Guermantes, turned to their guide-books to find out the period and the style of the palace, being shaken the while, as though upon the crest of a blue wave, by the wash of the glittering, swirling water, which took alarm on finding itself pent between the dancing gondola and the resounding marble."

The large foreign colony included a number of artists and writers and, with them, a predictable entourage of dilettantes, amateurs, rich but cultivated idlers. In the Palazzo Dario, just next to Duse's house, lived the wealthy and eccentric Comtesse de la Baume with her friend Madame Bulteau, described by one writer as "vigorous" and "of virile character and intelligence." Not far away was the palazzo of the Italianized Spanish painter and designer Mariano Fortuny, whose experiments with stuffs and design would make him one of the most sought-after couturiers of the day. (He made dresses for Duse in real life and, in fiction, for Proust's Albertine.)

Almost directly across the canal was the Casetta rossa, or Casina delle rose, the little eighteenth-century red house where the sculptor Antonio Canova had had his first studio. Now it belonged to the elegant Austrian aristocrat Friedrich ("Fritz") Hohenlohe, refined collector and exquisite host, friend of artists and poets including the Comtesse de Noailles and Gabriele D'Annunzio, who later—when Fritz was forced to leave Italy during the First World War—took over the house, and, during a period of temporary blindness, wrote his *Notturno* there.

In that autumn of 1894, as she settled into her first real home, Eleonora received a visit from Primoli who was in Venice with friends. As always, the Count brought his photographic equipment along and, at Duse's request, photographed the house and her in it. One of the photographs survives and shows her, in a sparsely furnished room, lying in a wicker chaise, an open book in her hands. On the wall next to her there is a delicate Madonna by Bernardino Fungai, one of her favorite possessions, which followed her for many years from one house to the next.

The visit was marred when one of Gégé's friends apparently asked for a copy of one of his photographs; Duse had to write to Gégé, refusing. "It may be childish of me," she said, "but the idea of *copying*, of *painting*, of advertising to some extent my house, distresses me, as if I were to lose its refuge, that *à part* from the world that I have wanted to create for myself."

At the same time she thanked him for taking the pictures. "I asked you to take some for me out of pure egoism, because of a presentiment of the nostalgia that will seize me and torment me, three months from now, when I will be *overseas*."

Another kindred friend whom Eleonora saw often in Venice was the writer and art historian Angelo Conti, recently appointed Director of the Royal Galleries, charged with ordering and cataloguing the Venice collections. Conti was a close friend of Fortuny and—though they had lately lost track of each other—of D'Annunzio.

D'Annunzio also arrived in Venice during that autumn, his second visit to the city that was to play a large part in his life and in his works. On this occasion, the purpose of his visit was to meet, for the first time, his devoted French translator Georges Hérelle, the man largely responsible for the writer's celebrity in France, where he was more discussed, and even more appreciated, than in Italy.

Shortly after his arrival, D'Annunzio got in touch with Conti (who had just published a book on Giorgione): "I am in Venice. I'm told you are here, too. Since time immemorial, O faithless friend, I have heard nothing! Yesterday I saw your name, under the name of *Giorgione*, in a bookseller's window. I would like to see you, embrace you again, and cover you with reproaches. Where can I find you?"

It may have been Conti (later to appear in D'Annunzio's *Il fuoco* as the character Daniele Glauro) who brought the poet and Duse together; or it may have been Hérelle, who was very much a member of the glittering international group that revolved around the Palazzo Dario.

Many romantic tales have been invented, and repeated, about the meeting of Duse and D'Annunzio. In one version they first met in Rome, after a performance of *La Dame aux camélias* (what else?) at the Teatro Valle. The poet, coming backstage, encountered the actress and exclaimed "*O grande amatrice!*" (O great lover!). D'Annunzio scholars have dismissed this as a typical fabrication, though, for that matter, it could also be a typical exclamation of this public figure who sometimes spoke in slogans.

Another story has the two meeting in Venice at dawn, when Duse, unable to sleep, had fled her apartment to drift restlessly in a gondola about the canals, as the great barges bearing fresh fish from the coast and vegetables from the country began to arrive at the Rialto. Stepping out of her gondola, she found another gondola releasing its passenger: D'Annunzio. The two recognized each other and, sleepless, in the first light, they walked and walked, discussing art and literature.

However it went, the encounter was inevitable. D'Annunzio had surely seen her act in Rome, where he never missed a social or cultural event of any significance. Duse followed his career, read his books. They had a number of mutual friends, including Primoli and Matilde Serao and also the poet and translator Adolfo De Bosis, who was often to act as counsellor and mediator in the tumultuous years that followed.

When D'Annunzio arrived in Venice, Hérelle was already there. Originally, the poet's plan had been to spend only a few days in the city (then, as now, Venice was not cheap; and D'Annunzio was short of funds, a frequent condition of his); but instead he lingered on for about a month, perhaps because, in addition to enjoying the company of old friends like Angelo Conti, he was also savoring the new friendship with Duse.

D'Annunzio was thirty-one, famous, controversial, extravagantly admired by some readers, loathed by others. In 1883, when he was barely twenty, he had shocked Roman society by eloping with the nineteen-year-old Duchessa Maria Hardouin di Gallese. By now they were long separated, and the poet had had a series of mistresses, to the delight of the cheap press. The latest was the Sicilian Principessa Maria Gravina, who had already borne D'Annunzio a daughter, Renata (known as Cicciuzza). He had settled them in a house at Francavilla, in Abruzzo (not far from his birthplace), where his old friend, the painter Francesco Paolo Michetti, could keep an eye on them. D'Annunzio was only too glad of the excuse of meeting Hérelle, which allowed him to escape to Venice; Maria Gravina's violent, almost insane temper, combined with an exhausting sexual appetite, was making the poet's home life intolerable.

Even if his meeting with Eleonora was less romantic than some writers have indicated, the presence of the actress inevitably directed the conversation to the theatre. Barely returned from one tour and already preparing to embark on another, Duse could not help thinking, with dismay, of her tired repertory, of those endless Marguerites and Fedoras and Frou-frous that she was doomed to repeat in country after country. True, there was Shakespeare, but even if *Antony and Cleopatra* had enjoyed abroad the success denied it in Italy, it remained an exception. She asked D'Annunzio why he had not written for the theatre.

Actually, he had already been thinking about the stage. Some months earlier, in March of that year, he had written to his publisher Emilio Treves and, in discussing future projects, had said, "To this series, later, there could be added the series of the Theatre, which begins with *La nemica*." This play, "The Enemy" (female), was never written; but D'Annunzio's confident announcement of it indicates that his meeting with Duse came at the opportune moment.

The excitement of the encounter underlies Eleonora's first letter to Gabriele, an undated note that clearly belongs to this brief period.

"I see the sun," she wrote impetuously, "and I thank all the good forces of the earth for having met you.

"To you, all good things and every good wish."

The "you" in this note is still the formal *voi*. In the next surviving letter Gabriele is addressed by the intimate *tu*. But the second letter was written a year later, and between the two communications Eleonora had a long journey to make.

In late October she left Venice for Germany. With the Rossi company (but without Rossi himself), she toured until 18 December, when, in Berlin, she gave her last performance of the year and dismissed the company. Seeking a mild climate—the Grand Canal in winter is not ideal for anyone with respiratory trouble—she went to Genoa for a period of rest; and there, from the Grand Hotel du Parc, on 7 January 1895, she answered a now-lost letter from Arrigo:

> The letter that you sent me—and that I asked for, and that I foresaw—is a letter that *resembles* you.
> Arrigo.
> It could intoxicate with (so sweet) sorrow a woman who is beginning to live—or could cause an ordinary Mary Magdalene to weep . . . *'hot tears'*!
> Alas! I don't know if you know me . . . (no) But I feel inside that I am neither of the *two* women to whom a letter like this one of yours could give *'breath'* to go on living.
> So nothing, not even the truth, will help the two of us understand each other—and help each other! . . .
> Except for kisses—nothing is possible, nothing is sayable between us!—Not the silence, the absence, or the return, oblivion, sorrow, or the *persecution* ensnared in the existence of the other.
> No—nothing.
> You remain for me (except for the San Giuseppe days . . .—and even then!)—you remain for me the ambiguous creature, who has understood nothing, who has allowed nothing to be understood!— Even when I wrote you, did you really read—(in *our* days)—my letters?

The tone is a far cry from the prattle, the diminutives, the private references of the early love letters. It is almost as if Lenor is begging Arrigo, for once, to bare his soul, to discuss the unmentionable obstacles between them. The letter concludes:

"All that is left for me then is to pick myself up once more, hoist myself on to my back—and pursue my way.

"And I will do it. And so be it. *Addio. And so be it.*"

There is no signature, and the tone is one of farewell, if not of dismissal. Still, Eleonora wrote him another short note two days later, to say she was ill, and then again on 11 January, at seven in the evening, she wrote a longer letter:

'I have just come back from the sea.

"'All day I have asked myself, in the face of such beauty . . . (I felt as if on my *knees*), I asked myself how it was ever possible to stray so far from the true meaning of life, to go off, oppressed, useless, neither towards death, nor within life . . .

"This is what I have never understood, and perhaps will not understand. Yes, perhaps, now, if you help me.

"But don't promise, don't promise anything, Arrigo!—The two of us have failed each other in *trust* and *truth*, and this is why life was tormented, and lost.

"I would have liked, today, Arrigo, to hold your hand—and remember nothing any more—I felt so deeply that *my anguish* was *ours*. . . .

'I would have liked to hold your hand . . . so . . . you are the stronger and weaker, and tell you—without words, and I was stronger and more defeated than you. . . .'"

At this point, as if to arrest the literary turn the letter was taking, Eleonora made a scrawl over the words of some text which she had copied out, and she wrote, with desperate emphasis, instead "*NO—no—useless!*"

On her return from the sea, she had also found papers, documents, lawyers' communications, all concerned with her legal separation from Tebaldo:

"So I am no longer able to write you the letter I wanted to write—So I send you only *one plea: I beg you not to come at this moment.*

"The reasons that force me to say this to you are too painful—and *repeating* them tortures me—as much as undergoing them."

In a few days, she said, she would be in Milan, on her way to Venice; they would meet then. Perhaps they did meet, because from Venice, on 26 January, she wrote of the possibility of their going together to the seaside for a few days, or even a few hours.

The same letter, a long one, is mostly about business, however, an unusually factual letter. A new manager had come to see her, a tour was arranged that would take her through Holland and Belgium into Germany. On her way to Paris, to begin the tour, she stopped over in Turin; Arrigo may have joined her there briefly. By 19 February she was in Paris, where she stayed about a week, buying *chiffons* (no doubt from the fashionable M. Worth, who became her lifelong friend). She kept writing to Arrigo, but the letters are discontented, at times peevish. She carped at her older rivals, Sarah Bernhardt and Coquelin, and also took the opportunity to criticize Arrigo's friends.

"Giacosa—and other of your friends—have declared those Two [Bernhardt and Coquelin] 'unparalleled'—true, unparalleled in everything, in nonsense too. For that matter, everything harmonizes so perfectly with their life, and a man like Giacosa, so limited in heart and in talent, *bourgeois* to the roots of his hair—*must* find that whole world *in excellent taste!*—Well, that's their business!"

As the tour proceeded, she complained also about her own leading man and other members of the company; but still she was a great success, especially in Belgium. In June she was in London, where Sarah was also playing.

The contemporary seasons of the two actresses gave reviewers an opportunity to dissect and compare their quite different styles. The writer who took greatest advantage of this occasion was Bernard Shaw, who—having virtually abandoned music criticism and his pseudonym Corno di Bassetto—was now contributing a weekly theatre column to *The Saturday Review*. The forty-year-old author, whose career as a playwright was just at its outset, not only reviewed the often stale theatrical fare of the West End but also exploited the paper's pages to advance his own ideas about what the theatre should be.

Shaw's first mention of Duse, on 8 June 1895, is a review of her Césarine in *La Femme de Claude* at the Theatre Royal, Drury Lane. It immediately declares his total partisanship: "The appearance of Duse at Drury Lane on Wednesday in La Femme de Claude is too recent for my judgment to have recovered from the emotional disturbance produced by such an appeal as she made to my passion for very fine acting. The furthest extremes of Duse's range as an artist must always, even in this greatest art centre in the world, remain a secret between herself and a few fine observers. I should say without qualification that it is the best modern acting I have ever seen."

Though Shaw had seen Salvini, Ristori, and Coquelin, he felt insufficiently familiar with their work to be able to judge it properly, and he added that, in any case, their art had been born in "the period before the theatre had advanced to the point at which Wagner and Ibsen became its master spirits. Duse is the first actress whom we have seen applying the method of the great school to characteristically modern parts or to characteristically modern conceptions of old parts."

Shaw was familiar, however, with the contemporary English theatre and with its leading lights such as Ellen Terry and Janet Achurch. "But Duse has been helped to her supremacy by the fortunate sternness of Nature in giving her nothing but genius. Miss Ellen Terry is a woman of quite peculiar and irresistible personal charm. Miss Achurch has been kept in constant danger of missing the highest distinction in her art by having, as an extra and cheaper string to her bow, an endowment of conventional good looks. . . . But in Duse you necessarily get the great school in its perfect integrity, because Duse without her genius would be a plain little woman of no use to any manager, whereas Miss Terry or Miss Achurch . . . would always find a certain degree of favor as pretty leading ladies. Duse, *with* her genius, is so fascinating that it is positively difficult to attend to the play instead of attending wholly to her. The extraordinary richness of her art can only be understood by those who have studied the process by which an actress is built up."

Shaw posited three kinds of actress: the lesser artist simply imitated old, successful effects; an ordinary performer studied a part, decided on certain points to be made, and, if intelligent, learned to do nothing between those points, so that the work would "play itself." But then, he said, "the great actress has a harder struggle. She goes on inventing her points and her business determinedly, constantly increasing the original half-dozen, and constantly executing them with greater force and smoothness. A time comes when she is always making points, and making them well; and with some actresses this is the end. But with the greatest artists there soon commences an integration of the points into a continuous whole, at which stage the actress appears to make no points at all, and to proceed in the most unstudied and 'natural' way. This rare consummation Duse has reached."

Duse herself would probably have called this consummation *la grazia*, a gift rather than a process, or perhaps a conscious utilization of unconscious promptings. Shaw, after generalizing, became specific: "Take, as a very simple illustration, the business of Camille's [Marguerite Gautier's] tying up the flowers in the third act. It seems the most natural thing in the world; but it is really the final development of a highly involved dance with the arms—even, when you watch it consciously, a rather prolonged and elaborate one. The strokes of character have grown up in just the same way. And this is the secret of the extraordinary interest of such acting. There are years of work, bodily and mental, behind every instant of it—work, mind, not mere practice and habit, which is quite a different thing. It is the rarity of the gigantic energy needed to sustain this work which makes Duse so exceptional; for the work is in her case highly intellectual work, and so requires energy of a quality altogether superior to the mere head of steam needed to produce Bernhardtian explosions with the requisite regularity."

Duse was appearing at Drury Lane; Bernhardt's season was at Daly's Theatre. The rivalry was now explicit, and Shaw's joy in being able to use Duse as a stick with which to beat Sarah and "stardom" is evident, especially in the long article he published in *The World* on 15 June 1895. It is worth quoting at some length, since the Duse–Bernhardt opposition was to continue—and dominate the European theatrical scene—for over a decade more.

This week began with the relapse of Sarah Bernhardt into her old profession of serious actress. She played Magda in Sudermann's *Heimat*, and was promptly challenged by Duse in the same part at Drury Lane on Wednesday. The contrast between the two Magdas is as extreme as any contrast could possibly be between artists who have finished their twenty years apprenticeship to the same profession under closely similar conditions. Madame Bernhardt has the charm of a jolly maturity, rather spoilt and petulant, perhaps, but always ready with a sunshine-through-the-clouds smile if only she is made much of. Her dresses and diamonds, if not exactly splendid, are at least splendacious; her figure, far too scantily upholstered in the old days, is at its best; and her complexion shews that she has not studied modern art in vain. Those charming roseate effects which French painters produce by giving flesh the pretty color of strawberries and cream, and painting the shadows pink and crimson, are cunningly reproduced by Madame Bernhardt in the living picture. She paints her ears crimson and allows them to peep enchantingly through a few loose braids of her auburn hair. Every dimple has its dab of pink; and her finger-tips are so delicately incarnadined that you fancy they are transparent like her ears, and that the light is shining through their delicate blood-vessels. Her lips are like a newly painted pillar box; her cheeks, right up to the languid lashes, have the bloom and surface of a peach; she is beautiful with the beauty of her school, and entirely inhuman and incredible. But the incredulity is pardonable, because, though it is all the greatest nonsense, nobody believing in it, the actress herself least of all, it is so artful, so clever, so well recognized a part of the business, and carried off with such a genial air, that it is impossible not to accept it with good humor. One feels, when the heroine bursts on the scene, a dazzling vision of beauty, that instead of imposing on you, she adds to her own piquancy by looking you straight in the face, and saying, in effect: 'Now who would ever suppose that I am a grandmother?' That, of course, is irresistible.

Shaw then calls her acting "childishly egotistical"; it makes no attempt to stimulate the spectator's mind or deeper feelings. It is "the art of making you admire her, pity her, champion her, weep with her, laugh at her jokes, follow her fortunes breathlessly, and applaud her wildly when the curtain falls. . . . She does not enter into the leading character: she substitutes herself for it."

This long, droll description of Bernhardt is really a preface to an even longer, serious description of her younger rival:

All this is precisely what does not happen in the case of Duse, whose every part is a separate creation. When she comes on the stage, you are quite welcome to take your opera-glass and count whatever lines time and care have so far traced on her. They are the credentials of her humanity; and she knows better than to obliterate that significant handwriting beneath a layer of peach-bloom from the chemist's. The shadows on her face are grey, not crimson; her lips are sometimes nearly grey also; there are neither dabs nor dimples; her charm could never be imitated by a barmaid with unlimited pin money and a row of footlights before her instead of the handles of a beer-engine. . . . Wilkes, who squinted atrociously, boasted that he was only quarter of an hour behind the handsomest man in Europe: Duse is not in action five minutes before she is quarter of a century ahead of the handsomest woman in the world. I grant that Sarah's elaborate Monna Lisa smile, with the conscious droop of the eyelashes and the long carmined lips coyly disclosing the brilliant row of teeth, is effective of its kind—that it not only appeals to your susceptibilities, but positively jogs them. And it lasts quite a minute, sometimes longer. But Duse, with a tremor of the lip which you feel rather than see, and which lasts half an instant, touches you straight on the very heart; and there is not a line in the face, or a cold tone in the grey shadow that does not give poignancy to that tremor.

Already Duse's refusal to use make-up had been seized on by the press as a sign of her eccentricity or her bold honesty (depending on the degree of the writer's admiration for her). Shaw took a different view: "it would be a critical blunder as well as personal folly on my part to suggest that Duse, any more than Sarah Bernhardt, neglects any art that could heighten the effect of her acting when she is impersonating young and pretty women. The truth is that in the art of being beautiful, Madame Bernhardt is a child beside her. The French artist's stock of attitudes and facial effects could be catalogued as easily as her stock of dramatic ideas: the counting would hardly go beyond the fingers of both hands. Duse produces the illusion of being infinite in variety of beautiful pose and motion. . . . She is ambidextrous and supple, like a gymnast or a panther; only the multitude of ideas which find physical expression in her movements are all of that high quality which marks off humanity from the animals, and, I fear I must add, from a good many gymnasts."

After describing Duse's "moral charm" as Camille, Shaw praised the actress's range, "extending from the depths of a mere predatory creature like Claude's wife up to Marguerite Gautier at her kindest or Magda at her bravest, so immeasurably dwarfs the poor little octave and a half on which Sarah Bernhardt plays such pretty canzonets and stirring marches."

Magda, in Sudermann's play *Heimat*, is an actress who has left home after becoming illegitimately pregnant. Having achieved great fame, she returns. At a certain point, the father of her child is announced by a servant.

"Sarah Bernhardt," Shaw writes, "played this scene very lightly and pleasantly: there was genuine good fellowship in the way in which she reassured the embarrassed gallant and made him understand that she was not going to play off the sorrows of Gretchen on him after all those years, and that she felt she owed him the priceless experience of maternity, even if she did not particularly respect him for it. Her self-possession at this point was immense: the peach-bloom never altered by a shade. Not so with Duse. The moment she read the card handed her by the servant, you realized what it was to have to face a meeting with the man. It was interesting to watch how she got through it when he came in, and how, on the whole she got through it pretty well. He paid his compliments and offered his flowers; they sat down; and she evidently felt that she had got it safely over and might allow herself to think at her ease, and to look at him to see how much he had altered. Then a terrible thing happened to her. She began to blush; and in another moment she was conscious of it, and the blush was slowly spreading and deepening until, after a few vain efforts to avert her face or to obstruct his view of it without seeming to do so, she gave up and hid the blush in her hands. After that feat of acting I did not need to be told why Duse does not paint an inch thick. I could detect no trick in it: it seemed to me a perfectly genuine effect of the dramatic imagination. In the third act of La Dame aux Camélias, where she produces a touching effect by throwing herself down, and presently rises with her face changed and flushed with weeping, the flush is secured by the preliminary plunge to a stooping attitude, imagination or no imagination; but Magda's blush did not admit of that explanation; and I must confess to an intense professional curiosity as to whether it always comes spontaneously."

Biographers have all insisted on Duse's ability to blush at will: it was part of the "naturalness" of her performances, like the ability—shared with many in the profession—to summon tears on command. Duse was photographed hundreds of times, but rarely on stage with her colleagues; and so these detailed descriptions registered by an eye as acute as Shaw's have a special value, documenting her interpretation in a way that few other reviewers were able to equal. A good reporter, Shaw also recorded the enthusiasm of the public: "there really was something to roar at this time. There was a real play, and an actress who understood the author and was a greater artist than he is. And for me, at least, there was a confirmation of my sometimes flagging faith that a dramatic critic is really the servant of a high art, and not a mere advertiser of entertainments of questionable respectability of motive."

10
Gabriele

While Eleonora was on tour that summer, her new friend D'Annunzio was restless. The liaison with Maria Gravina was more oppressive than ever, especially since the Principessa had learned of the friendship with Duse (still innocent; but as la Gravina had occasion to know, D'Annunzio's friendships with women tended not to remain innocent long). To escape the claustrophobic life of Francavilla, to breath a freer, more stimulating air, D'Annunzio found excuses to go to Rome.

There his friend—and Duse's—Adolfo De Bosis had founded a very D'Annunzian literary review, *Il Convito* (The Symposium), which was arguably the most elegant, the most beautifully produced magazine of its kind ever to appear in Italy. Though De Bosis was well-to-do (he was a successful businessman in addition to being a poet and translator), *Il Convito* led a precarious economic life, and its twelve numbers appeared at irregular intervals between January 1895 and December 1907. The contents were as notable as their presentation, and from the first issue—which began a serialization of his *Le vergini delle rocce*—D'Annunzio was a major influence.

Il Convito had handsome offices in the Palazzo Borghese, in the heart of aristocratic Rome, and they became a convenient meeting-place for literary friends. There, D'Annunzio was introduced to the older, more conservative poet Giovanni Pascoli; though the two expressed great reciprocal admiration, acquaintance never warmed into friendship. More often, D'Annunzio met Edoardo Scarfoglio, the painter-critic G.A. Sartorio, and Guido Boggiani, a painter who was also an ethnologist. (He died, at thirty-one, in the Chaco, in South America, apparently murdered by Indians.)

At one of these informal gatherings, the idea of a cruise to Greece was broached. Scarfoglio had recently bought a yacht, which he had named *Fantasia*, the title of the first novel by his wife, Matilde Serao (a rare example of conjugal devotion; Scarfoglio was not a good husband). He invited a Roman friend, Pasquale Nasciantonio, to come along, with D'Annunzio and Boggiani. With Scarfoglio's consent,

D'Annunzio invited his translator Hérelle to come from France, meet him at Francavilla, and join the party.

Hérelle, older than the others, a prim bachelor schoolteacher, spent a peculiar summer. First, at Francavilla, he had to hear the confidences and complaints of Principessa Gravina; he heard D'Annunzio's confidences as well, both sexual and literary, and Hérelle dutifully recorded all this information (later published in his *Notolette dannunziane*) before he and the poet set off for Gallipoli to meet the rest of the Greece excursion.

The *Fantasia* set sail on 29 July. The journey was generously documented: Scarfoglio sent off articles to his newspaper; D'Annunzio made notes in his *Taccuino*, and later referred to the trip in his first book of *Laudi*; and Boggiani kept a diary, recently discovered and published. But Hérelle's account is probably the most reliable; certainly it is the most shocked.

At D'Annunzio's suggestion, the French visitor was traveling light, but the poet had brought ten suits, eight pairs of shoes, and at least thirty shirts. Though all the travelers visited the noteworthy sights— Mycenae, Olympia, Nauplia, Tiryns—D'Annunzio and his companions spent much of their time, to Hérelle's discomfiture, seeking out prostitutes in the ports and bringing them back aboard. When they reached Athens, D'Annunzio, in impeccable black-tie, went to the Café Français for an ice, to cleanse his mouth of the taste of Greek food, which he found disgusting.

On 6 September, back in Italy, D'Annunzio wrote to Emilio Treves: "My long and vague—fluctuating—dream of a drama has finally crystallized. In Mycenae I reread Sophocles and Aeschylus, under the Gate of the Lions. The form of my drama is already clear, and set. The title: *La città morta* ("The Dead City").

At the end of that month D'Annunzio was at the Hotel Danieli in Venice. Duse was also in the city, at the Palazzo Wolkoff. And at this point their friendship turned into love. In the poet's notebooks there is a dated annotation: "Amori. et dolori. sacra [sacred to love and to pain].—26 September 1895—Hotel royal Danieli—Venezia."

D'Annunzio had a special talent for describing works he had not yet written (and, in some cases, never got around to writing); and no doubt during those Venice days he described to Eleonora his play, *La città morta*, a dense, morbid drama of incest and adultery set on the hot plain near the ruins of Mycenae. External details of the tragedy were inspired by the discoveries of Heinrich Schliemann twenty years before.

Between the famous actress and the aspiring—and totally self-confident—dramatist a "pact" was made: he would write great plays for her, and she would interpret them. *La città morta* would be only the first of these. And from this premise another dream grew. They would found together a festival theatre (the example of Bayreuth was still fresh), near Lake Albano, just south of Rome, and would perform—as D'Annunzio explained in an interview some time later—"only the works of those new artists who consider the drama to be a revelation of beauty communicated to the crowd, and the scenic arch to be a window opening upon an ideal transfiguration of life." It is easy to imagine how such a plan impressed Eleonora, about to set out on another round of Sardou and Dumas *fils*.

D'Annunzio had to go to Florence to instal his son Mario in the Collegio Cicognini, the severe institution at Prato where he himself had studied. He stayed at the Hotel de Russie on the Arno, and Duse soon joined him in the city that was later to become their home (when they *were* at home). Florence, in 1895, was unfamiliar to both of them, and they explored it together.

But the beauties of Florence and even the excitement of the love of Eleonora could not totally distract Gabriele from writing. In Florence he completed the text of a long speech he was to give in Venice—the *Allegory of Autumn*—and delivered the manuscript to a Florentine printer. Then family duties summoned him back to Francavilla.

On 8 November, in the course of the Esposizione Internazionale d'Arte in Venice (forerunner of the Biennale), D'Annunzio gave his long, elaborate, spellbinding address at the Teatro La Fenice. It was his first appearance as an orator, and he clearly enjoyed himself immensely. A few years later, in writing *Il fuoco*, he described this occasion as a central event in the novel, placing it, however, in the more august setting of the Ducal Palace.

The audience enjoyed him, too. And it was a large, distinguished gathering, including writers and painters, many of the poet's friends. Duse was in Venice, but did not attend. (Nor did Queen Margherita, though D'Annunzio has her present in the fictional reconstruction in *Il fuoco*.) After the ovations, the organizers of the Exposition and a number of critics and journalists sponsored a grand banquet in the poet's honor. His friend the painter Francesco Paolo Michetti, whose works were featured in the Exposition, was among the banqueters.

A short time later, Duse and D'Annunzio met in Milan, discreetly staying at separate hotels (he at the Milan, where Verdi lived; she at the Grand). Two surviving letters of Eleonora's—hand-delivered, since there are no stamps on the envelopes—seem to belong to these early days. The first narrates a disconcerting dream about a strange house, a garden without any flowers, a host of blind people; then the letter refers indirectly to the pact:

"You will help me, won't you?—oh—the beneficent strength—there it is! You thrust it back into my arms, this strength of mine, which is my art, and you make me worthy of it!—

"How to tell you the *thanks* I feel inside me."

And gratitude is the theme of the second letter, no more than a note, sent to the same hotel. Unlike Boito, who had so often expressed contempt for the theatre, for her profession, Gabriele exalted it—and her with it.

Both her letters are signed "Eleonora." D'Annunzio had not yet invented the fantastic, romantic names—Ghisola, Isa, Ghisolabella— by which he would later call her. In all of his affairs of some importance, he exploited this gift for inventing not only magic, talismanic names but a whole private world of secret references and hidden meanings in which he and his beloved could shut themselves away from mundane concerns.

Now mundane concerns occupied them both. The poet had to think of la Gravina and his daughter in Francavilla, his son Mario in boarding-school, his wife and his other legitimate children in Rome; he had to stave off creditors (an art in which he already had great experience) and cajole editors. Eleonora had to set off on tour with her impresario José Schurmann. They opened in Vienna with a performance of *Heimat*—a single matinee—at the historic Theater an der Wien, then went on to other Northern cities including the one she spelled "Stokkolm." She wrote to Gabriele that there was "nothing but cold and snow, and the trees are 'black on white' as in a *gravure*." She recalled their walks in unfamiliar Florence and how they had to ask a passing soldier for directions to reach the Cascine park.

Sometime before Christmas, as Duse's tour continued, D'Annunzio came to Florence to wait for her; but he did not await her return in solitude. He looked up several old friends, including the omnipresent, inevitable Carlo Placci. A sometime diplomat and occasional writer, the cosmopolite Placci made a profession of being the friend of all the right people and of bringing people together. His circle of acquaintance reached from London to Paris to Vienna; he spoke several languages, and played the piano decently. In Florence he knew the Anglo-American colony (the Actons, and eventually the young Berensons) and the art world. It was at his house that D'Annunzio met the absent

Duse's young friend Giulietta Gordigiani, twenty-four-year-old daughter of the painter Michele Gordigiani (if she *was* his daughter; Florentine gossip said her real father was a local music-critic called Cecchi). The poet immediately paid court to the tall, striking, temperamental girl, who was also a promising pianist; his advances were apparently repulsed, but the experience was not wasted, and in *Il fuoco* Giulietta reappears as the fascinating young Donatella Arvale.

Duse wrote to him from abroad: not love letters, not quite, not yet. After all, their relationship was still in a tentative stage: Gabriele was bound to Maria Gravina (a tie he was only too eager to sever), and Duse was somehow still in love with the patient, temporizing, exasperating Arrigo. Aware of Gabriele's complicated situation, Duse was careful not to press him. He is to write her, she says in a letter of 20 December 1895, only if his heart tells him to, "otherwise . . . not." And she adds, prophetically but in vain: "You must not lie—to me, you have *no* duty, no obligation—Never do it—"

With Gabriele, she felt free to write about the theatre.

"Every now and then I admit that it is good luck after all, my having a job that requires so much strength— . . . so much activity (made of idleness). . . . In the evening—the evenings when I work—I *plunge in*, and only you know, only you can understand through what *twists and turns* of soul and body an *expression* of art is made!—

"And a control, inexorable, must be invented for it.—*to harmonize oblivion with memory—*."

Early in January 1896 Eleonora arrived in Florence, as arranged. She could not stay long—ahead lay a long-planned, dreaded North American tour—and Gabriele devoted himself to her. From Florence they made an excursion to Pisa; D'Annunzio wrote to Treves of its "solar enchantment." But during those brief days their physical attachment also deepened.

From Paris, the night of 18–19 January, Eleonora wrote to him with a new abandon:

"I speak to you—I think of you—I see you again.

"Upon me, still, your touch—but the road is *there*, and it must be resumed."

After a ritual visit *chez* M. Worth to replenish her wardrobe, Duse went on to London for a few days, staying with her English friends the Seniors in Cheyne Walk. (Mabel Senior had accompanied her on the Northern tour.) Then she sailed on the *Majestic* for New York, where she arrived on 6 February. Her impresario, Schurmann, was already there to meet her, with a Mr J. Charles Davis, representative of Senator

H.C. Miner, owner of the Fifth Avenue Theater, the man responsible for bringing her to America this time.

As usual, Duse took refuge in her hotel, the Holland House at Fifth Avenue and 30th Street, and avoided the press. The *Daily Tribune*, which had been friendly during her 1893 visit, reminded its readers of the star's aversion to publicity and said, with heavy irony: "Yesterday she permitted Mr Schurmann to say that she was in good health and that for the last two days of her voyage the sea had been uncomfortably rough." On the same day (7 February) the Boston *Herald* quoted her as having said she "hated" America.

She opened with the inevitable *La Dame aux camélias*. The repertory, on this trip, was more limited than before: the Italian double bill (*Cavalleria* and *Locandiera*) and *Magda* (*Heimat*). She omitted the offensive *Femme de Claude* (except for a single performance, in Washington) and the Sardou dramas.

She did not really hate America, but she was unhappy there. She missed Gabriele. On 27–28 February she wrote to him: "The trouble, perhaps, is this—that I can no longer measure, *calculate* correctly how many years, or centuries—or days—or months—have passed since I arrived here."

She was still a little apprehensive of the future: "I ask and *require* that my soul not suffer."

D'Annunzio did not write often, but she forgave him; and she added a little, affectionate touch: "in Gordigiani's studio I saw a *Michetti*." In referring to Michetti, she was somehow linking herself with Gabriele's closest friend. The painter Edoardo Gordigiani, who lived in New York then, was the brother of Giulietta and perhaps this reference had an elusive significance, warning Gabri off the dangerous beauty.

Before the New York opening Duse had played a few performances in Washington, where President Grover Cleveland and his wife attended the opening night—17 February—at the Lafayette Square Opera House (convenient to the executive mansion). The presidential couple came back to the rest of her performances, impressing the small (260,000 inhabitants) and provincial capital. Mrs Cleveland also invited Duse to a tea party at the White House.

On returning to New York, the actress found huge advertisements for her performances fixed to the sides of the city's streetcars: "Eleonora Duse—The Passing Star." The slogan was later picked up by some of her biographers.

She was not the only star in New York then. Sarah Bernhardt was there on another of her sumptuous tours, which were more like royal progresses, with her special Pullman cars and her large menagerie, both human and animal. Again the two actresses shared pretty much the same repertory, both featuring *La Dame aux camélias* and *Magda*, as in London the previous summer. Here, as in London, the critics were divided. Some sided with Sarah, whose art had been familiar to American audiences for well over a decade; but the *Dramatic Mirror* said: "Duse's power is greater than Bernhardt's, for Duse's is the power of truth, while Bernhardt's is the power of theatricalism." The public seemed more impressed by Duse: to Schurmann's delight, her *Dame aux camélias* took in a much larger sum than Sarah's had done a few days earlier.

While Eleonora was in the United States, Gabriele was much concerned with *La città morta*. He had not yet written a word of the drama, but he was already thinking about the best way to launch it, and— calmly ignoring the "pact" with Duse—he came to the decision that the work should be given first in Paris, in French, and with Sarah. D'Annunzio's behavior was disloyal, but not unmotivated. It was a time when he was encountering even more hostility than usual in Italian literary circles; whereas in France, thanks largely to the prompt, effective translations of Hérelle, who also acted occasionally, discreetly, as editor and censor, D'Annunzio was fast becoming a celebrity. In Italy there was also the problem of casting. Though Duse would be ideal in the role of Anna, conceived for her, it would be difficult to assemble a troupe worthy of her and of the complex play. So D'Annunzio went to Rome, to his friend and Duse's, Gégé Primoli. Through Primoli's wide circle of friends in Paris, the poet hoped to reach Bernhardt.

In America, Eleonora's tour was triumphant. The New York newspapers commented on her health, better than it had been in 1893, when she had been forced to cancel a number of performances. And though the critics were divided—and some actually baffled—by her acting, she was, the *Times* said, the idol of the hour. All the celebrities who came to America, especially people from the theatre, were taken to visit Thomas Edison's studio in Orange Park, New Jersey. Duse paid the ritual call and, at the request of the famous inventor, recited some of the last act of *La Dame aux camélias* into a horn. Some time later a fire destroyed much of the Edison laboratory, and so this sole recording of Duse's voice was presumably lost.

From New York she went to Boston, where she opened on 6 April at the Museum Theater. *La Dame aux camélias* was the usual success, despite doubled prices. But success, now a familiar and discounted companion, was no shield against unhappiness and loneliness. The day after her Boston opening, she wrote to Gabriele:

"To salvage something of myself (that is the word)—a few evenings ago, in New York, I telegraphed *down there*, down there [Pescara] . . . —The light came from *down there*.

"I had so exhausted all strength—I was in the street, walking just for the sake of walking, without a destination, in the midst of an enormous racket, an enormous and repugnant crowd. . . .

"I felt an unspeakable anguish, and an enormous weight on my breast, without the strength to raise my arms—and I telegraphed a few words.

"It seemed to me that in doing this, asking help like that, I was SENDING AWAY myself, as if from a death that was tangible, in my sight, there, inevitable and immediate . . . —and *almost deserved*. . . ."

In this spell of anguish, though she had been granted a week's respite, she tried to persuade Schurmann to cancel her contract. She insisted she could not work; she tried to explain the reason to D'Annunzio: "So *unspeakable* is this suffering, this great sadness caused by your silence—that I cannot *live* in it. I find IT again, and I find ME again, at the dawn of every day, and I try to rescue myself from it, and I fail. . . ."

From Philadelphia, feeling better, she wrote to De Bosis, who was translating Shelley. (His version of *The Cenci*, published in 1898, was dedicated to Duse.) She felt that the part of Beatrice was not for her, but predicted that one day "an actress—(no!)—an *elect spirit* will come, young and beautiful—vibrant—" to interpret the heroine.

After a few more performances in New York (where her choice of plays was again criticized), she was ready to leave, but her departure had to be delayed. Her faithful maid Nina had to have an operation, and Duse would not leave her alone in a strange country. Finally, on 7 May 1896, they both sailed, once more on the *Majestic*.

In early June she met Gabriele in Venice, where she had hoped to be given a draft of *La città morta*. D'Annunzio arrived empty-handed. He had been working on other things, his mind more filled with his future novel, *Il fuoco*, than with his future drama. On 14 June, shortly after his reunion with Eleonora, he wrote an observation in his notebook, concerning the novel's hero, Stelio Effrena, and its heroine, la Foscarina: "His lucid, cruel view of her physical decline. Certain appearances of her face, her profile. Her wretched little chin." This observation was later expanded and underlined in the novel, in one of the passages that most wounded Eleonora and outraged her admirers.

Towards the end of June, Duse had to rush to Dresden, where Enrichetta seemed threatened by the tuberculosis that ran in the family. D'Annunzio went back to Francavilla. Then Duse had to go to Paris to succour a friend, a "poveretta," Duse calls her in a letter to the poet. (It seems to have been Giulietta Gordigiani.) "I am going," Duse wrote, "because she *begs* me to, but I will not stay with her—I am meeting her, but only to say goodbye and separate myself from her.—I *must*.—I can do nothing for her—nothing. . . ."

And, at the end of the letter, she added: "it is also true that, at a certain point in our life, sorrow and joy have the same price."

A few days later she left Paris to return to Venice, while Giulietta—if it was she—went on to Rome ("where she hopes to meet you," Duse said in a second letter). At about the time he received this letter, D'Annunzio finally started writing—not *La città morta* but *Il fuoco*.

Gabriele and Eleonora must have met again in the course of that summer, because in August or early September she wrote him a very loving letter, which ended: "Forgive me *also* this: that is, *feeling* only *my* joy when I am near you, but also *la gêne* [embarrassment], since I am incapable of giving joy to you! . . ." This letter was addressed to Milan; the letters sent to Francavilla—where la Gravina might read over Gabriele's shoulder (or behind his back)—were much more restrained.

At the same time, Eleonora was still writing to Arrigo, who was spending the summer at Quasso al Monte, in the area where he and Eleonora had summered together in the past. Unable to remain in Italy during the coming season and play *La città morta*, as she had hoped, Eleonora was hastily patching together a European tour. On 4 September, from the Hotel Cavour in Milan, she sent a letter to Arrigo. It was a rainy morning, and practical matters were irritating her: "The scoundrel agent from Paris writes and telegraphs lies after lies."

A few days later she joined Arrigo at Quasso for a brief, unsatisfactory visit. By 10 September she was back at the Cavour, in a gloomy mood: "The strongest is the most alone—the most alone is the strongest. Yesterday, as I *saw* you climb up to the sainted house, where I did not find peace, I said to myself for the *millionth* time in my life, that bread and spirit, and the *separation* from the world are salvation. But I SAW YOU *climb up*, you, towards the sainted house—I—in the midst of the tumult again, again!—I have lost so much of my strength!

"Thank you for everything, for so much compassion and goodness that I *feel* in you towards me!"

Though Eleonora did not yet know it, in July Sarah Bernhardt had accepted "avec enthousiasme" the still unwritten drama by D'Annunzio. (It is possible that the French actress had got wind of the D'Annunzio–Duse relationship and wanted to put one over on her professional rival.) When the contract came to be drawn up, D'Annunzio firmly insisted that Bernhardt should have the rights only for performances in France: he was still counting on Duse's presenting the work to Italian audiences.

Then, towards the end of September, in the days when Duse was between Milan and Quasso, D'Annunzio—in a sudden access of inspiration—furiously started writing his drama, and in six weeks it was finished. At about this same time he wrote to Eleonora, abruptly asking her to stage the play at once, that same November. The prospect caught her off guard, but she was bravely willing to undo all her tour negotiations, pay any penalties, and make the effort.

"Listen to me. Listen.—I am writing you only a few words so as not to lose time, not to postpone, and to *tell you* the great joy your letter brought me.

"Thank you! Yes, of course!

"Your work is something sacred—and we must speak of it, and, in every respect, the *truth*!

"Yes! Thank you—

"The truth is that *today* I don't have with me the *two actors* or the *actress* that the drama requires. But IF you *do not steal* this great joy from me, and, before leaving the theatre forever, I can *close* its door well *with* a work of yours—(God! what joy!)—and well—give me time, and we will find, we will find both the actors and the actress—

". . . The actors that I have—*today*, no, I have no one good or even tolerable—and I would assume no responsibility for them . . . but I repeat, one can *seek*!—

"And seek I will—"

Duse was in Rome. Obviously she had learned from some one, perhaps Primoli, about D'Annunzio's dealings with Bernhardt, hence the reference to his "stealing" the play from her. In the rest of the letter she proposed to break all her contracts: "I remain in Italy. I will perform a bit here and there and I will seek *à droite et à gauche* the persons needed for *La città morta*—(what joy to name it!)"

But D'Annunzio had already signed with Sarah and could not give Duse time. As quickly as the poet wrote the work, the faithful Hérelle translated it, generously allowing D'Annunzio to pretend he had written the play directly in French. It was quickly ready for Paris performance, and the author was confident that Sarah would rush it on to the stage. She did not. Ironically, Duse could have had all the time she wanted; Sarah did not appear in the play until 21 January 1898. Duse first played the part of Anna only in 1901.

From Rome, those last days of September and first days of October 1896, Eleonora wrote more frequently to Arrigo. She begins to call him "Arrigo santo." Though she did not yet know where she would go on her tour, she was already rehearsing and already tired. On the first day of October she wrote:

"I don't know how to tell everything I'd like to!—and what's the use—It's the old story! Prolonging the respiration of a shipwrecked person—this was my life!—What to do?

"I will see it through. The 'how' doesn't matter!—I *see* our house in its peacefulness! The hours of reading! The beautiful page of *music* that expresses the words that cannot be said . . .

"Your soul has some refuges—

"—mine—nothing. . . ."

Through October, despite the disappointment suffered through Gabriele's dealings with Bernhardt, Eleonora continued writing to him in Francavilla. The letters are less expansive now. On 14 October she wrote: "Lucky is the man who can produce art alone, by himself! . . . After all these days of rehearsal not one proper *intonation* in those who surround me . . . none vibrates." He wrote that he could not come to Rome and read her what he had written of the play. "That is settled, then," she replied sadly, and went on: "Here nothing and no one understands 'art,' and nobody around me yearns for it!"

Her letters to Arrigo were more open, and more depressed. "This life of mine is a farce," she wrote on 3 October; and the next day: "Say that I can still give you some joy! Say it, *anima bella!*" And, towards the end of the month, when Arrigo was visiting Verdi at his Villa Sant'Agata:

"You are in a house of peace—I . . . —where am I? I must set forth—and as soon as possible.

"—Tomorrow—

"And come back? When?—. . . *to stretch my arms, again, 'dans le vide'* [in the void] until the day of return—? . . ."

She had made every possible effort to remain in Italy, but all the best theatres were taken, and neither Ermete Novelli nor Flavio Andò, her former partner, would cede any houses to her or allow her to perform plays for which they had the Italian rights. Giulietta Gordigiani was in Rome with her, planning to accompany her on the tour.

Late one afternoon, a friend—"one of those women who always know everything," as Duse described her—casually mentioned that

1896

Boito was in Rome, that she had seen him and spoken with him. In the rain, with Giulietta, Eleonora made the rounds of all the hotels where Boito might conceivably be staying. To no avail. Then the next day, the same woman—who, of course, knew nothing of Duse's real interest in Boito—remarked that perhaps she had been mistaken.

"I wander the streets of Rome like someone seeking peace—making my adieux to so many streets, and stones and skies that I love! . . ."

She had hoped to leave at the end of October, but legal problems (an impresario was suing her for damages) and a brief spell of illness kept her in the city. It was late November before she set forth. The letters to D'Annunzio apparently stop, but those to Boito continue. Berlin, 24 November: "Arrigo! I don't know how to write, but only when I find you again beneath my hand do I feel I am living!" And now she signs herself "Lenor." Two days later, after she had received a letter (now lost) from him:

"Arrigo, I must try to make you find me attractive again – so I *must* find again the *inner harmony* that you urge me to have.

"En effet, the sensation I have concerning myself every now and then is as if I had struck with my fist the inner mirror we carry inside ourselves, and there, every now and then I see the world in fragments, or rather in smithereens.

"But—I would like so much for you to like me again, O Arrigo!"

The following night, sleepless, she again picked up her pen: "I have worked headlong, soul against the wind, all week.

"The so-called *work* succeeded (as they say backstage) quite perfectly, great, as to success—What big words!—The fact is . . . — . . . no, facts bore me, they burden me enough as I live them! . . .

"I'm dying to see you again!—no, no, no, everything that is postponed till later is lost. I have been dying for so many years of this hateful illness: *distance*—: *waiting!*— . . . at night, when I come in after my work, and, finally shut myself in my room, and shut out of my room all the nonsense of the day . . . then, as I *comb* my thoughts . . . the more I feel you and find you, the more everything gnaws at me inside. . . ."

In Berlin, Giulietta had been joined by another of Duse's "guardian angels," as she called the devoted young women who traveled with her as unpaid companions. This was Laurence Alma Tadema, daughter of the popular painter, friend of Henry James, and later a writer herself. For Duse, the girls were a mixed blessing: sympathetic company, but also a responsibility. It was probably during this Berlin stay that Duse introduced the lively, if unstable, Giulietta to the

142

German banker Robert von Mendelssohn, collateral descendant of the composer. Robert—Robi—had long admired Eleonora, and at first had been in love with her. She did not return his love, but cherished his loyal friendship. He and Giulietta married in 1899.

From Berlin, the Duse troupe went on to Russia, and from the Grand Hotel d'Europe, St Petersburg, Lenor wrote Arrigo on 15 December: "the road is still long." To reach the end of that road, retirement (with enough saved to support herself and Enrichetta), a sizable sum had to be earned.

"To stick to mundane matters, I can count for you, on my fingers, how in six nights in Berlin, Lenor drew (from the well) *37,000 marks* . . . (buckets of water) – And, figure it out for yourself: for me to collect 37,000, they had to take in *twice* that, because I have only 60 per cent of the total sales . . . So . . . we were saying? . . . 37,000 for me. Out of this, pay the troupe, the fares . . . enfin—add it up—I saved barely 8,000 marks . . .

"And, besides! with great anguish, not to mention the annual expenses of that Paris where I put together *chiffons* and laces . . . Devil take them! No way to make ends meet. . . ."

It was unlike Lenor to write to Arrigo of such material matters, but there are many times in her correspondence with others when she is clearly proud of her earning capacity—which grew enormous—and her independence. To the high-minded Boito all this talk of sums and percentages must have been distasteful. As Christmas approached and Duse stayed on in St Petersburg, she continued writing to him, more and more like her old self. On 20 December she wondered when she would see him again:

"when? I just telegraphed you—*'don't worry'*—to be sure, yes, I work, and I plug on

"It has been so many—years, Arrigo! . . .

"Here everyone wants me to play the women of *the one* who knows how to say everything—

"But I didn't bring *Shakespeare* with me this year either!!! Tonight I was rereading some scenes of *Rosalinda* ('*Comme il vous plaira*') et *Hélène* ('*Tout est bien.*')

"What grace! What joy!—But these are threads one must know how to *entwine.*—Reread *Rosalinde* and tell me the *tone*. I see it."

Then, the day after Christmas:

"Last night I was rereading the *Sonnets* of the *Father* of *Rosalinda*, and I found the words that *he* knew how to say, that YOU say to me, and I, myself, would like to say to you—

"Arrigo—beautiful soul—my soul—Arrigo! What good have I ever done in this world to deserve you again?

"Arrigo! some times I feel so . . . so . . . so— . . . (no, not unworthy, that's a base word – and it's better to *be* it (base) than to *imagine* it for oneself. . . .

"Arrigo! I want to *see you*, soon, soon. I will be leaving Russia at the end of *January*

"—We *must* meet, immediately, even *before* I come *back to Italy*.—One *day*, one *night*, no more than that—you will come—Yes, yes, I know!— You *will* come.—*Perhaps Berlin*, where I ought to stop over for some business matters (I'll tell you in another letter)—and you will

"shake me

"tight and close for a whole night. . . ."

The verb she uses here is *struccare*, a Venetian dialect word which in the private love-language of Lenor and Arrigo apparently meant to make love. It was a word she used very rarely, and in the copious surviving correspondence with Arrigo, this is one of the few physical letters. It is as if, feeling that their physical relationship—always problematical—was drawing to an end, she were trying to recapture it on paper before any attempted recapture in reality, in flesh and blood.

At the same time, Eleonora told Arrigo about her two traveling companions, especially the volatile Giulietta: "The dear creature . . . (she is young!) and believes that nothing exists in the world beyond her sorrows. *Her* personality absorbs HER, and to such a degree that the rest is invisible to her eyes, though she has a beautiful spirit, also disposed towards good."

Her whims, her gregariousness only exacerbated Duse's moodiness. As she wrote to Arrigo:

"The word 'homesickness' . . . yesterday evening . . . *flung* on stage between one speech and another in the dialogue of a play . . . *trilled* inside me . . . and I felt my hands turn pale

"—and I was ashamed to display (on stage) that true emotion.

"—I did not know it, before, and it had seemed to me only an expression. . . ."

During her last weeks in Russia, Duse was ill and had to cancel performances. She also cancelled scheduled appearances in Germany, and so could be back in Italy by late February. She and Arrigo met , briefly, on the Ligurian coast, but he had to dash off again to Turin for the opening night of *Tristan*, conducted by the young Arturo Toscanini. Eleonora was already besieged by proposed tours, including one to America.

But she was more dissatisfied than ever with her repertory. From Russia she had written to the Bolognese journalist and man of letters Enrico Panzacchi, asking him to prepare an Italian version of Maurice Maeterlinck's French translation of John Ford's *'Tis Pity She's a Whore*. (Duse called it *Annabella*.) She was also trying to lure Boito into making a translation of *As You Like It* (then virtually unknown in Italy), despite the near-catastrophe they had had with *Cleop*. She also wrote to Adolfo De Bosis, indicating that she still had not given up hope of *La città morta*. And on 28 March 1897, in Rome, under the eye of De Bosis, Duse signed a contract with D'Annunzio, who—on terms very favorable to him—ceded her exclusive Italian rights to the play.

Finally she and Gabriele met again. They went out to Albano—a charming hamlet in the country, where D'Annunzio had had trysts in the past—and there he read her the text of *La città morta*, near the lake where their ideal theatre was to rise. As D'Annunzio described to her the dream of a festival, she immediately was caught up in it and committed herself to its realization.

But first she had another important challenge to face. Through her agent Schurmann, and at the urging of Sardou, Sarah Bernhardt invited Duse to come to Paris and give a special season there. Though she had often visited the French capital and knew the city well, Duse had never performed there. (Parisian critics had traveled on occasion to Brussels in order to see her.) Paris was Sarah's territory, her domain, and Eleonora had been careful not to venture into it. She still felt some of the awe that had filled her, as a young girl, when she first succumbed to the older actress's spell; at the same time, the practical Duse was aware that Bernhardt had a fanatical following in Paris, headed by the doughty Francisque Sarcey, dean of French drama critics.

Primoli, who was seeing both Duse and D'Annunzio during that Roman spring, describes a dialogue that is supposed to have taken place after Sarah's invitation arrived. Since the account was published only a year later (in June 1897 in the *Revue de Paris*), it can be considered essentially correct, if not actually a verbatim record.

"You hesitate?" D'Annunzio asked her.

"Of course. I have never dared face the Parisian public: they are accustomed to such perfection of ensemble, to such personalities!"

"You are wrong . . . You well know what a noble and, I may say, unhoped-for welcome my own art has found in France. For that matter, it is a good French tradition to fling open their doors to artists from beyond the seas and beyond the mountains . . . I am sure that in

Paris, more than anywhere else, you will find alert ears and reflecting spirits."

"That may all be possible. But what use is the public's attention if they do not understand the language?"

"Even so! . . . You will amaze those sensitive minds even more by the multiple expressions of your countenance and the music of the Italian syllables."

"Fine music! My repertory consists of bad translations of familiar French plays. If I could at least give *La città morta*!"

"*La città morta* is reserved for the Renaissance."

"The Renaissance is the very theatre I have been offered."

"The theatre of Sarah Bernhardt?"

"She herself has kindly offered me her theatre."

"Your hesitations have no further reason to exist, when the doors of the Renaissance are being opened to you by Sarah la Magnifique."

"Well then! To honor the Queen of Poets, provide me with some rhythms and images. Improvise a work of poetry for me!"

"You cannot be serious! In a week? It's madness!"

"Then write me a madwoman's part."

"Will you go to Paris?"

"Only on that condition."

"Then we must try to satisfy you."

"I want a formal promise."

"Very well! In ten days you will have your madness!"

Duse went off to Capri for a rest, and D'Annunzio retired to his favorite little hotel in Albano, where he set to work. A short time later, under the date "Easter 1897" (Easter was 18 April that year), Count Primoli wrote in his diary: "Visit from G. D'Annunzio, back from Albano where he had taken refuge for a week to devote himself entirely to his drama of the Mad Girl. His eloquence gave me the illusion of sincerity and won me over. He was keyed-up, like someone who has lived away from all human contact or in the privacy of imaginary visions or with the mad. His impressions burst from every pore: awareness of his power coexisted with the genius that represented the future as it appeared to him. He was seer, prophet, poet, the *vates* in all his admirable intensity, with his second sight. I was won over, absorbed, without listening overmuch to the details of the plans he was expounding to me. . . . As the walls of Jericho fell to the blast of trumpets, the walls of his ideal theatre rose at the sound of his magic word. The wondrous cycle unrolled before my charmed, dazzled eyes. . . ."

Obviously Arrigo had heard of Eleonora's rapprochement with D'Annunzio—at least on the artistic level—and was hurt, upset. From the Hotel Quisisana she wrote to Boito on 9 April:

"—I do you harm!—It's like dying.

"After your first letter, and the first telegram, I felt SOMETHING LIKE blood all around my heart, drowning it.

"Arrigo!—Oh, *see me*! Speaking, writing, is so painful. I *saw you* every hour of these last few days, and after so much love between us, after the life lived, it seemed to me that now, after the *joy of art*, I would have found you again at the end of my road. At the end of my life!

"What would I do without you?!—And what would be my anguish today, at this *last* moment of my career, if I had to renounce the sublime work!?—Ahi! only the terrible pain of making you suffer could cause me, in suffering, to do that!—

"Only your *consent*, can give life again to my blood! . . .

"*See* my life! SEE PART of my *being*! Who will say the words, the unchangeable words of the sublime work, if not I?—I *know*, I KNOW—I UNDERSTAND. And I understand *you*, Arrigo!"

Once again, it was Arrigo who, in his contempt for the theatre (at least, for the modern theatre), could not understand Eleonora's excitement at having drawn Italy's most thrilling, most adventurous, most verbal writer into her art, her world. At this point she had not read a single word of *Il sogno d'un mattino di primavera* ("A Spring Morning's Dream"), still being written for her in Albano. She assumed it would be sublime. And she may also have been referring to *La città morta*, which D'Annunzio had read to her. Determined to persuade Arrigo, she wrote him another letter that same day:

". . . Oh—Arrigo! How to say it to you? Your mark will remain after you—I—Of me, on the contrary, nothing will remain except the terrible suffering, till now (you know it), of an endeavor not lofty, but worthy.

"Today a new power is in sight—oh—tell me *how* could I refuse?—*If it makes you suffer, I* WILL—but what after all is the thought of our wound (already so far off!) *today* when the joy of a beautiful work would make its effort worthy of our soul?—

"Oh! Arrigo—I feel terror at resuming my work with the eternal *Dame aux camélias*—my very *mouth*, at this point, refuses to say *those* words! Tedium, the tedium that is more *fatal* to the artist than any danger! . . ."

She sealed the letter, then reopened it to add a P.S. Telegrams were arriving in a stream from her Paris agent. It looked as if she might have to make a quick trip there, to settle some matters, before coming back to prepare her troupe. She begged Arrigo to wire her his assent, his reassurance. She needed a serene heart before facing the great challenge:

"I must have *wings*, and must be free to decide, and clear-spirited to build things that have meaning. Trust me. *Let me have my wings.* GIVE ME wings. *I will come back to you*—into the palm of your hand!"

To judge by the still-anxious tone of her next letters, Arrigo was reluctant to give her the sort of reassurance she sought. She stayed on in Capri another week, worrying also about practical matters, especially about the quality of her company (her fear that the Parisian audience was accustomed to greater "ensemble" was probably justified).

"I must also *style* the young actor who is with me," she wrote on 16 April. "Primoli wrote to Andò, suggesting he go to Paris with me for a week. Andò has refused, and I must *rehearse* the new actor—"

After receiving another dispiriting letter, the next day she wrote:

"I *beseech* you, give me time.

"Give me time. Only a few days, so that I can get myself together, and leave here—and go where I want, and do what I must—(*for years*) and afterwards we will have some days for ourselves. . . .

"For a moment's joy, in art, how many anxieties!—And it all came, like that, as if by *enchantment*! Your suffering (mine), the promise of the work, the proposal of Paris, the refusal of Andò, the petty demands of my entourage . . . the rain and hail on the island . . . and my head which is going away, away.

"I *beg* you. Give me time! Have trust—and trust in me. . . ."

By 29 April she was back in Rome: "The play was read to me. Alone, the other evening—How can I speak of it? The title—derived from Shakespeare—is the only one right for the distinguished work. Never, never, never was 'Dream of Spring' more sweet and cruel! You enter the dream, through those words . . . which Lenor has known for some time. These, 'For a little garland that I saw,' end the *Dream*, the same words, 'Per una ghirlandetta che io vidi'—Lenor will say things . . . that no one has heard her say before—and she must be beautiful, and all smiling (the first Scene) because *Isabella* (her name is Isabella) is BEYOND life. '*Her soul obeys laws that we do not know.*' But the 'mad' girl (mad for love) is sweet, sweet, sweet. . . .

"—No. I can't tell the story. I don't know how to!—I know that I, too, live in this Dream, and today I seem almost to keep life, which has always drowned me in too much joy or sorrow, at a distance from me

"Today, I remember—and I work!—

"Oh—you will see how beautiful I will be. *I* will be beautiful . . . Yes, yes, and the *'madness'* will be played so sweetly. . . ."

Though Duse did not have Sarah's famous flair for publicity, she took care to orchestrate her reception in Paris; and during her days in Rome she saw something of Primoli, who was writing a long biographical-critical article on her to appear in the *Revue de Paris* just as she arrived in the city. (The same issue would also print the text of D'Annunzio's one-act play.) In the article, Primoli describes a meeting with her; it is dated "1 May 1897," but it probably took place a bit earlier.

At the Hotel Bristol, I ask for Madame Duse. She is about to leave; she comes down the steps. Seeing me, she waves in her hand a magnificent folder bound in old brocade and tied with green moiré ribbons.

"I have it," she says to me triumphantly.

"What?"

"Gabriele D'Annunzio's manuscript!"

"What is it called?"

"A Spring Morning's Dream!"

"It's the right season."

"And to put it in shape, I am going to the country with my troupe, and we will rehearse on the fresh fields, under the trees, in the midst of the flowers . . . Ten days, just ten days' rest: and then, Paris!"

"And you will open with—?"

"I was hesitating between *Magda, La Femme de Claude, La Dame* . . ."

"All works admirably played by Sarah."

"Alas, I know that all too well!"

"A friendly piece of advice: for the Parisian public choose something else."

"Ah! What to perform then? . . . Is it my fault if the great, universal artist has touched everything, and has left her indelible mark on each of her creations? . . . I would prefer not to touch them any more myself: it is natural, however, that, since everything has passed through her hands, my repertory is made up of a little part of hers."

"Perform Italian plays."

"That's the question. Which? As you well know, I do not feel at home with the classics—mind you, I mean our tragedies of yesterday . . . One would have to go back to the Greeks . . . and the moment has not yet come." . . .

"And *La Locandiera*?"

"Ah, you're right! I was forgetting Goldoni! Yes, *La Locandiera* . . . the whole Venetian Settecento is there . . . beauty-patches and sidelong glances . . . it is a gust of fresh air, restful . . . One evening, perhaps: but I can't banter all the time . . . that is not my kind of beauty . . . Come! you don't want to send me back to my grandfather's house; once one had left it, it is not amusing to go back and shut oneself up there."

"Do modern Italian plays, then."

"Which?"

"*Cavalleria*."

"Yes, perhaps . . . That was a bold venture, ten years ago, a new view of the theatre . . . I created it with respect; I was perhaps one of the first to appreciate the work of a great and serious talent, and I perform it with pleasure . . . But today, in Paris, after the popularity of Mascagni's opera, wouldn't they miss the music?"

"Ah, no! If they know the story, so much the better . . . Come, you will perform it . . . But you have also performed other Italian plays."

"There is Giacosa's *Tristi amori*, and *La moglie ideale* of Praga, which are interesting attempts; but in those two works I play a petty bourgeoise whose character is local, essentially Italian, and could be of no interest beyond the Alps . . . And besides, though the plays may be beautiful, those are not roles. If I have some inner flame, how can I reveal it in them? This time, I must confine myself to offering the Parisian public, as samples of the Italian repertory, along with that *Cavalleria*, which is not unfamiliar to them, the comedy of Goldoni and the dramatic poem of Gabriele D'Annunzio: the theatre of yesterday and, perhaps, that of tomorrow . . . For the rest, I will give principally the French drama. It is only there that you find both a play and a role. There will be some interest, I hope, in seeing a French creation interpreted by an Italian temperament. . . ."

The conversation, clearly contrived to announce and justify Duse's choice of plays for Paris, also contains discreet flattery of Sarah, meant to soothe the feelings of her most violent partisans. Hérelle, meanwhile, was completing the French text of *Il sogno d'un mattino di primavera*.

And Duse was in rehearsal. She had found a vacant theatre in Frascati, a little town, like Albano, in the Roman campagna. There she put herself into the character of this new heroine, Isabella (Isa became one of Gabriele's pet names for her), a young girl who has gone mad after her lover was stabbed in her bed. The typically D'Annunzian mixture of violence and delicacy, of sensual poetry, was a far cry from her Magdas and Fernandes; and Duse embraced this new opportunity with ardor and confidence.

"If I speak of *art* . . . I become calm," she wrote to Arrigo at about this time, "as soon as I speak of *life*—my throat tightens . . . and I cannot talk any more!

"Oh Arrigo! We should have grasped it then! . . ."

Caught up in the preparation of the sublime work—and in the presence of the author—Eleonora probably had less time to worry about Arrigo and his dislike of D'Annunzio. In any case, Arrigo sent her a patient telegram with the requested reassurance, and on 14 May 1897, before leaving for Paris, she wired him from Frascati: "I received the telegram! Thank you—Thank you—Thank you! . . ."

11
Sarah

Duse hardly needed the *Revue de Paris* and the article by Gégé Primoli to stir up advance interest in her Paris season. The moment it was announced, the whole city—or rather, *le tout Paris*—seemed to talk of nothing else. There was a Proustian quality about the excitement, and several of Proust's friends (and models) were immediately in correspondence about the forthcoming cultural and social event. Duse had already acquired a reputation as an intellectual actress, and this fame was calculated to add to her snob appeal in the French capital. In the center of the stir, naturally, was Robert de Montesquiou, another friend of Primoli's, and a friend of everyone who counted in the city. Comtesse Edmond de Pourtalès wrote to him to expound a personal problem. She was in mourning; how could she manage not to miss the Duse performances?

"My dear friend," the letter begins, "the thought that la Duse is coming to Paris thrills me. So, despite my self-imposed rule of total retirement this year, I still cannot bring myself to give up the idea of going to hear the great genius.

"Yesterday I had a long talk with the dear Comtesse de Wolkenstein [wife of the Austrian ambassador, and also in strict mourning], and we have decided that the two of us, wrapped in our funereal pepla, will ask you to help us in satisfying our legitimate curiosity.

"The Comtesse wrote that you have promised to speak with Sarah about the possibility of slipping her into one of the boxes that have grilles. I ask you to do the same for me, and in that case the Ambassadress and I would go together, but concealed, with the greatest tranquillity, before or after the rest of the audience."

Montesquiou also arranged the first meeting between Sarah and Eleonora, after Primoli had written asking his friend to act as intermediary. Duse wrote to the Count from her hotel: "Oui et merci," the note says, "I will then expect you on Friday at quarter-past-six in order to go to her at six-thirty . . . And when we are at her house you will speak in my name."

Though he admired Duse's gifts, Montesquiou—who had met her some time before—was less taken with her character; he was too much a friend of Sarah's. Nevertheless, he duly stage-managed the meeting. The two actresses fell into each other's arms—the Count, describing the scene later, said it was more like a collision—and exchanged the suitable compliments. Duse, as often in those days, looked a little dowdy and wore no make-up; Sarah, who received them in her sculptress's atelier, was at her most glowing, her most mettlesome.

That night at her theatre Sarah was starring in *La Samaritaine*, a new vehicle written for her by Edmond Rostand. Duse was in the box of honor, decorated with orchids for the occasion; she rose to her feet at the star's entrance and—to the discomfiture of Montesquiou, her escort—remained standing for almost the whole performance. Sarah, with a grateful glance, acknowledged her colleague's visible (some said ostentatious) tribute.

Contrary to her habits, Duse participated in a certain amount of Parisian social life. She even received interviewers. One of them was the critic of *Le Figaro*, Jules Huret, who described her for his readers: "Her apartment smells of tar; a great fire burns in the fireplace, and from time to time the artist bends over a vaporizer, to inhale the tar steam with which she treats her throat. Then the slender, mystical fingers are raised to pull back the rebellious locks, as she speaks ardently with the friends surrounding her of the subjects that mean most to her, uttering in passionate accents the words *goodness, soul, life*."

With Montesquiou and Primoli, who had arrived in the city, Eleonora visited the salons of the leading Parisian hostesses. She also called on M. Worth for some smart new clothes. But her chief concern was the preparation for her debut at the Renaissance.

Boldly, or perhaps superstitiously, she decided to open with *La Dame aux camélias*, the work in which she felt most comfortable when making her debut in a new city. By now the play was almost half a century old, and the French knew it by heart. What's more, they knew Sarah's interpretation of it by heart. Marguerite Gautier and the Divine Sarah had become virtually identified with each other, and Duse was going to challenge this identification, in a foreign language and with a routine company. She was to some extent reassured by the presence of Andò, who had finally given in to her insistence and managed to be in Paris for a few days, to act yet again as her Armand Duval. Though he was forty-six, Andò remained the best romantic leading actor that the Italian theatre could offer.

The house glittered. In an account published the following year, the American correspondent Victor Mapes wrote: "From the first row in the orchestra to the last row, up there in the balcony, not a vacancy— one unbroken sea of animated faces. According to a custom, which makes all tickets complimentary for a first night, the desirable places have been tendered to notabilities, while friends of the theatre and their friends occupy the rest. All the faces near enough to be distinguished, therefore, have a claim to attention. . . ."

Sarah herself occupied a stage box. She was wearing a richly embroidered silk dress with a wreath of red roses in the famous red hair. Her son Maurice and his wife sat with her. Above, in separate boxes, were the actresses Réjane and Bartet. The spectators in the boxes also included Prince and Princesse Murat, Prince and Princesse de Poix, Duc and Duchesse de Gramont, Prince and Princesse de Bulgarie (again, the list sounds Proustian). Gégé Primoli's aunt, Princesse Mathilde Bonaparte, the great patroness of the arts, sat in the box directly over Sarah's.

Yvette Guilbert was there, and so were the widows of Dumas fils and Georges Bizet. And the critics: Jules Lemaître, Catulle Mendès, and the portly, white-maned Francisque Sarcey, who wrote for Le Temps. By a not-so-curious trick of lighting, Sarah seemed to be sitting in a halo. Mapes described her: "Bernhardt changes her pose—she puts one arm forward on the edge of the box, and after giving a nervous glance to see if she is still being observed, she leans her chin on her open palm and fixes the stage with her eyes. The curtain trembles, there is a sudden hush, and amid the silent intensity the memorable performance has begun."

The performance was memorable more for social and historical reasons than for dramatic ones. Duse was understandably nervous; among other things, she had had to undergo some petty harassments from Sarah (who had locked her own sumptuous dressing-room and given her paying guest a smaller, uncomfortable room). When Duse appeared, she seemed unusually pale, and—her enemies remarked— unusually elegant. Even her unruly hair was neatly coiffed.

Throughout the first of the play's five acts, Duse's nervousness was visible. During the brief interval, the audience was supposed to remain seated, but a number of Sarah's friends flocked to her box, and so the spectators were treated to another show—the words inaudible—as Bernhardt mimed her enthusiasm for her Italian colleague.

The second act went better, but in the longer interval that followed it the comments, as Mapes reported, agreed that "Duse's impersonation of Marguerite Gautier was essentially wide of the mark. She was not sufficiently a courtesan, and her 'transformation at the touch of love' was no transformation at all."

The third act aroused scant enthusiasm, and the major scene with Armand's father failed to impress, partly because it was heavily cut. The fourth act, where Armand throws money at Marguerite, saw the public's interest shift to Andò, who won a personal ovation. But finally, in the death-bed scene, Duse came into her own. It was too late. "If some one had triumphed," Mapes wrote, "it was not Duse."

The next day's reviews were measured, analytical, extended, but far from the overheated hymns to which the actress had become accustomed, especially from the foreign press. She had not taken Paris by storm. And all the notices implied—where they did not contain—comparisons with Sarah, in Sarah's favor.

Sarcey took his time. His review came out only the following Sunday, interesting because it was a French view of an Italian Marguerite Gautier; but his enthusiasm was no greater than his fellows', and his insular prejudices hardly less evident than those of New York or Boston. As he saw her, "La Duse (either because she has so conceived the character, or because she is incapable of rendering it otherwise) suggests a good little soul,—if I knew the Italian word that corresponds to *grisette* I would use it,—very sweet, not over tumultuous, who certainly must be sorry to be so cruel to Varville, and who can only be conceived as ruining her lovers by making them buy her macaroni. She is a tender creature, and it is only necessary for her to talk a few minutes with Armand in order to have her heart touched— her utterance becomes slower, and one feels in beholding her that such a woman was made, not to dissipate with reckless extravagance the millions of her passing admirers, but to live at the feet of a man she could adore. In the drama, as Dumas conceived it, matters are quite otherwise. . . . And yet, it is nevertheless delicious. For she excels in expressing tenderness, and her manner of offering a flower to Armand, though quite absurd if one follows the text, is in itself exquisitely graceful and tender."

Sarcey also reports that, in the third act, Duse lost her hold on the public and miscalculated the scene with Duval *père*. Sarcey did not share the enthusiasm for Andò, and added: "Frankly, if one of our actors played Armand like that in *La Dame aux camélias* in French, he would not be tolerated. It is not his little mustache, so much. . . ."

There were a number of Italians in the audience, all of them partisans, and they led the scant applause, Sarcey pointed out, at the end of the unsuccessful Act III. Among them was the Neapolitan playwright and critic Roberto Bracco, a friend of Duse's from her Naples days. His report, sent back to a Naples newspaper, was headed "Paris—the night between 2 and 3 June 1897" and gave a more roseate account of the evening. Bracco was particularly interested in picking up the brief comments of celebrities during the intermission. "The most profound sensation I have ever felt in the theatre," said the playwright Georges de Porto-Riche; and the widow of Dumas *fils* said: "If Dumas were still with us, what a great evening, what a great evening for him!" Duse's fellow-actresses, Réjane and Bartet, as well as Yvette Guilbert, expressed similar enthusiasm.

The next week Duse performed *Magda*, then—again following a familiar pattern—she fell ill and cancelled a second *Magda*, as well as performances of *Cavalleria rusticana* with *La Femme de Claude*. Sudermann's play, also familiar in Paris, was not a favorite with the French; but here the Duse–Bernhardt contrast could be more serenely appreciated, since both actresses had to play in translation. And this time the press was more favorable; several critics admitted that the part of Magda was more suited to Duse's temperament than Marguerite had been. "I think I am beginning to distinguish the characteristic traits of her peculiar talent," Sarcey wrote. "Before attempting to arrive at definite conclusions we were waiting to see her in *La Femme de Claude* and *Cavalleria rusticana*."

By the time this piece came out Duse, confined for several days to her hotel room, was recovering. But Sarah—evidently reacting to the implied challenge of Duse's presence—did not consider the battle won. She simply sharpened her weapons. Two years before, at the time of the death of Dumas *fils*, a committee had been formed to raise funds for a monument. The sum had still not been collected, so Sarah had a word with the men involved. She suggested a gala benefit in her theatre, for which she, of course, volunteered her services.

As Duse learned from the newspapers (which had been immediately and deliberately informed), Sarah had decided to do the last two acts of *La Dame aux camélias* and was inviting Duse to present Acts II and III (the very ones in which she had not shone on her opening night at the Renaissance). Duse had to accept the invitation somehow, but she balked at Sarah's selection and insisted that she would do, instead, the second act of *La Femme de Claude* (which, because of her illness, the French public still had not seen in her interpretation). Sarah tried to stick to her own plan, but Duse stood firm and the committee agreed with her.

It was an all-star occasion. The final bill opened with Sarah in a one-act play she had written herself, *L'Aveu*. Then Tamagno and Héglon came from the Opéra to sing a duet from *Il trovatore*, after which Emma Nevada sang an aria from *Lucia di Lammermoor*. Yvette Guilbert, the reigning diseuse of the Chat Noir, displayed her talent as an actress, reading a piece by Marcel Prévost. Then came Duse in *La Femme de Claude*, Sarah in the last two acts of *La Dame aux camélias*, and the Intermission. After that, Coquelin recited some poems; there were further operatic selections; and—as the splendid conclusion—an *Hommage* "to Alexandre Dumas from Marguerite Gautier," verses by Rostand recited by Sarah, with all her illustrious guests on stage, surrounding her. At the end of the recitation, the audience sprang to its feet; she went over to Duse, took her by the hand and led her to the bust, where the two stars made a reverent bow together.

In France, *La Femme de Claude* had been less than a success, and it was the second act—the one Duse did—that had aroused most controversy. The author had felt called on to defend it in two pamphlets, *L'Homme-femme* and *Tue-la*. But in Italy the play had long been one of Eleonora's greatest triumphs. Now, in the role of the husband Claude, she enlisted an old friend and longtime colleague, Carlo Rosaspina, who also took over the role of Armand when Andò had to return to Italy. Years later Rosaspina recalled: "The rest of the performance (which began at 1 a.m., after the other theatres had closed) took place amid general indifference as everyone waited for la Duse, who then won such a raving success that, two evenings later, when she performed the entire *Femme de Claude*, the Parisians paid as much as 250 francs for an orchestra seat."

The Paris season was virtually over, and Bernhardt went off to give some performances in London, including Alfred de Musset's *Lorenzaccio* (in which she played the title role, in breeches). But Eleonora still had another great hurdle before her: D'Annunzio's *Il sogno*. It would be the first time a work of his had appeared in the theatre. Fortunately the premiere would be in Paris, a city that knew and admired his work.

But the French knew his work in translation, and Duse was naturally giving the little drama in the original, incomprehensible to most of the audience. Gabriele was in Italy and did not plan to come for the opening: he was about to embark on a lively political campaign, which would end in August with his election to the Italian Chamber of Deputies as the representative of the district of Ortona-sul-mare, in his native Abruzzo.

Il sogno is the story of a girl whose clandestine lover is killed while they are making love; she lies till dawn beneath his dead body, as his blood soaks into her nightdress; and in the morning, when the couple are found, she has gone mad. All this has happened before the curtain rises. When the play begins, some years have passed, and the mad girl is living in a secluded Tuscan villa—the time is vaguely Renaissance—in the care of a sister and some devoted servants. But as the title implies, the work is not so much a story as a dream, a rhapsody, a verbal delirium; and if the words are lost—as they were on the French public—the play is lost with them. Even an audience that understands the words might find the play antidramatic: this, in fact, was the reaction both of the Italians, when Duse gave it in Italy a few months later, and of the French, when Sarah gave it in translation at the Renaissance some time after Duse's departure.

The gala opening, on 15 June, was a great occasion. Even President Faure of France was there, and at the end of the play he declared he had understood everything. "Did you play in Italian, Madame?" he flatteringly asked Eleonora. Enthusiastic telegrams were despatched to the author in Rome, giving the idea of an overwhelming success, though the outcome was more cordial than triumphant. Still the reports were an encouragement to Gabriele, whom Eleonora wanted to keep in the realm of the theatre.

Duse's season, which was to have lasted less than two weeks, was stretching on. "Arrigo!" she wrote to Boito on 24 June, "How long this fifth act of my life is! When will it end?"

Before it could end—and it was hardly the fifth act—*Le Temps* published a Letter to the Editor, signed with the pseudonym Sganarelle, a waggish concealment of the identity of Sarcey himself. In the letter, full of praise of Duse, the critic expressed his regret that the actress was about to leave Paris when, because of conflicting schedules, few of the actresses and actors of France had had the pleasure of seeing her. He suggested that, before leaving, she should offer a matinee to them, by invitation. Though professional matinees, as they were called, were then customary in other countries, in Paris they were unknown. Duse would also be establishing a precedent.

She hestitated. It seemed pretentious, she thought, for *her* to invite fellow-artists to come and see her perform. To a friend she wrote: "For my performance there will be no invitations! I cannot invite my fellow-artists to come and hear me and applaud me! It would be a bit ridiculous, wouldn't it? It is they who are inviting me: I put myself at their disposal. That is all I can do."

Sarah, back from London, got wind of the plan, and —according to Mapes—wanted to put her name on the invitations (which was why Eleonora wanted no invitations at all). Then she made further trouble. Duse's temporary lease of the Renaissance had expired. When Schurmann asked for the theatre on the usual terms, Sarah said it was impossible. Needless to say, word of this refusal reached the press, adding fuel to the blaze of gossip. In July, when it was all over, Sarah wrote a letter to Robert de Montesquiou, who seemed to have gone over to the enemy. It gives her side of the story (Sarah was not, however, known for adamantine veracity) and justifies some of her irritation:

> You are the one who introduced me to la Duse. I was utterly courteous and polite towards her. She was supposed to perform ten times in eleven days; she performed ten times in thirty days. This meant a very heavy increase in expenses for me, since I kept my theatre open, though it was to have been closed. And I paid my staff even more than usual, since they were entitled to a holiday. I did all that, my dear friend, *de bonne grâce*, without even mentioning it to anyone.
>
> You are aware of all the pettinesses and infamies I have had to put up with since la Duse's arrival. Having been given my apotheosis, they wanted to give me my burial. You are aware that I was forced to sue that Schurmann, who prompted a hateful and defamatory article against me in the press.
>
> You are aware of all the moral suffering I underwent for a month! And yet I bore everything with perfect patience and loyalty, and now la Duse goes elsewhere to give her farewell performance; and what is odious, these people to whom I gave my theatre, my lighting, and my employees for nothing [*sic*] give a performance half to a paying audience. Schurmann called on that old fool Sarcey, who declares my theatre too small, and allows seats to be sold to a half-private performance. All this is improper, and la Duse has played a shrewd role, oh! how shrewd! I did not want Schurmann to be named on the invitations, and she told mutual friends that I wanted to put myself in charge of the event. You know me, friend, and you know how it is. I find this all very base, very *lâche*, and the Italian artist lacking a straightforward and noble character; she didn't even write me a word of thanks or farewell.
>
> I am sad at heart. . . .

Nearly thirty years later, when Camillo Antona Traversi was writing his book on Duse, he questioned José Schurmann about the matter. The impresario replied: "When la Duse arrived, the Paris press was not kind to Sarah. I had nothing to do with it.

"Sarah, who wanted to have the Légion d'honneur, was exasperated when she learned from Adrien Bernheim that I was about to be given the cross and she wasn't. . . ."

According to Schurmann, then, the defamation charge had been brought to impede his decoration. But Sarah finally lost the case, was ordered to pay 1 franc damages, and Schurmann got his cross.

When the Renaissance became unavailable, Schurmann found a larger house, the Théâtre de la Porte Saint-Martin, also more conveniently located. The program was Duse's final Parisian vindication; her colleagues applauded her in *Cavalleria*, Act V of *La Dame aux camélias*, and Act II of *La Femme de Claude*. Sarah's complaint about paid admissions was based on fact: a few seats—a hundred in all—were sold to members of the aristocracy, to help defray the considerable expenses. The other 1,400 seats were given away to the invited guests (about ten times that many applications had been received).

Now completely won over, Sarcey wrote in *Le Temps*: "La Duse then leaves victorious; from the general viewpoint of the theatre, she leaves behind her an example which it would be well for all to profit by. . . . She has won us by the sheer power of the truth."

The troupe left for Italy the day after the performance. Eleonora stayed behind for a farewell breakfast offered in her honor by the Comédie Française at the Pavillon d'Armenonville in the Bois de Boulogne. Wearing one of her smart new French toilettes, a bouquet in her hand, she posed afterwards for a souvenir photograph, sitting between Mounet-Sully and Worms, two stars of the Comédie, surrounded by her festive colleagues.

Then it was Eleonora's turn to leave Paris. She was eager to get back to Italy and Gabriele.

1 Duse, on her first tour of Russia (1891). It was there that the foundations of her international career were laid.

2 Eleonora's father, Alessandro Duse, though he was an actor and the son of an actor, did not like his profession (and apparently was not very good at it). Once his daughter's success was established, she was able to support him. He retired to Venice, where this picture was taken, and died there in 1892, while Eleonora was on a Russian tour.

3 Angelica Duse, Eleonora's mother, died young, in 1875, before her daughter had become famous. Eleonora felt a lasting veneration for her mother and frequently mentioned her in letters, especially to her own daughter Enrichetta. This photograph showing Eleonora as a child with Angelica was in Duse's possession at her death, then in Enrichetta's.

4 Duse used to say "Je suis belle quand je veux," but she
was never a classic beauty. Her face was remarkably
mobile, capable of endless nuance; and thus photographs—
especially an early one like this—can give, in their fixity,
only a pallid idea of what she must really have looked like.

5 It was in Naples, at the end of the 1870s, that Duse finally began to be recognized as a promising young actress of exceptional qualities. There, too, she fell in love for the first time, with the brilliant journalist Martino Cafiero, some years her senior. For Eleonora this was a great passion; for Cafiero, a man of the world, it was a passing affair. The affair had ended by the time Eleonora bore Cafiero's child, who survived only a day or so.

6 Cesare Rossi (1829–98) was a successful actor-manager when he recognized Duse's talents and took her into his Compagnia della Città di Torino in 1880. She was soon the prima donna of the troupe and went with it to South America. She left Rossi's company in 1886, to form her own troupe. Rossi later acted with Duse during a season in London, but with scant success. The disparity between Duse's style and his more old-fashioned acting was by then too evident.

7 Another member of the Rossi company was Tebaldo Checchi (a professional name, his real surname being Marchetti). Born in 1844, Tebaldo also came from a family of actors; and though he was never a star, he had a solid reputation, especially as an interpreter of character parts. After Cafiero abandoned Eleonora, Tebaldo became her companion and mentor. In 1881 they were married; their daughter Enrichetta was born in 1882. The marriage was not a success, and during the South American tour of the Rossi company in 1885 Duse and Tebaldo separated, with some bitterness. He died in 1918.

8 Flavio Andò (1851–1915) was the leading man in the Rossi company, Armand to Duse's Marguerite Gautier, Turiddu to her Santuzza. During the South American tour, as her marriage was disintegrating, she had a brief affair with Andò. After it ended, he continued to be her leading man; and when she formed her own company in 1886, Andò was the principal actor. In 1894 he left Duse to join another company, but he acted again with her—at her insistence—at the opening of her 1897 Paris season in *La Dame aux camélias*.

9 Duse was devoted to her daughter, Enrichetta, but professional obligations kept mother and child separated for most of Enrichetta's early life. During Duse's affair with Arrigo Boito, the child became fond also of the austere poet-composer. This photograph was sent to him by Duse and was found among his papers after his death.

10 This photograph of Arrigo Boito (1842–1918) belonged to Duse and was presumably given to her by Boito at some point during their affair, which began in 1887 and ended a decade later.

11 Duse as Mirandolina in Goldoni's *La locandiera*. Duse's family came from the Venice area, and Goldoni had been a favourite author of her grandfather. This was one of the first parts in which Boito saw her (he had taken the Verdis with him to the theatre).

12 Many of Boito's letters to Duse—like this one—were concerned with arrangements for a meeting, choice of hotels, schedules of trains. This letter ends: "Lenor—This time you were the one who lit the fire with your own hands. Don't complain if it still burns."

13 Duse as Santuzza in the play *Cavalleria rusticana*, written by Giovanni Verga, a friend of Boito's. Cesare Rossi—in whose company Duse was then acting—was reluctant to stage the unconventional work, but Duse insisted and triumphed in the leading part.

14 Italian troupes and Italian audiences of a century ago consumed quantities of drama, and repertoires were large. Like other leading performers, Duse was always on the look-out for new plays and new writers. In 1890 she met the twenty-eight-year-old Marco Praga, then at the beginning of his career. He read the manuscript of *La moglie ideale* to her, listened to her suggestions, made revisions, and she presented his play triumphantly in November of that year.

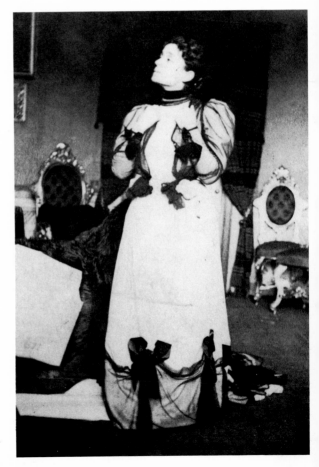

15 Duse as Shakespeare's Cleopatra. Shakespeare was a favorite author of Boito's and also of Duse's (though she played him rarely). Boito's translation of the play turned it into a vehicle for Duse, and the Italian critics castigated both translator and actress. Duse took the production on tour. Since foreign critics and audiences could not follow the Italian text, the work enjoyed more success abroad. Duse also considered doing *Macbeth* and *Romeo and Juliet* in translations by Boito, but those projects were abandoned.

16 Duse in a studio photograph, *c.* 1890. The photograph was given, with an inscription, to Marco Praga's mother, Anna, a friend of Boito's.

17 Duse in San Remo, in the late 1890s. At left is the
French playwright Maurice Donnay (Duse gave his play
L'autre danger in the early 1900s). Duse is standing next to
her old friend, the Neapolitan journalist and writer Matilde
Serao. The half-hidden man behind them cannot be
identified. At right, holding the bicycle, is Count Joseph
Primoli (Gégé).

18 Duse as Sardou's *Théodora*. The actress assumed this role—created by Sarah Bernhardt—early in 1885, shortly after its Paris premiere. The lavish production involved dozens of extras, great expense, and an immense physical effort on Duse's part. The effort proved too much for her, and she had to drop the play.

19 Duse as *Odette*, another of the Sardou parts she came to dislike intensely, though it was very popular with audiences and she played it often.

20,21 The Italian painter Edoardo
Gordigiani, brother of Duse's friend
Giulietta (later wife of Robert Mendelssohn),
painted this portrait in New York in 1896,
during the actress's second North American
tour. He also took some preliminary
photographs in preparation for the work.

22 Duse in *La Dame aux
camélias*. Throughout the
early part of her career,
Duse was particularly
attached to the part of
Marguerite Gautier; and
she often chose the Dumas
drama as her debut vehicle
in a city where she was not
known. She even opened
with it on her first visit to
Paris, in 1897, challenging
Sarah Bernhardt on her
home ground and in a part
with which the French
actress was intimately
associated.

23,24 Duse in Venice, photographed by Count Joseph Primoli. Late in 1894 Duse took an apartment in Venice, the top floor of the little Palazzo Barbaro-Wolkoff. The rest of the building, which has a view along the Grand Canal, belonged to the family of the painter Wolkoff, Duse's friends. Other friends lived nearby. Shortly after she had settled in, Gégé Primoli came up from Rome and took a number of photographs of her and of the house. Above, she is seen in her apartment in her most characteristic attitude, as a reader. At left, she is in a gondola.

25 Gabriele D'Annunzio, in Rome, photograph by Primoli, *c.* 1895. The poet surely saw Duse perform in Rome when he was living there, and they may have met then. They had a number of mutual friends, including Primoli and Matilde Serao. But their real friendship—which soon developed into a passionate affair—began with their meeting in Venice in 1894.

26 Letter from Duse to Boito: "*I do you harm!—It's like dying.*" Even after her affair with D'Annunzio had begun, Eleonora continued to write to Arrigo and—on rare occasions—to see him. But Gabriele represented her future, in the theatre as well as in her private life. This letter was written from Capri on 9 April 1897, as she was preparing to go to Paris, where she was to perform D'Annunzio's *Sogno di un mattino di primavera*, his first play to be seen on a stage. In November 1898 Eleonora and Arrigo met in Rome and their affair officially ended.

27 After an uncertain start, Duse's Paris season in 1897 was a triumph. Before leaving the city, she gave a special matinée for her French colleagues. The troupe of the Comédie-Française then sponsored a luncheon in her honor at the Pavillon d'Armenonville in the Bois de Boulogne. In the souvenir photograph taken on the occasion, she is seated, in the center, between two leading figures of the company, Worms and Mounet-Sully. The third person to her left is Le Bargy, who later encountered Duse and D'Annunzio during a stormy stay in Switzerland.

28,29 After giving up her apartment in
Venice, Duse settled in a house she called
''La Porziuncola'' near Settignano, on a
hill just above Florence. A short time later
D'Annunzio leased the more splendid
Villa Capponcina, across the road. Their
proximity did not arrest their
correspondence. The poet invented new
names for the houses—''The House of
the Swallows'' and ''The House of the
Evening''—and notes, messages, letters
were constantly exchanged between
them. Duse's letters were on occasion

bitter or reproachful; but the lovers also
had periods of unalloyed happiness, as is
borne out by these lines, written by the
poet at ''dawn of 9 July 1899.'' They begin:
''Dear dear companion, every day more
beautiful and every day more beloved.''

30 D'Annunzio at La Capponcina with two
of his greyhounds. The poet was surrounded at
the villa by animals, especially dogs and
horses. In his novel *Il fuoco* several pages are
devoted to describing the beauty and mystery
of greyhounds.

31 Duse in the garden of La Capponcina. The photograph was taken by D'Annunzio, whose shadow—his head, wearing a cap—can be seen on the ground.

32 D'Annunzio in the garden of La Capponcina. The photograph was taken by Duse, on the same day as the above.

33 Duse as Silvia Settala in *La Gioconda*, 1899. At first
D'Annunzio's drama, written for Duse, was not a success;
but with tenacity and devotion she continued to play it
until, eventually, it achieved a certain popularity, at least
with Italian audiences.

34 D'Annunzio's *Francesca da Rimini*, first performed on 9
December 1901 with Duse in the title role, was a cultural
event of great interest. Sparing no expenditure (of Duse's
money), the poet carefully supervised every detail of the
sumptuous costumes and the elaborate staging. First reactions were mixed; but eventually the work—and Duse's
interpretation—won praise and support. Some of her
photographs in the drama indicate signs of her premature
aging (she was in her early forties), which D'Annunzio had
implacably—and, her friends felt, unpardonably—
described in *Il fuoco*.

35,36 Duse as Anna in *La Città morta*. Given originally in French by Sarah Bernhardt in 1898, the D'Annunzio tragedy was a failure. Duse, who first played it in 1901, finally imposed it on audiences in Italy and abroad, though its theme of adultery and incest was considered shocking. She revived the play, judiciously cut (with the author's approval), for her last tours.

37 After her rupture with D'Annunzio in the spring of 1904, Duse found herself with a much reduced repertory. (For five years or so she had devoted herself largely to his plays.) She was reluctant to return to her old vehicles, the works of Sardou and Dumas; and she explored new paths. One venture was Gorky's *The Lower Depths*, which she played in France (seen here) and in Milan, but then gave up.

38 Ibsen had always been a favorite author of Duse's; and in her post-D'Annunzio period she explored his works more and more. In the winter of 1906 she actually took a troupe to Kristiania (now Oslo), where she hoped to meet Ibsen. The hope was frustrated by the dramatist's ill-health (he died soon afterwards); but she gave several Ibsen performances, including *Rosmersholm*. This photograph was taken at the time.

39 In her solitude, after the break with D'Annunzio, Eleonora relied more and more on the support of friends, such as Gégé Primoli, who came to see her in Paris—where this photograph was taken—in the spring of 1905.

40 In the winter of 1909, Duse stopped performing—she apparently did not consider this a definitive, formal retirement—and a restless period in her life began. One of the several cures she adopted for her poor health caused her to put on weight briefly, as can be seen in this photograph taken during a seaside holiday with her daughter, Enrichetta, and her friends from Berlin, the Mendelssohns. Enrichetta is holding Angelica Mendelssohn, while little Eleonora Mendelssohn—Duse's godchild (and herself later a famous actress)—is standing in front of Duse at left. In the background is an Italian nurse, standing beside Robert Mendelssohn. Giulietta Gordigiani Mendelssohn is holding her son Francesco. The gentleman at right is identified (in Enrichetta's handwriting on the back of the photograph) as "Adami, a friend of the Mendelssohns."

41,42,43 Like many other stage actors of the time, Duse was fascinated by the new medium, cinema. But unlike most of her colleagues, she studied it carefully and adapted her style to its requirements and limitations. Though she wrote or conceived a number of scripts (for silent films, of course), she made only one picture, *Cenere*, in 1916. Febo Mari, her leading man, was the titular director, but she actually directed the picture herself. It was not a commercial success, and producers were not encouraged to make further films with her.

44 Duse with Selva, *c.* 1913. Unlike Bernhardt, who always traveled with a menagerie, Duse had no pets during her touring years. But in her period of inactivity, she adopted a near-setter mongrel named Selva (because he had appeared from the woods, a stray), to whom she became very attached.

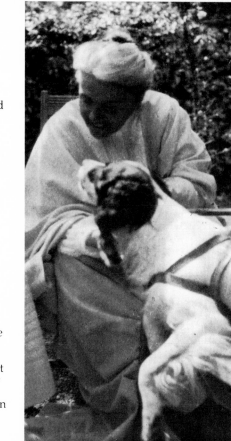

45 Duse on the set of *Cenere*, 1916. Long after she had apparently left the stage, Duse continued to be written about in the newspapers. During the making of her film, there was an erroneous report of her being dangerously ill, near death. To show Enrichetta (who was in England) the fine state of her health, Duse made a brief movie—of herself in street clothes—to be sent to Enrichetta. It never got to England and was lost, except for a few frames that survive in a private collection.

46 Duse at the front, 1917. Duse followed the events of the First World War with a mixture of intense, unquestioning patriotism and profound human suffering. When asked to take part in a program for entertaining the troops, Duse refused, but she went to the front anyway, to make herself useful, writing letters, talking with the sick (and the homesick), and—within her limited resources—helping the soldiers with small sums. To Enrichetta she complained that her black dress (seen in this photograph of her, with the critic Renato Simoni) made her seem "disguised as a priest." After this first visit, she bought a blue one.

47 Duse did not go to the front as a tourist. She was actually in a danger zone; and on one occasion her hotel room—while she was fortunately out—was destroyed by a shell.

48 Duse had many friends among her fellow-actresses. She particularly admired Cécile Sorel, with whom she was photographed at the front.

49 During the war years, Duse was separated from Enrichetta, now married and living in England. Soon after the armistice, Duse made the toilsome journey from Florence to Cambridge, where she spent seven weeks in the summer of 1919. This photograph, taken in the garden of Enrichetta's house in Huntingdon Road, shows Duse with her son-in-law Edward Bullough and her granddaughter Eleonora (now Sister Mary Mark).

50 Duse in Turin, 1922. This photograph was taken shortly after her return to the stage (with Ibsen's *The Lady from the Sea*, Turin, 5 May 1921), before she set out touring again, first in Europe, then the United States.

51 Duse, photographed by Alice Boughton, New York, 1923.

52 Duse, photographed by Arnold Genthe in New York,
1924, shortly before she set out on the cross-country tour
that led her finally to Pittsburgh and her death.

53 After a solemn funeral mass at the Church of St
Vincent Ferrer in New York, Duse's remains were put on
the Italian ship *Duilio* and returned to Italy. There was
another solemn service in Santa Maria degli Angeli in
Rome, and another in Asolo, the little town north of Venice
where the actress had bought a house and where she had
chosen to be buried. This photograph was taken at the
Asolo service.

12
Settignano

Rimini in 1897, according to a Baedeker published that year, boasted "Handsome public rooms with a café and restaurant, and numerous lodging-houses have been erected on the beach, to which a tree-shaded avenue leads from Porta Marina." This is where Eleonora and Gabriele met, after she had stopped off briefly in Venice on her return from Paris.

In those days, the Adriatic town had 11,000 inhabitants and was only beginning to attract attention as a bathing resort. It was easy for D'Annunzio to come up from Francavilla, where he was then in the midst of his electioneering, and the very name of Rimini had its magic, suggesting the romantic story of Francesca and Paolo which the poet would soon use for one of his dramas. The meeting with Eleonora had been preceded by the usual telegrams ("*Horrible peine*," one of Duse's said), and it did not last long. By 20 July D'Annunzio was back in Francavilla, where she wrote him: "Yesterday I couldn't bear the anguish of watching you go away, so I sacrificed even the *one minute* that remained, and I went off before the train moved. . . ."

During this meeting, the two of them obviously discussed the future, but they must have discussed, more urgently, the present. D'Annunzio's present, as always, was complicated. Principessa Gravina had recently given birth to another child, but the poet had refused to give the baby his name, insisting that the actual father was a coachman. He was determined to break with la Gravina for good, but it was impossible to do so at once. Among other problems, there was the question of where he would live. Venice—though Eleonora had her little apartment there—was not suitable; life was too public, too social. He and Duse would have had no privacy, and he would not have been able to write, any more than he could amid the domestic scenes and nagging responsibilities of Francavilla. Florence—or rather its out-skirts, the lovely hills—provided the solution.

After D'Annunzio left Rimini, Eleonora stayed on for a few days. She wrote to him, and she also wrote to Boito. Her letter of 22 July, three days after the poet's departure, is tedious, mostly about her health, the medicines she was taking (atropine and morphine), and her troubles with a London agent who was suing her. But she also suggested that she and Arrigo might meet. Just as Gabriele's situation with la Gravina was still unclear, so Eleonora seemed as yet reluctant to make a clean break with the past.

"I will leave as soon as I can bear the *railroad*. I will stop at Interlaken for a week. There, we will meet—There is a Hotel . . . the name of the chief mountain . . . the *Jong-Frau*. Is that how you spell it?—I don't know. Anyway, there is the Hotel of the Virgin Mountain, and there we will meet. There all is green, and peace—. . . There I will speak to you, beautiful soul, whom I still cost so much pain—whereas here, the apathy of suffering, and the *enormous* effort it is for me to write a letter prevent me—. . ."

They do not seem to have met at Interlaken, which Eleonora soon left. From Mürren, on 10 August, she wrote again to Arrigo, who was in Aix-les-Bains.

"Write?

"I am here, under fog, and without rudder, and out at sea.

"I feel profoundly grateful to the one [Arrigo] who wrote to me yesterday, who three times wanted to come to my aid and support.

"But for the moment it was, and is impossible. Oh! don't think I'm an ingrate! But this whole hateful tangle of things revolts, revolts, revolts me, and all my blood is poisoned.

"I have none of the virtues fate requires of me at this moment! No patience (ah!) or a stupid religion that would plunge me into prayer, no illusion of *conquering* this stupid nature in order to keep alive (to be torn to pieces in due course) a creature beginning now to live [Enrichetta, who was with her in Mürren, also ill], and another, myself, at the last steps, close to the door through which you leave. . . ."

In Mürren, besides her health and Enrichetta's, she also had to worry about work; she was pursued by telegrams, claims, demands for decisions. "I read all these epistles, and then I fling myself on the bed to seek sleep. For today, then, it's impossible to write. My hand, my head, everything aches—and I can't—but I thank, and bless *him*, to whom I could (in another life) have given so much sweetness."

Sometimes Boito's letters arrived in the same mail as the daily ones from Gabriele which she answered in long, ecstatic replies. On 6 August, she wrote: "What is the point of living if I am not working for you? . . . Will I *still* be here, in this delicious world, in two years' time?—For to arrange everything for the great plan [the festival theatre in Albano] it will take two years, at least!—*La città morta* will be only 'to open the doors', but it is the *Temple* that must be built. . . .

"Alas, do not take offense, dear soul—if I insist always on: *taking action*

"*doing, helping* you.

"I know well that these words revolt you, but if you reflect and calculate how much calm and seclusion you need, then you will understand all my humble and worthy offer. . . .

"You should have around you people who are eager but calm, avoiding every shock, every *loss* of time, so that you can prepare the *holy bread*—which is necessary *to you* to provide, if you want to live in the great joy of expending yourself."

She was worried also about the "new *parliamentary* idea," which might rob more of that time she wanted so much for him to have for himself, for the holy task of writing. Clearly, she was already thinking of creating a refuge for him, where she could spare him shocks and surround him with her eagerness for his work. In the same letter she discussed possible casting for *La città morta*. D'Annunzio had thought of the beautiful, rising young actress Tina Di Lorenzo for the secondary female role, and for the men Flavio Andò and Ermete Zacconi. It was impossible to assemble such a trio, but Eleonora tried all the same. Discussing Andò, she spelled his surname with a small "a" to indicate her contempt for what she considered his pettiness:

"How like him to *stall for time* till the 15th. He should have accepted at once, on his knees. *He* is the one who must be hitched to the wagon, not the wagon to him—and I can't tell you how *disgusted* I am by that manner of his, and how surprised I am that neither you nor Boutet [the critic-manager who would present *La città morta*] *lashed* him with some words suited to his hide. . . .

"He is only a performer, in the most *utilitarian*, and *wretched* sense of the word. What he *performs* today seems to him most opportune also for TOMORROW, and he *seeks* no farther. . . ."

Some strangers in Mürren, discovering she was there, sent her a bouquet of mountain flowers as a welcome, with a little note saying that her art had been "the greatest consolation" to them. The note cheered her, as she said to Gabriele:

"You see—you see, you see, it is possible, it really is possible to *open the doors*—and I . . . I swear to you that I did it, *ennobling* those stupid, clumsy plays I have played till now! . . ."

And she confessed that, in filling the pages of her letter, she had used the manuscript of *La città morta* as her writing-desk.

D'Annunzio was briefly in Rome, but by 9 August he was back in Francavilla (he had to make an important campaign speech on 14 August), and Duse wrote to him there:

"How much strength it takes to live against one's own strength!

"And that Paris! That too: what a waste of energy! What contrast between them and me in the *pitch of art* and of *life!*—Every day the holy madness had to win, to keep me from abandoning everything and going off without argument. I loathe 'la politesse' when it hides disgust. And the opposition to every idea and ideal. And yet, what attraction I found there, at the same time! Like a kind of intoxication necessary to the artist, a *something* I can't describe, when I appeared (freed from the entourage) alone and with myself, *against* the crowd. It was like a shudder, so sweet, so *troublant*, which I prolonged *with* and *for* art, as if I felt that it would never, never again be possible, now, for me to act before the epidermis of another audience . . .

"This is what one lives on, when one is inflamed by it.

"I speak obscurely, but you know how to decipher.

"And that fever reminds me of the other, the one that made me ask *when* I will see you again. . . ."

They would meet again in September: that was settled during this month of August. Boutet wrote her that the "tragedia" could not be given until 24 November, for box-office reasons. And on 19 August, she begged Gabriele: "Don't let these *yesses* and *nos* of the profession disgust you meanwhile, or deflect you from the *work of art.*"

On the last day of that month she wrote to him from Basel, as she traveled to Munich. There a friend met her and collected Enrichetta, who was going back to Dresden temporarily until a suitable sanatorium could be found. Though Duse found Davos "a prison," that was where the child was sent and treated, with success, for incipient tuberculosis.

Returning in September, Eleonora took possession of her new home, in Settignano, just above Florence. The rustic house had a garden and a view of the city; but work had to be done, so she spent a few days in a Florence hotel. Earlier, in a letter to Liliana De Bosis, Adolfo's wife, she had described the place:

"In Florence I've rented an old house, among olive trees, very simple, but not poor, quite secluded though not far out. You reach it by a little road, as if it were a convent, and the gate is hidden among the jasmines.—Swallows on the roof, and a vine on the wall of the house, and wistaria. A great farm, amid wheat and cypresses, climbs and descends the lovely hill.

"*All the hills* of Florence and Fiesole behind the house . . . roses everywhere, and a greenhouse of orange trees opposite the window of my room.

"Peace.—Peace could enter there. Now they are whitewashing it. The days spent amid dust and the burning lime—I ran off to the sea."

She renamed the house La Porziuncola, after the original convent of Francis of Assisi. Since the publication of Paul Sabatier's highly popular *Vie de saint François* in 1893, the *Poverello* of Assisi had become almost fashionable; pilgrimages to the Umbrian town were in vogue, especially among intellectuals. In her letters to Boito Eleonora had copied whole passages of the life, and Gabriele was also under the saint's spell. (In later life he actually wore a monk's habit about his villa, the Vittoriale, and adopted Franciscan speech, though not Franciscan behavior.)

On the walls of the house, all decorated in neo-Gothic style with suitable mottos, Eleonora hung reproductions or photographs of her favorite works of art, including some by Desiderio da Settignano. The study was filled with her books and with other literary souvenirs, a portrait of Keats, and one of Shakespeare. In a special case she kept the letters of Boito, the manuscript of his translation of *Antony and Cleopatra*, and a miniature portrait of Matilde Acton. Mary Costelloe (later to be Mrs Bernard Berenson), who was a neighbor, described the house in her diary, some time later, as being "a little too Museum-y and a little too barbaric below, but upstairs, where she lives, furnished just like a cultivated undergraduate's room. . . . Rather too many casts, however, and enlarged photos, but very sympathetic, on the whole, and remarkable for an Actress. She has a mania for calling everything 'Francescano.' . . . I don't think she half knows what she means. . . ."

Soon Eleonora and Gabriele were to make their own pilgrimage to Assisi. On 13 September 1897, D'Annunzio wrote in his notebook: "A little while ago Illuminata [one of his many fantastic names for Duse] said that in no other part of the world is nature so close to us as in this Franciscan countryside . . . The horizon gazes on us with the conscious goodness of a blue iris."

They separated. Gabriele went to Francavilla, Isa-Illuminata-Eleonora to Rome, where she wrote to him on 20 September: "I love you—I love you. These are the only words my spirit cries out. I suffer a nameless sorrow in saying it to you—I suffer an anguish that undoes me when, as I kiss you, I don't *dare* say it to you any more! . . . Even the *Dream*, even the certitude of your victory, were not enough for me yesterday, and I seemed to be lying to myself, lowering myself, eluding my heart, speaking to it of art, when it wants only love."

After two weeks they met again in Rome. At nearby Albano, Gabriele—with Duse hovering near—gave an interview to James Gordon Bennett, owner of the New York *Herald*. The article, which appeared in the Paris edition of 10 October 1897, filled five columns of the fifth page, with a prominent headline: "Talks with Gabriele D'Annunzio—Although Now "in Politics" He Will Continue His Work." And below, in upper case: "CANNOT SEPARATE ART AND LIFE." Reporting a conversation that had taken place "a few days ago," Bennett describes the setting: "we were standing on the slope of the ancient volcano, whose crater is the cup that holds Lake Albano. Down below at our feet stretched the lake, a strangely attractive opalescent picture."

Duse and Gégé Primoli were also present. "La Duse is dressed in gray and looks as pretty as a woman so intelligent should ever allow herself to look. . . . D'Annunzio . . . is wearing a costume of pure white *piqué*. . . .'

At the beginning of the interview D'Annunzio had seemed to behave strangely, striding across the ground as if he were measuring it off. Finally, he announced to the journalist that he was planning to build there a temple "to the tragic muse." And he went on: "Here, in fact, is the best refutation of any rumors about my deserting literature. . . . Even amid the ardor of the electoral struggle, after a tumultuous day, I could sit down to the joy of translating the great scene of Cassandra in the 'Agamemnon' of Aeschylus for our glorious *tragédienne*."

Bennett continues: "And D'Annunzio glanced at Signora Duse, who listened in silence gazing dreamily across the waters of the lake, only a faint smile from time to time evidencing that she heard the conversation or, rather, monologue."

D'Annunzio talked on, about the mistake of appointing a mere politician as Minister of Education, about the lack of funds for restoring art works, about naval power, his poems, the recent scandal of the Banca Romana, the influence of the former prime minister, Francesco Crispi. But chiefly he talked about the "temerarious enterprise," the Albano temple.

We are going to build in this solitary and solemn spot a Festival Theatre which will remain open during the two mildest months of the Roman spring. Only the works of those new artists who consider the drama to be a revelation of beauty communicated to the crowd, and the scenic arch to be a window opening upon an ideal transfiguration of life, will be played in it.

In building this isolated theatre we hope to co-operate in the renaissance of tragedy. We wish to restore to the representation of the drama its ancient ceremonial character. . . . 'Open the windows! Let the wind and the sun enter!' That is the cry of a man suffocating in a closed room. . . . The Drama, although now descended to the lowest depth of abjection, although now become an ignoble industry in the hands of traffickers devoid of all intelligence, bereft of all culture, although now condemned to the secret artifices of the adroit courtesan seeking to excite senile lust, the Drama, I say, is always the one living form given to the poet in which he can embody for the crowd, by which he can communicate to the multitude, the revelations of Beauty. . . .

We are going, then, to consecrate a temple to the Tragic Muse upon the shores of the lake, among these olive trees, these fig trees, among the plants whose distorted branches imitate the convulsions of the Menades. We would, thus, recall the rural and Dionysiac origin of the Drama. . . . What a distance will separate this Festival Theatre, built upon the serene hillside, from the cramped urban theatres, where, amid a suffocating heat impregnated with all the impurities, before a crowd of stupid imbecility, actors and actresses display their attainments. . . . When the first stone of the temple has been laid here we shall send forth a cry into all Latin countries: 'O Poets! Bring us your masterpieces!' ''

With these words still ringing in her ears, Duse left for Venice, where she still had her little refuge under the eaves of Palazzo Wolkoff. On 13 October, Gabriele arrived in the city and stayed at the Hotel Britannia. There, a few days later, he gave an interview to a young admirer, Mario Morasso, who published it on 18 October in the *Gazzetta di Venezia*. It appeared on the front page, though it was largely a repetition of what the poet had said the previous week to Bennett.

Both interviews, the one in English and the one in Italian, were widely commented on in other newspapers and aroused considerable interest and polemics. Committees were promptly formed—after the model of the Wagner Societies that supported Bayreuth, but less effective—and funds were offered. The names of the sponsors were impressive: the Principessa di Venosa, Contessa Pasolini, Donna Giacinta Martini, Comtesse de Vogüé, Comtesse de Béarn, Principessa Pia di Savoia. The architects, D'Annunzio said, would be "Latin," chosen by an international competition.

The opening was scheduled for 21 March, the first day of spring, two years hence. For the occasion the poet promised a new tragedy, *Persefone*. He never got around to writing it, but he did use the idea and the title for a work by his fictional alter ego Stelio Effrena, hero of *Il fuoco*, the novel he was then pondering.

He also announced that he had translated the *Agamemnon* of Aeschylus and the *Antigone* of Sophocles and was finishing *La città morta* (actually finished). The Albano festival repertory would also include the cycle of his four one-act *Dreams*, beginning with the *Sogno d'un mattino di primavera*, which Duse had just introduced in Paris, and continuing with the *Sogno d'un tramonto d'autunno*, which—as the poet now revealed—he had just completed.

Eleonora was already back at work. Earlier in the autumn she had appeared in Genoa, and at the beginning of November, after her brief holiday with Gabriele, she appeared in Venice at the Teatro Rossini in *La Dame aux camélias*, and in *La Femme de Claude* on a double bill with the *Sogno d'un mattino di primavera*. This was the little play's Italian premiere, and it was not a success.

Duse herself was received with some reservations. Several critics felt that the Paris experience had changed her; she seemed "less human, less true, more affected." Even some details of her performance had been modified. In the fourth act of *La Dame aux camélias*, in the scene where Armand throws his winnings at Marguerite, Duse had become famous for her repetition, three times, of "Armando" (her own inter-polation into Dumas's text). The three Armandos were still there, but instead of murmuring them from a seated position, she paced after the actor. At the Renaissance, this new effect had deeply moved the audi-ence; at the Rossini it was a puzzlement. And yet the Venice critics should have known by now that Duse never fixed business rigidly, and no two performances of the same play were ever exactly alike.

During these Venice days, Gabriele brought her the text of the second *Sogno*, set in an autumn sunset. In some respects the brief piece is a sketch for *Il fuoco*, with its rhapsodic evocation of a past Venice and its pitiless study of an aging woman's passion for a younger man.

Eleonora was thirty-nine. Gabriele was less than five years her junior. Not a great difference, but it clearly disturbed Duse. At times, she exaggerated it, assuming a maternal role, calling Gabriele *figlio*, "son." He, too, exaggerated it, less sweetly. And soon, in *Il fuoco*, the fictionalization of their lives, he was to be cruelly explicit. The leading character in the second *Dream*, the impassioned, near-crazed Dogaressa, a noble widow reduced almost to madness by the lover who has abandoned her, was temperamentally removed from Eleonora's dramatic range; and in fact, she never played the role. (It was not performed until 1905, after she and D'Annunzio had parted.)

The next stop was Milan, where Eleonora had not played for some years. She was warmly welcomed, though the *Sogno* was no more successful here than in Venice. Then Rome, then Naples, city of many memories. At the Teatro Mercadante, she gave *Magda* and *La seconda moglie* (Pinero's *The Second Mrs Tanqueray* in Italian dress); and the papers were full of warm, welcoming articles, including some by her old friend Matilde Serao.

After a few appearances in Monte Carlo, she was back in Rome, where a great test faced her: the Roman premiere of the *Sogno*, scheduled for 11 January 1898. Preparing prospective audiences for it, she gave an interview, shortly before the opening, to a critic of the *Tribuna*, who signed himself Rastignac, repeating to him for publication what she had long been saying privately: "I need to try something new. What I have done till now, what I continue to do, no longer satisfies me. I feel something dying within me and something coming to birth; I feel all the false, fleeting—indeed, already fled—aspect of the productions in which I act; and I feel, at the same time, the still vague desire, the still undefined aspiration for a form of art that corresponds more directly and deeply to the present state of my spirit."

She referred to a new movement in the theatre—perhaps alluding to activity in France, to Maeterlinck—and insisted that a new movement could begin in Italy. "I will appeal to all the determination and all the intelligence of my colleagues, to help me in this magnificent enterprise."

In fact, she was still trying to assemble an Italian cast for *La città morta* (it would take her years) and, no doubt, she was also thinking of *La Gioconda*, another new full-length tragedy that D'Annunzio was planning to write for her.

Neither the Roman public nor the Roman critics received the *Sogno* favorably, but since Queen Margherita was present at the Teatro Valle on opening night, the audience restrained its hostility to snickers and shuffling of feet. After D'Annunzio came *La locandiera*, and when the curtain went up there were polemical cries of "Viva Duse" and "Viva Goldoni."

A few days later, at the Renaissance, Sarah Bernhardt gave the world premiere, in French of course, of *La città morta*, *La ville morte*. Once she had wrested the rights from her younger Italian rival, the actress seems to have lost interest in the play, and the production was perfunctory, even though D'Annunzio had journeyed to Paris to be present for the occasion.

In Rome, Duse and a group of friends stayed up late at the Palazzo Primoli, waiting with Gégé for news, which was to be telegraphed promptly. The party included a bright, malicious young journalist, Ugo Ojetti (later to become a leading Italian cultural figure under Fascism). After the fiasco of the *Sogno*, Ojetti had written a defense of the play—or rather a justified attack on the hostile Roman public—in a leading magazine. Matilde Serao was also present; her husband, Scarfoglio, was in Paris with his poet friend.

"La Duse was dressed in gray," Ojetti wrote afterwards;

she stretched out on a sofa, with a hot water bottle on her stomach, her hair already slightly disheveled by her constant drawing her hand over her brow, baring her ears. Count Primoli had received a telegram from Paris announcing the good reception of the first act.

At the beginning la Duse spoke of the drama calmly, scene by scene, at times quoting the words of the text as if she already knew them by heart, and telling anecdotes about Sarah. We were all prepared to speak ill of Sarah Bernhardt, even Primoli; but Signora Eleonora drove chivalry to the point of defending her. Looking at the ceiling, she declared: "She is the mistress of the public because first and foremost she is mistress of herself. A hundred performances: always the same in every gesture, precise as clockwork. In *La Dame aux camélias* I saw her three times. When she asks Armand to go back to his father, she sits down at a table on which there is a coffer and she nervously starts twisting the little key. In all three performances, she turned it the same number of times: five. I counted."

And she sighed, as if to say that she, alas, had not been born for such mechanics. Then the other telegrams arrived. The success seemed great. La Duse was seated. She raised her eyebrows halfway up her forehead. The nostrils of her little snub nose fluttered like wings. Her lips were white, but her broad slavic cheekbones, which were the feral part of her anxious face, flushed as if with fever. Primoli, who knew her well, tried to distract her. Louis Ganderax had written to him that Sarah's actors called 'The Dead City' the 'Deadly City.' And la Duse laughed cruelly, that throaty laugh of hers that sounded like a brief whinny, and she repeated the foolish remark as she moved about the salon, touching a flower, a dish of bonbons, a photograph, without seeing them. Suddenly she stopped, looked us in the face, overcame her jealous suffering over her rival, sat down again, smoothed her hair, adjusted her skirt, and began a eulogy of D'Annunzio as poet so noble, confident, and heartfelt that, had he heard it from those pallid lips at that hour, the applause of Paris would have seemed vanity to him. It was only when she fell silent that I realized that, as she had spoken, she had taken, one by one, all the flowers from a nearby vase and ripped off the petals with her nails.

It was dawn when she and the others left Primoli's house by the Tiber. Scarfoglio's telegrams had not given an accurate account of the play's reception. At best, it was a *succès d'estime*, and some of the critics were brutal. Sarah gave the play fourteen times that season, then dropped it from her repertory.

D'Annunzio did not stay in Paris long. In early February he was briefly back in Rome, then in Santa Margherita, where Eleonora was recuperating from a bout of illness. From there, she had written him:

"I lose the *harmony* of my soul—and of the world (there is a harmony—it exists!) when I go away from you.

"—What to do?

"—Perhaps I would not love you—or would love you wrongly (—or perfectly?) if this were not so?"

After he left, she wrote to him again, on 11 February 1898, sending him a copy of his hotel bill for one night. Itemized, it included: "candles—2 lire," "broken pot—16," "coffee, two eggs, served in the room."

Two days later, she wrote more seriously about theatre plans, recalling the Roman fiasco of the *Sogno*, and on other nights "the boredom, the boredom more murderous than repulsion,—no, no, I can't do it any more." She wrote, too, about them:

"Here, after the heart-pang of your departure (the room, next door, empty), the spell of the sea has opened my eyes again—. . . .

"Since yesterday, this *sea*, so calm for you, has been murky, gasping—and I remain, like this, alone and with you—looking at it and listening to it, feeling it. Where, where would I go, dear soul, without the great promise? . . .

"You must not believe I lack strength.

"On the contrary, IT IS *this* strength that becomes 'art' in me. . . .

"I cannot tell you! Only you know how to say beautiful things; I know only how to listen to you! This *anguish*, and joy, and *harmony* of *listening* to you, nothing but you . . . oh!—it must not be taken from me! . . ."

He had gone to Rome, but soon he rejoined her and they went on to Nice and Cannes. At the end of February they were back at Settignano, where Gabriele's friends De Bosis and Benigno Palmerio had found him what promised to be a suitable refuge, the Villa Capponcina, just across a narrow country lane from Eleonora's Porziuncola. "Peace and hope," Duse wired De Bosis.

The villa's owner, the Marchese Giacinto Viviani della Robbia, offered it furnished to the poet for 1,000 lire per annum. Though he was already immersed in debts, D'Annunzio grandly raised the rent to 1,200 lire, provided the Marchese removed all the furniture.

Then, presumably with money given him by Duse, Gabriele bought horses, dogs, and the superfluities that, as he wrote to his publisher Treves, were his necessities. At Santa Margherita he had composed two sonnets dedicated to Eleonora, and he composed a third in Florence on 22 February. According to the D'Annunzio expert, Emilio Mariano, these marked the final sealing of their pact.

From 6 to 8 March Duse was in Paris, where she had been invited to participate in a homage to the actress Suzanne Reichenberg of the Comédie Française, who was retiring from the stage. Duse, as her contribution, performed beautifully the last act of *Adrienne Lecouvreur*, an old piece that had long been in her repertory (and in the repertory of the Comédie and of Sarah). The next day she left for a tour along the Southern coast: Nice, Cannes, Marseilles, then on to Lisbon and Oporto.

She was raising money for Gabriele, who had initiated an elaborate renovation of La Capponcina, and she worried about his financial situation. From Nice she wired De Bosis: "Dear Adolfo, if my work is not enough to build our Città in our way, that work belongs to you for our house. I resume tomorrow. I have lost almost a week. Unable to tolerate anything or anyone I beg Adolfo to come to Nice for one day and I will hand over what is needed without the mediation of posts and maids. . . ."

The days in Paris had been "feverish," she wrote Gabriele, and she had realized she could never live there any more. She wired him constantly, repeating how she longed to see him and how she was concerned about the suitable arrangement of the house so that he could finally begin to work in ideal surroundings.

Much of this time he was in Rome. He had been sworn in as a Deputy on 11 December 1897, but had taken small part in the debates of the Chamber. His contempt for the whole parliamentary process was evident in the novel *Le vergini delle rocce*, which De Bosis had published in

Il Convito and Treves had brought out as a separate volume. In Rome, D'Annunzio pursued, as always, a few Roman ladies; and naturally some of Duse's friends wrote to her about these escapades. Occasionally her jealousy flickers in her letters, now unabashed love letters, which she wrote almost daily and which he answered with equal regularity. From Marseilles, a city she hated, she wrote on 31 March:

"How do you want me to love you?

"Do you want me to love you without suffering? Without cruelty, without sorrow?—without weeping?—

"(but what about joy, then?)

"What a *beautiful* love I would like to give you, loving you!

"alas! I *look at* the hours I live!—There is then something *cruel* in every love—even in mine! . . ."

The flow of letters and telegrams did not cease. Again on 31 March she wrote in answer to a telegram in which the "holy" word (presumably *amo*) was thrice repeated:

"It is the word that when you have me beneath your hand . . . mouth to mouth, neither you nor I dare say!—

"So it is! Near, a sweetness bans the word . . . and far, the erosion of art, which exasperates—the *tone* of the inner life, so much *higher* than the life surrounding it . . . and then we yell, along a telegraph wire—words (you to me, I to you) that, close, mouth to mouth, we dare not touch, *saying* them. We know so well their value, danger, purity, secrecy, expectation. . . ."

Her tour was beset by worries, troubles with the unreliable Schurmann ("the worst kind of liar," as she described him, "because his lies always have a basis of truth"), and concern for Enrichetta in Davos. Her mother wanted to get the child out of that "prison" for part of the summer; and from Marseilles, on 2 April, she wrote to a friend, the psychologist and writer Marchesa Laura Groppallo, who lived in Nervi, the seaside resort near Genoa: "For what I am about to ask I may have found something in *Cannes* . . . but certain circumstances . . . advise me to postpone *Cannes* till later. My dear, *soyons pratiques*. I am asking you for: a *Hotel, a pension, a kind of boarding-house for young ladies*—and for *two months*—voilà tout—If this place exists in Nervi, here is what I would do—On May first I would have Enrichetta *descend* from Davos . . .—she would arrive *alone and serene* (I like to give Enrichetta *tests of character*, and Enrichetta, yes . . . of course, would arrive *alone and serene*, perfectly responsible for herself, out of her love of earning my respect) in Nervi—I would send her, for one day, one of my trustworthy maids (Elisa) to introduce her to you, simply. After 10 May, I would be between *15 and 20 May* in Milan to perform. I would then come to Nervi for three days, towards that date, between *the 15th and the 25th*. . . ."

Provincial Lisbon, where she now had to play, was hardly preferable to dreary Marseilles, and Eleonora was looking forward to her freedom later in the summer, which she planned to spend in Settignano. Gabriele was already installed there. In the past she had divided her periods of rest between Enrichetta and Boito (the child usually receiving the larger share) or, in earlier days, she had kept the little girl with her while enjoying the hidden mountain retreats that the prudent Boito found for them.

But now Enrichetta was seventeen, growing into a beauty, with a mind of her own. The previous summer, when they were together in Mürren, Eleonora had sometimes perceived, in moments of passing irritation, the awful shadow of Tebaldo in her daughter. As she wrote to the Marchesa, "Once in *Italy*, having freed Enrichetta of the homesickness for Davos, and me of the useless suffering, having given the sun to somebody who asks for it, then I would breathe!!! I must give Enrichetta the *illusion* (which is such a great part of certain realities!) of being *cured*, to help her be cured; and *taking her away from Davos*, . . . the mere fact of *leaving* that place inhabited by the sick will make her hopeful of living!— . . ."

Prophetically (since Enrichetta was to become English), Duse wrote that she wanted the girl to live "en *Miss* anglaise, *tranquille et pratique*."

The Italy Duse was longing for was not a happy country that spring. At the beginning of May, the ineptitude and corruption of the government, the stubborn insensitivity of the monarchy, the disastrous economic situation, had brought the nation to the point of explosion. There were strikes and demonstrations in all the large cities. Milan was the most violent, and the forces of General Bava-Beccaris fired on the unarmed demonstrators, with many casualties. The King sent him a telegram of congratulations, and for the conservatives the general was a hero. Boito wrote to a friend: "Don't believe this was a riot for bread (Milan is a rich and hard-working city); they eat their fill. The aim of this fuss was rather jam. But, thank God, the leaders (almost all Deputies) were defeated from the first, and now are meditating on the difficulties of a social revolution in the dungeons of the Sforza castle. We are still in a state of siege, which is not without its charm, first of all it offers the illusion of a return to the Middle Ages. One comes home before midnight, one encounters patrols, the bicycle has vanished, the automobile as well. For myself, I am overjoyed and feel four centuries younger."

D'Annunzio was hardly more sensitive to the profound meaning of the unrest. Though he now sat on the far left in Parliament (having taken his seat there with the declaration that he was moving "towards life"), he still looked at politics from his own, eccentric position. He sent his friend James Gordon Bennett an article for the New York *Herald* entitled "La primavera di sangue," in which he complained mostly that a stone, hurled in a riot in Florence, had struck the *Perseus* of Cellini in the Loggia dei Lanzi.

In June he was installed in La Capponcina, and Duse was at La Porziuncola. She wrote to her friend Laura Groppallo: "Florence and the hills and all the surrounding countryside are in flower. I would like to stay in this peace and this warm land, but I have to leave!" From Settignano, during the early summer, she made brief dashes to Italian cities—Genoa, Bologna—for a few, money-making performances. In June, in Bologna, the historic Teatro Brunetti was renamed Teatro Duse, and Eleonora gave a double bill of the D'Annunzio *Sogno* and *La locandiera* on the festive occasion.

On 17 June (five days after the Bologna ceremony) she wrote to Donna Laura in Nervi. She was concerned about Enrichetta; obviously the situation with D'Annunzio was affecting the child.

"Life is no longer possible for me, except at the price of the most absolute truth. And I alone *know* to what I refer, to what truth. My dear, I have never lied to others, but to endure life, *to defeat it*, how many times have I been able to lie to myself! Now the double power of this *divine lie* has vanished in me, like a dream.—Life and I are *two things, one separate from the other*.

"This is why the hour in which I write you is, perhaps, a very grave hour!—the sense of feeling, *alone*, judge of my soul, myself, *alone*, facing everything, because the possession of my *soul* is, today, more lucid and more profound than ever! . . ."

And, in a practical P.S., she added: "Tomorrow I will send a *chèque* to Henriette for 1,500 lire. I believe that almost 500 lire will go for the Pensione Sanitas. She should keep the rest for her journey. She must learn to count, because everything is uncertain . . . in my life and in hers. Tell me if Henriè is a burden to you."

Though Enrichetta's Pensione was certainly expensive, D'Annunzio was, of course, the one who should have learned to count. He never did. But Enrichetta, as Eleonora wrote Donna Laura, represented reality; the poet was the dream. Part of the reality connected with

Enrichetta was her father, who chose this summer of passions to write to Eleonora and suggest—after a decade or so—a reconciliation. He seems also to have asked her for money. Unwilling to answer him herself, Eleonora shifted the task to Enrichetta, explaining (in a letter to Donna Laura):

"This morning I wrote a long letter to Enrichetta. I have charged her with an important mission between her father and me. The daughter of the two whom the law keeps bound can speak to the one in the name of the other, without wounding.

"For me to write directly to her father (to answer a letter received from him) is something I really do *not* want to do any more. I did it when my strength was greater, and ready for the help that was asked of me—today, I can do it no longer.—

"I hope that Enrichetta will answer with calm, with kindness, with impartiality. When you see her don't mention her father's letter . . . if it is possible for you—steer the conversation to questions of *finance*. . . ."

Duse feared that Enrichetta was taking money—and her mother's earning capacity—for granted. In any case, the girl soon returned to Zurich and resumed her studies. But in late October a friend of Eleonora's, passing through the Swiss city, saw Enrichetta and found her run down, coughing, studying too hard. Her mother brought her at once to the mild climate of San Remo. From the West End Hotel, on 20 October, she wrote to Liliana and Adolfo De Bosis: "I am here by the sea, seeking help for this poor daughter of mine . . . who is so uncomfortable in this world! . . . I arrived here, breathless with suffering. The sea *howled* the night I arrived—and the greatest threat I felt *inside* me."

But the sea calmed down, and so did Eleonora. In the same letter she spoke of D'Annunzio. "I left our beloved friend in Florence, and at this moment I could predict nothing about him . . . I remember last spring, when I arrived from Paris! He was in an agony of work: you remember?—Now,—*now*, he *wants his book* 'Il Fuoco', but he wants to *enjoy himself* also, his life and his being. . . . Perhaps he also suffers. . . ."

A few days later she was in Rome with her daughter. The famous doctor Pietro Grocco had advised a warm climate, so she was planning to sail from Naples for Cairo, taking Enrichetta with her as well as an English *Miss* to act as chaperone. Next spring, if Enrichetta was still not well, she would return to San Remo where the Englishwoman was co-owner of a villa; if the trip cured her, she could go back to Zurich and her studies. After endless negotiations, the contract with Ermete Zacconi was apparently ready, and so Duse would join him on her return from Egypt and tour in a mainly D'Annunzian repertory.

While she was in Rome, she learned that Boito was also in the city on one of his official errands. He was involved in meetings at the Ministry of Education in Piazza della Minerva. From the Hotel Hassler, she sent him a note by hand. Three lines:

"Please tell me if I am allowed to speak for a moment.

"I must leave tomorrow for Naples and Cairo.

"Please send a word in reply."

And a formal "Eleonora" below.

The reply must have been affirmative, for they met that same afternoon. This was the definitive break. Whatever was said, they both knew everything was finally over. On a slip of paper, which he preserved with her letters until his death, Boito wrote: "Last time/Thursday 24 November 98—/at six in the afternoon have seen/for the last time, in her room/at the Hotel Hassler, Lenor." Then, another paragraph: "In the night between 24 and 25/seen again in a nightmare/where the dominant impression/was of a fatal departure."

Duse also wrote a few lines, which she sent to him; and he kept them in the same envelope. She wrote: "It is like death—exactly like—"

And he wrote an answer, but may not have sent it, since it, too, was found among his letters, many years later:

"It is more than death, because it was more than life!

"It is more than death, Lenor, because one suffers more than in dying.—

"The dead have peace, do not remember, do not feel the annihilation—

"Lenor answers no more, will never again answer the familiar voice, the familiar words, ready still on the lips.

"Above every thing and *always*. This is more than death."

Like their love, their rupture was lofty, literary, verbal. They spoke of death, but the love they talked about had already been buried. Duse continued to write to him on occasion, and—though no more letters from him survive—he evidently replied. But it was years before they met again, and by then he had been enshrined, the "Saint," in her private pantheon. He had found another (equally difficult, but less brilliant) companion in Velleda Ferretti, whom he also kept discreetly at arm's length.

D'Annunzio had been left behind in Settignano, to write. There he quickly finished the new drama, *La Gioconda*, on which he had been working at intervals for some time; and he drafted the outline of another, *La gloria*, inspired by his aloof observation of Italian politics. Before Duse sailed from Naples, she asked him to join her later in Egypt. He wired his assent, borrowed some money from the patient Treves, and on 24 December he also sailed from Naples for Alexandria. The December Mediterranean was rough, and despite his many ecstatic verses about the sea, D'Annunzio was a poor sailor. The trip exhausted him.

Before he arrived, Eleonora wrote a letter to Boito in a nostalgic tone. "I can speak thanks to the sweetness of the air around me, the magic of the light . . . and the memory of a happiness . . . painful even 'then' perhaps, but yet so full of hope! . . .

"I am trying my fate again—here, too. Having conquered it too many times, having worked so many years, has changed the destiny of these recent times—(it was predictable)—and everything I had gathered, was scattered—So I must remain bent beneath the yoke.— But, youth has passed—health, passed!—and hope. . . ."

D'Annunzio's stay with her in Egypt—which lasted until the end of January—was fairly serene. During the day the poet rode out into the desert or visited ancient monuments. Sometimes she went with him; they snapped each other with his camera. In Cairo, Eleonora played at the Khedival Theatre, inaugurated some thirty years before to mark the opening of the Suez Canal, the theatre where Verdi's *Aida* had had its world premiere in 1871. As in the days of *Aida*, the theatre audience was almost totally foreign.

One night Eleonora was standing in the wings, waiting for her cue. Next to her was Augusto Jandolo, the youngest member of the company, hired for walk-on parts. (He later became a well-known antique-dealer in Rome.) Suddenly—as he recalled in his *Memoirs*—she confided in him: "I had such a fright today, you couldn't believe! What a fright! A friend and I went to visit the Khedive's garden! I got lost in the maze I insisted on visiting. I've never suffered so much. I found myself, all of a sudden, alone, in a passage with thick, green walls. So cramped! What torture! Desperately, after trying again and again to get out, I started shouting! I had the terrible sensation that I would never find the right path. Deathly silence . . . only the swallows overhead seemed to laugh at my anguish. Look at the scratches on my hands: I thrust them uselessly into the yew! And I cried out in a loud, distressed voice: 'Enough! Enough! I can't bear any more, D'Annunzio!' "

Though the company was well aware of her attachment to the poet, and of his presence in the city, this was the first time his name had been mentioned to any of them. It had escaped her involuntarily. There was a moment's awkwardness, then "fortunately we both appeared in the last scene. She took me by the hand and led me on stage."

The sadistic scene in the labyrinth of hedges—shifted geographically from Cairo to the Villa Pisani at Strà—recurs at a crucial point in *Il fuoco*, another instance of the autobiographical inspiration of the novel. If Duse was working during their Egyptian sojourn, so was the poet, whose notebooks were filling up with jottings for later exploitation in his work.

Enrichetta and her English companion were sent back to Europe at some point, while Duse and her troupe—with D'Annunzio, more or less discreetly, in their train—went on to Athens.

Duse and D'Annunzio were both enthusiastically received there. At a special gathering of the Parnassòs Society, a cultural association, Duse recited some scenes from the *Sogno d'un mattino di primavera* and D'Annunzio read an Oration to the Athenians, in Italian. Between performances and social events, they religiously visited museums and monuments, as the young Jandolo—who kept running into them—recorded in his Memoirs.

In Athens the tour ended and the company was dismissed. Duse was free to go with Gabriele for a brief rest on Corfu, where they found a villa. Under Eleonora's devoted but watchful eye, D'Annunzio worked hard on *La gloria*—which Duse was planning to stage soon—and on *Il fuoco*. On 26 March 1899, in a letter to Treves, D'Annunzio announced the completion of the drama: "I have masterworked . . . This Drama is bound to arouse much debate. An old conservative like you will be overcome with horror . . ."

Duse, on Corfu, was not in good health. The tour had taken its toll, and she was coughing. "I am going straight to *Rome*," she wrote to Donna Laura Groppallo; ". . . I'm going to join Zacconi—and I hope, in person, to smooth out some difficulties, perhaps misunderstandings, which have arisen between him and me—and which keep me uncertain and uneasy about much of our project. I will write you, dear Laura, from Rome as soon as I have a specific plan to be communicated. Now the only thing decided is that we will go to Sicily. A mere two months of *union* between me and Zacconi is a ridiculous amount of time if we want to do something that has *form*, and I have decided to start in Sicily so as to have a *few days* (at least) for us to 'get into step with each other.' . . ."

A few days before, on 5 March, obviously with Eleonora looking over his shoulder, D'Annunzio had written directly to Zacconi:

"Dear Zacconi, since our pleasant evenings in Florence I haven't had another opportunity to meet you, but I have communicated with you in spirit; because during this period of separation, I have been pondering the moulding of a new 'character' in accord with the prodigious expressive powers in you, in your art. . . .

"I am sending you a copy of La Gioconda. This tragedy will be performed—Signora Duse tells me—next April. In drawing the character of Lucio Settala, so mercurial, ardent, bold, I was thinking of Ermete Zacconi as the ideal interpreter. Now I am counting on you not only for the 'creation' of that character, but also for the staging of the whole drama, not an easy preparation, for it requires a lively sense of harmony and sobriety of style. . . ."

In 1899, Ermete Zacconi, only a year Duse's senior, was almost as celebrated as she, at least in Italy. Like her, he had been born into a family of poor, errant actors, and had come up the hard way. He too was largely self-educated, but he did not really share her intellectual interests or her passion for the new and adventurous. D'Annunzio's talk of harmony and sobriety—surely inspired by Eleonora—was really meant as a warning, for Zacconi was the archetypical verismo actor. If Duse's acting was poetry, Zacconi's was vigorous prose.

For him the offer to join forces with Duse and D'Annunzio was flattering. Zacconi was in a kind of trough in his career; his first foreign tour, to Austria and Hungary in 1898, had been only moderately successful.

In La Gioconda he would have a meaty, if not sympathetic role (the brilliant, sensual, egocentric sculptor); in La gloria—which D'Annunzio went on to discuss in the letter—Zacconi would be the real protagonist. "This tragedy is different from my previous ones; it is vaster, more full of movement, murkier. It could be called a 'national' tragedy, because it depicts a tragic hour in the life of a people and the violent actions and reactions between the soul of the people and the will of a hero."

D'Annunzio hinted that, in the central figure of the dictator, Zacconi might "recognize the traits of some well-known personage." He meant the politician Francesco Crispi. Zacconi would play this character—who appears only in the second act—and also the young rebel Ruggero Flamma, who appears in the other acts. Duse would have a long, larger-than-life role, as the fatal older woman, la Comnèna, an unusually disagreeable part for her.

Zacconi would manage the company and divide the profits equally with Duse. "It was a contract . . . ," he wrote later, "that honored me, and I accepted it." In addition to the two D'Annúnzio plays, the repertory would also include some money-making Dumas pieces, *La Femme de Claude* and *Le Demi-monde*, both chosen by Duse.

Zacconi went first to Sicily. From Naples, on her way to join him, Duse sent a wire to Liliana and Adolfo De Bosis: "Palm Sunday. Melancholy, here alone." The same day, she wrote them a letter, telling how she had gone out for a moment to look for an olive twig (Italian churches distribute such twigs on Palm Sunday rather than the bits of palm frond customary in other countries). "All of my vagabond life stirred in my heart as I touched that little olive twig. Peace exists."

But at that point it seemed beyond her grasp. Despite the persistent cough, she was to set off for Messina the next day. She had forebodings about the two-month tour ahead of her. "If I am unable to *finish* these two months, where will we be?"

She was worried about Enrichetta, but Gabriele was an even more immediate concern. She had heard he was in danger of being evicted from La Capponcina for debts, and she begged Adolfo to find out the truth (not always an easy enterprise with the poet) and tell her. "Between Adolfo and me, we will find a solution, one that is also *decorous* for all, right for *each* of the three."

In Messina she found the menagerie—as she contemptuously called it in another letter to Adolfo and Liliana De Bosis—and an indescribable confusion. The theatre where they were to open two days later was not free. And they started rehearsing *Le Demi-monde*, which was Zacconi's property for Italy. The script was mislaid; Duse had to accept his cuts and changes. "The rehearsals we have held these past two days were the most colorless, petty, ignorant, listless, blurred, with no impetus, no tomorrow, present or future. . . ."

The prompter had to yell from his box. Actors and stagehands chattered on stage, and the rehearsal dragged on until eleven in the evening. The cast knew their lines, since they had done the piece often, but "there was no *fusion*, no *thread* to guide the 'puppets' from the first word to the last. The play, as a result, is reduced to some '*duets*' between Zacconi and me."

It had been years since she had acted with a company other than her own, and—as she went on to tell her friends in the same letter—she had forgotten the Italian penchant for improvising, or muddling through.

This had to happen just when she was aiming at something out of the ordinary, something that would lift the theatre out of its routine and serve as a guide, a banner for others.

Her hope was to make enough money with the Dumas pieces to pay the troupe for the whole Sicilian period; then, in a closed theatre, giving no performances, to rehearse *La Gioconda* again and again until it was ready, vibrant.

D'Annunzio had joined her in Sicily, but his presence brought little joy, because some of his lies—apparently about economic matters—came to light, and were a source of distress. Then on 2 April the company opened in Messina.

"We haven't yet begun playing, and the porters are already in my room to collect the trunks for Catania. Madness."

And she concluded bitterly: "Here, as always, I am the 'femme à barbe' [the bearded lady or sideshow freak], squeezing my soul out over the framework of a rotten, vulgar piece."

Finally, on the night of 15 April, at the Teatro Bellini in Palermo, *La Gioconda* opened. Though D'Annunzio attached great importance to the sets and had insisted Zacconi engage painters rather than a regular stage-designer, in the end one of the scenes—the garden room of the last act—was impossible to construct from the drawings, and a further delay was threatened.

That evening Zacconi received a letter from Duse, carried by hand to his hotel: "Dear Signor Zacconi, I expect from you the resolution necessary to get us out of the present awkwardness; I am certain, confident that you will decide for the best."

In the all-purpose collection of sets that Zacconi—like all actor-managers of the time—carried around with him, there was a "jardin d'hiver" of sorts. "Not ideal," Zacconi recalled later, "but it could do, and the next morning I informed Duse that we could rehearse with all the sets."

The opening night was a disaster. The shabby Bellini, with its greasy seats and threadbare curtain, was packed, even though the prices were astronomical. Zacconi's memoirs suggest that *La Gioconda* was a success, despite some scattered hostility from the audience; but other accounts indicate quite a different story. Despite their respect for Duse, the public had a hard time accepting D'Annunzio's grim tale of a sculptor torn between his mistress, who inspires him, and his loyal wife (Duse), who loves him blindly and actually sacrifices her hands to save his statue, his masterpiece. There was something particularly sadistic in making Duse play the last act with her famous hands concealed in voluminous sleeves. This was strong, even repellent fare for audiences used to seeing their beloved actress as the noble heroines of Dumas *fils* or the sophisticated "Ideal Wife" of Marco Praga.

In Naples, less than two weeks later, they presented *La gloria*. This curiously prescient drama of a modern dictator, couched in luxuriant prose, with its sinister Byzantine heroine, outraged the Neapolitan public (and, admittedly, the drama is perhaps the least successful, surely the least winning, of D'Annunzio's stage works). According to Scarfoglio, while Duse was on stage fighting to save the play from the vocal fury of the public, D'Annunzio—in the wings—enjoyed a quick fornication with a young actress of the troupe. Duse's valiant efforts failed: *La gloria* was a total fiasco and was revived only very rarely thereafter (never again by Duse).

The red boxes of correspondence carefully preserved at the Vittoriale, the villa-museum where D'Annunzio spent the last decades of his life, contain no letters from Duse for the first months of 1899, largely because she and the poet were seldom apart then. He followed the exhausting tour from Sicily northwards, even though his presence—always trim, dapper, self-assured—was sometimes more of a provocation than an inducement to listen objectively to his work.

His presence only exacerbated Eleonora's jealousy, which did not abate even as the reception of *La Gioconda* gradually became warmer. On 6 May, at the Teatro Valle in Rome, the piece was fairly well received; in Bologna it went still better, and the next morning—19 May—Eleonora was able to wire Adolfo: ". . . Last night was a very rewarding performance because everything was in accord. Complete fusion between work and public result sincere and noble without painful and odious things as elsewhere. . . ." The success was repeated in Venice, at the Teatro Rossini; but Duse's jealous mood persisted.

The next morning, 24 May, D'Annunzio wrote a letter to Angelo Conti:

"Here in Venice, too, *La Gioconda* last night had alert listeners who allowed themselves to be swept on to unusual enthusiasm.

"For me, for our friend, no joy. After the performance I spent some of the saddest, most tragic hours of my life. She is in the grip of a kind of evil demon that gives her no peace. The most profound tenderness, the purest devotion, are of no avail! She sees, on all sides, falsehood and intrigue around her.

"The sweet creature becomes unjust and cruel towards herself and towards me, irreparably.

"What shall I do?

"This morning I waken dazed and dull, as if after an immense misfortune. . . ."

In Venice there were also peaceful moments: with their friend Fortuny, they visited the third Biennale and saw a portrait of Eleonora by Franz von Lenbach, as well as the immense works of Primoli's friend, the Roman painter Giulio Aristide Sartorio, including a triptych, *The Wise and Foolish Virgins*, one of whom (presumably a foolish virgin) was a portrait of D'Annunzio's wife Maria di Gallese. Fortuny also had a picture in the exhibit, as did D'Annunzio's friends Michetti and De Maria.

In a note to De Maria, D'Annunzio asked him to suggest "some quiet little house near a beautiful garden" in Venice. Already the solitude of La Capponcina, with Eleonora vigilant nearby, was becoming less attractive.

In Venice Eleonora also spent some time with a friend and admirer, Emma Calvé. The great soprano was seeking consolation after a sentimental misadventure, and Duse listened with understanding, then wrote her:

"Your tears, as you were telling me your misfortunes, have remained in my heart. . . . One who possesses, to express herself, a voice unique in the world, composed of all the colors of the rainbow, pure as mountain springs, no longer has a right to cry. What pride, to believe that a soul and a heart could belong to us for a lifetime! This means shackling the freedom of a human being.

"Become his dearest, best friend: this is the only revenge suited to women of heart. . . ."

And she urged her friend to concentrate on her work. Duse might have been writing to herself; a few years later, when her heart was broken for the last time, work was the temporary solution she adopted.

After Venice, in Milan and, finally, in Turin, the tour went well. And so did the professional association with Zacconi, for at the end she wrote him a note of thanks. "In the pettiness of the theatre world, among some mistakes and the many injustices of these days, there remains *only* in my heart the memory of you, dear companion, who were *perfect* and *most noble* towards the artistic ventures we agreed to undertake. *This* is all that matters, and for this I thank you affectionately."

The tour was also a success financially, so D'Annunzio was able to send some money ahead of him to La Capponcina.

There they returned, Eleonora and Gabriele, weary, battered by the tour and their reciprocal torment, in early June. The writer had planned to get back to *Il fuoco*, the novel that had been on the stocks since July 1896, but he hesitated. To Hérelle he wrote that the novel "would cause great sorrow;" and instead of working on it, in a sudden access of inspiration, he wrote some of his finest poems, including "La sera fiesolana" and "Il silenzio di Ravenna," later included in the *Laudi*.

The poetic vein continued when, in July, they went briefly to Bocca d'Arno on the Tuscan coast, renting an old customs house cheaply. There D'Annunzio wrote one of his most beautiful and celebrated poems, "La Tenzone" (The Combat), and the equally popular "Bocca d'Arno": "Woman's mouth (except yours, yours here) was never so sweet in the loving path as the pale and silent mouth of the little river . . ."

By the end of the month they were back in Settignano, and, having written a great part of the *Laudi*, D'Annunzio determined to devote himself at last to *Il fuoco*.

Duse then set off to begin a European tour. This time she had taken over a company organized by Luigi Rasi, which included two of "her" actors, Carlo Rosaspina and Ciro Galvani. The first rehearsals were in Vichy (she spelled it Vichi), and were toilsome, as she promptly informed Gabriele.

"And now, to pick up my whip again!", she wrote on 22 August. "I have to pick up the whip, Gabri, for my *entourage*; they take such advantage, *all* of them, of the fact that I haven't done so before.

"Here, again, everything has to be put into shape, with the mediocre *Rasi*, who has started off on such a foundation of . . . *insincerity* that it must be cut short, today, or it will mean a poisoning as with Zacconi, and with no result. . . ."

Though Duse calls him "mediocre," Luigi Rasi should have been an actor after her own heart, for he was unusually cultivated, a classical scholar and translator, much admired for his poetry recitations and for the clarity of his diction. By now he had half-abandoned the stage in order to direct an important School of Acting in Florence, though he appeared frequently in one-man shows (writing his own monologues, later collected in a volume). In 1901 he published the first biography of Duse, which remains a valuable study of her art by an intelligent contemporary.

The company he had formed in May 1899—which Duse now became responsible for—existed chiefly to display the talents of his gifted pupil Teresa Franchini, then barely eighteen. (Later she was to create D'Annunzio's *Fedra* with outstanding success.) Rasi also acted occasionally with the troupe; his parts included Lucio Settala in *La Gioconda*.

In Vichy it was not always easy for Eleonora to write letters. The life of the fashionable spa disturbed her; and—to complete her misery—an orchestra and singers performed "atrocious Neapolitan songs" under her window from 8 to midnight.

On 24 August she was pressing Gabriele to work and promising, once more, to work for him. In a kind of triangle she wrote the names Antigone and Cassandra (which he was to translate from the Greek) and Anna (of La città morta), all three underlined. On the next page she outlined a schedule for him: September, October, November—Il fuoco ("Cast it to the rabble," she wrote, "which is waiting for it".) December and January were reserved for the adaptation of Antigone.

Exhortations to work alternated with love letters, interspersed with the usual avalanche of telegrams. These telegrams became an obsession. Some time later, Mary Berenson noted in her diary: "Carlo Placci came to dinner and he was very diverting. He said that Duse insists on having a telegram from D'Annunzio every day . . . and that as it is very chic to pay no heed to expense in telegrams, they spend about 200 francs a day sending messages like this 'Ave ave ave cara cara cara—io penso a te a te penso sempre a te cara.'" Unfortunately, the gossipy Placci was close to the truth.

Then there were Boito-like arrangements for a meeting in Zurich, where D'Annunzio joined her for a few days at the elegant hotel Baur-au-Lac. The other guests of the hotel included Romain Rolland and his wife Clothilde Bréal, and the actor Charles Le Bargy with his actress-wife, the young and intelligent Simone Benda. It was not a happy encounter, all in all. There are two accounts of those days, one in Rolland's Journal intime (as yet unpublished in its entirety) and one in Simone Benda's volume of memoirs, Sous de nouveaux soleils.

Simone—as she signs herself—was not impressed by the sparkling compliments D'Annunzio paid her when Le Bargy introduced her to the poet in the lobby of the hotel. Instead, her observant, detached eye was taking in his appearance:

"Overdressed, with a tight-waisted suit, silk shirt and handkerchief, jeweled cuff links, complicated two-tone fabric shoes, he disconcerted you as much by this feminine vanity as by his short stature, his narrow shoulders (narrower than his rounded hips), his tiny feet, and the plumpness of his arms, thighs and legs, which afflicted his body with an androgynous softness.

"His head, on the contrary, had the full, manly form of an antique bust. There can be no doubt that, in the hands of a sculptor, the forehead with its fine curve, the powerful nose, the mouth with its regular outline, the determined chin, would have become objects of beauty. But in life, deprived of the matt perfection of marble, these noble forms could arouse no admiration because of their deplorable coloring. His sparse hair, of a washed-out chestnut color, dwindled to a horrid point. His prominent eyes, with no lashes or eyebrows, were neither gray nor blue; they looked like soapy water. His pale lips revealed funny, irregular, unhealthy little teeth; his complexion was coarse and patchy, ranging from pallor to a pinkish tinge, and set off by a beard trimmed in sixteenth-century style."

Having written this far from alluring description of the poet, Simone then reminds the reader of his countless successes with beautiful, much-courted women. "These victories have no possible explanation except the power of his dazzling eloquence, in which the timbre of the voice, the forcefulness of the delivery, served the ends of an oratory devoted exclusively to the attractions of art and of emotional excess." And she added: "Must I yet again denounce the diabolical hold that language has over those of my sex—their animal need to be tamed by the music of words?"

After giving Le Bargy's young wife a sample of this music, D'Annunzio immediately invited the couple to lunch the next day in Duse's suite (without consulting Duse, as Simone noted with surprise). When they got there, it was D'Annunzio who received them in the sitting-room of the suite, where four musicians were playing ancient instruments and the table was laid clearly for three. The room had also been decorated with a portrait of Dante, some magnificently bound books, flowers and old brocades, to make it more artistic.

Duse, the guests were told, was tired and would join them later. When she did appear, after the coffee, it was obvious that the presence of outsiders did not please her. Unsmiling, making no effort to conceal her fatigue, she greeted the couple, as Simone carefully observed her:

"I gazed my fill on the most extraordinary face that nature ever created in an actress.

"At that time, oral tradition had it that Eleonora Duse faced the public without any make-up whatsoever. It is true that on the stage no suspicion of rouge lent false fire to her cheeks, although an ivory foundation, covered by a layer of powder, unified and clarified her sunburnt Calabrian [sic!] complexion. Away from the footlights, out of pride or sheer disdain, she scorned to embellish her skin at all.

"This wild coloring of hers was all the more striking as her tawny throat emerged from a thick, soft, white dressing gown, rather like the woollen wraps in which the people taking the waters at Mont-Dore swathe themselves when they come out of the baths. . . ."

Rolland, in his diary entry for 4 September, also describes meeting D'Annunzio at the hotel and finding him "aged, his skin tired, head almost entirely bald, eyes very nearsighted, wrinkled and blinking, front teeth spoiled and filled." But his intelligence, insisted Rolland (three years the poet's junior), was as brilliant as ever.

D'Annunzio insisted that this was the first time in six months that he had left his solitude in Settignano, but Rolland apparently took this declaration with several grains of salt. And he was in no hurry to introduce his French friends to la Duse (perhaps he was wary after the chilly luncheon for the Le Bargys).

Duse was performing in Zurich at the Grand Théâtre in *La Dame aux camélias* and *The Second Mrs Tanqueray*. Her new acquaintances naturally went to see her and recorded their impressions. Rolland was negative about the Dumas play:

"The piece is so inept that no actress, even a genius, can bring it to life for me. But this actress does not charm me, as she charms some others. She has a personal attraction, there is goodness in her lips and her eyes; but hers is an elegiac art which lacks force and health. Little moans, little convulsive movements, a tremor of the lip, hands which shake feverishly, a strained expression, sighs, subsidings: the genius of neuraesthenia."

He liked her better as Paula Tanqueray: "She plays her part with a tenderness, a lassitude, a weariness of life, and a goodness, which pierce the soul like music." And he referred to her "exquisite heart."

Rolland was even more impressed by his conversation with Duse in her dressing room after the performance. "She is kind, simple, welcoming. She quotes (!) Plotinus (!)—saying that death should always be concealed, that it should not be shown on stage: that is a profanation. Whenever she has to play a death-bed scene, she reflects that one day she will really die, and that on that day she will remember that she once acted a parody of her own dying moments. 'When the soul remembers, what will it say?' "

Simone Le Bargy was even more excited by the performances, which she observed with the knowledge of a professional (although one who was still at the outset of her career). "Listening to and watching Madame Duse, I discovered, behind the decidedly mediocre work that she was performing, a boundless landscape, that of the soul. Obscure leanings, unconscious fears, smothered aspirations, all glimpsed in the subtlety of an intonation, the singularity of a gesture, a look, a silence, beyond and behind the essential line of her performance."

After describing Duse's hands and the range and musicality of her voice, Simone added:

"Her strength, which was great and profound, seemed to spring not so much from the nerves, which is the case with most actresses, as from the muscles and the blood.

"If the word 'femininity' means the graceful pretense of weakness, aggravated by all the affectations that spring from coquetry and the desire to please, then Madame Duse possessed no femininity. Her powerful being scorned such feeble weapons; and yet her ability to charm was immense. . . ."

But if Simone's admiration for the older actress was unconfined, Duse's attitude towards her rising young colleague was less enthusiastic. D'Annunzio was tormenting her, keeping impossible hours (while she, exhausted from her work, retired early), and evidently commenting insistently on the charms, the attractiveness of the pretty little Madame Le Bargy. One day, Eleonora's nerves got the better of her, and there was a scene as dramatic as anything in her repertory.

The Rollands and the Le Bargys were lunching on a little terrace, when suddenly, as Simone related the event, "abruptly as the breaking of a storm, Madame Duse appeared. Without a word, and so quickly that no one could have stopped her in time, she caught me in her arms, rushed me full tilt down a corridor, opened the door of a room, and hurled me on to the bed like a parcel, shouting at the petrified D'Annunzio: 'There you are, you love her, so there she is!'—and disappeared, double-locking the door after her."

"Our friend is mad," was D'Annunzio's comment, while the rest of the luncheon party, finding the trapped pair, arranged for a ladder to be placed outside the window of the room so that they could escape. The poet went off in search of Eleonora, but not finding her, blithely joined the French party for coffee. After lunch they learned that Duse, cancelling the rest of her Zurich appearances, had left the city.

D'Annunzio's fleeting infidelities, his open admiration of other women, were not the only source of Duse's unhappiness. Gabriele had almost finished Il fuoco. During much of its composition, Eleonora had been at his side, urging him on, even though she knew that it was largely about her, and even though she must have suspected it would reveal parts of her life that she wanted to keep private. "I thought that it was true art; I tried to defend it," she told Clothilde Rolland, in an outburst of self-revelation. "It's terrible, terrible." But this was only the beginning of her unhappiness over *Il fuoco*; the real distress would not come for several more months, not until the book appeared, to considerable sensation.

By 12 September D'Annunzio was back at La Capponcina, as Eleonora continued her tour. In early October she was in Berlin, where, with a company of German actors, she played Klärchen in Goethe's *Egmont* (she was a Goethe admirer and had quoted *Wilhelm Meister* to Rolland during their Zurich conversations); she performed in Italian, while the others spoke the original text. From Berlin, on 2 October, she wrote to Gabriele in Settignano. They were already planning a brief meeting in Vienna.

"No—we will not speak! I need only to *feel* that you live—.

"*This* hour, of dawn, is the most bitter of my day. Everything screams louder, after some hours of oblivion in sleep.

"—how many times have I

"*re-found* you at this hour!"

The letter is unusually physical for the reticent Eleonora, who obviously missed Gabriele's bodily presence. "Who is it who gives you your bath in the morning? I caressed you like a little child, at Corfu! Sweet eyes, my head aches so this morning. Life is long!"

And the next day: "Cleopatra had caused me an acute fever of work, and I *was beautiful*, and I was *worthy*!

"You know that *grace* [*grazia*]

"does not come to me often!

"But *that evening* I had it, complete—and afterwards, a suffering of love, dark and deep, consumed my voice and strength in regrets—

"Art, too, like love, is insatiable and inconsolable, at times."

The letter ended with the bitter news that the production of *La Gioconda* had to be postponed. In reply, D'Annunzio reproached her severely, and she answered with a telegram, still from Berlin, on 6 October: "Do not deserve and never thought to receive such observation. No vacillations or delays but only profound interest in the beautiful work. Neither sets nor performance were worthy and thought best to postpone will inaugurate return engagement here with Gioconda."

On 9 October they met briefly in Vienna. But Duse left the next day; "a cold morning—Isa gone," Gabriele wrote in his notebook, and then set out to find the Albertina gallery. She had gone on to join the company in Bucharest, but peasant riots there closed the theatres. She had to face a worse rebellion in her own ranks. D'Annunzio had unwisely granted an interview to an Italian newspaper, in which he had made some unflattering remarks about the ability of Italian actors. One of his many enemies, eager to make trouble, had promptly mailed the article to the Rasi company. And so, on 12 October from Bucharest, the poet received an outraged telegram from the troupe:

"On eve of interpreting your Gioconda we read in the press your opinion of Italian actors. This reading deprives us of solicitude and faith conditions indispensable to our work. We ask explicitly if author of article reported your thoughts and if you confirm vulgar insults. All the members of Duse–Rasi company."

At the same time, Duse wired him privately: "I hope it will be easy for you to clarify distasteful contretemps."

Since D'Annunzio had stopped off in Venice, to visit Wagner's bedroom and take notes for *Il fuoco*, before returning to La Capponcina, he could not reply to these telegrams, which he found a week after they had been sent. Somehow Duse managed to salve the wounded feelings, and so he also found a telegram, dated 13 October, which said: "Stupid rebellion has calmed down."

The company had opened in Bucharest on the 12th, and on the 13th Duse also wrote Gabriele a long and beautiful letter, describing the trip to Bucharest, the endless train journey over the *plaine*, then the performance—the inevitable *La Dame aux camélias*—and then:

"As I was coming out of my dressing room to go back to the hotel, halfway across the stage, all the actors stopped me—the lights were out, the furniture was piled in one corner, the rugs rolled up against the wall. It looked like after a fire, after a rout.

"And the poor actors spoke to me!—*Each of them* (mine, not the new ones of the Rasi troupe), confronting me and recalling the years of loyal collaboration, spent traveling at my side.

"And in *each* of them, I felt a *gratitude* and a *plea*—Oh! Gabri!

"How *powerful* is human folly, pettiness—What drove those poor things to seek me out was their having read an *ignoble* article, and the most ignoble and vulgar citations of an '*interview*' that is attributed to you. They, my poor companions in art, read *every word* to me—and repeated it, and commented on it! . . ."

The actors had other complaints: some of them were lodged in an uncomfortable hotel, others still bore grudges dating from the tour with Zacconi. And each of them asked to be released from the obligation to play in *La Gioconda*. Patiently, Duse heard them out, and at two o'clock in the morning she was able to go to bed, having persuaded them to go on with the D'Annunzio rehearsals.

She wrote him two more letters on the 13th. On the 14th the performance was canceled "for lack of audience." Only ten or twelve seats had been sold, because prices were high and because Bucharest society was in mourning for the death of Prince Ghika, a high court official. In any case, she hated the gloomy city and was pestered by increasing difficulties with Rasi, whom she calls ironically *l'onesto Rasi*. In his dislike for D'Annunzio, he was stirring up the actors and tirelessly exploiting the offensive interview.

"Today, again today," Isa wrote Gabri on 22 October, still in Bucharest, "while I was *seeking oblivion* in work, nothing but oblivion—there, that gnat, that ant, that *mosquito* of a man starts all over again.

"I was there—tired, *alone*—far, far away from everything.

"And my heart was yearning for an *instant* of oblivion—

"And there is the mosquito—

"I was insisting with 'Francesca' [a character in *La Gioconda*, played by Adele Garaviglia, one of Rasi's actresses] to make her say a speech the way I wanted—and I began once more, ardently but patiently, to teach it to the actress.—The dream seized me again—the *pause*—the rest—and there he is: addressing the little *actress Francesca*, and saying to her: 'Well, what are you about?'—

" 'Haven't you understood yet *what the Signora wants?*' . . .

"The *honest* man was speaking to the little actress, but it was *meant* for me. . . ."

La Gioconda had been presented two nights before, and Schurmann had wired the author: "Gioconda enormous success twelve calls Duse acclaimed initiator modern art literature. . . ."

Rasi, whose book on Duse says nothing of the actors' rebellion or his disputes with Duse, wrote enthusiastically about the premiere: "Almost all the university students had gathered at the National Theatre; and every now and then it was like being present at one of our student celebrations. . . . Standing up, leaning from the boxes, from the highest gallery, the deep stalls, at the end of every act they called for the enchantress with cries, applause, the waving of hand-kerchiefs."

The Queen, Carmen Sylva (her pen name), was unable to come because the prince, her son, was ill; so she sent a special message by her secretary. Outside the theatre, the public gathered around Duse's carriage in silence, because they knew that if the artist heard a great commotion she would manage to slip away. Finally she appeared and was greeted, Rasi says, by "a single cry, loud, frenzied, long," which accompanied her to the hotel, until "she disappeared up the great staircase." She had to be at the railroad station early the next morning, to catch the 5.25 train for Budapest.

After some performances in Vienna, she was back in La Porziuncola by the end of December. D'Annunzio, next door, was hard at work and, as usual, fighting off creditors. On 25 January he wrote to Treves: "*Il fuoco* will be completed within ten days," and he declared that it would be his best book. Still, he put it aside to begin another prose work, *Il compagno dagli occhi senza cigli* (The Comrade Whose Eyes Had No Lashes). Finally, on 13 February 1900, he was able to write the last page of *Il fuoco*—page 1004 of the manuscript—and the date at the bottom of its eight lines.

By then Duse had gone to Rome for a series of performances and had resumed writing to Boito. Even before leaving Florence, on the first day of the year she had sent him a sad note ("Every good wish to Arrigo, every oblivion"); and from Rome, on 1 February, she wrote at greater length, largely about her work and her disappointment in the unadventurous Italian public.

"I wanted to *found* (!!!) in Italy something that would be art, and free flight towards something that was art, and expectation of new forces!—

"But nothing was understood. I was up to here in mire, up to the throat! and the venture was ruinous—and my soul, today, cannot be paired with its art any more!

"—*Art* of what?—I have nothing left (oh life!) but a *name* I have made, and bound to the old rubbishy works by Sardou and Dumas— no—not possible any more!—I would like to *yell* my revolt, because I am *sure* I am right in this— . . ."

A few days later Gabriele wrote her that the novel was finished; then he came to Rome himself, to read it, all of it, to the living model of its heroine.

"I know the book, and I have authorized its publication," Duse had written, some time before, to Schurmann, who had got wind of its contents and warned of the possible ill-effects the novel could have on Duse's career. "Because my suffering, whatever it may be, does not count, when it is a question of giving another masterpiece to Italian literature." Thus far, her letter seems written as much to the press as to her impresario; but then, the last sentence is suddenly naked: "And besides, I am forty years old . . . and I am in love!"

Her age—forty-one by the time *Il fuoco* appeared—is underlined in the novel. The hero, Stelio, is D'Annunzio's stand-in, but is portrayed as even more overwhelming and brilliant (and much more handsome) than the poet. His virility, his vigor, mental and physical, seem inexhaustible.

La Foscarina, the famous actress, is older, and the signs of decay are already evident. Age brings a quality of desperation to her love and her love-making, and the author implacably, clinically, describes her physical eagerness: "And now, by a violent, sudden impact of fate, she had been thrown on him, a female in heat, with all her quivering flesh. She had mingled with him with all her harsh blood. She had seen him sleep on the same pillow the heavy sleep of love-fatigue; she had known at his side sudden wakings, troubled by cruel dismay, and the impossibility of closing her weary eyelids again, for fear that he might observe her sleep, and seek in her face the marks of the years, and be repelled by them, and yearn for a fresh, unaware youthfulness."

To the reader today, eight decades after its publication, *Il fuoco* remains alive chiefly for the characterization of la Foscarina and the lyrical descriptions of Venice, its surrounding country, and its legends, rather than for Stelio-Gabriele, whose asserted greatness often seems to reflect D'Annunzio's megalomania more than his undeniable genius.

Though it is set in 1883 (to allow Wagner to appear as a symbolic supernumerary), the book is based on people and events of the following decade, and the readers of 1900 had no trouble identifying them. Like D'Annunzio, Stelio was also planning a great festival theatre for his plays and for la Foscarina. Stelio's tastes in art, interior decoration reflect accurately the D'Annunzian taste, which was already becoming an identifiable fashion trend.

Like all successful performing artists, Duse had created—or rather there had been created, had accreted, around her—an ever-expanding circle of admirers, worshipers, many of them women. "She unleashed a sort of fanaticism," Simone Le Bargy wrote, "the moment she was settled in a city." She herself called it "l'état dusien." For her cult she was more than an artist: she was virtually a saint. Already the news of the liaison with D'Annunzio had given these admiring ranks a disagreeable shock: the angelic interpreter in the power of the diabolical, immoral libertine. And many of her friends—including some who were also friends of Gabriele—felt that his influence, burdensome in her private life, was having a calamitous effect on her art. His unpopular dramas, these critics believed, were distracting her from a more suitable repertory.

In mid-May 1899, for example, Gégé Primoli had written in his Journal that Duse was "totally under the spell and in the clutches of the Poet, who is dragging her down a fatal slope. There, she is gradually losing all the fertile seeds that Genius had sown in her beautiful soul.

She has undertaken a tour in Italy with the man who is said to be our best actor [Zacconi], to perform the works of her author. With the power of her genius she has imposed a mediocre play called *La Gioconda*. But encouraged by this low-quality success, Poet and Artist thought they could impose on the Neapolitan public a vulgar, absolutely foolish drama derisively entitled *La gloria*, in which la Duse heard herself booed and whistled at by the crowd, which made her say she had been sent 'to the slaughter.'" And he repeated the story of D'Annunzio's fornication in the wings during the performance.

Matilde Serao, with characteristic frankness, said to Eleonora: "If you want to give him money, perform Dumas. But don't mix your love and your art: don't play these works, which are bad and which you perform badly, and which do you economic and artistic harm." Quoting this in his Journal, Primoli commented that in fact she was "too modern to play fake antique; it is a perpetual contradiction, a false note all along the line. She does violence to her nature, her talent; she contradicts herself."

Though *Il fuoco* is not always an easy book to read, the scandalous subject matter ensured its immediate success, and it became news even outside Italy. The French translation was soon to appear, making the work available to a wide, international audience more likely to read French than Italian. Within the year the book was also translated into English and published as *The Flame of Life*.

Through all the polemics the book sparked everywhere it appeared, Duse maintained a dignified silence in public, or if she was forced to express an opinion, she confirmed the belief in *Il fuoco*'s supreme artistic value. Among friends she was for the most part silent, only rarely—as with Clothilde Rolland—revealing her distress at the poet's destruction of their privacy.

In Italy, publication date was 5 March. Before the month was out, Eleonora left on a foreign tour, returning to Berlin and Vienna. She wrote and wired to Gabriele constantly. Having remembered that he was a member of Parliament, he spent some time in Rome attending debates, but he was planning a trip to Vienna, for another brief meeting with Eleonora.

In Berlin she met Enrichetta, who was understandably troubled by the publication of *Il fuoco*. "I have two arms," Duse is supposed to have said to her daughter, "one is called Enrichetta, the other Gabriele D'Annunzio. I cannot cut one off without dying." Temporarily appeased, Enrichetta continued to harbor a dislike and distrust of the poet. Many years later, after her mother's death, before going to see him at the Vittoriale, she took care to put her missal and a little bottle of holy water in her purse. (He charmed her, all the same.)

In Rome, D'Annunzio stayed at 79 Via del Babuino, not far from the Spanish Steps and the Pincio, the setting of many scenes in his novels. There, on 20 March, Duse wired him from Berlin, signing the telegram "Isa": "success last night [of *La Gioconda*] enormous. Am told today's press unanimous and enthusiastic. The mob begins to hear. This is what I wanted." So delaying the Berlin premiere of the work had proved a good idea.

On 31 March she opened in Vienna at the Theatre an der Wien, with *The Second Mrs Tanqueray*. This was to be followed by *Cleop* and *La Gioconda*. The D'Annunzio drama was to be repeated on 11 April at a special performance in the Burgtheater, with the Emperor and the court attending.

D'Annunzio came in time for the event, a moment of particular happiness. The night before, the poet wrote in his notebook: "Remember 10 April, as a *climax* of your life." And, under the same date, cryptically: "Isa, speaking of the variety, the awesomeness, and the fullness of her life in these days, says: Madness is not *richer*."

The diary continues: "11 April—At the Burgtheater this evening they are giving *La Gioconda*. I pass in front of the old, monumental, gray stone theatre. In the heavy bronze frames, locked beneath bronze grilles, are the announcements of the performance, with my name and that of my friend. A singular sensation! Something so *living* on that old, dead hulk, on that traditional seat of official art, of the academic, of everything that is past forever!"

That night, when Isa had gone to the theatre, Gabri took a cab and roamed the city: the Prater, the Danube, then back to the centre of Vienna. "I pass again in front of the Burgtheater, where the performance has begun. The words of my poetry echo in the vast hall, over the multitude that does not understand them and does not know me. Solitude. A slight mental fever. Weariness. Passion. And that old Emperor, there in his box, mummified!"

The next day he wrote in the diary: "God protect my love!" And, still in the Vienna pages, Isa wrote her next address (she was returning briefly to Berlin): "Reinicherhof—Wilhelmstrasse—Berlin." There, the Vienna happiness lingered in her thoughts, and on 21 April she wrote to him, perhaps echoing unconsciously—and reversing—the conclusive exchange with Arrigo: "It is more than living! More than dying!"

She asked him not to join her in Frankfurt, where she would be surrounded; but he came anyway, and she *was* surrounded. From her room in the Frankfurterhof, on 1 May, she wrote to him just after his arrival in the city. Their meeting had to be arranged with familiar precautions:

"Gabri. I will be free about 11½ or midnight.

"The door to the right (as you look at the windows) opens into my sitting room—the same large balcony outside leads to my rooms. I will come back about 11, but, at about 10 some people who know Gabri will be reentering the hotel, and it is not a good idea for them, now, to meet Gabri— . . ."

Then, having explained the practical matters, she could write more intimately, and sadly, about problems that had arisen because of *Il fuoco*:

"Only this (at this point) I would like to say to you: that I would have given my *whole life* to be spared these last few days, not to hear you accused, in my presence, and to be able to defend you with all joy, not to feel this *stain* in the soul!

"—But . . . by you, only by you, sweet son—*so* beloved, only by you was I disarmed—"

The furor over *Il fuoco*, now exploding in the papers in Italy and in Paris, had affected their relationship. Her letters—and their life—had always had violent swings between happiness and despair, ecstasy and rage; but now the alternation became more frequent, and the unhappiness, the veiled reproaches, more regular. From London, she wrote on 21 May:

"The *only* great, deep sorrow . . . was just one: here it is:

"—the *secret*

"*given*, to the mob.

"—Everyone talked about it, and

"knew it. You

"will say—ha!—

"Ah, no!

"the *secret* was

"ours

"now!

" 'c'est fait. . . .,' "

One cause of gossip—and, for Eleonora, surely of humiliation—was the idealization of Giulietta Gordigiani into Donatella Arvale, whose youth and beauty are described in the book as a contrast to the fading Foscarina. The London letter goes on:

"If, then, you loved the beautiful creature—you were justified— within your rights. I, first, (—and only I, perhaps) understood it!

"If you have praised her in your book—you did well—this, too, was your right. . . .

"*Sing* what you loved—and what has beautified life! and gave hope! . . ."

D'Annunzio's letters to her also contained reproaches, especially for not giving more performances of *La Gioconda*. (She was paying him generous royalties, and he wanted the money.) On 31 May, she wrote to him frankly about the economics of her situation: the winter tour, interrupted by an illness in Vienna, had been a disaster, leaving her with 52,000 francs' debt, some of it owed to Worth and Paquin, some to the suppliers of the scant furniture—the "broken chairs," as she said—for La Porziuncola. Now she had scraped together 32,000 and the other 20,000 would have to come from "that stupid, cheap *Fédora*."

It was during this season, when she played at Sir Henry Irving's elegant Lyceum Theatre, that she was reviewed by Max Beerbohm, the young successor of G.B.S. on *The Saturday Review*. Beerbohm's view of Duse was different from Shaw's. "I could not bow down before the demi-goddess," the iconoclastic wit wrote, confessing that he was unable to discuss her technique because of his lack of Italian. "I am the only critic who labours under this difficulty," he added, going on to say that Magda, Paula Tanqueray, Fédora, and the Princesse Georges were all, in Duse's hands, "vehicles for expression of absolute self. From first to last she is the same in Fédora as in Magda, in Magda as in Paula, in Paula as in the Princesse Georges, and in the Princesse Georges as in La Gioconda."

But he slightly preferred her in the D'Annunzio play: "La Gioconda (known to me, as I have said, only through a synopsis) happens to be an Italian part, and it happens to suit Duse. It might well be realized otherwise than by her, but it could not, I imagine, be realized so fully. If I had never seen her in any other part, I should have raved about her conception. 'She *is* La Gioconda,' I should have exclaimed. As it is, I can only remark that La Gioconda is she."

Still insisting that he was not overwhelmed, as others were, by Duse's personality, he could nevertheless see "the power and nobility in her face; and the little shrill soft voice, which is in such strange contrast with it, has a certain charm for me. I admire, too, her movements, full of grace and strength. But my prevailing emotion is hostile to her. I cannot surrender myself, and see in her the 'incarnate womanhood' and the 'very spirit of the world's tears' and all those other things which other critics see in her. My prevailing impression is of a great egoistic force; of a woman overriding, with an air of sombre unconcern, plays, mimes, critics and public. In a man I should admire this tremendous egoism very much indeed. In a woman it only makes me uncomfortable. I dislike it. I resent it. In the name of art, I protest against it . . . Thus do I, the devil's advocate, resume my seat, trusting to the judge to suppress any disturbance in the court."

Today Beerbohm's conclusion, though no doubt written with tongue in cheek, sounds sexist. Still, his attitude may explain, indirectly, why Duse did appeal especially to women, and to feminists, though she was not a feminist herself. For the rest, Beerbohm's testimony has to be added to the conflicting evidence about Duse: he says her voice was shrill, others say it was musical. He says her movements were graceful; others described them as lurching. (Simone Le Bargy actually thought Duse limped—though gracefully.)

Duse appealed to men as well as to women, and that spring she made a profound impression on the eighteen-year-old James Joyce, visiting London with his father. The future author of *Ulysses* sent her a poem, which she neither saved nor acknowledged, and bought a photograph of her, which he kept on his desk back in Dublin.

In spite of D'Annunzio's complaints, Duse was not neglecting his work. In the same letter about money quoted above, she informed him, "by the end of this season *La Gioconda* will have been given *five* times." Not bad, she might have added, for a play in which the text was more important than the action (most of which takes place off stage), being performed for audiences that could understand not a word of that text. "If, another year, *Gioconda* were translated into English, performed first in English, and *then* in our language, I am *sure* it would run for many, many, many nights. Now, they barely understand a few lines. . . ."

The heat, that summer, was too oppressive for them to stay in Settignano, so they escaped together to a little villa on the Tuscan coast near Viareggio, a place called Il Secco. The poet brought his dogs and horses with him, and this menagerie caused talk in what was then a quiet, remote seaside locality. Rumors, as always, surrounded him, and people said he used to ride his favorite horse naked along the beach. The truth is that he was again working. Here he wrote the famous poem "La pioggia nel pineto" and some of the finest parts of *Alcyone*. He was also beginning another tragedy for Isa-Eleonora, *Francesca da Rimini*.

Before the summer ended, the lovers had another of their dramatic quarrels. D'Annunzio went off to the Villa Consigli in Viareggio, Duse to Venice, then on to Tegernsee to her friend Sophie Drechsel and, probably, to meet Enrichetta. The meeting was not happy. "How many bitter words—and futile!" she wrote to Gabriele, with whom, once they were apart, she had been quickly reconciled.

From Lucerne, where she was already performing, she wrote Gabriele that things were going well, a box-office take of 5,000 francs nightly. "Which begins to make up the 80,000 needed for the wheels of the wagon——I have already put aside 10 . . ." She was saving up to buy a year's freedom for them both. "*You will work—You will rest—*," she added.

The Rollands were in Lucerne, and so was Matilde Serao. Duse told Gabriele that she was disenchanted with all three of them. From Berlin, she wrote again about the proposed year of freedom, which did not much appeal to Gabriele, now in the heat of work on *Francesca*, which he obviously wanted to see on the stage—with Isa—as soon as possible.

In fact, he was already thinking of the cast, and he recommended a young actor to Duse. After asking first "how much does he cost?" she wrote:

"Now that you glimpse a new possibility for your work—here I am again, *ready*, to keep my word—

"—that is what matters—

"*Eleonora* has never rested in her life—nor has she rejoiced in freedom—a year more or a year less for one who has already been in prison so long—what is that??"

Then she discussed an actor she had just auditioned.

"He wanted to do *La città morta* (he said he knew it by heart) and he *zacconi-ized* methodically. . . . Frankly, from that *cabotin* [ham] manner, that 'voice' that 'acted' even when *speaking*, I received an impression so . . . *repulsive*—that the recollection and suspicion of it, embarrass me. . . .

"I repeat, my son, that—since it is a question of your work, I am ready to smother and strangle, once again, "Eleonora" to make "la Duse" work and slave—but we must be *demanding* and *proud*—and *prudent* in admitting *baritones* to our table—."

On the last day of September she gave what was to have been the final performance of the tour, in Berlin; but then—obviously making "la Duse" earn some money for Eleonora and Gabri, she continued touring. From Bucharest again, on 15 October, she wrote: ". . . my life belongs to you—and everything will be given to make yours triumph.

"But don't take from me the flame of work—the hope of being necessary to you!—"

The tour went on to Genoa (where she wrote him another long love letter), then to Nice, where Gabriele joined her. In Milan, on 27 January 1901, Giuseppe Verdi died, after a long and glorious career. Like all Italians D'Annunzio was moved, and he began writing an Ode probably while on the Nice-bound train. Its composition was part of his self-appointed role as Italian laureate. A few months before, on the death of Umberto I, the poet had composed a perfunctory Ode to the Young King; but the Verdi Ode was inspired. D'Annunzio finished it, back in Settignano, on 24 February, and three days later he recited it in Florence to an enthusiastic public. It appeared in the *Tribuna*, and within a few days Treves had brought it out in a handsome little volume.

In January Eleonora had briefly interrupted her tour in order to take part in yet another benefit for the Dumas *fils* monument in Paris. In February, back in Italy and again in partnership with Zacconi, she was preparing, at last, *La città morta*. Whatever she may have thought of Zacconi's style of acting, she liked him personally; and this time it was he who joined her company, not the other way round (though several of the actors were the same in both cases).

After over two weeks of intense rehearsal, the play opened at the Teatro Lirico in Milan on 20 March. In Zacconi's recollection (when he wrote his autobiography), there was still a certain hostility towards the poet; but the opening was a success. The play then went on to Genoa, Bologna, Florence, Rome, and—concluding the tour—Venice, where D'Annunzio had usually fared best in previous theatrical attempts.

On 8 May they opened at the Teatro Rossini. The success, according to Gino Damerini, was "indescribable." Certainly it surpassed anything the Duse–D'Annunzio combination had achieved before, and it was a genuine personal triumph for the poet, who received countless curtain calls amid salvos of "Viva D'Annunzio!" There was an added, non-literary reason for some of this enthusiasm. Only two evenings previously, at the Teatro La Fenice, D'Annunzio had made a belligerent speech in favor of Italian naval rearmament and had read his *Canzone di Garibaldi*. Two nights after the play's premiere, as guest of honor at a banquet, he spoke again aggressively about Italian expansion.

That summer Isa and Gabri divided their time between Settignano, the Villa Secco, and a remote spot in the Euganean hills in the Veneto, the area that later became Duse's choice for her last home and her final resting-place. In September, from Venice, they visited the lovely Teatro Olimpico in Vicenza; the Palladian building was to be restored, and D'Annunzio announced the title of the tragedy he would write for the opening: *Re Numa*. The tragedy never got written, and D'Annunzio never used the Teatro Olimpico.

It would, in any case, have been unsuitable for *Francesca da Rimini*, which he completed that summer. This mammoth work, a historical pageant, required twenty-six actors, and included scenes of warfare, all accompanied by specially composed music: a conception somewhere between D'Annunzio's beloved Wagner and the still-unknown Cecil B. DeMille. A celebration of medieval Italy, the play contained references to Dante and (anachronistically) Vivaldi, as well as elements of folk culture from the poet's own Adriatic country.

He was in Vicenza on 28 September. Apparently he had completed the drama by then, because on 1 October he read it aloud to a small group of intimates amid the suitably medieval trappings of La Capponcina. It was dedicated to Eleonora, not only with a formal inscription ("A Eleonora Duse dalle belle mani") but also with a trio of elegant sonnets. For the reading, she sat on a kind of throne, while D'Annunzio stood at a lectern and read the 12,000 verses. Gustavo Salvini, son of the great Tommaso, was present (he was to play Paolo), as well as Luigi and Teresa Rasi, who would also be associated with the production. As the reading progressed, Duse became nervous and occasionally left the salon to retire to an adjacent room where she could lie down on a sofa and ease the accumulated tension. This drama was also a reward for her trust and her sacrifice, and the several dedications bore witness to her share in its creation.

Though the gathering was private, news immediately spread, and the Italian papers published secondhand, highly colored accounts of the event. D'Annunzio, already concerned with questions of staging, took time to write indignantly to the editor of the *Tribuna* on 9 October, belaboring the public and issuing a broader complaint: "In Italy, he who dares direct his strength towards any ideal work sees himself deprived even of the rights enjoyed by the most humble citizen; and further he is exposed to the insults of the countless rogues and clowns who infest our beautiful country. . . ."

This burst of wrath was soon forgotten, however, in the fever of preparing *Francesca*. Eleonora was not only the star and co-director (with Gabriele); she was also the backer, and ruled that no expense should be spared. None was. The final cost is supposed to have come to about 400,000 lire, an enormous figure (when you bear in mind that D'Annunzio rented his capacious villa for 1,200 lire per annum). For rehearsals, Duse hired the historic Teatro della Pergola, Florence's opera house, and to play the smaller, choral roles—handmaidens and swordsmen—she engaged the students from the Rasi academy. (One of them was the future writer Aldo Palazzeschi.)

D'Annunzio was constantly present. In those hectic days Eleonora may have recalled—with nostalgia or bitterness—the time when she prepared *Cleop* in Milan, settling all the questions of costumes and staging while Arrigo kept a safe distance and sent her advice by letter. In the thick of the work, Gabriele created choreography, gave fencing lessons, found props, read lines; he even worried about the drape or the color of the dress. His willingness also to perform humble tasks impressed the cast.

But his determination to have his say in the staging—according to Teresa Rasi—sometimes made Eleonora, used to directing her own productions, tetchy and irritated. On at least one occasion she threatened to walk out, to turn over the part to another actress. But D'Annunzio apparently remained calm through it all: the work kept him serene, and a Roman caricaturist of the time—D'Annunzio and Duse were an endless reservoir of material for cartoonists and humorists—shows him, cloth cap over his bald head, sawing, hammering, dusting, combing an actress's hair, cobbling. He discussed the incidental music with Maestro Antonio Scontrino, the composer who was also the director of the Florence Conservatory, and the sets with his great friend, the painter and designer Adolfo De Carolis. To the latter D'Annunzio sent countless, finicky instructions: "On the slave's tunic I would like some black decoration, rather barbaric and with oriental *flavor*. On Ostasio's red surplice I would like, on the chest, the eagle of the Polenta family, among the other decorations. . . . Among the gems you will find some amethysts, which must decorate the embroidery of that little tunic of iridescent color, around the neck (as in the angels of Benozzo [Gozzoli], in Palazzo Riccardi.)"

Specialists were hired for the woodcarving, the armor; the patient Worth sent one of his most trusted assistants to Florence. And to supervise the hairstyles the poet summoned the president of the Académie Française de Coiffure (who also did the hair of the troupe of the Comédie) from Paris to Florence.

After almost two months of rehearsal, the play was finally to open in Rome on 10 December 1901. The theatre chosen was the Teatro Costanzi, where Duse and Zacconi had appeared in *La città morta* the previous April. Primarily an opera house (Puccini's *Tosca* had received its world premiere there the year before), the Costanzi was Rome's newest and largest theatre, and certainly the best for the wide-ranging innovations of the D'Annunzio tragedy.

In spite of the long rehearsals and the superior technical equipment of the Costanzi, the first performance of *Francesca da Rimini* did not go smoothly. The expectation was immense ("all Italy talked of nothing else," the editor of the *Giornale d'Italia* said) and the house was full. The first act proceeded well; the poet had three curtain calls alone and another for the company. But in the second act, with its complex battle scene, there was trouble. The incident was described by Tom Antongini, D'Annunzio's sometime secretary and biographer:

"He had insisted on having real mortars and genuine war-mangonels to go into action during the siege of the Malatesta stronghold.

"What happened is indescribable and unique in the annals of the theatre.

"A thick, acrid smoke, scientifically obtained by the chemist Helbig, blinded and left breathless some hapless spectators, who abandoned the theatre, howling and booing. However, a big stone hurled by a mangonel simply knocked down a wall of the stage. The tragedy, already endangered on its own, took advantage of this to collapse also, clamorously."

Other accounts ignore the technical mishap, and the failure was less clamorous than Antongini—writing years later—suggests. True, after the aggressive second act, which ends with the shouts of the fortress's defenders, there was an echoed shouting from the house, both favorable and hostile, until D'Annunzio finally appeared. There were more calls after the other three acts, but the premiere could not be counted a great success.

A balanced judgment was expressed, in the *Giornale d'Italia* (which had sent four critics to cover the drama from different aspects), by the literary critic Domenico Oliva. In his long article he wrote: "Great, noble, is the attempt to lead us back to tragedy, to the greatest expression of dramatic poetry; and it is worthy of the poet we all admire. But the tragedy must be there, the soul of tragedy, not only appearance, not only plot." Oliva also criticized the characterization of the lovers: Paolo he described as a "tenor," and Francesca, instead of being the ideal woman immortalized by Dante, is a confused series of aspects: ideal in the first act, then a bellicose fury, then a romantic lover with violent (read D'Annunzian) accents.

The young Luigi Pirandello, also in the audience, later wrote: "I believe I have never suffered so much in the theatre. The art of the great actress seemed paralyzed, indeed downright shattered by the character the poet drew with heavy strokes. . . . For me, and I believe for many others, the impression then provoked a deep and sad nostalgia for the Marguerite Gautier that Duse had brought back to life a short time before on our Italian stage."

Duse came in for even sharper criticism and was blamed for not having asserted herself as director, for having allowed D'Annunzio to crush her, and for not having perceived—and adjusted—the untheatrical quality of the play. Depressed, she thought again of passing the part to another actress; but the mood was short-lived. She helped the poet make cuts (in the first scene of Act I and then in Act V), reducing the play by about a thousand verses. The Roman audiences followed the remaining three performances in the city more calmly and warmly. Now undisturbed by catcalls and technical mishaps, the actors—including Duse—were able to polish their performances. The reception improved; after all, the play was, if nothing else, a dazzling spectacle.

Present at one of these performances was Marchesa Capranica del Grillo, the ennobled retired actress Adelaide Ristori, about to celebrate her eighty-sixth birthday. The doyenne of the Italian theatre, who had been kind to Duse at the time of her first South American visit with the Cesare Rossi company, now expressed some reservations about the work within the hearing of a journalist, who printed them. The Marchesa promptly denied the unkind words; but they must have reminded Eleonora of some previous remarks by Ristori, published in 1897 on the eve of Duse's Paris debut. Relations between the two artists were cool.

But now, in January 1902, for Ristori's birthday, a Paris paper—*Le Gaulois*—asked Duse to write a sentiment appropriate to the occasion. Duse hesitated; then, on 25 January, she wrote:

"I find admirable and consoling, in the cruelty of our rapid and forgetful life, this great movement of love and gratitude which impels not only my own country but all countries of lofty culture towards a beautiful image of time past, towards the calm and happy riches once capable of intoxicating the world with her gestures. . . ."

After thus sweetly relegating Ristori to the past, Duse stressed that she had always found her older colleague in every way perfect, both as artist and as woman; but she went on to say: "I could not read without astonishment and incredulity the strange remarks that a Russian journalist reported yesterday on the subject of my personal efforts and the modern Italian theatre.

237

"The great tragedienne, in fact, has just denied that imagined conversation, which, like a sudden gust of wind, came to trouble the beautiful and serene lines of the image that our love and our reverence have consecrated forever."

Then Duse spoke of her devotion to a work of pure poetry—*Francesca*—and the duty of a modern actress in the changing Italian literary scene.

"For some time now, Italian literature has emerged from the romantic and patriotic period, rich in generous spirit but poor in enduring forms. Men like Giacometti, Montanelli, Marenco . . . [i.e. the authors of Ristori's repertory] are dead and forgotten. . . . And one feels on all sides today, in young Italy, an eager yearning for that renascence announced by one of our most eloquent writers. In the theatre one has been content with bad translations or mediocre provincial dramas written in barbarous jargon.

"Now, on the old boards, between potboilers, one hails the unexpected reappearance of poetry. . . .

"As an artist and as an Italian, I consider it a great honor to be able to give my name and my firm determination to this effort of renewal. As an artist and as an Italian in my country, I am doing only my duty, placing myself at the service of a beautiful and fertile idea.

"Sensible people reproach me for having abandoned my old repertory, which won my fame. . . . I scorn to be the virtuosa who parades her skill. I disdain to place my personal success above the work. . . ."

The handwriting and the signature were Eleonora's, but the words bear the stamp of Gabriele, though there could be no doubt that she shared his ideas. Bravely she took *Francesca* on tour. First she visited the major Italian cities, where it failed to please; even in Venice, their lucky city, Eleonora and Gabriele had to face catcalls amid the applause. For a long time afterwards, D'Annunzio refused to attend a Venetian performance of a work of his.

Francesca fared better abroad. In Berlin, where Duse played from 8 to 28 April, she concluded her season with a triumphant *Francesca*, after which she was called out before the curtain more than thirty times, in a rain of flowers. In Vienna the success was repeated, and on 6 May she was hailed in Trieste. The ledger of the Teatro Verdi, still preserved, shows that D'Annunzio's twelve per cent of the take (an exceptionally high cut, at Duse's insistence) brought him 1,176 lire—almost a year's rent—for a single performance of *Francesca*, and only slightly less for *La Gioconda*.

Gabriele was there to participate in the acclaim. On the last night of the run and of *Francesca*, poet and actress were presented with silver plaques; in a speech of thanks, D'Annunzio promised the theatre two new tragedies. Poet, interpreter and plays were received with equal warmth at the next stop, Gorizia; D'Annunzio's intensely patriotic ideas had made him a hero in that part of Austro-Hungary that irredentists wanted to make Italian.

In the course of the journey, Gabriele also encountered the famous actress-courtesan Liane de Pougy, with whom he made a rendezvous for later in the summer, as Duse was to discover to her chagrin and fury.

Duse and Gabriele went to the Villa Secco again that summer, and then—with Enrichetta and the English "miss" installed nearby—to the castle of Romena in the Casentino valley, above Arezzo. Duse was still concerned with business matters: her contract with Schurmann had expired, and she was reluctant to renew it. "That is the last rope I want to hang myself with," she wrote to her company manager. There were offers from Täncer, the man who had first taken her abroad on her own, and from the French impresario Ulmann.

And another American tour lay ahead. She had been invited back by the New York impresario George C. Tyler, and negotiations were in progress with Tyler's European representative, Joseph Smith. Smith also discussed with D'Annunzio the idea of a lecture tour, but the poet's demands were so excessive that the plan was quickly dropped. In America, too, the English translation of *Il fuoco* had been read and had created the predictable scandal. Tyler sent word to Duse that if she was unwilling to come to America alone (that is, without Gabriele), she had better not come at all.

She gave in. She would leave Gabriele in Europe, but she would take his plays with her. She would tour the States in an exclusively D'Annunzian repertory: *La città morta, La Gioconda,* and *Francesca da Rimini,* the new poetic theatre for which she was conducting her courageous, unequal battle.

She battled privately, too. When she learned, at Romena, of Gabriele's encounter with Liane de Pougy in Milan, Duse packed and left abruptly. But she went only as far as Arezzo, where she wrote to a mutual friend: "I felt I was losing him, not days *rightly* given to *another,* but something of his soul." In theory, she respected Gabriele's freedom, but in practice she suffered.

She turned back, and when Gabriele arrived at Romena she was there to receive him and to forgive.

At the end of August they returned to Settignano, where she had more forgiving to do. In his *Libro segreto*, a kind of random diary published years later, D'Annunzio described a characteristic escapade of his:

Perdita [another of Gabriele's names for Eleonora] lingered on the ivy-covered stairs. Beyond her waist, the thick, dark ivy climbed, as if it were clinging to her, binding her to the iron of the railing.

'Where are you going?'

'Off, at random. As always.'

'But where?'

'Don't ask.'

It was Silvia's reply to Sirenetta in the drama [*La Gioconda*] in which she had seemed sublime with her mutilated hands and a whitened tress.

Along the old Fiesole road I was going to the Della Robbias of Sant'Ansano. I went down to the gate of a villa enclosed in precise boxwood, where two sisters awaited me, players of virginal and lute, pupils of Arnold Dolmetsch, experts in perverse games. 'One always makes progress by teaching.'

I returned after three hours, eager.

From the drive I called to my unique companion, I cried my love with the tenderest of elect names: 'Ghisola! Ghisolabella!'

Dropping my reins, I jumped down to the gravel. 'Ghisola!' I was mad for her, oblivious, not guilty. The fleeting infidelity gave love an intoxicating novelty. I raged against all delay as I bathed. 'Ghisola, I love you, I love, always, only you. . . .'

At the end of September they both left Settignano for Bologna, then Milan. There they parted again. Eleonora journeyed on to Genoa, where on 29 September she sailed on the *Kronprinz Wilhelm* for New York.

13
Transgression

She landed on 14 October. As usual, the company had sailed on another ship; Eleonora traveled with her secretary and her maid. Smith met the ship, and Helena Gilder was also there to receive her friend. Duse was greeted by a wave of publicity, somewhat different this time from the explosions of naive curiosity on past visits.

The translation of *Il fuoco* had preceded her, shocking the American reading public; and that shock was reflected in the press. When the rumor spread of a possible tour with D'Annunzio, straitlaced theatre-goers were outraged. One of them, for example, wrote to the editor of the *Dramatic Mirror*, who published the letter. It expressed the hope that the rumor was untrue:

"The friends and admirers of the distinguished Italian actress are unwilling to believe that she would so recklessly affront decency or cast so careless and brutal a slur upon the women of the stage. . . .

"There is no doubt that the actress in question is as 'moral' a woman and probably a far more honest and less hypocritical woman than many a woman who lives and moves and has her being in the most exclusive circles of society. Nevertheless the free public exhibition of the attachment of the actress and the author would, in the peculiar circumstances, mean something more than the mere offense, repelling that part of the public which loves the theatre and its actors intelligently. It would mean the spreading of a dangerous and mischievous influence among the weak-kneed youth of the stage—the sort of youth that is already eager to shed tears over the tumults and distresses of the heroines of nasty Italian novels. For there is nothing noble or warming or lofty or genial in these books."

Obviously, the nasty novels in question were those of D'Annunzio. And the author of the letter made this even more clear in his next paragraph: "Circumstances spiritual or material may render the devotion of a woman to a man who is not her husband an admirable thing, but the devotion of a woman to a man who has ruthlessly paraded her on the bookstalls as the licentious heroine of an obscene novel is not a pleasing spectacle. Will enterprising business management see to it that the book is sold in the lobby? . . ."

Following her custom, Duse gave no outward sign that she was aware of the press and the public, hostile or friendly. She spent the first days mostly in the Holland House, did some sightseeeing (she admired the brand-new Flatiron Building), saw friends, and discussed business with her agents. George C. Tyler, who had arranged this tour, later described his first meetings with her:

"Her hands were wonderful—she could do anything with them. I remember when I first negotiated with her through an interpreter. Thinking that the interpreter was incompetent, she pushed him aside and explained to me herself the distress which it gave her to play more than five performances. So eloquent was her pantomime that I understood what she said although I could not speak Italian."

For Duse, five performances weekly were an absolute maximum, which impresarios seldom managed to wrest from her; but this tour was specially important, partly for artistic reasons—she was introducing D'Annunzio to America as a dramatist—and partly for economic ones. She wanted to buy him more serenity for writing; and she had all her own usual expenses. The dream of Albano and the festival may not have entirely faded either.

Boston had always been a welcoming city, so she began her tour there, not with *La Dame aux camélias* as in the old days, but with the new and difficult *Gioconda*. Curiosity and anticipation were high; sales for the first three performances of her brief season netted over $2,000.

She arrived by train and was escorted by her agent's representative to the Hotel Somerset. That night, at the Tremont Theater, she finally met the company, to rehearse for the next day's opening. The scenery, shipped from Italy on big rolls of paper, was mounted and hung.

The audience on opening night was elegant and friendly, but *La Gioconda* did not please. Indeed, it puzzled and irritated the critics. In the Boston *Herald*, the reviewer called the hero "a weakling and decadent," though Silvia—Duse's part—was sympathetic. "The great artist seemed as before except that in face, figure and action she showed a large and fortunate gain in health and strength." And he continued his praise: "in the indication of delicate shades and varieties of emotion no face on the stage of our day has equaled the face of Madame Duse."

La Gioconda was at least a success for the actress, but *La città morta*— which was given at the Tremont on 24 October—was a virtual failure. Seeing it, the *Herald* critic wrote, "was like going through the worst wards of a hospital for incurables under the guidance of a very clever physician who possesses an immense gift in delusive euphemism." He did admit that the play had "passages of high emotional power and rare picturesque beauty." Another critic simply found the play "revolting." And these objections to both of the D'Annunzio plays would be repeated by critics in other cities in the course of Duse's tour. Audiences were discouraged, and Duse encountered less than full houses. Loyally, she kept this situation from Gabriele and sent him royalties calculated on sold-out theatres.

For her last week in Boston she scheduled five performances of *Francesca da Rimini* (reduced to four because of an indisposition); and this play proved the most successful of the three. The kernel of the story, at least, was familiar to the audience. A routine play on the same subject by George Boker had been interpreted by several American actors, including Otis Skinner; and two other writers—Stephen Phillips and F. Marion Crawford—had produced modern settings of the story. But the beautiful and elaborate staging probably drew more people to the theatre, and Duse triumphed as the tragic heroine.

From Boston she returned to New York, and on 2 November the *New York Times* ran a long article, preparing the city's audiences for the "new" Duse, considerably different—the article warned—from the actress they had seen six years previously.

"Duse is now in the prime of life and is enjoying better health than for many years. Her art is said to be at its best. In Boston . . . she gave five performances a week as she promises to do here—something almost unprecedented for her.

"D'Annunzio's plays are as yet unknown to American theatre goers. Several of his poems and novels have been translated, but their subject matter and their manner of treatment has made it necessary to suppress considerable portions of them. . . .

"In the writing of his plays, as in his novels, D'Annunzio has worked along lines of realism which has gained for him in English-speaking countries the reputation of perhaps a great but degenerate artist. In his poetry, however, the sumptuous reproduction of beauty has caused him to be likened unto the English Keats. . . ."

The physical description of Duse in the *Times* article interestingly recalls, to some extent, the descriptions of la Foscarina that were so offensive to her in *Il fuoco*: "There are lines of illness in her cheeks and beneath her eyes; the increasing years have made it advisable to add a suggestion of color in her face; and her own hair, which is said to be tinged with gray, is covered in a coiffure of brown. Yet her throat is as firm and soft as in a young girl, her profile as spiritually transparent as ever. It is the same calm, mobile face, so individually beautiful and expressive as to surpass a thousandfold all portraits that have been made of her. Her voice, which has no great native strength and sweetness, retains all of its old refinement and charm. The resources of her expression are as varied and as accurate. In a word, Duse of today is a trifle older, perhaps, but by virtue of the fact her art is the more mature."

In New York, Duse opened on 4 November at Hammerstein's Victoria Theatre. It was not a happy choice of date, because it was election night (Benjamin B. Odell was reelected governor), and at least one review mentions the din of "fish horns and rattles" in the streets outside. D'Annunzio's plays were ill received. The *Daily Tribune* called *La Gioconda* "a great lachrymal opportunity" and "odoriferous," and *La città morta* fared no better. There were letters to the editors about the morbid and decadent dramas.

The tour continued: to Baltimore, Washington, where the Theodore Roosevelts invited Duse to the White House; and Chicago, where she was more warmly received than in any other American city. The Chicago stay was marked by a humorous mishap, when five of Duse's sixteen trunks were delivered to Harry Doose's grocery store at 163 Larrabee Street (the incident was amply covered in the press). Then St Louis, and back to New York for seven concluding performances.

In New York she was now performing not at Hammerstein's Victoria but in the Metropolitan Opera House, where her audiences looked even scantier. By popular demand, and no doubt after some urging from her disappointed impresarios, she agreed to depart from her announced repertory and give a special performance of *Magda*, favorite vehicle for the "old" Duse. The sets had to be sent from Italy, and cables were despatched in December. Meanwhile she gave *Francesca* with no better results than before. On 14 January 1903, *Magda* finally drew a full, enthusiastic house.

The next day was her farewell, a mixed bill including the second act of *Magda*, the third act of *La città morta*, and the third of *La Femme de Claude*. Again—perhaps because of the D'Annunzio—the audience dwindled, though the star received many curtain calls. As the *Daily Tribune* summed up the results of the tour, "The distinguished Italian actress has had a season of variable fortune, making known some of the worst plays that have ever been seen, and she will now return to Europe." Two days later she sailed on the *Savoie*.

The churlishness of the daily newspapers, the poor attendance, the sometimes spiteful gossip, did not tell the whole story. If the Duse of 1902 was no longer the romantic actress who had timidly approached the North American shores in 1893 and had returned to conquer the nation's audiences in 1896, the America of the nascent twentieth century was also different from the brawling country of the 1890s.

The American theatre was creating a more sophisticated public and, for it, a new generation of actors. And, to record and even guide this movement, there were serious, thinking writers on the theatre. Among the most original and rewarding was James Huneker, born in Philadelphia in 1860 of Hungarian–Irish background, and trained in Paris.

In 1902 Huneker had just joined the New York *Sun*, after twelve years as drama and music critic on other local papers. His views of D'Annunzio and of Eleonora, expressed at the time, were summed up two years later in his book *Iconoclasts*, a series of essays on contemporary drama. It is interesting to place Huneker's study beside the long Shaw article on Duse written seven years earlier, in pre-Gabriele days. First Huneker discussed her physical gifts and her old repertory:

Without special comeliness, without the golden ductile voice of Bernhardt, Duse so drilled her bodily organs that her gestures, angular if executed by another, become potent instruments; her voice, once rather thin, siccant, now gives a soft, surprised speech; and her face is the mirror of her soul. Across it flit the agonies, the joys, of the modern anaemic, overwrought woman. She excels in the delineation of listless, nervous, hysterical, and half-mad souls. She passes easily from the passionate creatures of Dumas and Sardou to the chillier-blooded women of Ibsen and Sudermann, unbalanced and out of tune with their surroundings. Shall we ever forget her reading of Vladimir's letter in Fédora? And yet her assumption of the Russian was a tour-de-force of technic; temperamentally the rôle belongs to the hotter-tongued Bernhardt. With Santuzza, a primitive nature, she accomplished wonders. That miserable, deserted girl, in a lowly Sicilian village, with her qualms of conscience, her nausea, her hunted looks—here was Verga's heroine stripped of all Mascagni's rustling music, the soul showing clear and naked against the sordid background of Cavalleria Rusticana.

The slinking ferocity of Césarine's entrance into her husband's atelier; the scene with Antonine; the interview of Camille with Armand's father; the gracious gayety of Goldoni's La Locandiera:

that hideous battle of an exasperated man and woman before the closed doors in Fernande; Magda's wonderful blush as she meets Kellar, the cold-hearted prig who ruined her—all these stale situations and well-worn types, Magda being an honourable exception, Duse literally recreated.

Then Huneker faced the question that Duse's friends discussed privately and audiences debated publicly: was the D'Annunzio repertory right for her?

"The wisdom of her choice in selecting only D'Annunzio's dramas is not altogether apparent. She will listen to no advice; perhaps she is on a mission; perhaps she wishes to make known everywhere the genius of her young countryman, and to go back with the means to raise upon the border of Lake Albano a great independent theatre, the poet's dream of a dramatic Bayreuth. The D'Annunzio plays are not of the kind that appeal to the larger public. For the student of contemporary drama they are of surpassing interest in their freedom from conventional stage trickery and characterization; La Gioconda, La Città Morta, are really lyric masterpieces in little, though many will wince at the themes, at their bold development and treatment."

In analyzing the plays one after the other, Huneker dwells on the special relationship between D'Annunzio's work and its great interpreter, and he refers briefly to Il fuoco, which, as he says, "set wagging the tongues of the curious by its carefully exposed portraits of a celebrated Italian actress and D'Annunzio himself. In that astonishing performance, the taste of which can hardly be gauged by any but Latin standards, one of the D'Annunzio plays—The Dead City—is set forth in detail. Whether the betrayal of a woman's soul—for D'Annunzio is a true soul-hunter—was made with the concurrence of the subject, no one seems to know. Of the psychologic value of the study there can be but one opinion. It is unique, it is painful, it is appallingly true."

In his analysis of La Gioconda, Huneker describes the sculptor Lucio, his devoted wife Silvia (played by Duse), and the young model and inspiration who gives the play its title. In the central scene, the "wife meets the woman, who is young, beautiful, strange, and absolutely enamoured of the sculptor. Of her sincerity there is no doubt."

This situation—the basic triangle—prefigured the real-life situation that was to confront Duse not many months later. In the theatre she dealt with the drama in what Huneker calls a revelation of "imagination and technic." And he says further: "Her entire assumption is on the plane of exalted realism. . . . D'Annunzio has not before created such a noble woman. Lucio is only a variant of his typical man. . . . Silvia is unique. Silvia is adorable as Duse presents her. Throughout this most human among actresses is in constant modulation; her very silence is pregnant with suggestion. She is the exponent of an art that is baffling in its coincidence with nature. From nature what secret accounts has this Italian not overheard?"

Duse's American mission had not achieved its main purpose, and she did not return to Italy with large sums of dollars. They were needed not so much for the chimeric festival theatre as to pay off the immense debts incurred for the lavish *Francesca* production.

She also returned exhausted. She rested briefly in Paris and was hoping for further rest and peace at La Porziuncola. But peace was not in D'Annunzio's gift; and her stay in Settignano, also brief, was tense and uneasy as usual. To others it was already clear that the poet was tiring of his muse. He had taken a small apartment in Florence for his fugitive love affairs.

In late March Duse was in Vienna, playing *Hedda Gabler* by her beloved Ibsen, as well as *La città morta* and *Francesca*. On the last day of that month she wrote to him: "like those who *will believe* in *your book—so* I will believe in you—because life cannot be separated from art!"

The book she mentions may have been the first book of the *Laudi*, which he completed on 18 April 1903 (the last day of her Viennese season). In the same letter, as if to reassure him, she wrote: "*You are free towards me* as *towards life itself.*"

D'Annunzio may not have taken this guarantee of his freedom entirely seriously; he knew Eleonora's jealousy too well. And as if sensing that her presence in Settignano would disturb him (and his distress her), she stopped off on her return from Vienna at Rapallo, on the balmy Ligurian coast, for some repose. From a letter of his she learned he was preparing to go to Milan, and she wrote: "I plan therefore to go on Monday to the house [La Porziuncola]—because *that same Monday* you are leaving . . ., so I will arrive at the gate of the house without the slightest upset to your plans—not wanting, my son, to disturb them . . . I need privacy, and the house—therefore—*far from you*—that's the only place—home—where I love going."

His book, *Laus vitae*, handsomely produced, appeared in May, and in June Duse went to Rome so he could have Settignano to himself. They had been discussing their usual summer holiday together, and for the months of July and August D'Annunzio planned to take a splendid seventeenth-century house at Nettuno, the Villa del

Bell'Aspetto, built in 1660 by Cardinal Costaguti, purchased by Camillo Borghese, husband of Pauline Bonaparte, and at that time still in the Borghese family. Eleonora went out to Nettuno to take a look at the house and wired her approval. She also wired that she would return to Settignano only when he made it clear that he wanted her there.

But even when she got there the situation was unstable. D'Annunzio was involved in one or more affairs, making no effort to keep them a secret from her. From the solitude of La Porziuncola she sent notes, delivered by her long-suffering maid Nina, to the more splendid Capponcina: ". . . you *know* that to *graft* one love on to another means to risk the life and the death of both—*you know it*—*you know it*. . . . Have you really *exhausted* the desired . . . *experience?*—And if it isn't exhausted, distance will only make it more acute—not to mention the fact that I will be at your side, sighing. You will continue—if we do go away—to inoculate *me* with the anguish of the letters that will arrive. . . . Of all of us (perhaps) I *alone truly love.* . . . While I *bow* before—and exalt—your art—and bless having served it faithfully and nobly, I implore you—for a moment—to think also about *my* art, I mean the strength I need for it!— . . . You have believed me too *generous* or too *passive*—As a woman, I am only a poor woman who loves you—and as artist, I need for you to be proud of me—so as not to lose the *voice of my art!* . . ."

He apparently asked her to come with him to Anzio but also to allow his other *experience* to continue. From her house to his, she answered on 24 June: "Gabri—to accept living in Anzio on the terms so *lucidly* expressed in your letter—is absolutely impossible for me. Pointless to discuss it further.—I begged you—You have replied—All is said—The only thing left for me is to go away—"

But D'Annunzio was contemplating a new drama, and Eleonora would sooner leave the poet than abandon the poet's art. "If in three or four months' time, your work is finished, let it then remind you that you need a *soldier.* If it happens, you will write me—summoning me—if not, not. All will be over. . . ."

The two of them reached some sort of agreement, and on 4 July D'Annunzio went to Rome, then on to the villa at Nettuno, where Eleonora joined him. Soon they were joined, too, by the poet's little daughter Cicciuzza. The child's mother, Principessa Gravina, had been behaving more and more strangely. (A jeweler had brought suit for fraud; D'Annunzio had paid the man off, with money borrowed from Treves.) Convinced that the unbalanced mother's influence was affecting the little girl, D'Annunzio took her over for the summer, before enrolling her in the elegant boarding school at Poggio Imperiale, outside Florence.

Years later, Cicciuzza recalled that summer: "My father was writing *La figlia di Jorio*. He had created a study for himself in an attic of the villa with a door that opened on the terrace that was the roof of the building, and the window looked out over the sea. He worked there most of the night; in the morning after an icy 'tub' [the author uses the English word, no doubt quoting her father], he rested until lunch time. The Signora devoted her morning to the infinite treatments her delicate health required, and I went to the sea."

D'Annunzio's new drama, a pastoral tragedy, was set in his native region; it was an idea he had long pondered. Some years previously, he and his old friend, the painter Michetti, had witnessed a horrible scene in the mountain village of Tocco da Casuaria, when a young woman had been chased by a band of drunken, lusting farm-workers in the blazing summer heat. Michetti had made a large painting and a number of studies based on the scene, entitling it *Jorio's Daughter*. The picture was exhibited at the Venice Biennale of 1895.

Now, after years of brooding on the subject, D'Annunzio completed the drama in less than a month. But not all his time at Nettuno was spent in the study. He had brought dogs and horses with him. "Some times all of us went to the riding ring," Cicciuzza wrote, "and my father would ride, while we watched him. I realized that the Signora didn't like these exhibitions; she observed with anxiety all the rider's turns, and every time he took a fence she would turn pale and tremble, but she would stand there even for two hours because she knew he liked it and she would force herself to show him a smiling face."

Whatever his defects as husband or lover, D'Annunzio could be an enchanting father; and for Cicciuzza those summer weeks were unforgettable. The poet played games with her, carved boats from corks for naval battles in his tub; and on one occasion he bought her a puppet theatre and wrote a little play for her. It was to honor Duse's return after an absence, and the text was about the arrival of a desired guest: "The little September roses have already recognized her." "Who can it be?" went the refrain, and the jubilant answer was: "La Signora! La Signora!"

On the night of 29 August he wrote the last lines of *La figlia di Jorio*, as the strange, gypsy-like heroine Mila, sacrificing her life for her lover, cries "La fiamma è bella!," "The flame is beautiful!"—a line that was to become famous in Italy, imitated, parodied, and even carved in Gothic script over the fake medieval fireplaces fashionable in many turn-of-the-century villas.

On finishing an important work, D'Annunzio liked to celebrate by reading it for a few friends. For the first hearing of *La figlia di Jorio*, the little audience at the villa included, of course, Duse (for whom the part of Mila was written), Michetti, Scarfoglio, and a faithful friend, Tenneroni. Matilde Serao, Scarfoglio's wife, was not present; his infidelities, even more numerous and sordid than D'Annunzio's, would soon lead to a legal separation.

There was another, secret listener: Cicciuzza, who had silently got out of bed and climbed to the studio, where she stayed behind the closed door. "The harmonious voice recited the verses, and I would have stayed there all night, but accidentally I bumped against the door. Signora Duse, as if impelled by a presentiment, came and opened and I found myself clasped to her heart, as she covered with kisses my eager face, raised to her."

One morning Cicciuzza couldn't find the Signora in the house. "She's left us, and she won't come back again," her father said with some exaggeration. Actually, she had gone to Settignano to pack her trunks for a little tour that would take her to Switzerland, Germany, and London.

From Zurich on 8 September 1903, she wrote: "Ah, why does your *so-called 'joie de vivre'* have to massacre my soul so?" And in the same envelope she enclosed an article from an Italian paper on the Keats–Fanny Brawne letters. Later, from London, she tells of going to Westminster Abbey: "I looked for the written name of him who resembles you [Shelley], and as I hunted, I was thinking of Gabri, of Cicciuzza, of Mila di Codra."

In the archives of the D'Annunzio villa, the Vittoriale, among Duse's countless letters and telegrams (D'Annunzio saved everything, even the most trivial scrap of paper), there is an undated letter, perhaps written during this tour. In it, Eleonora finally opens her heart on the subject of *Il fuoco*:

". . . If I ask too much of you, remember it's because you promised so much—so much you promised, remember. Remember, *after the Book*, how much you promised.

"How could I have *lived* if you hadn't promised? . . . Ever since the book, *you, you* promised me to change your life. . . .

"Remember that I faced the mob, still believing, still concealing in my heart *the secret of the two of us*—which is *not*, not that of the Book—

"The Book is *perverse* in its feeling (I am not speaking of *art*, alas!!!)

"It is a book based on the physical disgust for an old woman, in a *young* man, who desires a young girl—

"nothing else!—

"For the victory of *your art*, something quite different would have been of far more use to you!

"If you had written a *Book of love* and of *Praise* for her, for the one whom we hoped was '*ours*,'

"I swear to you that I would have *blessed the book.* . . ."

While Eleonora continued her tour, Gabriele was already thinking of the cast for *La figlia di Jorio*. At the beginning of August, even before completing the drama, he had written to Michetti: "To perform such a tragedy, virgin actors are necessary, full of pent-up life, with sober and eloquent gestures, with a voice sustained by the laws of inner song. Because here all is song and mime. Where to find them?"

Does this sound like a description of Duse? Her voice was no doubt sustained by the law of inner song; but D'Annunzio—after publishing a novel describing her physical aging—could hardly have thought of her now as a "virgin" actress. Perhaps, though the play was officially inspired by her, he was already harboring other ideas. At the beginning of their pact, he had betrayed her professionally with Bernhardt; now a worse betrayal, at the end of their love, awaited her.

In September he was back at La Capponcina, and one evening he went to see the actor Virgilio Talli, playing at the Arena Nazionale in Florence. During an interval, D'Annunzio sent Talli a message, asking him to come up to Settignano the next day for a talk.

Actually, poet and actor had known each other as boys. A rarity among Italian actors, Talli had received a serious formal education and had been a classmate of D'Annunzio's at the prestigious Collegio Cicognini in Prato. As their conversation began the next day, the poet recalled those old times and their few encounters since then. Talli records in his autobiography:

"Afterwards he revealed his intention of entrusting to me his *Figlia di Jorio* provided I would make possible (and he made no secret of the importance of his request) the splendid collaboration of Eleonora Duse in the first performances of the tragedy, which, at a later meeting, would be scheduled for Milan, Florence, and Rome. Since, at the outset, he said he was well aware of the 'tormenting sensibilities' of the stage and was afraid of troubling them, it was easy for me to reply that his invitation was the fulfilment of a cherished dream, not only of mine, but also of Calabresi and Irma Gramatica [other members of Talli's troupe]; and still, as far as the collaboration of Signora Duse was concerned, I could not answer him then and there without some hesitation. . . ."

At this time, Irma Gramatica was in her early thirties (her birth-date is reported variously as 1870 and 1873), and already famous. Daughter of a prompter and of a dresser, she had grown up in the theatre, and—as a child—had known Duse during the first South American tour with Cesare Rossi. She had already played opposite Zacconi in a repertory that ranged from the usual French dramas to Schiller and Shakespeare. And Talli was right to suspect she would be reluctant to step back into the ranks and allow the illustrious older actress to take first place. Talli may have had some reservations of his own. As 'artistic director' of his company, he staged all the productions; and he was particularly admired for the coherence, the fusion, he was able to create. It was unlikely that Duse, at this time in her life and with her dominant personality, could fuse easily with actors she had not known long. Though she often berated and maligned her own company—players like Rosaspina, Galvani, Mazzanti—many of them had been with her for years and knew how to do her bidding.

Talli spoke with Gramatica that same evening; and as he had anticipated, the actress was less than overjoyed. The Milan opening, yes. That she would cede to Duse. But Florence? Rome? They would have to wait and see. For the moment Talli pressed her no further. It was simply agreed that D'Annunzio and Duse would collaborate with the Talli–Gramatica–Calabresi company. Gabriele seems not to have told Eleonora immediately about this step. The pile of telegrams she sent him from London contain no reference to Talli or Gramatica, though she says she is "all ready for Mila."

As usual, Gabriele had personal concerns on his mind. In September, during a fox hunt in the Roman Campagna, he had met a fascinating, beautiful young widow, Marchesa Alessandra di Rudinì Carlotti. Daughter of a former prime minister of Italy, Alessandra was twenty-seven; her husband, Marchese Carlotti, had been dead for three years. The marriage had been stormy, but had produced two children. Mercurial (there was madness in the family), blonde and blue-eyed, an expert horsewoman, the Marchesa was calculated to arouse the interest of the poet, who—with his mania for nicknames—immediately began calling her "Nike," presumably because she reminded him of the Winged Victory.

After the talk with Talli in Settignano, D'Annunzio returned to the Villa Borghese at Nettuno, then to Rome and to the courting of Alessandra. The two of them were in Florence that September for the marriage of Alessandra's brother; and their affair, consummated shortly thereafter, was soon openly mentioned in the newspapers.

Word of *La figlia di Jorio* was also circulating. Talli received telegrams from solicitous friends, advising him against trying to work with Duse. For the crucial part of Aligi, the young shepherd-artist, D'Annunzio wanted Talli to engage an inexperienced young apprentice lawyer, Gualtiero Tumiati, whom D'Annunzio had seen in an amateur performance that summer. Unwilling to risk a completely raw recruit in a major part, Talli insisted on Ruggero Ruggeri, a member of his company. D'Annunzio gave in; but he continued making suggestions. Now he wanted Giacinta Pezzana, the older actress who had encouraged Eleonora in the early days in Naples; but Pezzana, in spite of her economic difficulties, asked an exorbitant fee and thus eliminated herself.

To prepare the role of Mila, Eleonora—on returning from London—visited the Abruzzo, where she studied the speech and movements of the women of that remote and, in those days, exotic region. But the trip caused further exhaustion; when she returned to Settignano she was at the end of her strength. D'Annunzio was in residence part of the time, with Cicciuzza, who would not enter Poggio Imperiale until December. The poet and Marchesa Rudini were in constant secret correspondence; they met in Milan sometime before Christmas.

But D'Annunzio spent the holidays at La Capponcina, with Eleonora next door. This is perhaps when she wrote the undated note, sent by hand to D'Annunzio (and now preserved at the Vittoriale): "I am here, suffering, *dying* of my life, and I don't even have the apparent freedom of a few hours' pause, amid the *green* that I love so, and am worthy of loving. You suffer (you say) and are repelled (I know) at *seeing me on those cursed boards*. I suffered at it long before you—all my childhood, all my youth—feeling I deserved to *live* life, and not only to simulate it."

Immediately after the New Year, she left for Marseilles and opened there on 3 January; she remained in the hated city for the inside of a week. Her poor health was now a matter of public concern, discussed freely in the newspapers. On 20 January, Marco Praga wrote to Talli: "Is Duse really seriously ill? Or is something concealed behind the illness? Is it absolutely certain she won't play in Milan?"

Praga went on to point out a danger in Duse's brief appearance in the new work: if it should succeed when she played Mila, then fail after she left the troupe, the drama and the other interpreters would suffer.

Michetti, at the poet's insistence, had designed the sets, which were under construction in Milan. Another artist had gone to Francavilla to work with the painter on costumes, props, and other items. Friends of D'Annunzio and of Michetti had contributed authentic fabrics, shawls, jewels, to enhance the realism and beauty of the staging.

The premiere was set for 2 March, and rehearsals were already under way in Verona, where D'Annunzio had given a special reading to the assembled troupe. Duse, in her distant hotel rooms, had already learned her lines; sometimes she slept with the manuscript under her pillow. Then, from Marseilles, she wrote to Gabri, asking him to postpone the premiere a short time, so that she could have a few days' rest.

D'Annunzio's reply was curt: impossible. And from Cannes, on 9 January, she wrote him a letter giving up the part. "With this, I will have given everything to your beautiful destiny—and my heart breaks—now, this last time, so be it!"

From Cannes to Nice, Nice to Menton: each brief appearance brought her closer to Italy, to home, and to the reality of her situation. In Genoa, fatigue and the emotional strain felled her. Ill, she took to her bed; and she lay in the hotel room, suffering, for nearly a month.

Her friends came to her aid: Laura Groppallo from Nervi, Matilde Serao from Naples. But Gabri did not come. On 25 February she wrote to him in Milan: "horrible—horrible."

She had received a telegram from him, from Rome, where he had obviously gone to see Alessandra.

> . . . while for *22 days* I have been imprisoned between bed and window of a horrid hotel room—While for *six weeks, ever since Cannes,* I have begged, I have telegraphed to have an hour's talk—in the days when I was *dying of grief* in Cannes, in Menton, in Nice—where I wired you those true words, not receiving permission to see you:
> *the heart dies*
> from San Remo—where I told you I was in agony . . . then *here,* where I arrived with a fever, and almost unconscious of my words and actions—and *here* . . . where, in going from Rome to Milan and from Milan to Rome, you have to make a *special effort* not to pass— here—where you find the hotel address to complain at a moment when your work seems to you (though it isn't) in danger—
> here, finally—where I felt the agony of every hour— alone— alone—alone—alone—

always alone—with my strength, with my faith—with the loyalty of the *pact* I made with you (and maintained)

alone—while, forced into it, I gave *even Mila* to your 'beautiful destiny' rather than delay it one hour!—while I struggle not to see, not to live what my destiny and your spirit, blind and furious, are making of my life! . . . You found the way to go to Rome (for the 4th time)—but not for *one hour* to the person who was risking death *here*, alone—and who has worked, *worked* for you, and has given her all for your destiny! . . .

Go,—go—God save you from yourself!

From *your self* may God save you!

From today on—assume that the *death* of the whole body has freed me from this death of the soul!—assume that I am *really dead* for you— . . .

D'Annunzio managed to deliver another blow when he sent someone to collect the Mila costume Duse had already had prepared. Matilde Serao was there to witness the event, and to hear her recite, from beginning to end, the entire *Figlia di Jorio.* "It was mine," Duse said, "mine, and they took it from me!"

She continued writing to Gabriele, sometimes more calmly, as in the letter of 26 February, when she was thinking of going to Sicily for her convalescence. Instead, she went to Rome, settling in the Hotel Bristol. Gabriele was already in Milan, supervising the final, feverish rehearsals. On the day of her arrival in Rome, 28 February, she dashed off a letter to him, still resentfully analyzing his soul: ". . . pride, healthy and pestilential . . . no loyalty of the man in you towards woman . . . if you do not have pleasure, either through art or through the flesh (which, the more you feed it, the hungrier it is), you feel *no* impulse of tender pity for the creatures that you *know* love you!"

The letter is signed simply *io.* I.

The same day, or night, she wrote again, to speak of the imminent opening:

"Alas! I send *every good wish.* If my own ill-fate has prevented me from being able to share risks and sufferings for the beautiful work—if my own ill-fate has robbed me of the possibility of playing, even a *few lines* in the beautiful work—

". . . If after six years of assuming responsibilities, with the fortunes of work sometimes good sometimes not; if after six years, the material means—namely, money—and the actors, suitable ones, were lacking to me . . . —alas!—After having *ventured everything* in order to go ahead, my arms fell to my sides, and now, like one who has accepted disaster, I will make amends, working—the one thing I can say is this, the one thing that consoles me: I have not delayed the *beautiful destiny*; and the day when it was impossible for me to keep *Mila*, I donated her—But at the hour of that gift, which was owed and sacred, my heart died. . . ."

And at the end of the letter, after repeating *ogni augurio* (every good wish) three times, she took a separate sheet of paper for a P.S.: "I ask a great favor—The evening of the *first performance*, please do not have me telegraphed by any of those friends who will be charged with sending wires.—I beg you to spare me this—I will wait till *the next day* for a telegram, but a personal one—without having been a burden in the hour of anxiety— . . ."

The premieres of D'Annunzio's plays had always been evenings of tension, of battle; and the cast, on the night of the 2 March opening at the Teatro Lirico, was understandably nervous.

Years later Ruggero Ruggeri, the Aligi, described the event:

"When the curtain rose, the immense crowd plunged into a deep silence from which it never emerged, not even for a moment, during the whole first act, which is quite long. And I well remember what I and everyone else felt. As the curtains closed, a sepulchral silence followed, in the house. We looked at one another, all of us dumbfounded. Was it possible? What was happening? Was the work being received by a cold, hostile silence? But it was as if the audience, under the poetic spell of the work of art, had to make a collective effort to recover itself, to emerge from the stage fiction, and see again the theatre, the actors, the performance behind the poetry.

"The ovation exploded in a formidable din. When the curtains parted once more, we found the whole immense public on its feet, calling for the poet in a tumult of shouts. He appeared, smiling and calm, in his impeccable evening dress, a flower in his buttonhole."

D'Annunzio, after the years of struggle and even of ridicule, had finally triumphed in the theatre; the play was an immense, complete success. Eleonora, who had been in the front line of so many of his battles, was not there to share the conquest, so much of which was also hers. A telegram was despatched—probably by Gabriele himself—to Rome; and in her room at the Bristol, she wrote to him immediately:

"It's almost two—*The victory is yours!* The anxiety stops—my soul is mine again—

"*You have won!* and I bless the fact that nothing was lost on my account—I have lived all day in agony—hours—everything stops—no longer that suffering I felt in inaction. . . . We can say farewell to each other. . . . I say farewell to you—I seem to see my *self* far, far, far away, as if at the bottom of the sea. . . . During these hours as La F. di J. was being performed, I tried to think of a certain wall in *Chioggia*—yes—which is directly over the sea, I remember it so well!—When I was little, three or four years old, my Papà would drop me from there, into the sea, throwing himself in with me—Oh! how my father and I loved each other. . . ."

Then, in a shift of mood, from reminiscent she became accusatory: "Learn—learn that *lying is not possible—in the hour* of the solemn test of hearts—the lie is revealed. You lied to me, and I know it—and you have never been able to conceal the truth—and today I say to you: *farewell.*

"—we are *two*—But I—dead."

After a few performances in Milan the play went on tour, and D'Annunzio promptly returned to Rome. He moved into room 337 of the Grand Hotel, while Alessandra was conveniently close, in number 341 *bis*. Totally involved with his new love, Gabri still did not go to see Eleonora, who bombarded him with letters, sending Nina to the Grand Hotel two, three, even four times a day. Duse's moods were a kaleidoscope, constantly shifting, but always tinged with the hysteria of despair. Eighty years later, the letters are still painful, almost intolerable to read. There is little talk of art. She had been robbed of the pleasure of giving him, at last, an unalloyed triumph. A younger actress had been praised as Mila di Codra; and a younger woman was sharing the poet's love, with shameless publicity that was another mortal blow to Eleonora's pride and privacy.

Still she hoped that this was just another of the passing affairs she had already survived. "Tell me—repeat to me that you *want* me to *wait for you*. . . ."

She even wrote to Alessandra, whom she had never met, a humble, begging letter:

"For love, which absolves and equalizes everything—for love, which understands all and can do all—for a life that is *sacred* to me—and from which I will be separated only in death. . . .

"For the profound respect and the profound compassion I have for a woman's heart, for the respect I have for you, whom I address *soul to soul*—to you, woman and lover at this hour—to you I speak, and what I say to you and ask of you—*with loyal spirit*—ready and determined to understand all, I wish for you—for me—that for love and with love what I say to you may be received, above any petty indulgence and ridiculous formality. . . . I cannot interrogate the person I love, he cannot answer, he cannot because love itself prevents him—Whatever the flight of his spirit may be, he has the right to love, he is worthy of it—

"Believe me, believe me, it is not your secret I ask of you. . . . I cannot help asking you: Tell me, in the name of life itself, are you prepared to sacrifice everything to this love? FOREVER?—totally?—as he merits—forever. . . . I turn to you, to ask if my waiting for the beloved, who is sacred to me, whom—I repeat—I will leave only in death—tell me, measuring *your* love for him, if my waiting will or will not be hopeless. . . ."

Giddy young Alessandra must have been taken aback by this flood of words, this bared emotion, naked suffering. She sent an answer, and it must have been unsatisfactory, for on 11 March Eleonora wrote her again, asking her this time to come and see her. There is no evidence that Alessandra came.

In the Hotel Bristol, again confined to bed, feverish, Duse wrote to Gabri, too. On the same day as her second letter to Alessandra, Eleonora sent him a letter written at dawn: "Now what has happened—that has separated me from you? Am I dead?—no—Where have you gone? Why—why?

"Must I know, I, that *all day*, in the perfume of the air; in the vibrant life of the fields, at races and in joy; that you are with another? What is this that makes you sleep next to her, door by door, in the same hotel?—And I here? . . . Now life appeals to me no more—no more—no more. . . ."

If he did not come to see her, he at least sent her violets and a note, "the *only* thing that could heal me." And she insisted: "Tell me—repeat to me that you *want* me to *wait* for you." And, as in several of her letters during these terrible days, she asked after Cicciuzza, whose loss she also feared: "Ah! don't let her be stolen from me."

Alessandra accompanied Gabriele on visits to Anzio, to Albano—places associated with Eleonora. Still in her hotel room, Duse received visits of condolence from her friends (some of whom may have gloated a little at the fulfillment of their worst predictions); and she vaguely planned a return to work. "I hope to begin work in May," she wrote Gabri, promising to resume "our" work, the plays written for her. Among them she even included La Figlia di Jorio: "O wait for her too, *also* for Mila."

The new play was repeating its Milanese success throughout Italy. After the first four performances, Irma Gramatica, the Mila, had fallen ill and been replaced by Teresa Franchini, the young actress who had been playing the mother, Candia delle Leonesse. On 24 March D'Annunzio was in Florence for the gala opening there. The play arrived in Rome on 2 April.

But Eleonora, still weak, had left the city for Palermo and warmer weather. From Sicily she continued to write and wire Gabriele, but now she spoke chiefly about her resumption of her work. Notes of anguish still creep into the letters, as if in spite of herself: "I swear I have never done you any harm, not I, and I *cannot understand* when you *know* you are making me suffer. Help me." She asked him to remove from La Porziuncola any objects that might wound her, by their associations, on her return there. *"Don't take the photographs* of the dogs," was another plea.

On 15 April, back in Rome at the Bristol, she wrote that she was going that night to *Mila,* as she called the play, in the box of some English friends. Did she actually go? The subsequent letters curiously say nothing. It is logical to suppose that, at the last minute, her nerve failed her and she stayed home. A week later she was in Settignano, where she wrote to a friend asking about a translation of "Ceckov." And thence to Paris; she had to see Worth and buy some dresses for appearances in contemporary plays. Because of Francesca and Anna, "and in the hope of Mila," she had bought nothing from her couturier friend for several years.

The telegrams go on, all through the year 1904. From Paris she wired him, from Germany, from other stops on her travels. Sometimes the communications are practical—she needs trunks from La Capponcina with Cleopatra costumes and props—at other times they are wistful ("Never rancor," she telegraphed from Paris in late May). Gradually they peter out. In the summer there was an exchange of letters that marked the end, practically speaking, of their correspondence for more than a decade. Only a war would restore contact between them.

In mid-July of 1904 Eleonora was at Borca, in the Dolomites. D'Annunzio wrote to her there, from Marina di Pisa (another place rich in associations). He referred to a previous letter: "Now I remember having sent you that greeting, in Rome, with the purest feeling of melancholy and regret. I felt that you were separating from me, the friend, and also from me, the artist, joining the life of your heart and the life of your spirit with a transgression which you yourself should suffer by. . . . The poet—far more proud than the man, by divine right—wanted to give you back absolute freedom with regard to his poetry."

In other words, Duse was free to perform his works or not, and by this time she had chosen—it seemed permanently—not to do so again. This hurt Gabri (who was also hoping she would play in future works of his). He went on to speak of the past:

"You lived at my side for years and years. It seemed to me sometimes that you looked into the depth of my nature and you felt sometimes in me that 'innocence' which I cannot mention, even to those who consider themselves fraternal friends, without their smiling, in mocking incredulity! You looked at me as you looked at trees; and often I felt myself live in your gaze as in the air, with a perfect transparence. . . .

"My imperious need of the violent life—carnal life, the life of pleasure, physical danger, gaiety—has taken me far away. And you—who were sometimes moved to tears at an instinctive movement of mine as you are moved by an animal's hunger or the efforts of a plant to climb over a sad wall—can you hold this need against me? . . ."

The letter is long and, in D'Annunzio's way, persuasive. But Eleonora was not persuaded. Her reply, if it was sent, is not among the hundreds of her letters preserved at the Vittoriale. But her draft of it exists (and drafts of her letters are rare, for she usually wrote in a single outburst). It begins: "Alas!—*Don't alter the truth.*' Don't write the word: *Transgression*

"It was not transgression.

"You wrote me this same word when I was in Marseilles—and there my illness began—"

And she defends her decision not to perform his plays. "Now, for the ill-luck of those days in Rome, blind days, cruel and base, I thought that the best *tone* to adopt among my friends, and enemies, for the mob and the press, and all the human ballast, was to declare myself, on my own initiative, NO LONGER NECESSARY to your work, now that you have won—and will win—I thought that was the only word *suitable* for all—since to disappear from those cursed boards of the stage is not possible for me!

"And all is said.

"—I have nothing further to say that is sayable.

"—The rest dies and lives, lives and dies, every day, with me, *like me.* . . .

"Don't defend yourself, son, because I am not accusing you. . . . Don't speak to me of the dominion, of the *reason* of your 'carnal life,' of your thirst for 'joyous life.'

"—I am sated with those words. For years I have listened to you say them. . . . If the 'life of pleasure' arouses such a thirst in you, in what corner of the world do you delude yourself that you will find it, worthy and enduring? Among what people, who do not have roots in human suffering, will you go and seek to live? . . . What woman's love can you find that is not bound to the same laws of life?—What love, worthy and profound, that lives *only* on pleasure? . . . I leave here tomorrow. To this letter of mine there is no reply. . . ."

Part Three
1904–1924

14
Farewell to the stage

"La Duse announces to me her arrival in Paris," Gégé Primoli wrote in his diary. (The entry is dated simply "1904," but it clearly refers to the spring of that year.) "Edgy, as I know her to be, she is quite the opposite of a restful friend. But we have been friends for twenty-five years, and I have a very sincere admiration and affection for her: she is the most honourable man [le plus honnête homme] and the greatest lady that I know. I left her in Rome distracted, at a loss, on the brink of suicide: she had even bought a pistol, to end it all, for she found herself on the verge of moral and material failure. Now I find her revived, alleviated, calm, healed . . .

"Gratitude overflows from her heart through her eyes and lips. She feels impelled to cry out in gratitude. It's the first time, she says, that she feels this sentiment of *material* gratitude; till now she had felt only moral gratitude. There is a great and generous Jew (the husband of a friend of hers), a noble soul, who made a beautiful gesture. He sounded the depths where the poor woman was drowning, he stretched out a hand to save her. She had contracted 200,000 francs of debts to produce the *Figlia di Jorio*, which her health did not then allow her to play. He paid them, he settled her affairs, he has given her back the peace necessary for her to go on living."

The generous friend was Robi Mendelssohn, who had come to Rome from Berlin during the most tormented days of the separation from Gabriele. In the course of his visit to the Hotel Bristol, Robi had made these practical arrangements, and he took over the management of Eleonora's affairs from then until his death over a decade later.

"Look at life," she said in Paris to Primoli. "For five years I worked to help a being in whose genius I believed; and it is another, who owed me nothing, who helps me. It is the chain of nature . . . I feel the need to thank God—who perhaps doesn't exist! I ask myself what I have done to deserve this deliverance? . . . I had told the *Other* that I was virtually bankrupt. . . . To continue supporting his work I was forced to resume *La Dame aux camélias*—7,000 francs of guaranteed takings. I asked his authorization, since I had contracted to give only his plays. He accepted, but didn't reply directly. Then I gave the *Dame*, whose performance would plug some holes. Before the third act I received a telegram signed Gabriel: 'Is it true you have changed, have renounced the mission?' That wire was a blow straight to the heart. I answered, but how could I go on performing in the state into which that reproach plunged me? Where would I find the strength to go on stage, to say the words and make the gestures? Well, though I was beside myself, I was Marguerite as I had never been before, and I brought the house to its feet. . . ."

She was slowly regaining her physical strength, and Robi had freed her from economic concerns. But there was the question of her repertory. She was no longer "necessary" to Gabriele; but she still looked back on the old plays, those Odettes and Frou-frous, with horror. She thought of Tolstoy, of Chekhov, and of Maeterlinck. At her insistence, Adolfo De Bosis urgently translated Maeterlinck's *Monna Vanna* for her; and to him, too, she cried out her gratitude. "I asked for your help, and you stretched out your hands to me."

On 3 May, only a few weeks after the definitive break with Gabri, Duse bravely opened in Milan, at the Teatro Lirico, the very theatre where, two months previously, *La figlia di Jorio* had had its success. Her repertory now included *Monna Vanna* and *A Doll's House* (Ibsen would become more important than ever to her), but it also included the inevitable *La Dame aux camélias*, with which she began her season.

The critic who signed himself Leporello in the *Illustrazione italiana* found her interpretation of Marguerite different, revitalized; and in his review he also commented favorably on the *chiffons* from *chez* Worth. "In this new incarnation Marguerite moves, enfolded in white pepla, starred with rainbows of diamonds, like a figure of dreams and poetry. . . . You would say the actress means to comprehend the figure and physiognomy of the character in the symbol of that white camellia she offers Armand. . . ."

Her Nora, according to the same critic, was also changed, subtler, gentler, deeper. "She triumphed also in *Monna Vanna*, though even her personal triumph as an actress could not raise the value, the significance of the work, which did not please when it was given in French with Georgette Leblanc, and to which all the talent of our great actress could give only an ephemeral life."

Later that summer, when she was resting in the Tyrol, she wrote to De Bosis again; she had been rereading, probably in a French translation, Ibsen's *John Gabriel Borkman*, and she asked her friend to put it into Italian: "I have reread the work in this first peace of the mountains, and it seems to me that I could *attempt* it. But I need the word, the living, lived *word*, like a sword here and there, but *true* always—"

Actually it was several years before *John Gabriel Borkman* appeared in Duse's repertory, and then only briefly. In autumn of 1904, she resumed touring, once more abroad, where she could count on her audience more than in Italy. On 18 October, she wrote to an old friend and colleague, Emma Garzes, after a passing quarrel had created a silence between them:

"I am still I, and I have resumed working, as tenaciously, as never before.

"I go, in the wind, like someone who *knows* his way, though, on the contrary, at the bottom of my heart, I am only obeying an inner rhythm that carries me *always forward*!

"What will I find at the end of such a long race? Perhaps . . . the secret sweetness of having *obeyed* my *fate*—perhaps—. . ."

After appearances in Vienna and Budapest, she played for two weeks in Berlin, opening on 30 October. Ugo Ojetti saw her at this period and described her, in *L'illustrazione italiana* of 7 November:

> By now there is much silver in her black hair, but in her eyes there is perhaps more kindness; her face is paler, but in her voice there is more fervor than ever. Life has refined her and wearied her: her art today, when she chooses, strikes at the heart like a blade. The sky at sunset is deeper than at dawn and gives to him who contemplates it an almost religious anxiousness. I use the word religious. Those who have not heard foreigners speak of Duse do not know the almost fanatical devotion certain audiences have for this miraculous woman. In Italy we admire her, we love her, we are perhaps proud of her as a voice and a countenance that for twenty years have revealed to the world the best of our soul: the spontaneous and mortal passion, the omnipotence of a smile amid tears, a gaze in an anguished silence. . . .
>
> But only the foreigners have adored her. Every time she has returned to Italy, it has seemed that the public, the majority of the public, went to the theatre to judge her coldly, as if she were making her debut that evening and her fame almost harmed her. . . .
>
> Now, at the peak of her glory, she has in Italy neither a theatre nor an audience that is hers. Every time she performs she has to hire the theatre, win the public.

The Italian public was like most of the Italian repertory: it was staid, provincial, timid, unresponsive to international reputations. Though

Duse's endless tours exhausted her, they also stimulated her. In the course of her travels, she met writers, painters, sculptors; in Paris she visited Rodin, went to the Théâtre de l'Oeuvre, where Lugné-Poe was putting on the best of modern drama. On her tour she encountered again her long-time admirer Hugo von Hofmannsthal, now—at thirty—a famous writer. His adaptation of the Greek tragedy *Elektra* had been staged at the Kleines Theater in Berlin in October 1903, under the direction of Max Reinhardt, then at the brilliant outset of his career.

During her Berlin season in the early winter of 1904, Duse saw Hofmannsthal and sought to acquire the rights to *Elektra* in Italian. They had already been given to an Italian director named Fumagalli, but the playwright, through the good offices of Marco Praga, director of the Italian Society of Authors, recovered the rights and gave them to Duse. For her, he prepared a literal French translation of the drama, which Praga then passed on to the critic of the *Corriere della sera*, Giovanni Pozza, to turn into Italian.

While she was in Berlin Duse also met the thirty-two-year-old Gordon Craig, son of Ellen Terry, an artist she much admired. Craig was already acquiring some fame as a stage designer, though his actual theatre experience was still limited. Duse may have met him before, during one of her London seasons; but now she saw him as a possible colleague, and they were soon discussing his designing *Elektra* for her. With him, Duse got to know and admire Isadora Duncan, already very famous, and the exquisite art patron Count Harry Kessler, who had brought Craig to Germany and now commissioned him to prepare the drawings for the projected production of Hofmannsthal's work.

Sometime the following spring Craig sent the preliminary drawings off to Italy (and was paid £300 by Kessler). Duse continued to ponder *Elektra* for another year or so before abandoning the idea. But she did not abandon the idea of using the exciting young Craig; the project remained in the back of her mind, as she continued her tour.

In Vienna, on 8 January 1905, she signed a contract with Lugné-Poe to appear at the little Nouveau-Théâtre in Paris, the performances of her company alternating with performances of Lugné's Oeuvre company, starring his wife Suzanne Desprès and presenting three Ibsen works, *The Master Builder*, *A Doll's House*, and *The Enemy of the People*. Duse would be seen in her old repertory: *La Femme de Claude*, *La Dame aux camélias*, *Magda*, *The Second Mrs Tanqueray*, *Une Visite de noces*, *La locandiera*, *Odette*, and—for one self-indulgent performance—an Ibsen production of her own, *Hedda Gabler*.

The moment Duse reached Paris, in early March, Bernhardt called on her, offering her the Renaissance, because the Nouveau would be too small. "Ma petite, je suis désolée, désolée, désolée," she said, predicting that Duse would have scanty audiences. But Eleonora politely rejected the invitation. The politeness was a shade chilly because, since their last meeting, Sarah had allowed the publication of some *Memoirs*, in which, among other things, she claimed that Duse was a "great actress, but not a great artist," because she had never created anything. Now, in writing a letter to Sarah that began "Pas d'oubli dans mon coeur," Duse referred to that opinion: "At this point, I cannot ignore the judgment you expressed on my art—I cannot ignore it or admit it or forget it, because we do not like to forget that which sets vibrating in us the most fertile of our powers—But . . . the memory of your artistic judgment must not make me forget your first kindnesses, *for each hour in life has its own worth*, and at this moment I like to recall the hour when, to me, you were perfect and good. . . ."

Though she complained about the cramped conditions in the Nouveau-Théâtre, Eleonora enjoyed the collaboration with Lugné and his wife. She had met them the previous year in Turin, but in the course of these weeks in Paris she developed a warm, even intense friendship towards them. And as she did with all her close friends, she affectionately tyrannized them. Lugné carefully preserved the dozens of letters—mostly brief notes—that she sent him during this period. "Take a carriage and come at once," she would command, in a note carried by hand by her maid or the *chasseur* of the Hôtel Continental.

"Today I want to see you. Come at 2. If the weather is good, we'll go out for some air, or we'll fix something else.

"Perhaps this evening we could go to some theatre to see what the other imbeciles are doing. But come."

One of her actors, Ciro Galvani, started keeping a diary at this time (he stopped a few weeks later). He scrawled his notes on scraps of paper—even on the back of his laundry-list—and though they are confused, they give a life-like picture of Duse, the "Signora" as he and all the company called her, at this time, a year after the lacerating break with Gabri, in the full spate of her revived activity.

"On the evening of the 13th called at 9 to the Hôtel Continental to rehearse for the first performance—*La Femme de Claude*. . . . Good impression received from the Signora. Converses a bit with us about the inventions the newspapers print about her. Requests to visit her. . . . She's in good humor—all dressed and with little furpiece—Encouraging words for us. She is sure we'll work with our finest commitment—Away from certain cliques of journalists and rejected authors she is convinced they will see that hers is also a fine company and has excellent members. . . ."

Galvani had to ask her for a 700 lire advance because his wife was ill. With her characteristic generosity towards colleagues, she sent it to him at once; when he tried to thank her, "with a courteous gesture she won't let me finish and asks about my wife's health."

From Paris they went to Brussels, but all performances there were canceled. Duse was indisposed: an abscess on her thigh caused by an infected syringe. It had to be lanced. ("The blood came out with such force," Galvani wrote, "that it struck the wall beyond the bed.") It was twenty-four days before Duse appeared again, and then it was in London, at the elegant new Waldorf Theatre (now the Strand). In addition to the plays done in Paris, she actually revived a play by D'Annunzio, *La Gioconda*, for two performances. The critic of *The Times* said: "The grievous fate of Silvia Settala gives Signora Duse the opportunity for what is, we think, her highest achievement in pure pathos." She also gave two performances of *Hedda Gabler*.

The season was such a success that she extended it through July and into early August; she also appeared at a reception given by Sir Ernest Cassel in honor of King Edward VII. For her appearance she received £500 (she performed the last act of *Adrienne Lecouvreur*). Enrichetta was also in London, and so Duse spent much time with her daughter.

After London she went back to Paris, where the Oeuvre company was rehearsing Maxim Gorky's *The Lower Depths*. The play was two years old and had already been staged in the West by Reinhardt in Berlin. Gorky was much in Eleonora's thoughts (she was reading him in French); and he was also in the news, for he had just been sent into exile, after arrest and imprisonment.

"Bon travail, bon travail, bon travail," she wrote to Lugné, on a day when she was unable to attend rehearsals. "Work with all your heart and your head. Eliminate . . . eliminate that little gray 'scialle' [i.e., shawl—she wrote in French, but dotted her letters with Italian words] with pompons, for Wassilissa. Give her a darker shawl. Eliminate the tiresome stirring of that *Tatare*, who should sleep without snoring so loud. . . . A few more words must be cut at the end of the 2nd act, after the death of Anne, too long; also the speech of the actor, but he isn't bad, it's only the *white shirt* the actor had!

"Tell Luka he's being *Augier*! . . ."

By now Eleonora had adopted Lugné and Suzanne, and was virtually in love with them. "The two of you possess the *best* of happiness," she wrote, "working together, struggling together. I know the worth of dreams and of realities—Assez!"

Though Lugné's Gorky was a great critical success, the struggle continued. At the fourth performance the take dropped to nothing; "it became preferable," he recalls in his memoirs, "for me to pay and not perform." Duse learned of his straits, and with one of her familiar notes, she summoned him to her hotel. She wanted to make him a proposal: she would join the Oeuvre company for one performance, a benefit, taking over the role of Wassilissa, which she would play in Italian with the French-speaking cast.

"Snobisme aidant," Lugné says, the house was crammed. But what most surprised the director was the abnegation of Duse, who kept herself in the background, allowing Suzanne Desprès, in a lesser role, to shine. Ticket sales enabled the company to pay all its debts, and Lugné asked Duse what her *cachet*—her fee—would be.

"What do you pay the child who plays the fool so well in the first act?" she asked.

Ten francs, she was told. "I want the fool's *cachet*," she said then. She had the two écus mounted in a crystal block and kept them always on her bureau. She also took to signing herself, when she wrote to Lugné, "Sociétaire de l'Oeuvre." She and the director had long talks about Ibsen, whom they both revered. Lugné had introduced a number of the great man's plays to France and had actually met him in Oslo some years earlier. Eleonora and Lugné discussed *Peer Gynt*, Eleonora revised the Italian translation of *Rosmersholm*, and the Frenchman introduced her to *When We Dead Awaken*. "My head is Rosmerizing itself," she wrote to him, ". . . But Rebecca is more pure and more . . . (what?) than Hedda. But Hedda is right. Every WILL is right."

Even as she was immersed in their work and in her own, she was looking back over her life and career, and in that August of 1905 she wrote to Suzanne:

"I write at the moment when I am going to my work. I believe you can understand how much 'life' there is in that word 'work.'

"I feel and I hope that 'a tomorrow' of our work and our art lies in you—and this is why I speak to you and tell you—you alone—the sweet sorrow there is for me in this decision—now taken—to leave my work.

"It is said.

"I look at my day! It is beautiful, for I have given it everything, all of myself. To my art I have given my love, my strength, my youth, my life: all—all—I have therefore decided that, this year, my work will be directed towards freedom. Your friend [Lugné] will tell you the details.

"You will find me always, when you want—at the hour of your strength, of your joy, of your work, and of the art that will have Victory."

But the year she predicted was to stretch out and become four years before she retired, and then the retirement was only temporary. First she made yet another attempt to find her place in Italy, in the Italian theatre. And on 1 October 1905 she joined Virgilio Talli, the actor-director whose company had given *La figlia di Jorio*. She appeared in one of her old war-horses, Sardou's *Fernande*, but at the end of that month she performed *The Lower Depths* at the Teatro Manzoni in Milan, with Talli. Her success in Italy equaled her success in Paris.

Talli apparently had different ideas from Lugné about the work, and at the first rehearsal there were difficulties with Duse. As soon as she was back in her hotel she wrote him an apology: "This morning I didn't *know* what you wanted and I cost you irritation and effort . . . now I have understood the *whole mechanism* of the third act, and I will do my best—and well—to avoid *betraying the conception*. I hope that my 'super-accursed' quality of prima donna will not be a burden for you or me. You believe I am 'alive' and therefore capable of comprehending and *obeying* one who has the light and grace of art in his soul."

She was hoping to form a company with Talli for further productions in Italy, but somehow it did not come about. He went off on tour with Ruggeri and Irma Gramatica, and Duse again went abroad.

In August 1905, after the London appearances and before returning to Paris, Duse had dismissed her company and her company-manager Ettore Mazzanti. Now she asked Lugné-Poe to take on the job. Though he had managed his own company for some years and had taken it on tours abroad, Lugné was anything but an experienced impresario. Still, he was a friend, an admirer, and a man of sensitivity and culture. His memoirs also suggest that he was something of a diplomat, good at handling the often difficult and demanding Signora. He was to organize an itinerary including Copenhagen and Stockholm, where Duse had not been seen for a decade, and also Kristiania (as Oslo was then called), where she had never played: the city of Ibsen. For Eleonora the journey to Kristiania was to be not just a tour but a pilgrimage. As Lugné later wrote: "The excitement of that journey, the enthusiasm, warmed Eleonora Duse's heart for five months. A strange fever took possession of her, no doubt the last of her life."

She was rehearsing *Rosmersholm* in Florence that late autumn of 1905, and she wired Lugné to come at once. He came and helped her rehearse the play between her performances at the Teatro della Per-gola. *Rosmersholm*, Lugné reported, aroused "the hilarity of the old Tuscan city. Poor Eleonora!" "Yesterday they booed Ibsen," she wired him. "It would serve them right to give Augier!"

In Bologna, Milan, Turin, it was the same. They wanted *Odette*, *La Femme de Claude*, but she insisted on giving them Ibsen. Finally, in Trieste she encountered success. It had been reported in the news-papers that Ibsen was gravely ill, and before the performance of *Rosmersholm* Duse asked the critic Silvio Benco to read an *augurio* addressed to the author. The anonymous chronicler of the Teatro Verdi recorded in the ledger: "The initiative was considered inopportune by the public, though the work was inspired by the loft-iest ideas. The performance then ensued triumphantly. . . ." She sent off a happy telegram to Paris, where she then went to meet Lugné.

The tour began in Brussels and Amsterdam. On her way to the next appearances in Copenhagen, Eleonora stopped off in Berlin, where she saw Enrichetta, who was studying there, and the Mendelssohns. Giulietta Mendelssohn had become a friend and supporter of Isadora Duncan and had even defended her when, because of her illegitimate pregnancy (by Gordon Craig), the stiff Berlin aristocracy wanted to close Isadora's "immoral" school of the dance. One evening Isadora and Craig came to the Mendelssohns' for dinner, along with Enrichetta and Duse. Enrichetta appealed to Craig, saying, "Do help Mother; she has no one to help her." Isadora added her pleas to Enrichetta's.

In Berlin, Duse learned from the Danish author Herman Bang that Ibsen was paralyzed. The news saddened her, and her gloom increased when she reached Copenhagen only to find that Georg Bran-des, the country's leading intellectual, was out of the city, and his brother, the playwright Edvard, seemed to avoid her. She was not allowed to play in the Royal Theatre. Then old King Christian IX died, and the court went into mourning. Duse did not appear at all, and moved forward her journey to Oslo.

She arrived there ill. Nevertheless, she was touched, on entering the Grand Hotel, to see Ibsen's chair proudly displayed. She was eager to see the man himself. Despite her poor health, she wrote a note the first morning and sent it off to Ibsen's wife, with some flowers: "My first greeting, the homage of my visit to Kristiania, belongs to you. I have come to offer a few hours of my work and my respect to the genius who permits us to believe in the fertility of our talents and who, for that same reason, gives me faith in my efforts and light in my hours of interpretation and good will."

Madame Ibsen accepted the flowers, but sent no reply beyond a telephone message to the hotel: Ibsen could no longer receive guests or even greetings.

"I entered her room," Lugné recounted, "I found her in the huge white greatcoat that she liked to wear. She was frightened, distraught, her features drawn, haggard, as if life were eluding her."

She asked him: "What to do? What to do? What to do?"

Lugné did his best to cheer her up, but she felt really ill. She had already postponed her opening from 2 February to 5 February. Now she postponed it again to the 7th. Fortunately her inventive manager succeeded in finding an exceptional doctor whose idea of treating Duse was to play the 'cello for her. Soon he had her laughing, and she began to feel more fit.

"The next morning we set out, Duse and I, around noon for the street where Henrik Ibsen lived. She had bought some Norwegian boots; she was determined to go on foot. We walked around the castle, turned left; and at noon we were opposite the corner window where, each day at about noon, it was possible to see Dr Ibsen himself, sometimes with a secretary or an assistant.

"Despite the cold, despite the glare, Eleonora Duse waited.

"Who is the man who would not be profoundly moved, even thirty years later, at the memory of witnessing that mute, pathetic interview . . . On the sidewalk, facing his house, Eleonora Duse waiting for the silhouette of the old poet behind the great window!"

Not even the outline of the writer was to be seen. Lugné and Duse went back to the hotel in silence. In Kristiania, at the National Theatre, Duse gave three performances in four days: *Rosmersholm*, *Hedda Gabler*, and *La Gioconda*. She managed to squeeze in the D'Annunzio play by giving a 1 p.m. matinée, before taking the evening train. "She was in a kind of frenzy," according to Lugné, "recalling all the stages of work of her earlier life." The Norwegian critics were puzzled by her Ibsen: some said she had found the true Norwegian spirit, others praised her Mediterranean warmth.

While she was in Kristiania she insisted on buying some pieces of old furniture, heavy wooden chairs and cupboards—adding to the troupe's already considerable baggage—for her future Ibsen productions. Norway captivated her: she allowed photographers to take her picture on stage, and she was delighted when a crowd of students and admirers accompanied her to the station. From the platform of the train, where she stood a long time in the icy air, she kept crying "au revoir, au revoir!"

Stockholm, where she was to play in the Royal Opera House, brought her abruptly back to earth. The theatre's directors had decreed her repertory: *La Dame aux camélias*, *La Femme de Claude*, *Magda*, *La locandiera*, *Une Visite de noces*, the old, tired standbys. She fell ill and kept to her bed for two weeks, without performing. Then she did, reluctantly, appear, before returning to Copenhagen to give the performances canceled because of the king's death.

When the tour ended in late February, she came back to Florence. She had already given up La Porziuncola and taken a little house with a garden and some roses (to compensate for the loss of the famous roses of La Porziuncola) in Via della Robbia, not far from the studio of Michele Gordigiani (father of Giulietta Mendelssohn), in what was then suburban Florence, near the Cimitero degli Inglesi.

In June she went to London to take part in the jubilee of Ellen Terry, Craig's mother and an old friend. To celebrate the fifty years of the great actress's career, there was a gala matinée at Drury Lane. "The two things about it which touched me most deeply," Ellen Terry wrote in her memoirs, "were my reception by the crowd who were waiting to get into the gallery when I visited them at two in the morning, and the presence of Eleonora Duse, who came all the way from Florence just to honour me. She told me afterwards that she would have come from South Africa or from Heaven, had she been there!" The gala performance lasted five hours and included not only performances by Duse and Caruso, but also scenes from Shakespeare, some Gilbert and Sullivan, and a minstrel-show performance of "O Dem Golden Slippers."

Isadora Duncan's *My Life* is not a reliable source (it appeared posthumously and was rewritten—or, in part, written—by other hands); but her description of the collaboration between Duse and Gordon Craig in Florence, that summer of 1906, has the ring of accuracy, especially to those familiar with the personalities involved. First of all—though Isadora does not say this—Craig must have made Eleonora scrap all that heavy, authentic Nordic furniture she had bought in Kristiania and expensively shipped to Italy. "The first discussions began," Isadora writes, "discussions in which I played the interpreter for Craig, who could understand neither French nor Italian, and Duse, who knew not a word of English. . . . I only hoped to make each happy and to please both. This I accomplished by a certain amount of misrepresentation. I hope some of the lies which I told in interpreting may be forgiven me, for they were in a holy cause. I wanted this great production to come off, and it would never have done so if I had really told Eleonora Duse what Craig said to her; and if I had repeated Duse's orders to Craig exactly as she expressed them."

Ibsen's description of the first-act setting of *Rosmersholm* reads like this (in Rolf Fjelde's translation): "The living room at Rosmersholm, spacious, old-fashioned and comfortable. Down-stage right, against the wall, is a tiled heating stove decorated with fresh-cut birch boughs and wild flowers. . . . Around the walls hang portraits, both old and more recent, of clergymen, military officers and public officials in uniform. The window is open; likewise the doors to the hall, and the front door to the house. Outside, an avenue of huge, ancient trees is visible, leading out to the estate. The twilight, of a summer evening, after sundown."

Craig, as Isadora reports, "had been pleased to see the interior of a great Egyptian temple with enormously high ceiling, extending upward to the skies, with walls receding into the distance. Only, unlike an Egyptian temple, at the far end there was a great, square window. In Ibsen's description, the window looks out into an avenue of old trees. . . . Craig had been pleased to see this in dimensions of ten metres by twelve. It looked out upon a flaming landscape of yellows, reds and greens, which might have been some scene in Morocco. . . ."

Duse, presented with the design, was disconcerted. "I see this as a small window."

Craig, according to Isadora, thundered in English: "Tell her I won't have any damned woman interfering with my work!"

Isadora's discreet translation was: "He says he admires your opinions and will do everything to please you."

She assured Craig further that Duse considered him a great genius and would not make any further suggestions. Though Isadora was still nursing Deirdre, her daughter by Craig, she managed to spend long hours interpreting—or rather pretending to interpret—for the two artists. Finally Craig shut himself up in the theatre to paint the sets, giving Isadora strict orders to keep Duse out.

The dancer took the actress for long walks in the Boboli Gardens, among the statues and the great beds of flowers. "I shall never forget the picture of Duse, walking through those gardens. She did not look like a woman of this world, but rather like some divine image of Petrarch or Dante, who found herself upon the terrestrial sphere by some mischance. All the populace made way for her and stared at us with respectful but curious eyes. Duse did not like to be stared at by the public. She took all the little by-paths and small alleys, to avoid the popular gaze. . . . As soon as we found ourselves alone, she would pull off her hat and let her raven locks, just turning grey, free to the breeze. Her wonderfully intellectual forehead and her marvellous eyes—I shall never forget them. Sorrowful eyes, yet when this face lit up in enthusiasm, I have never seen a more beatific expression of joy."

The sets were ready, and Duse was allowed to see them. "She met me in the lobby of her hotel. She was enveloped in a big brown fur coat, with a brown fur cap which resembled that of a Russian Cossack. It was placed at an angle over her eyes. For although Duse at times in her life by the advice of her kind friends patronized the fashionable dressmakers, she could never wear a modish dress or look in any way chic. Her dress was always up on one side and down on the other. Her hat was always crooked. No matter how costly her garments, she never seemed to wear them, but appeared to condescend to carry them on her. . . ."

Craig was already at the theatre, and when they got there they could hear his voice inside, behind the curtain, yelling at his assistants. "The curtain slowly rose. . . . Never have I seen such a vision of loveliness. Through vast blue spaces, celestial harmonies, mounting lines, colossal heights, one's soul was drawn toward the light of this great window which showed beyond, no little avenue but the infinite universe. Within these blue spaces was all the thought, the meditation, the earthly sorrow of man. . . . Eleonora's hand grasped mine. I felt her arms around me. . . ."

When Eleonora could recover her voice, she rushed to the stage, called Craig from the wings, and poured out her praises in a flood of Italian superlatives that Isadora was hard put to translate. Then Duse assembled the whole company and, according to Isadora, said: "It is my destiny to have found this great genius, Gordon Craig. I now intend to spend the rest of my career (*sempre, sempre*) devoting myself only to showing the world his great art."

Whatever Duse's actual words, her joy and admiration were genuine and immense; and she was soon broaching further projects, more Ibsen productions, with the young genius who seemed to offer— as, in a different way, D'Annunzio had—a new vision of the theatre and her art.

Only a few weeks before the Florence opening of *Rosmersholm*, Duse had engaged a new actor, the twenty-three-year-old Guido Noccioli, a former Rasi pupil. Noccioli played only bit parts, but he kept a diary, which survives and gives a backstage view of the actress, seen, of course, from a certain distance. Noccioli did not appear in *Rosmersholm*, but he observed and described the preparations. On 4 December, the day before the opening, he recorded: "Terrible day. Rehearsal with the new set for *Rosmersholm*, the Ibsen drama. The Signora adores this work. The new set of which I speak is conceived by a young English painter: Gordon Craig, natural son of the great actor Irving. [Noccioli gets this wrong; Craig was the son of the architect Edward Godwin.] It is a strange set, all green and illuminated by 10 spotlights. The furniture is green, of canvas like the scenery: at the rear a big glass door is covered by a blue veil. More veils at the sides. A dream! Will the public like it? The Signora is enthusiastic."

The next night, he continued, "Usual capacity audience. The Signora is incredibly nervous. At 7 she is already dressed and made up; she sends for Orlandini [a leading actor in the troupe] and rehearses with him a scene in the second act, suggesting many new things; then she sends for the actor Robert and with him rehearses a scene in the fourth act. At a certain point, she stops and corrects the actor, who keeps answering: 'Yes, Signora! Yes, Signora! . . .' The Signora continues and at a certain point the actor forgets to say 'Yes, Signora' and says simply 'Yes, yes.' The Signora gives him a withering look, then says sharply: 'You are being disrespectful!' And she goes and shuts herself up in her dressing room."

Isadora Duncan's eye was sharper to catch visual details: "Duse, with her marvelous instinct, had donned a gown of white with great wide sleeves that fell at her sides. When she appeared, she looked less like Rebecca West than a Delphic Sybil. With her unerring genius, she adapted herself to every great line and to each shaft of light which enveloped her. She changed all her gestures and movements. She moved in the scene like some prophetess announcing great tidings."

Craig, too, was delighted. After the performance he wrote to his friend and musical collaborator Martin Shaw: "It was a success & is—Duse was magnificent—threw her details to the winds and went in. She has the courage of 25! She, Ibsen and I played our little trio out and came home happy. I have this morning rec'd a lovely letter from her—she asks me to work with her in joy & freedom and do 3 more Ibsen plays at once. She says 'I will never have any other scenes—any more of that other *horrid family*!' Is it not happiness to find this still alive in the theatre. What I talk—and I think it's *necessary* to talk—is not always what I do. One must shout out *Passage to India*! in order to book travellers to Dover or Maidstone."

The reviews in the Florence papers were also favorable, though the audience seemed to have some reservations, shared by young Noccioli. But he, like the Florentines, was lost in admiration of the Signora, whose acting achieved, he said, "dizzying heights." When the performance was over, he noted, she was in excellent humor. With Craig, she seemed to be making a fresh start, heading in a new direction. As she would soon discover, she had reached another dead end.

By three o'clock on the day after the premiere, she was rehearsing a new Italian play, *Maria Salvestri*, by a Florentine critic, Enrico Corradini. It went on that night, and flopped. She was also rehearsing other repertory plays—*Monna Vanna*, *Une Visite de noces*, and *La locandiera*—because some members of the troupe were new.

After Florence there was a benefit performance in Milan; then the troupe moved on to Genoa, where *Rosmersholm* was to be given at the Teatro Paganini. Noccioli recorded the events of the day:

"A black evening at first. The Signora's nerves were incredibly tense. She had the set shifted two or three times. According to her, it has been cut down. Since all the props for this production have already been shipped to Vienna, the property man had to manage as best he could. This caused worse nerves. Finally we began. Magnificent house and big success, especially in the third act. The Signora calms down again. As she goes out to bow, she says to Orlandini: 'You see how they understand? All people of the sea are pensive, meditative. They love Ibsen, they have more poetry. The sea, the sea makes them poets.' Orlandini nods, but after the Signora has gone, I realize he does not share her view."

Neither did the Genoese critics. Duse's "nerves" returned, and she went off at Christmas to Rapallo—with its memories of Boito—for some rest. She felt ill, returned to Genoa, where Enrichetta joined her; then went to Nervi.

In Nice early in February 1907, *Rosmersholm* was again included in the repertory. Craig had left Florence after the premiere there, but he and Duse had been exchanging telegrams. She confirmed that he was to design *The Lady from the Sea* for her, and, instead of a Tintagel project they had discussed, she now had a new play in mind. She wanted to talk it over with him in person. "Can you make a dash to Nice?" she wired from Cap Martin in January. "Will be there to give Rosmer nine February."

Craig's reply was a request for a thousand dollars, which Duse must have sent, because by 8 February he was in Nice, and furious. Noccioli's diary: "Needless to say, he found the set horribly mounted

. . . Therefore big scenes with the stagehand, the electrician, the business manager, the stage manager, the property man. Great chaos of horrible languages back and forth. The English of Gordon Craig had, indeed, some strange analogies with the pure Bolognese dialect of the stagehand Pompeo Giordani, but it was not in harmony with the Florentine of the stage manager, the Italian of the business manager; the Niçois of the electrician, the Milanese of the props. Countless insults flew about! Finally the painter went off only to return almost immediately with the Signora's daughter. Change of scene! Gordon Craig spoke some English with the Signorina, who spoke in French, to the business manager, who spoke in Italian to the stagehand, who cursed in Bolognese. The stage manager at a certain point vanished. Heroic decision! I don't know what happened next."

Accounts of what happened next differ. According to Isadora, who was not there, Craig had found his scenery cut down to half its height, "amputated, massacred before his eyes." And he complained to Duse: "you have destroyed my art!" According to Duse's biographers, her answer was, in effect: That's what's been done to *my* art all my life. Craig was not one to face the realities of theatrical life, the touring and the necessity of adapting productions to different houses; in fact, except for two other productions—a *Hamlet* with Stanislavsky in 1911 and an Ibsen (*The Pretenders*) with Johannes Poulsen in Copenhagen in 1926—his work for the drama was now to be in the realm of theory and the unfettered imagination. He exhorted more than he produced. In any case, Duse told Isadora later that Craig said "fearful things" to her (presumably with Enrichetta translating). Duse pointed to the door, and replied: "Go. I never want to see you again." He subsequently revised his opinion of her acting, which he described to the Berensons as "horrible."

At the time, however, she must have felt Craig had some justification for his rage. According to Noccioli, the night of 8 February— when *Rosmersholm* was performed in Nice—was "stormy as never before, not least because of all the pandemonium of yesterday. . . . The Signora, irritated, released her anger on the stagehand, who defended himself violently, and on the business manager, who . . . didn't give a damn." The reception of the play was cold, despite Duse's fervor. She fired the stagehand, the business manager, and the secretary of the company.

As the tour continued to Marseilles, San Remo, Milan, and then Vienna, *Rosmersholm* was temporarily dropped; Duse returned to the usual Camilles and Magdas. When she did resume the Ibsen play, on

18 March 1907 at the Theatre an der Wien, the Craig sets had been abandoned, and the familiar old sets by the firm of Rovescalli in Milan (the *horrid family*) were back in service. The Viennese were still cool to the play.

After touring the Balkans, the Duse company returned to Italy, and in late May sailed for South America. But without Duse. As usual, she traveled separately, accompanied only by her personal staff and by Lugné-Poe, who was managing the tour for her.

Three accounts of this South American tour survive: Noccioli's, with his distanced description of the "Signora"; Lugné's, written some years after the event but based on close, daily communion; and the diary of Tony Lamberg, a Viennese salesgirl to whom Duse had taken a shine and whom she had engaged as a kind of companion and errand-runner (the sort of position that Giulietta had occupied earlier and that Katherine Onslow would occupy later). All three are interesting, and different. Noccioli reports the humors of the troupe, the gossip and envy and enmities, the varying temperature of the Signora's performances, the dreadful provincialism of the audiences, who disliked Ibsen even more than the Italians did. Lugné, sometimes with a hint of desperation but usually with good humor, tells of the actress's caprices, her illnesses, some real and some imaginary, and the problems of reconciling them with the necessities of the tour; and Lamberg—whose diary is included, to some extent, in Lugné's Memoirs—narrates the private Duse.

Lugné sometimes took Duse's fragility with a certain skepticism; and on one occasion—as he recounts—he told her to her face that she had the strength of ten and would bury them all. Shocked then at his own daring, he braced himself for her fury; but instead, she laughed and admitted he was right.

He was right only up to a point. Her strength was more nervous than physical. She could take punishment because she was used to it, ever since they had taken a switch to her bare legs and pushed her onto the stage as a small child. But she also had a sense of humor, and Lugné gives some welcome examples of it. (The mournful, tragic Duse—though real—was always emphasized by commentators.) On one occasion, when he insisted that, to satisfy a local impresario, she had to perform the detested *Fédora*, she agreed, but when he offered to fetch her a script she cried: "Basta! . . . you can make me perform it, but you can't make me reread it!" Instead she read Goethe, and Wilde's *De profundis*, which affected her deeply. ("I too feel I am in such a prison of soul and body," she said to Lugné, showing him long passages she had copied out.) Lugné describes what he calls one of her "normal" days:

Around 7 in the morning—never later—at the hour when all her other confidants, defeated by sleep, by fatigue, can no longer appear (I discovered it only after two years work together), Duse received a secretary attached to the company, who would appear as if to report, and already in a dinner jacket! . . . (I never understood why he was ordered to appear in such a get-up.) He brought her the papers, the gossip-sheets of the theatre, the local papers, the Paris papers, the cheapest backstage talk; she read them along with *L'arte drammatica* . . . and all the others. Some of the papers were quickly destroyed; she kept only two or three that she considered suitable for display; the *Figaro*, the *Corriere della sera*, and the *Marzocco* of Florence (published by her friend [Angiolo] Orvieto).

She was careful to send (without mentioning it to anyone during the day) little sums to everyone, in the theatrical world or the social world, she thought might be susceptible to a little blackmail in her favor. She took care to deal with the "mafias" of the Italian theatres—she confided to me one day—for she was afraid of them. Finally she dictated a series of telegrams to all her grand lady friends in the great capitals. . . .

When the secretary went off, he also carried the answers, the replies that had to be distributed somehow during the day for all the little confessions that she had wrested, the little events of her own troupe: a very special task that could only work in an Italian company.

She also measured the town's excitement about her presence; and she would decide, on that basis, whether or not she would perform that evening. "She would not go on stage," Lugné wrote, "unless the public came into the theatre in a state of grace, to collaborate."

Her bedroom, with its vapors redolent of pine or turpentine, its photographic reproductions of Velázquez or Rembrandt, with the plaster death mask of Beethoven in its opened traveling-case, became a council chamber, a throne room, as she received the people she had summoned: her maid, managers, the director of whatever Grand Hotel she was staying in (frequently to insist on changing her room; she might change it as often as three times in a single day).

But to Tony Lamberg she was a different person. A pair of entries in this diary are particularly arresting: "23 June—Sunday, matinée at 2.30. *La Dame aux camélias*. During dinner, she starts to pour out her heart, that heart so simple and loving. The words came out so simply, so comprehensible, without pose, without theatrical artifice; she is so upright as a woman that she feels more intensely. She suffers horrible homesickness. After her jaundice in Paris, she got up too quickly and today she has a relapse. 'Why try to revive a broken life? What's broken is broken. One can at best patch it up, at the price of great effort. And to the very people who are hurting one, one can make no reproaches; they are doing nothing wrong, though another's happiness is forever destroyed. The only way not to suffer is to be only materialistic, to live, eat, and start over again twenty times being only materialistic. Naturally, for that, health is necessary. As for me, apart from the foolish mistake I made in marrying my husband, I have loved only twice. . . .''

And then, three days later: "Today she was calm, charming, but said not a word about last night, which, to tell the truth, hurt me a bit. At 5 o'clock, during dinner, she spoke to me a great deal about her work: 'Out of the two hundred plays I have performed, there are barely ten that I love. Ibsen, yes, Ibsen, and always and only Ibsen.' I interrupt her, saying: 'But there are others. *La Gioconda*.' The name had barely escaped my lips when she sat up straight, crying: 'Oh, that is true poetry . . . We lived only for art. That cost me my reputation and my health, not to mention my three million francs.' And she added: 'One cannot win celebrity twice: one has become too accustomed to the thought of seeing me die. The press has been hateful to me, but what does that matter? I want to prepare the work of the next century. It is like Wagner's music, which was understood only later.'''

Enrichetta joined her in Buenos Aires after the tour had been in progress for almost two months. But Duse's nerves were still taut: with Orlandini, the leading man, there was a terrible quarrel after a performance of *La Dame aux camélias* in which the money he flung, as Armand, actually hit Duse in the face (and it was not paper money). *Rosmersholm* was essayed again, and again received coldly. *Hedda Gabler* was more successful, but *La Dame aux camélias* and *Adrienne Lecouvreur* went best of all. The final performance of the tour was *La Dame aux camélias*, in Montevideo on 13 October.

In one of the notebooks into which Enrichetta, years later, copied many of her mother's letters, she also wrote a little note of her own, recalling the return from South America that winter. Duse was carrying the sum of £8,000 in gold sovereigns—the earnings of the tour, after the actors had been paid off—tied up in bags containing £500 each. Half the sum was given to Enrichetta, who was about to marry (and "throw away that stupid married name of your mother and that stupid *Duse as well,*" her mother wrote); the other half was sent to Robi Mendelssohn to be invested. Obviously, this was the nest-egg Duse had dreamed of since the long-past Boito days, the sum that would allow her to retire.

But before this could be achieved, she had more traveling to do: Germany, Austria, and—at the end of the year—Russia. The Russian tour was a success; from St Petersburg in January 1908 she wrote to Enrichetta that this was "one of the most beautiful tours of my life." The same letter mentioned a visit from Giulietta and Robi, which apparently had not gone well. "What an abyss between us and them," Duse wrote, probably thinking more of the neurotic, unstable Giulietta than of her husband.

In St Petersburg, just as Lugné described, she began her days by reading newspapers and magazines of every description. One morning, she read in the highbrow *Marzocco* that the magazine was collecting funds to underwrite a search for ancient papyruses in Egypt, in the hope of discovering lost classical works. With her usual impulsiveness, she dashed off a letter to Angiolo Orvieto with a contribution of 100 francs:

". . . See here, mind you, I know nothing about *papyruses*, and unfortunately, of many treasures of ancient books I know only a few words, picked up here and there . . . But I know the *joy* and the *eagerness* of *journeying afar*, in search of something (unknown or beautiful). This is all I know (and deeply); and therefore I felt something *stir* in my spirit, as I was reading your article. . . .

"Accept, Signor Angiolo, I beg you, the contribution of someone who likes to remain concealed behind you, but responds to what you are seeking. Accept this 'response' not as the pose of a papyrus-lover, but as the true response of one who loves and *understands* those who go far off, in the illusion of searching for something (an ideal) that is worth the trouble."

After the Russian tour and a rest in Italy, she took to the road again, to Vienna, and then, in the autumn of 1908, to Brussels, a half-dozen other cities, and finally Berlin. She was scheduled to give five performances, but the fifth—*La Gioconda*—was canceled because of illness. And so she closed her season on 25 January 1909 with *The Lady from the Sea*. And with it, she seemed to close her career; for a long absence from the stage then began. Duse was now fifty years old; she had been acting for forty-six years.

15
A new life

Vita nuova Eleonora had written to Enrichetta in February 1908, on her daughter's marriage to Edward Bullough, a young teacher in Cambridge; and she had underscored the two words heavily. Secretly, she may have been thinking of herself, of the new life she was hoping to find when she left the theatre. It is not clear—and perhaps was not clear to Duse then either—whether she was planning actually to retire or simply to withdraw from acting for a period of meditation before returning to it in some new guise. A letter she wrote Enrichetta a year later reflects this ambivalent state of mind:

"I would need to know your *plans* for the current season. Here are mine:

"none—

"Since for the present I am free of any contract for work, I would like to realize my freedom, to look at the sky the way a sailor does, asking if the wind will be favorable or not.

"The only *probable* things are the following:

"Perhaps I will need a water cure during the summer—

"Perhaps I will have to go to a *civilized* place to take baths—but the stupidity of the life in a Hotel or a *Kurhaus* distresses me. . . .

"I must go to Paris . . . to get *rid* of all the chiffons of my *French repertory*, which I wish never to see again—"

A few weeks later she wrote again, "my solitude enchants me." And mother and daughter arranged to meet in June in Paris.

But that solitude, her freedom from work, from the crowns of Fédora and other French protagonists, from the *ménagerie* and the *rampe*, soon turned to emptiness. Now under no obligation to tour, liberated from the slavery of trains and timetables, she traveled frequently, restlessly, often without apparent purpose. Her friend Gemma Ferruggia wrote of this period: "Some years of illness, of obscure suffering, of futile flights. Every so often, rumors in the newspapers . . . and not always on pleasant matters. Her faithful friends grieved at some of the acquaintances she made. Ladies, friends of hers, lamented having seen her with a young woman, actually so unsavory that she [Duse] had to get rid of her through legal means."

This young woman was the poet Cordula—or Lina—Poletti, then in her twenties, already an active figure in the feminist movement. Duse may have met her through another young friend and feminist, Alberta Alberti, daughter of the actress Giovannina Aliprandi whom Duse had known since her early days in Naples. "Berta" Alberti was one of those surrogate daughters Duse seemed to collect. Duse signed her letters to Berta "Mamma" and tried to comfort her in her apparently frequent bouts of unhappiness. But Duse also sometimes lost patience; a letter dated 6 September 1910 is indicative:

"You need tenderness and love—and where you might find them you lock yourself up—and there is no way to make you understand your mistake—

"You think you live in the truth—and you live in blindness—and I wear myself out trying to convince you.

"I have always said to you, if you don't have happiness, if you don't have *love*, take all the *profound and maternal* tenderness I offer you—and you kick instead—and don't know how much pain you cause me. . . ."

This letter was written not long after Duse's meeting with Berta's friend, Lina Poletti. If Berta—to judge by Eleonora's letters to her—seemed frustrated and bitter, Lina was quite a different sort of person. While still a student she had participated in the first Women's Congress, held in Rome in 1908, and had taken an active role in collecting funds in support of schools for peasants, venturing into the worst malarial zones south of the city. Her private life was just as adventurous. At that same time, she met and fell in love with the beautiful Sibilla Aleramo, poet, novelist, and freethinker. Aleramo's affair with the writer Giovanni Cena was well known, but did not discourage—or prevent—the younger woman from courting and seducing her. Sibilla's letters to Lina seem as bewildered as they are enamored (she accuses Lina, at one point, of wishing to assume "the harsh role of Don Juan"). Their affair continued until the summer of 1910, when Lina married a brilliant young scholar from her native Ravenna, Santi Muratori. It was a marriage of convenience for both, and they separated—remaining good friends—almost immediately.

During the same summer Lina seems to have first met Eleonora, and a series of notes from the young aspiring poet to the actress survive. The first are simply friendly ("How are you, Leor? When are you thinking of coming to Rome?"). But then the tone grows more insistent. On 21 July, from Ravenna, Lina wrote to Belluno, where Duse was resting: "I came home yesterday evening—Last night I listened to the *Walküre* on the piano from beginning to end, in a friend's house. Now I am in the pine woods and I carry in my memory the Walhall motif and the death motif. What an unfortunate intrusion, this friend of yours, in our two lives at a moment like this! You forgive me, don't you? for not knowing how to take things lightly and for needing a bit of time to adjust my thoughts reasonably? Be patient, be patient. I know that with me it is difficult to live, but my whole inner world is made up of *absolutes*. Eleor, I love you. Wait for me—"

In September Lina wrote a brief note, which also survives: "Eleor, I love you. Eleor, I have faith in you. Eleor, I am coming.—I will take a rather long way round, but in a few days I am there. Eleor, my soul!"

Among Duse's papers—which were preserved in a random way for the most part, so that neither losses nor survivals can be regarded as meaningful—there is one other item connnected with Lina Poletti, a poem, written in Florence on 16 May 1910, called "Gli inviti" (The Invitations). It is not a good poem, a series of imperatives addressed to a friend, urging the addressee to enjoy life, to give way to instinct.

All her life, Duse had been admired by women as much as by men; and she had always formed close female friendships, but her true love had been men, and—as her letters to D'Annunzio clearly demonstrate—she was a woman of profound, physical attachments. Now, away from her work, separated from that kind of family that was the troupe (even when she had kept her distance from it), she was forming new friendships and she sought new occupations. Lina Poletti can only have fascinated her: young, a writer, a person who *did* things. Eleonora had always hated idleness.

According to Alessandra Cenni, in her Introduction to a collection of Sibilla Aleramo's letters, Lina—after leaving Sibilla—became Duse's lover. There is no documentary evidence for this assertion. And, given Duse's character, it seems unlikely. Lina was her frequent traveling-companion, as Giulietta and Tony Lamberg, among others, had been before her; the quarrels may have stemmed from Lina's dissatisfaction with the surrogate daughter role Duse tended to assign to her younger women friends. In writing to Enrichetta, Duse referred to Lina by the nickname "Pineta" (after the famous pine woods of Lina's native Ravenna); the tone is ironic.

During this period Eleonora's health had good periods and bad. One of the latter inspired her friend Arthur Acton, the *italianizzato* English collector who knew everybody in Florence, to arrange for her to stay in a friend's airy and spacious villa. The friend was Mabel Dodge (later Luhan), who in her not always reliable book *European Experiences* described the fairly unsuccessful visit.

"In the white, cold room, Duse, in a flowing, wide-sleeved dress of ivory-colored, Capri, homespun wool, looking like an ascetic abbess. Her face was yellow-pale with darkened lids and brownish shadows. The corners of her mouth drooped dolorously, her hair was silvered all through and wound in a melancholy coil about her transparent-looking forehead.

"Only her hands and her eyes had any life in them—and the life in her hands was like that of two exhausted birds; but in her eyes it was a blue flame at the end of a black night. . . . Duse's being was beyond, in vibration, the speed of the lower range of mortals."

Lina—Mabel Dodge does not mention her by name, but calls her, as Duse did, "la petite"—arrived on her own, on her bicycle, "and dressed as nearly like a man as was possible in those days. She wore a man's straw hat with its black ribbon band, a narrow skirt which was made to hang like a pair of trousers when she stood . . . Her face was pale and narrow and her hair was parted and brushed straight back into a flat knot. Her intelligent eyes were reddish brown . . ., and they were merry and self-assured."

With the same self-assurance, Lina told Mabel of her plans to write plays for Duse, who would return to the stage to perform them. The first was to be an *Ariadne*, then one to be called *Incest* (Duse would be a Jocasta figure). Neither seems to have got beyond the title.

The visit to the Dodges' Villa Curonia did not last long, and Mabel did not remember it with pleasure. Duse and Lina spent much of the time in their rooms, quarreling; Lina made a verbal pass at her hostess. Unaware of this, Duse still apologized for her friend's eccentric behavior: "I am responsible to her mother for her," she said to Mabel. "C'est une créature de génie—mais aussi c'est une créature de suicide . . . de la folie . . . de la mort. [She's a creature of genius—but she's also a creature of suicide . . . madness . . . death.]"

In Florence, even when her health improved, Duse was bored. The newspapers themselves seemed unadventurous. "The *Marzocco* irks me," she wrote to Enrichetta on New Year's Eve 1910. "It has become old and conservative. The other *'personages'* of Florence?—Alas, they don't amount to much—Ibsen could make no use of all these characters for his plays . . ."

She was hoping her daughter could come to Italy, but Enrichetta was now the mother of a young son, Hugh, or "Halley," who was teething just then. Duse wrote, in a letter that is an indirect, unsolicited apology for all the years when she had to leave little Enrichetta in the care of others, "Don't be, *like me*, a *heartless maman*, and don't leave your *poupon* even for your *mother!!!*"

She continued the letter, writing in the third person, as if seeing herself, the herself of other days, in perspective:

"The only case when it is necessary, right, painful and noble, sad and comforting, is—you know when?—It is when one has—not a little English boy, but a very little, little, little, little Italian . . . daughter. When one, despite oneself, and despite marriage, is all alone in loving her and protecting her—then one would like to give her the world and the angels, and one has nothing—nothing but *her* poor heart heavy with love—

"—and yet—

"*even while loving her,* one leaves her, and goes far away—in the *illusion* of ennobling her life, guaranteeing her daily bread, and setting an example of courage—

"—Love *can* do that. . . ."

While Eleonora sought her private peace and moved from city to city, her absence from the stage was the subject of public discussion and regret. In late July 1911 the magazine *Comoedia* openly referred to her retirement; she caused a denial to be published immediately in the *Corriere della sera*: "The interruption of Eleonora Duse's work for the past two years has been due to the condition of her health and the necessity for Signora Duse to follow an aerotherapeutic cure under Dr Francesco Carloni in Florence. The distinguished physician hopes to restore her to the stage in a short time. . . . This is good news for Italian art."

Even people who had never met her were eager to persuade her to resume her career. One of these distant admirers was Rainer Maria Rilke, who had rewritten his play *The White Princess* with her in mind, and had dedicated it to her on its appearance in 1904. There are also elusive references to her in other writings of his.

Finally, in Venice in the summer of 1912, Rilke met her. She was with Lina Poletti. (The friendship was visibly fraying and would soon end.) Rilke's friend Prince Thurn und Taxis, brother of his great patroness, was also in the city, and so was the actor Alexander Moissi. Rilke, sometimes with others, sometimes by himself, spent almost every day with his new friend Duse for a period of about three weeks. They spoke of *The White Princess*, and when the poet gave her a verbal summary, Duse insisted he have a translation made for her. But he was really no longer interested in having the youthful work performed. In any case, before anything could be done, a quarrel between Duse and Lina—"an emotional hurricane," as Rilke's biographer E.M. Butler calls it— swept them from Venice in different directions.

Duse continued to follow the women's movement, though at a distance. To one of the several conferences in these prewar years, she sent a "communication," defining her position on the woman's situation. The communication was not calculated to please her more militant feminist friends, like Lina and Berta.

"The error of feminism," she wrote, "as it has been created and established in our country, is its having moved immediately on to a terrain of petty competitions and practical satisfactions. Thus the two sexes come to seem two parties, which can actually fight, one at the expense of the other. For the present, political demands have no reason to exist or are secondary considerations; social demands do exist, obviously indispensable and useful ones. But reciprocal esteem and trust will bring the solution of the problem, in the realm of the loftiest virtues and energies of life. . . ."

Eleonora talked about love and its importance, and about the "pariahs of love", perhaps thinking of Lina or of Berta Alberti, "those women who feel deprived and rebellious, because they have never conquered. . . .

"And thus are created the *feminists*, as they are called with a faintly sarcastic smile. But the women who today aspire to raise their own consciousness and their mission in the family and society—as many have already done through countless efforts and against immeasurable hostility—and who ask that the loftiness of their ideals and the nobility of their work be recognized: they are not feminists; they are true women, they are all women. . . ."

She complained of the narrowness of Italian horizons, the "scant friendship" in Italian houses; and she spoke of the unhappy women who "cannot find a field in which to be active" and are unable to resign themselves to loneliness and renunciation. Here she may have been thinking of herself. Her attempts to return to the stage, if she were really making any, seemed to come to nothing. Still, she was intent on finding a way of emerging from inactivity, of making herself useful, of exploiting her noble and considerable energy.

As early as 1911 she had begun pondering a plan, a charitable enterprise. It was to be called La Libreria delle Attrici, the Actresses' Library, an enterprise of which she was the founder, manager, and—practically speaking—sole supporter. It was a bold project: to create a refuge where young, itinerant actresses (as she had been) could come and rest, improve their minds, read and converse in handsome, peaceful surroundings. The project was to cause her headaches and bitterness; but it also brought her, by lucky chance, one of her most satisfying friendships, the most devoted and least demanding of her surrogate daughters.

In Rome, one November day in 1911, Duse went to inspect a little villa in the then remote neighborhood of Piazza Caprera; friends had told her that it might be a suitable home for the Libreria, and that the owner—a young woman recently widowed—might be prepared to rent or sell it. The widow, Maria Osti Giambruni, later described her first meeting with Duse:

"In the silent room, where I often spent long, immobile hours, closed in my grief, I saw some people enter. I waited for them to move on, to look round the house. But they stopped, facing me. I heard them utter words about the *patria* [Maria's officer husband had died in Africa a month before] and sacrifice; but I couldn't follow their talk and didn't try to. I heard only the hollowness of the words. Nor did I ask myself who the person talking to me was. I did notice, on the other hand, a noble figure, a woman with gray hair, dressed in black velvet, who remained off to one side, looking at me, moved. Simple and silent, she gave me a long, intense look before going out."

Realizing then who the visitor was, Maria Osti pulled herself together and followed. "I went down the few steps that separated us and I joined her. And so we met there, on the steps, in a tender, wordless embrace, which I felt was a kind of benediction."

A little later, Maria's elder daughter Pierina came into the room carrying an immense bouquet of white roses, which Duse had managed to find somewhere nearby. She had brought them back to the house and told the little child, "Take these to your Mamma."

The friendship was forged at once, and Duse—not always successful in managing her own life—took over the direction of Maria's: she arranged for the young mother to meet Maria Montessori, who was just opening her first school near Piazza del Popolo. Pierina was promptly enrolled. Duse sent Maria books to read, Christmas presents for the two girls; she invited Maria to call on her at the modest Pensione where she was staying. And, as with all her friends, she began charging Maria with little errands and responsibilities, including the keeping of Selva, her mongrel bird dog (called "Forest" because he had appeared from some woods and entered Duse's life). Her visits to Piazza Caprera became more frequent, and continued when the young mother transferred her family, which included her own mother and some aunts and sisters, to a large, rambling villa near Tivoli.

That winter Duse began to devote herself more seriously to the Libreria. She hired a watchman, Giulio (also occasionally charged with looking after Selva), and a librarian, Signorina Le Maire. Désirée, Duse's faithful if dull companion, acquired some years before in Vienna, lent a hand; and Eleonora's talkative old friend, Emma Garzes, an actor's widow, was also pressed into service.

But Duse's continuing bouts of ill-health delayed the work on the Library. Often she had to take time off to rest or to follow some cure for what had been diagnosed as emphysema. (One of these cures made her first uncomfortably portly, then alarmingly thin.) From Florence she sent some of her furniture and many crates of books, depriving herself of those faithful, silent companions of her years of travel.

Duse's inactivity as an actress did not bring any lessening of her fame. If anything, her legend grew; and with it the process of sanctification that was to continue after her death. One admirer, a writer named Sofia Bisi Albini, actually sent her a letter, meant apparently to flatter her, saying how she was "suffering from a secret, proud, superb torment" and ascribing her retirement to this noble suffering.

Duse's reply was sharp: "I beg you to alter your memory, to change the values in your recollection of me, and consider me someone who had always accepted a law of life which alternates hope and action, daring and silence, for all of us. Now, if illness has imposed the time of silence on me, this cannot place me (in your memory, that is) among the sufferers of a secret, proud, superb torment, as you choose to put it. No, thank you very much. In that niche you may place other women more deserving than I of such a fate. . . . If there was a time when, for some instants, I could glimpse the harmony between art and life, what is this importunate and unsought weeping over it now, and in my presence?"

"Life," Duse went on to say, "is composed only to be scattered."

If her admiring ladies had been shocked by D'Annunzio and had looked askance at Lina Poletti, they were even more dismayed by her friendship with Isadora Duncan, "l'orrenda," as Gemma Ferruggia insensitively calls her. Like so many other fellow-artists, Duse realized the elusive greatness of Isadora's art and, at the same time, respected her courage and independence as a woman. On 19 April 1913, when both of Isadora's children were drowned in a stupid accident, how could the maternal Eleonora fail to respond? Immediately after the tragedy, Isadora traveled aimlessly, to Corfu, England, and finally

Italy. There she received a telegram: "Isadora, I know you are wandering through Italy. I beg you to come to me. I will do my best to comfort you."

The telegram was from Eleonora. She had taken a little house that summer in Viareggio, near some friends, the painter Plinio Nomellini and his wife. They were in a lonely, beautiful locality on the sea called Fosso dell'Abate. She was often to take refuge there during the next few years, until the area began to be developed.

"I knew that Eleonora Duse was the one person whom I might wish to see," Isadora wrote in *My Life*. "I drove out to see Duse, who was living in a rose-colored villa behind a vineyard. She came down a vine-covered walk to meet me, like a glorious angel. She took me in her arms and her wonderful eyes beamed upon me such love and tenderness that I felt just as Dante must have felt when, in the 'Paradiso,' he encounters the Divine Beatrice."

Unlike other would-be comforters, who tried to keep Isadora's mind off what had happened, Duse asked her straightforwardly: "Tell me about Deirdre and Patrick." As Isadora said: "For the first time since their death, I felt I was not alone. For Eleonora Duse was a super-being. Her heart was so great it could receive the tragedy of the world, her spirit the most radiant that has ever shone through the dark sorrows of this earth. Often when I walked with her by the sea, it seemed to me that her head was among the stars, her hands reached to the mountain tops."

Duse also gave her sound, if not exactly sweet, advice: "Isadora, don't, don't seek happiness again. You have on your brow the mark of the great unhappy ones of the earth. What has happened to you is but the Prologue. Do not tempt Fate again."

Isadora was not the sort of person who takes advice. In *My Life* she—or her ghost-writer—tells a romantic story of how a beautiful young man came from the sea, asked if he could help her, and—then and there—she asked him to give her a child. The actual story was a bit more prosaic. The beautiful man was a sculptor named Romano Romanelli, to whom Duse introduced Isadora. He made a bust of her, and she deliberately arranged to conceive a child by him. The baby was born the following July: a boy, who lived only a few hours.

In the summer of 1913, to be near Duse at Viareggio, Isadora took a huge, gloomy villa, hired a piano, and summoned her old friend, the musician Hener Skene. Duse would come in the evening to hear him play Chopin, Schumann, Schubert, Beethoven. "Sometimes she would sing in a low, exquisitely toned voice, her favourite song,

293

'In questa tomba oscura' . . . and, at the last words—'Ingrata'
—'Ingrata'—her tone and looks took on such a deeply tragic and reproachful expression that one could not look at her without tears."

Late one summer afternoon Isadora suddenly asked Skene to play
the slow movement of the Pathétique Sonata. She rose and danced, for
the first time in the months since the children's death.

"Duse thanked me by taking me in her arms and kissing me." And
she said: "You must return to your Art. It is your only salvation." Then
she added: "If you knew how short life is and how there can be long
years of ennui, ennui—nothing but ennui! Escape from the sorrow and
ennui—escape!"

The advice was given to Isadora, but the emotion behind it came
from Duse's lonely experience of those empty years of absence from
her art. When the chill autumn drove them from the seaside, Isadora
eventually went back to Paris. Duse went to Florence and resumed her
preparations for the Libreria.

She had formed a committee, including illustrious names in Roman
society as well as in the theatre. But other well-known actresses were
skeptical about her plan. Her feelings were deeply hurt (though she
kept them to herself), when the actress Emma Gramatica, whom Duse
had known as a child, published an open letter to her in the *Giornale
d'Italia*. Gramatica refused to be a part of the committee, saying to
Eleonora (and addressing her with the intimate *tu*): "For too long a
time you have been living apart from us, alien to us; you have lost the
feeling and even the knowledge of what was, nevertheless, your life at
one time. Your project is a chimera."

An even worse blow was the defection of Gemma Ferruggia, the
journalist Eleonora had known for more than twenty years. Her article,
in a Florentine paper, was called "La casa inutile," the useless house.

Of course, Gramatica and Ferruggia were right. The plan was a
chimera; the house was useless. It would have been a paradise, thirty
years or more earlier, for the idealistic young Eleonora, who would
have asked for nothing better than a secluded corner and a vast library
for her hours of freedom from the poverty and toil of her early years in
the theatre. But Duse was unique, and the young actresses of 1914
included few bookworms.

Braving disapproval and cynicism, Eleonora went ahead. And in
May she sent out elegant printed invitations, which read: "I would be
happy if you could be present at the inauguration of the Actresses'
Library, which will take place on 27 May 1914 at five o'clock in the
afternoon, at Via Pietralata no. 14—Eleonora Duse." Beside the

printed words there was a little map, showing how to find the out-of-the-way address from Porta Pia.

"The house looks out on the Roman campagna. The horizon is vast, marked by the characteristics of the great Roman paintings." This description of the Libreria was printed in *La Tribuna* shortly after the opening. "Inside the house are some small, bright rooms that seem unaware of any season that is not spring. Everything is arranged to create the most complete tranquility. The books, which we saw piled up in great abundance, will soon be placed in the shelves and offered to the guests by the hands of the ladies helping Eleonora Duse in her most noble undertaking."

The inauguration was a great success, a simple, friendly ceremony (though the errant Ferruggia dared to come, and was received by a withering look from the hostess). When it was over Eleonora left for Florence, and then Viareggio. The Library remained open, but few people came. In Florence she had moved from the ground floor of the Via della Robbia house to an apartment at the top, sacrificing the garden. So poor Selva had to be left with friends. He died there, to his mistress's grief: "Selva is a lost friend!" she wrote to Maria Osti.

"August—24—evening . . . The war: no one is alone any more; no one belongs only to himself now."

Already in July, she had grown worried about the disruption of communication between Germany and Italy, as war was imminent. Germany was where her income arrived from. She thought of selling some pearls she had left with Enrichetta and wrote to her about them; but the sum that could be realized was too low. "You understand that between 17,000 and 10,000 there is a difference. I need that difference, which amounts to a year's support of the Libreria. I hope my daughter will not detach herself from the very depths of my heart and, when I say Libreria, she will understand." The letter was to Enrichetta, who, in her practicality, might have harbored a certain distrust of her mother's plan. "Not a forgetting of self, and of those responsibilities of life, but a human solidarity, something that uplifts every existence."

In September 1914 Duse was back in Rome, and on the 8th, she wrote again to Enrichetta: "So far I've been unable to conclude anything. They all ask for money, not refuge.—It's true, though, that September is still the dead season for theatres. We'll see later. We, Désirée and I, have tried staying in the villa, but at night it isn't prudent. Until there are many people living in the house, it is not prudent to spend the night there. . . . the whole quarter is in the deepest darkness, and after the beauty of the sun in the daytime, you remain in a darkness of anguish, because being unable to see increases the insecurity. . . . So for the moment Désirée and I sleep in two little rooms at the Eden, which has remained partly open—We have taken only our rooms, and—to avoid debts—no board at the Hotel. We eat here and there, in trattorias."

On 19 September she wrote Enrichetta: "My health is good, and I work at Pietralata. But actresses do not want to come to the refuge; they ask only for money; and more money. And I have only books, and three or 5 rooms available! I've had electric light installed, and will pay the bill as soon as I can!"

The news from friends was not heartening. Yvette Guilbert, who had been one of the most persistent in encouraging Duse to return to the stage, now wrote that she had been left with only thirty-two francs and had been given shelter by a friend. Isadora wired about the death of the baby. "This war," Duse wrote to Enrichetta, "gives me a terrible awareness of the necessity of things—The first days I saw only death and ruin—and the moral and physical terror of it . . . now . . . My heart is still swollen and heavy as I say so, but I see it as something *innate* in the human soul. Yesterday, in the despised Libreria delle Attrici I was re-reading some pages of *Tacitus*, and there it is like today! Everything returns! . . . Ask ton cher Ed. to read you some Tacitus—. . ."

Finally, in January 1915, she decided the Libreria was an impossibility. Rather than ship her books back to Florence, she gave them to a library, chiefly for schoolteachers, run by the National Committee of Italian Women and directed by Signorina Le Maire. Duse's noble plan had come to a sad end. Later, other contents of the villa were given to charity, after a terrible earthquake in the Abruzzo. The lease on the villa was allowed to lapse.

The war was coming closer to Italy, though the country was still officially neutral. In Rome, the society ladies of Duse's acquaintance were, as she said, already in a "fever of benefaction." But, she wrote to Enrichetta, "Charity? Alas! I love the equality of all beings, and I detest the word 'charity.'"

Boito came to Rome at the beginning of February, but she missed him. He returned to the capital in late May, when she was in Florence. As a Senator of the Realm—one of those appointed for cultural distinction and not an elected representative—Boito was in Rome to take part in the debate on war between neutralists and interventionists. He wrote to Camille Bellaigue: "On the 20th I had the joy of casting my vote for the beautiful war!"

On 23 May Italy formally declared war on the Central Powers, and on the 24th Duse wrote to Enrichetta: "My daughter, today is the first day of war: no futile words. All of us in the world are gripped by the same hope and each must do his duty. I have spent these days in silence and alone in the house—a sole book helped me: *Mazzini*. May his light and faith descend in every heart. The bells of Florence gave the signal and the salute, and the boys, soldiers, have rushed to the war. Alone in this room, I could see them (not seeing them), hearing in the distance the blast of trumpets, shrill and gay. . . ."

Duse was an ardent patriot and wrote *Viva l'Italia* more often than ever in her letters (now without the hint of irony there had sometimes been in the past; still, she would probably not have called the war *bella*, as Boito did). She was upset, at the very beginning of the war, when a Berlin paper accused her of ingratitude towards Germany, a country that had given her so much. And in Berlin, too, there was the beloved Robi. So it was impossible for her really to hate Germans.

That summer she went off to Boscolungo in the Tuscan mountains, where her American-born friend, the Marchesa Etta De Viti De Marco, had a house. Duse did not stay with her friend, but took a little place of her own. "You know," she said to Enrichetta, "dressing in the evening tires me and I am no longer capable of talking. When the evening, grave, sweet, and tranquil, descends on the mountain, my only desire is to be silent and to think of the soldiers of the world, swept away in such madness."

She had moments of despair, too. Her friends—in particular the surrogate daughters—did not get along, in their rivalry for her attention and affection. Sometimes she was fed up with the whole lot. "Your old mother would like only her Pupa—(and the Santo!)—"

From Boscolungo she moved to Bagni di Lucca, then to Viareggio. Boito, the Santo, was much in her mind. "Here in Viareggio, at the hotel where Isadora stayed, there is an elderly lady of the Milanese aristocracy, an old and faithful friend of the Santo." In a note on this letter, Enrichetta identifies the lady as Vittoria Cima. "Placci was here the other day, and as she knows him, she asked to meet me. We have known each other, the lady and I, for—27 or 28 years—but by name, through a heart; never personally before. She wanted to receive me; I went. I hoped to discover in her something of that unforgettable nature . . . but my heart remained closed. With respect and tenderness, I looked and I listened to this women he used to speak of, so many long years. But each soul is inviolable, and alas! I found nothing of Him! It is quite right and beautiful that it should be thus. Coming from her hotel,

I was a little sad—like a person who opens a door in a strange house—and afterwards, my feeling of sadness was soothed as I said to myself: each soul speaks to the *soul*, never through another person! I will understand nothing of the beauty of life. . . ."

Now, after forty years, in the midst of the war, Lenor had made a private peace with that Milanese society that had excluded her years before and separted her from Arrigo, enclosing him in a world where she had been forbidden to follow.

Other peaces would be made in the next years: with Gabriele, with the theatre, and finally with herself.

16
'Cenere'

While she was maintaining contact with old friends (even, indirectly, with Robi in Berlin), during these war years, Duse made a number of new friends, men and women, old and young, rich and poor. In Rome, besides the Osti family, she met Camille Mallarmé, young niece of the poet and herself a graceful writer of children's stories. Through Camille, she was later to meet the French playwright and diplomat Paul Claudel. And in Rome, at the house of her friend Etta, she met a young critic and journalist, Giuseppe Prezzolini. He gave his impression of Eleonora in a letter to his hostess; Etta quoted it to Eleonora, who then wrote it to her daughter: "If you only knew, Marchesa, for us young people, how often a too-familiar name brings disappointment and sorrow; but E.D. seems to me real, and human, and profound, and her every word, as she spoke it, was of truth!" And Duse's comment to Enrichetta was: "Still the bearded lady?"

In Rome also she met a young doctor, Angelo Signorelli, and his Russian-born wife Olga, who introduced her to a circle of writers, artists and musicians. Through the Signorellis, she also met—in Florence—Giovanni Papini, already a catalytic literary figure. And with Claudel, who visited her there in May 1915, she met the young university professor Gaetano Salvemini, with Madame Luchaire, who was to be his second wife. Describing Salvemini, she wrote: "that Mazzinian, totally pure, a brave and magnificent citizen of our country; and may many like him emerge after this war. He has a head like Socrates, and warm, persuasive speech. In the *Messina earthquake he lost wife, sister, and 5 children*—and now he has patched up a kind of life with Madame Luchaire. . . ."

Though Duse still thought of the war with horror at times, she wrote in the same letter: "But there is *beautiful harmony in the accord of all Italy*. Now our national life begins. How sorry I am that I can't send you all the papers. I read them all, from morning to evening, to accompany the soldiers with my thoughts. . . ."

After Duse's death, when Enrichetta was clearing up her things, she found all the letters she had written to her mother from childhood on. Enrichetta destroyed them, as she destroyed most of Duse's letters to her. But she saved those written during the war years, copying them carefully (and legibly) into a series of notebooks—in which she also added a few marginal comments and explanations—for her children to read in later life. These notebooks, now preserved in the Fondazione Cini in Venice, provide a virtual diary of Duse's life during those crucial years. She wrote several times a week, often daily. And though she would protest. "I am unable to write proper letters," these pages have a spontaneity and honesty and zest that constitute an irresistible moral portrait of their author. Another favorite phrase of hers was "trop long à raconter" (too long to tell), though she frequently told long and charming stories. Sometimes she wrote to Enrichetta's husband, consulting him about literary matters. A typical letter of this period suggests the range of her interests: "Tell me please in which volume Renan speaks of Gotama [*sic*] Buddha, I don't have my books with me. . . . Who translated Novalis into French?"

On 21 November 1915, from her room at the Hotel Eden in Rome, she wrote: "Ma pupa, the Santo is here!" The letters are written in a characteristic jumble of French and Italian, with French predominating. "He arrived Thursday, and Thursday evening and yesterday evening, Saturday, at this table with this pen, seeing the things I see as I write you, we talked of you. The soul rediscovers its path and its vitality.—Joy in sorrow, serene acceptance of the inexorability of life, and goodness and greatness, *everything*. I understand when I see that being again. What oblivion, and what awareness of life—that enormous thing that Life is, to find room for all. My daughter, a kiss from Maman, who would like to live and have suffered everything, to deserve the sweet and peaceful balm of word of goodness and greatness of heart. . . ."

That same day, to Enrichetta again: "The Santo is still here. He has extended his stay; nearly every evening he has come to see me. We talk, we look at each other, we are sad sometimes, and sometimes we laugh like children. Everything is changed, and nothing is changed. . . . I have tried talking to him about work, but it's best not to. Soul and work—that, for me, is like the charm, the secret of Life itself. I shall have to *do*, and not speak any more. . . ."

On 2 December Boito returned to Milan, and Duse told her daughter: "seeing him leave, voilà, I glimpsed, for an instant, how much strength, in the heart, vital strength, was lost and won during your far-off childhood, in those endless separations and departures . . . but so it is! I have gone white—I have done everything in life between one departure and another—the heart has remained motionless, turned towards that suffering, that light, that thing that is *everything* and that is *nothing*—. . . that *being*, magnificent, is Life itself, and it is *outside* life. . . . I try to find again in my heart the charm and the *sorrow* (horrible, at times, in those days) of that *charm* . . . that animated my life, and my life as an artist—it is a *living* thing like life = *dead* like death—I can't say it. . . ."

Just before Christmas, the first Christmas of the war, she thought of going to the front to visit a field hospital where a friend of hers was a nurse, but she put it off. Boito was in Rome again, and his presence inspired constant thoughts of "long ago" (*jadis*). Though she knew he was no good at discussing the practical work of the theatre, she still made him read a play that interested her, W.B. Yeats's *Cathleen ni Houlihan*. "The Santo didn't know it; I gave it to him to read. But, for him, there is only Shakespeare . . . but I, who am smaller, have always discovered contemporaries, after Verlaine, whom the Santo refused to know, and then, 10 years later, he said to me one day (long ago) '*yes, you are right, Verlaine is a poet*'—Enfin—I am *seeking* on our poor earth . . . and so is *he*—for understanding. . . ."

Boito also wrote to Enrichetta, describing Duse's life in Rome: "I saw your Maman several times. She is well, you must have no fear for her. She lives serenely in a quiet Hotel, her balconies (where she grows flowers) overlook some marvelous gardens; she sees frequently an excellent friend, who is devoted to her [Maria Osti], she meets at times some very great artists. She reads, as always, very beautiful books; but I think you know all that. . . ."

Her thoughts were constantly of the war—Verdun, and the poor Serbian refugees she was helping in Rome—but her thoughts were also of work. The Yeats play was an idea. Rightly worried about her mother's health, Enrichetta tried to dissuade her from any thought of returning to the stage. Duse's reply was almost sharp:

"*I have always lived by my work*—at the age of 5—I lived on my own bread, earned by myself (A child's work, in the environment of those days, was still work, and I could also relieve my Maman!)"

A young friend, Ofelia Mazzoni, had been giving some poetic readings; they made a deep impression on Duse, who asked Enrichetta if
she knew the works of Selma Lagerlöf. "Find the volume *Les Liens
invisibles*. . . . Then, in that book there is "old Agneta." Try to read it.
Very beautiful ending. . . . There is a *monologue* to be made, very effective in the theatre, and I am *working it up* . . . La petite blonde Mallarmé
is helping me prepare it—for to take words from the *book* and turn them
into words for the *stage* is not my job; I need a hand. . . . Naturally,
some days ago I had the Santo read it—but . . . Selma Lagerlöf is not
Shakespeare. . . ."

Enrichetta was also apparently discouraging about this idea, but
Duse herself had soon grown cool to it. The role was "sad without
being moving." Claudel, in Rome at this time, tried to persuade her to
play his *Annonce faite à Marie*, but as Duse said, "Violaine [the role] is 18
years old!!" Lucien Guitry had visited Rome and spoken of work, and
from Paris—after Guitry's return—Duse received a telegram from
"that fox Lugné," saying only "Amitié."

Duse, who in the past had spurned dinner invitations, partly
because food meant little to her and she preferred eating alone, now
began to go out more often in society. At one dinner party, about this
time, she met the art patron, the Conte di San Martino. In the course of
the conversation, as he recalls in his memoirs, he made a casual,
disparaging remark about the cinema, the upstart among the arts. To
his surprise, Duse defended the movies with considerable heat and
enthusiasm.

In fact, they were also in her thoughts. Sometime in 1914 Gemma
Ferruggia had suggested writing a script for Duse based on the life of
St Catherine of Siena; Duse's reply had been a curt "absurd." Her
sharpness may also have been inspired by her feelings towards Ferruggia at that moment. But, at about this time, she became an assiduous
movie-goer, both in Florence and in Rome. One afternoon, she was
observed by a French visitor to the capital, the writer Colette:

"I had sought, in a dark and cool cinema, a refuge from the Roman
spring, which had burst out everywhere in wistaria, in iris, lilac, and so
warm that the *ponentino* breeze did not refresh it. A friend said to me in
a whisper: 'Behind us, that lady in black is Eleonora Duse.' I recognized the luminous hair, combed back, flamelike, across her forehead,
and held in check by a black hat, and the great, deep hollows that set off
the brilliance of her eyes by enclosing them in shadow. Only her little
nose remained a young woman's nose, an exacting, ironic nose, quick
to convey anger or distaste.

"That celebrated face, inclined first to one side and then to the other, was following the episodes of a miserable film drama with an expression of great, tender, trusting naivety. The intermission, when the lights went up, brought Duse a gathering of admirers. She stood to receive their homage and shook a few hands. She did not smile, but lowered her head defensively, and her little nose, insulted, quivered with disdain. 'You see,' whispered my Italian companion, 'you see what a *lady* she is!' "

Duse was not just following the mediocre film; she was studying the medium. In September 1915 she received a cabled invitation to the United States, as she wrote to Enrichetta, to work "on I don't know what, in the cinema. If I were able to go . . . Doing—that was all my wealth. Now here I am, without enough breath to close a suitcase. . . ."

Two weeks later she added some details: "They have cabled me from America to go for 3 months to Los Angelos [*sic*], Califor. with this famous Griffith of the cinema: to do what? Today, with the help of Adolfo [De Bosis], I am composing and he translating into English a cable for New York. I can choose the work. Which? And if that can be settled: should I leave? How many journeys I have made in my life, awaiting 'The Journey'—the real one, the deliverance! But, after all, if I could still sell my soul a little, as I did in my youth (when you were so little and pretty, and relying on my help). Then, before my *emphysema* worsens, I could cable to Am. to be specific about what they are proposing for me. . . ."

In Florence, a short while before, she had pawned her rings and raised 2,000 francs, which would last her till Christmas, when "either Robi le Bon will have arranged things, or I will be en route to America (with Griffith-Cinema). . . ."

In a P.S. she asked Enrichetta to send any information she could garner about "this Griffith." The organization proposing the contract for fifteen weeks in "Los Angelos" was the "Banque Lincoln National, New York." To the bank, or rather to Miss Alice Kanser, who handled D.W. Griffith's affairs there, Duse wrote about possible film subjects, insisting that, in any case, she was determined "to exclude any subject from the usual dramatic repertory."

She was hoping that Griffith would be coming to Europe, where they could meet and talk; but the war made travel, and even correspondence, difficult. She sent Griffith some "scripts" she had written, but unfortunately these scenarios—brief descriptions for silent films—have not survived.

She wanted her films to be poems. One idea was to make a moving picture inspired by the frescoes of the Sistine Chapel. "I have found the draperies and colors of the dress—gold—and the white turban. Oh, it would be too long to explain, but to console you (a little) for my idea of working, I show you the source, a beautiful one, in Michelangelo." Apparently she enclosed a postcard illustration in the letter. "If this Griffith is the man they say, after the war we could meet in London and film (with ma pupa in London) the Sistine Chapel. There is an idea, but we will talk about it when hearts are less wounded and I can see you, after the war!"

She was also contemplating "Two figures (phantoms) of Aeschylus. *Hecuba* and another woman—but am not yet quite sure of the role; but in two weeks I will have studied it well. And also: the poor *Cathleen ni Houlihan*—of W.B. Yeats. It is modern, timely (even), but there is poetry. . . ."

To fulfil her request for information about Griffith, the best Enrichetta could do was send her the program of *The Birth of a Nation*. Duse was unimpressed: "Nothing beautiful in it." But this did not dampen her cinema fever. It was a difficult prospect, because, as she said, "I want to do nothing that resembles, even remotely, my work of the past.—The depths of the soul see the way, but it is almost impossible to clarify it for others."

She was also receiving film offers in Italy. The time was propitious. For some years the Italian cinema had been booming, and it was making a certain effort to rise above the level of mere consumer entertainment. D'Annunzio had lent his name, if not much of his talent, to the spectacular film *Cabiria*, for which his protégé, the composer Ildebrando Pizzetti, had written special music. Duse's old colleagues from the stage, Ermete Zacconi and Ermete Novelli, among others, were making pictures. And even her one-time mentor, the great and difficult Giacinta Pezzana, now living in Rome in proud poverty, made a film of *Thérèse Raquin*, from the Zola drama in which she had appeared with the young Duse.

Enrichetta wrote about Vachel Lindsay's pioneering book on cinema, and Duse was delighted to discover that many of the ideas she had worked out by herself in her long meditations about film were shared by the American writer. Lindsay was convinced, for example, that "the motion picture art is a great high art, not a process of commercial manufacture." He wanted to persuade art museums and universities—prophetic vision!—that movies were serious, and he insisted that people liked Mary Pickford because they caught in her beauty a hint of Botticelli and the ideal of the beautiful. This was exactly in line with Duse's idea of "cinematographing" the Sistine ceiling.

Lindsay also made an appeal to the literary world; here, too, the Italian scene looked propitious. Besides D'Annunzio, other writers were taking an interest in moving pictures; and among the first to write about them had been Duse's new friend, the polemical, original Giovanni Papini. Duse wrote to him often about films. In one letter—undated, as nearly all her letters are, but surely from the war years—she wrote that, "in order to have an idea of what this word, cinema, is", she had gone to see a film of Sardou's *Odette*, once a mainstay of her repertory, now a silent vehicle for the popular star Francesca Bertini. "I went to see *how* Odette would make the journey from *word* to *cinema*—And I saw this:—But—I can't narrate it—"

Then, as an example, she discussed the last act:

in that drama of Sardou, there is the usual faithful family friend who always arrives just at the right moment . . ., and in the theatre, in the piece by Sardou, he says, more or less, this: 'The sailors who found the body in the water asked where they should carry the poor dead woman, and I said: Here—receive her in the house, I beg you—'

These *few* and *clear* words can be spoken in a simple tone, fairly close to the truth—that is, I have heard them spoken a number of times, and they were heard in silence and also (theatrical weapon) with emotion. To *say* them, one minute suffices. But here, sapristi! an *hour* or more of cinema, to illustrate all this. Here, you *see*. Here there are *actions*, not *words*. It's all here: the sea, the wind, the boat, the sail and the woman—The woman with hat and veil, then without a hat or veil any more, but '*with desperation*' (says the title that explains)—

You see everything

The hesitation, the terror, the plunge, and away!

and the sailors who go out, and the woman, floating, then pulled, dripping, to the shore—and all the funereal stuff that follows, and the whimpering of all the relatives, who always cry, afterwards. There's everything—all is seen, experienced: documents, evidence in hand—

—a news item. The exterior of a poor life, displayed by machine, every evening in the same way. Trash—shame! And nothing that stimulates the soul—nothing that, after the word, frees the imagination!—Nothing of what is *not* seen and weaves life; nothing of the inevitabilities that form it, that grip it in a vise—

In a word: what I saw is not art—I was so worn out and fed up! And who is—right? They, or I? . . .

For Duse, in these commercial films, the pace was wrong, the fact of the picture's silence was not exploited. Cinema could be illustration for her, and was closer to painting than to the theatre. Far, in any case, from the spoken word. When she finally did find a film to make, she thought of it as a book to be illustrated, a story more of character and mood than of plot and action.

On 30 March 1916, she wrote to Enrichetta: "Yesterday, 29 March—day of my *crise*, when I felt that something had to be done, to bestir myself, I did it.—I *contracted for some work*: not theatre, no play, no words to speak. For a long time, here in Rome, they wanted me, to start up a large firm to make '*contre-cinéma*,' that is, to initiate something beautiful and worthy, against the stupidity of stupid pieces!—but too long to tell. . . ."

The financial side of the project would be handled by her lawyer Orlandi, while she would be in charge of the artistic aspects. "I believe I have found something beautiful—it is no longer Michelangelo—but I learned, after following that path, to seek something of a human beauty, and within our grasp. This is a book I am going to 'illustrate,' a *beautiful book*, which I have given my word not to name. So—don't be cross, my child—I will tell you in a week, when I am released from my word. A beautiful book, you will see! I will send it to you—and you will understand. You are going to cry, when you read it, ma bonne Pupa. It will be a brief and eternal story of love and sorrow—as always in the world. And this woman will have a child, and Life will force her to part from her baby. And Life will be the key to everything. All will go well then. I don't want to talk about it—Baisers, Maman."

But she did want to talk about it, so she picked up the letter and continued: "I would have to write pages to tell you how the contract came about, and the plan, and the search for the right book—but I can't. Don't worry: it's just that I've given myself a shake—and I will start work on a beautiful film in two months, in the summer—in a *magnificent landscape in Italy*. Viva l'Italia! . . . I will work on my film with the remembrance of our love, ma fille, and of our (since your infancy) long separation. ah! . . ."

Even this prospect of work, less exhausting than a stage return, did not rouse the enthusiasm of Enrichetta, who repeated an invitation to England. Her mother made excuses. "Today [it was 11 April 1916] I thought of *you, of the Santo, and of my film all day*. Tomorrow I'll send you the book."

But her next letter was not written until 2 May, after a spell of confinement to her bed. The film still dominated her thoughts. "But to begin a film, I'd have to go to an Italian island, Sardinia, and at this moment, to travel even for one night on the sea is out of the question. So all is suspended."

Things were proceeding slowly; there was some difficulty in raising money, but at least Duse could announce the title of the book:

"The *Book* is: *Cenere*
                       by
             Grazia Deledda"

It is a beautiful book set on the island of Sardinia. I read it in the past—I remember—on tour. You, Henriette (let's say) were little, a young girl—and it seemed to me that many of the things in the book—however, one *had* to *live* them. I will tell you: The Book is based on the necessity (no matter why) of a *separation* of a mother from her son. The mother—alone and poor—is brutalized by the death of her heart without love. But the son, sent—at the mother's wish—*among books*, undergoing a practical and poetic growth, becomes a Man, a true man—made of action, of dreams, and without sensual cruelty, but understanding *pity*. Something between the *Rolla* of de Musset, the *René* of Chateaubriand, and naturally something of the *thirst* for love (and sufferings) of Nietzsche. Then, when Life, his work, the moral development of his spirit, and the love of his heart *act* strongly on him (for he loves Margherita, a young girl). Then one must *act* in Life. But his ideal of woman is so lofty that he wants: first of all to *find his mother again*, who abandoned him (for his good, the mother says, *but* abandoned); and then, he wants to establish, with his wife and his mother, a way of working and living . . . but the two forces abandon him. The *fiancée*, out of *shame* in sharing Life with a beggar like the young man's mother, and the *Mother*, who on her own recognizes herself as unworthy to share the Life of her son, and in the *pride* of poverty—

In the last pages of the book there is a *noble love of Life*, of Life, no matter from whom we receive that divine gift, and *the mother*, any mother, is the *depositary*, blind but blessed, of vital form . . . Enfin, there are here, some pages of *reality* and *poetry*, which assail my heart and imagination, and which, I believe, *without speaking*, I will be able to make people understand!—. . .

Grazia Deledda had been living in Rome since 1900, but at this time it seems that Duse had never met her. The actress was certainly familiar with the works of the novelist, who was already gaining international fame, to be sealed, a decade later, by the Nobel Prize. Duse studied *Cenere* (Ashes), one of Deledda's finest works, with great care. Later, she wrote out the script in her own hand, using the impressionistic text, in a second phase, for the final scenario with the help of a professional screen writer.

As part of her preparation, Duse sought the help of another Sardinian writer, Paolo Orano, friend, and later husband, of Camille Mallarmé. The enthusiastic, scatterbrained Orano duly swamped her in Sardinian history and lore, prompting her to write to him:

"Yesterday evening, as you spoke, I was so *amazed* by the number of Sardinian scenes that, in the tumult of things glimpsed, I could only listen and admire. But this morning, I am trying to use the sieve, to sort out the fundamental difficulties, which to me seem *countless*. . . .

"The novel I have chosen—do you remember it?—is *in itself* a work of art; it possesses already, *in itself*, since birth, a specific aim; for years it has had an individual life of its own. . . .

"We love the books we love . . . for that something that cannot be grasped, that the soul does not find in life.

"But really, to enrich the story, even with an admirable vision such as you expounded to me yesterday evening, which, if inserted into the text, would somehow remain alien to it—does that seem to you possible? . . ."

Orano was presumably thinking of a great spectacle-film, rich in Sardinian local color. But the book, Duse insisted, was "only a story of sorrow and of love." She would do without Orano's help—and his folklore.

Instead, she redoubled her movie-going, often with Camille in attendance; and, also with Camille, she visited the studios of Cines (a Rome producing firm), to talk with the technicians and to become familiar with the practical aspects of making films. Camille later recalled "her discontent with the intermezzos of 'luxurious life, dinner parties, and décolleté ladies' that they wanted her to introduce into the film which she had conceived of as steeped in peasant sobriety.

"The producer says that a film without beautiful women can't have success in our country.—'And what does Grazia Deledda think about it?' 'There's a war on; she'll accept anything, provided they pay.'"

Shortly after sending Enrichetta the long summary of the story, Duse broke off all discussions with Cines, and went off to stay in Tivoli with Maria Osti for three weeks. But she wrote on 2 June: "I haven't thrown out the basic idea, which is to *Work* as soon as possible. My strength must be employed, no longer in *destroying myself*, but in *rebuilding*. I am having very serious negotiations with *three* producing firms. Each is good, but, so far I haven't signed, because I was ill, and because making a film is a *spiritual problem. . . ."*

And eight days later, still in Tivoli, she wrote: "I must learn the technical *things*. I have no lack of ideas for scripts, but I want the *execution* to be *modern*." She asked Enrichetta to put her in correspondence with "ce Lindsay", or rather, she wanted Enrichetta to write him, because "for me, to write in an orderly way is painful." And she announced that she was signing with the Ambrosio company of Turin, though she would be her own titular producer. In another letter, postmarked the same day, she described the firm she was dealing with: "It is a *Piedmontese* firm [Duse had the Northern Italian's characteristic distrust of Southern Italian business methods], headed by an honest workman who has risen, by his work, to real wealth—I knew that this Ambrosio was and still is (even though a bit out of fashion) the *honest firm* as far as regards *choice* of film—seriousness of choice—and *financial honesty. . . .* The firm has never produced banal and vulgar films. . . . Enfin, I am engaged—for a single film—to try—in partnership with the firm itself. I have become a partner—voilà! . . . I have been engaged avec tous les honneurs, of course—I will do what I like, the contract says, and I am given 50 per cent of the takings—and I am advanced 40,000—and 20,000 for my expenses. . . ."

Now that the prospect of work was assured, Eleonora could tell Enrichetta about the depression and confusion her enforced idleness had caused her: "I closed my eyes at night, sleepless. *I said: All right, calm down. Eleonora, you have always worked*, so retrace your steps.—If your health prevents the work of jadis—and if your cough prevents you from *speaking*, then make films! *The art of silence!* The fever in my heart, ever since Griffith's offer, I have dreamed only of films—Well, all of a sudden, in the night, *I said to myself: Turin!"*

So she wired Ambrosio, and the next day he came to Rome to discuss business. Though she was later to revise her opinion of his taste, his seriousness, and even of his honesty, she had not made a bad choice for her film partnership. Arturo Ambrosio, at the turn of the century, had been, not a workman, as Duse said, but the proprietor of a camera and optical shop in Turin, a gathering-place for the city's photography enthusiasts. In 1904, with another photographer, Roberto Omegna, he had filmed an important automobile race and—that same year—the maneuvers of the Alpine troops. These pioneering films are a part of Italian cinema history; and though Ambrosio soon was not alone in

Turin and already had rival producers in Naples and Rome, he quickly rose to a preeminent position in the field.

Ambrosio's films became popular abroad (in silent days, there were no problems of dubbing or subtitles), and he even imported Mrs Leslie Carter from Broadway to make a film in Turin, *La Du Barry*, based on a successful play by David Belasco, Mrs Carter's mentor. By 1914, the year of this film, Ambrosio had impressive new studios and was turning out twelve films a month. In addition to signing up some leading directors, he also persuaded several theatre stars to work for him, including a young friend of Duse's, the beautiful Tina Di Lorenzo.

"*He wept,*" Duse wrote to Enrichetta, "as he kissed my hand, saying that he, who had been making films all his life, had never understood as well as I, who have never made films."

In June 1916 she went to Viareggio, and there her film work began, as she supervised the experimental shooting of some outdoor scenes. In mid-July she went to Turin to see the results and to start work in earnest. On 16 July she wired Maria Osti: "Arrived at nine, at nine-thirty was at the studio. Great joy."

Letters, to Maria and to Enrichetta, followed the next day. To Maria she said: "One of the films [the sequences shot in Viareggio] has come out very well. It's the one I told you about, in the field of beans, with the silvery flowers, the stalks as high as wheat—and the woman reaping. The silver of my hair harmonizes, as well, with the silver of the flowers of the field."

Writing to Enrichetta, she was more practical. "The studio is very interesting! What a world! In the morning I was introduced to all the personnel, 204 people employed on my film. The film is 'passionelle' (mother and son), *but it takes 204 people to make it live.* I think I'm dreaming; my soul returns to me! Ah! who can say what I have lost of my soul during these 5 years without work. . . ."

She was pleased with the actor, Febo Mari, who was to play her son. "Half the trial films cannot be used, but there is something—which is not bad—a certain abandonment of stock movie gestures."

At four the next morning, she was up and on her way to a mountain village, to shoot a scene in a country omnibus, where the mother, babe in arms, abandons the village. In her few free moments she took pleasure in being back in Turin: "Yesterday I saw again the street where I used to walk when you . . . you were about to be born. How one has worked since then!"

There was a break later in July and in early August, but the film remained on her mind. As she wrote to Maria Osti from Milan: "I have learned a lot. *Technique* alone is not enough, as *inspiration* alone is not enough. I am eager to resume." Meanwhile the week in Milan had allowed her to see Boito, "a week of light!"

Four days later, back in Turin, she was *"furiously* at work." Febo Mari, besides being her leading man, also acted officially as director. Duse kept an eye on him, and they became friendly. She also made friends with the lighting man Luigi Florio, and with the gifted young writer Riccardo Artuffo, who worked on the script with her. Much of the shooting was done in little, remote Piedmont villages, and so for a while she was out of touch with Enrichetta. As ill luck would have it, during one of these absences from the city, *The Times* in London published a fanciful story about Signora Duse lying gravely ill in Lugano. Enrichetta sent an anxious wire, but received no answer.

Finally Duse replied, from the Grand Hotel at Ala di Stura, on 17 August. "Child! Enrichetta! How did that false story reach you? *I am not ill, ma chère fille, but on the contrary, I have been at work on my film for 3 weeks in 4 little villages,* black with poverty—as Claudel says—to 'establish' my scenes—. . ."

One of the joys of film-making was being able to work in contact with nature, in the stimulating mountain air. "Le bon Ambrosio" had driven four hours in his car to bring Enrichetta's cable. "When at Ambrosio's in Turin," Duse's answer continues, "I go into the darkened room *to see myself,* it has an odd effect on me—I am so detached that only the character (Rosalia) speaks to my eyes." After another week's work in Turin, the picture would be finished; then, after a stop in Milan to see the Santo, she would go back to Viareggio.

But when she saw the whole film in Turin, she was not satisfied with certain parts of it. To Enrichetta: "Some things in the film are really beautiful. And one part must be redone. Why? Because Maman, in a moment of fatigue, allowed some group scenes to be shot—and this, in the midst of my film. Two different hands are visible; almost, I would say, two souls. And I want the full responsibility for my film. *So it's another month's work.*"

With great hesitation, Eleonora asked Enrichetta to lend her some money until the completion of the film, when she would receive the rest of her advance. She suggested pawning a pearl necklace she had given Enrichetta some years before.

As a little surprise, and with the help of Ambrosio, she had shot a few minutes of film of herself in street clothes, outside the studio. It was meant to reassure Enrichetta about her health. "In the film, I speak to you, and I say to you: *'Courage, Henriette, au revoir, Maman.'*"

The little film apparently never got to London, and Enrichetta never saw it (a few inches survive in Maria Osti's villa); but she did manage to procure the money without pawning the necklace.

Meanwhile, even in its unfinished—or unsatisfactory—state, *Cenere* could be seen; and Grazia Deledda came up from Rome for a private showing. At Duse's insistence, Maria also came. Duse herself seemed to view it with new eyes, and she wrote objectively to her daughter: "The first film is finished—minus a single *raccord*, that is to say, not a central scene, but a transition between two. And voilà, *the rain has prevented it, and the wind.* Yesterday I saw it complete (minus the one scene). In the little viewing room. Maria Osti came from the country to see it. She cried and cried, unable to speak. She says the film is beautiful. There are a number of defects, but the empreinte is beautiful. One thing is an innovation (for this country; I don't know if the great Griffith has already done it, because the Americans are way ahead in film-making). It is this: throughout the whole film *I never speak.* My mouth remains shut; a yes or no with the head—and there are some very sad *no's*—All the Ambrosio personnel, the poor working girls and the clerks asked to see the film of *la patronne*; then the women came into the dark room and voilà, the *mamans* understood. So let us hope it is a success of *art and of heart.* I have already begun the second film, *The Lady from the Sea. . . ."*

She meant she had begun thinking about it. But her relations with the good Ambrosio were deteriorating. In financial difficulties—the war caused a crisis in the whole Italian film industry—Ambrosio was delaying payment, while urging her to go ahead with the next picture.

She was still waiting for the rain to stop so that she could shoot the little *raccord.* There were other touches she wanted to make, as she explained to Enrichetta: "for example, a window that doesn't open the way I want, and which must open on to a certain light and not another. . . ." Finally she left Turin and, after stopping off in Milan and Florence, went to Viareggio. There, "in the Apuan alps there are 3 little villages that are inhabited by peasants from Sardinia. And that would suit me, because the husbands are off at war or in America to earn their bread."

It was Grazia Deledda who had told her about these villages, where Duse spent a week "redoing the first part, the scene with the child, the one directed by Mari . . . was simply ridiculous and absurd and *without heart.* I redid it alone with that cameraman Omegna and I hope it is more in key with the soul of the film—which does *have* a soul—. . . ."

On 11 October she went to Alassio, up the coast, to begin preliminary work on *The Lady from the Sea*, examining locations and working on the script, which she had already outlined. "I am here to study the new film," she wrote Enrichetta. "I have with me 2 men from the Ambrosio company, one to decide the scenes, the other to frame them in the landscape. . . . I've made some trips in the automobile to look for the little house and the appropriate atmosphere. . . ."

Throughout all this work, however, she had not forgotten the war. She kept up a steady, time-consuming correspondence with a number of soldiers (including a young Duse, a distant cousin); and in Alassio, where she had spent a winter years before, she ran into her former cook, Rosetta, who cried out to her: "Signora! Signora! Look at my beautiful baby girl! And my husband's at the front!" And Duse wrote to her own daughter: "The baby is a few months old, and the woman is alone and brave. The heart shrivels, seeing them. *The whole war is on the backs of women, who must bear it.*" She decided to stay on in Alassio a while, to help Rosetta. "That at least would be something not wasted!—*How many sorrows remain unknown in this massacre*—ah, at night I think at times that some soldier is calling me!!"

From the Duchess of Aosta she learned that *Cenere* had been shown in the military hospital at Moncalieri, and had been warmly received. "Bon—" Duse gloated to Enrichetta, "for the soldiers, it works. In 2–3 months it will go to the mob. In a few days it will be shown at the front—that is, in the field hospitals, and the evenings are so long for the soldiers. . . ."

Her letter of 19 October to Enrichetta is long, weary-sounding; in a P.S. she explains the reason for her condition: "For about the ten days I have been here, I have basted together some work. . . . Pupetta, I prefer to tell you this myself, because those stupid newspapers say all sorts of things. But the situation is this: (1) I am well, (2) nothing bad has happened to me, (3) it is stupid to tell these things, but I'm afraid of the newspapers, so I will tell you myself, (4) voilà: a little auto accident, nothing bad, nothing serious. But the road was steep, and in turning, the driver made a mistake, and another auto, coming towards us, broke the windshield of mine. And so, naturally, I was rather shaken up and received a few splinters of the glass. And I was thrown forward and banged a bit, nothing serious, I give you my word. But enfin, for a few days, I must rest. Here I have found some very fine people. The thing happened on a mountain curve, *sheer drop to the sea*—the village where I had sought the location for the film is called *Cervo*. . . . There is nothing to tell. Now I am bandaged—the windshield—not agreeable, of course. I banged my face against it, but *nothing* to the *eyes*; only I have

19 little wounds, nothing at all, on the face. . . . I must tell you, to my honor, that I found a *sang-froid and a calm I didn't know I had*. Got out of the auto, and walked to an osteria, where some good people (ah, the heart of the poor) washed me, took care of me, gave me coffee, and much tenderness. The peasants called the village doctor, who came in an hour; and I was immediately treated with sublimate and tincture of iodine. The auto was . . . *not in the best of health*, and I gave up the idea of using it. With an old, rickety *closed carriage of a bishop*, I went back to Alassio. The young man from the Ambrosio studios was very kind and in despair, poor man, to see me bandaged like that. As for him, *his nose is a bit broken*. . . ."

Another victim of the accident was her eyeglasses, and their loss made letter-writing difficult for a while, though it did not cease altogether. She brought Enrichetta up to date not only on the film, but also on her problems of lodging. (The landlords of her Florence apartment were selling the building.) And on 20 October 1916 she wrote about a visit to the Santo in Milan. His brother Camillo Boito had died in 1914, and Arrigo asked her to deliver a photograph of him to an old friend, the lawyer and cabinet minister Giovanni Rosadi, in Rome.

So that evening, before leaving Milan, I arrive at 5 o'clock at the Santo's house. I walk very, very slowly, and I arrive in the courtyard—an aristocratic entrance, yes, his entrance, but the courtyard, so sad. So sad—grass among the stones, pots set in a row, like soldiers—three cats, tiny, very tiny, on the ground, sleeping on the grass; and in the courtyard, one opening into another, for there are two buildings joined to make a single one—I see—directly opposite the little door in the corner, which is the Santo's ground-floor entrance—I see a poor dog, white and black like Selva, also a setter, prisoner in a wire cage, set against the wall, sad, damp, stifling. Such sorrow. And I look, to catch my breath; and I hear the voice, and the footstep of the Santo, as if he were angry . . . I stood there perhaps two minutes, which seemed eternally long to me, and then I rang. The Santo, who was already in the vestibule, opens the door to me—he facing, me with my back turned—and the poor dog, opposite me, looking at me, with his poor tail, hoping for some help from me in his sorrow. What sadness—The Santo opens and sees nothing—and I, I see his manservant, one Pietro—who if he isn't a canaille, then truly I'm a fool. Well—now comes what I don't know how to relate—there was a whiff of an argument in the air, between master and servant; and I enter, making myself small (keeping quiet about the dog episode), thinking I am a nuisance; and voilà, the

Santo—cher Santo—He has me sit in his chair, and I see him, without speaking, sad, very very sad, those beautiful shoulders of long ago—hunched at the top like a tree that refuses to bend. I remain silent. He sits at his desk to write (he says) a letter for Rosadi, 'for it is 5 o'clock' . . . he says, 'and I haven't had time to do it.' That rogue of a Pietro comes and goes, reenters the vestibule. . . . This exasperates the Santo—who finally with all his energy (restrained) calls him, sharply 'Pietro!' There is Pietro—'go find me some string!' (an order!) 'Why?' asks Pietro!!! And here you would have to have a fine book on 'how Italians handle domestics'—a book of moeurs, which would be very useful, especially *after* the war! Bref, Pietro is despatched politely, but sent home, firmly (sharply, sharply) and voilà—the thing that gripped my heart—Voilà then the Santo, seeking by himself, left and right, a piece of string—He hunts and hunts, all the drawers of his desk, in the vestibule, in his little bedroom. Nothing. He goes, he comes, he turns, restless, confused. I, motionless—in his chair, making myself invisible so as not to annoy him, and there he is—alone—in the middle of the room, unnerved by the previous quarrel with the servant which I know nothing about, and by his searching—There he is with that *sudden* fatigue that strikes the old, as it does children—alone, bewildered, in the midst of the room . . . with his eyes, coming from afar, afar, looking at an invisible light, alone, his arms hanging at his sides, dejected, and his beautiful head as if forgetting the very thing that was making him suffer so—! I saw it! For a long time he remained like that; the September light, so mild, so peaceful, enters through the closed window and shutters (always, everything closed); and I, in the corner, looking at him—like two ghosts—after a few minutes, he recovered himself, and then—he sat, with a kind of moan, quite soft, at his desk. He says: 'You are there, Lenor? I don't know any more.' Then I, pretending to be indifferent and as if I hadn't seen, I answer: 'Yes, I'm here, yes, I'm resting, we have plenty of time, write your letter for Rosadi calmly, I'll wait'—and he, ah!, as if dreaming: 'what a good word, yes; sleep, sleep there in my chair; sleep; I'll write calmly—'

After a good half-hour he gave me the photo of Camillo and the letter for Rosadi—We were silent, the room and the street were peaceful, and the light—The portrait of a young woman, of *thirty years ago* (mine, of long ago) at his right, and a portrait of Verdi—on his desk, that's all—and some books, books everywhere.

'You are leaving?'

'Yes, at eight.'

'Yes, when one has to leave, one has already left—'

At the beginning of November, Ambrosio finally paid up and Duse was able to redeem some pearls she had pawned ("Pupa, I write you with the Duchess's pearls around my neck"); but she gave up all thought of a second film with him, as he had proved less upright and Piedmontese than she had imagined. So she had to abandon the idea of a film based on *The Lady from the Sea*, though she did not abandon the idea of making movies. First she set her hopes on Claudel to provide a script, but after dining with him in Rome she realized nothing would come from him. "I talked and talked with him," she wrote Enrichetta, "but for the moment he *detests and scorns cinematography.*"

Cenere had not yet been released, but was scheduled to open early in January. On 5 January she wrote: "I delayed leaving also because of my film—I wanted to *remake the last scene*, which, in September had not come out well in Turin—but . . . I had to write, telegraph, get someone to speak to *Ambrosio*—Enfin!—The other day I was given permission, and in an automobile, at 7.30 I drove outside Rome to film. The effort of going and coming (4 hours) was *a bit too much for my back*—and this is why I don't yet feel up to a 7 hour train journey to Florence! Tomorrow I would like to see if the scene is successful, but I don't think it is. The right landscape isn't there, and the people, so stupid—and me, so distant. . . ."

For the launching of *Cenere*, Ambrosio underwrote a special issue of the review *L'Arte muta*. The introduction spoke of the greatness of the actress and the importance of her film debut. "Cinema is not only giving birth to a work of art, but is winning a battle, that battle that has now been raging, undecided, for a decade. . . . Reverent audiences will bow at the passage of this great thing achieved through the passion of the Great Italian Woman and her intense love."

This fulsome preface was followed by a number of articles, some reprinted from past publications on Duse, others—including a piece by Matilde Serao—written especially for the occasion.

But once he had made this effort, Ambrosio—beset by other problems—seemed to lose interest in *Cenere*. (Duse's perfectionism may also have exhausted his patience.) He soon sold off the distribution rights, and the picture passed more or less unnoticed. Duse's friends loyally went to see it. Papini went with Olga Signorelli, who much later recalled: "It was a June afternoon, in 1917. . . . I remember especially the last scene, in the mountains. She dies as they are carrying her. It comes back to my memory as if I had seen it yesterday: Duse appears there, standing erect, in a garden of flowers. She is old, impressive, with her face of a *Madonna addolorata*. The snow-white hair, transfixed by the light, surrounds the proud head like a halo. Later the action shifts to the past. We see Duse young, everything around her is radiant. On her face a very delicate white kerchief flutters . . . the soft, agile movements of her slender, supple form make you believe she is young. . . . Now she is seated on a stone wall. She is cradling her child, and seems to live on that love; her hands are as light as the petals of a flower; tenderness flows from her. . . . We came out in silence, moved. Papini bought some white roses for Duse and I took them to her at the Hotel Eden."

Duse then discussed the film with Olga Signorelli: "They reproach me for the poverty of the story. Did they expect me to play Lady Macbeth or Cleopatra? . . . As if everything didn't come down finally to a handful of ashes [*cenere*] . . ."

In later years, Duse occasionally spoke of the film disparagingly; and after her death, some of her friends—Yvette Guilbert, in particular—insisted that it gave no idea of her art, though others, including the acute writer and theatre expert Rosamond Gilder, who knew Duse and saw her act, confirm that *Cenere* does convey something of the actress's genius and style. A legend—yet another Duse legend—grew up that she tried to buy up the prints in order to destroy them; but no evidence confirms this story, and a great deal of evidence, on the contrary, demonstrates Duse's affection for *Cenere*, which even today remains a striking picture, quite unlike any other of its period.

After breaking with Ambrosio and giving up hope of Claudel, she pondered further projects of her own, and started new conversations with Cines in Rome. She wrote to Enrichetta that she was thinking of "a composition of tableaux; for the period I have chosen is the Italian Trecento, full of beautiful things—frescoes, Italian churches, Umbrian countryside, for a tale of love and passion of the soul . . ."

The protagonist of the film was to be Angela da Foligno, an Umbrian saint who died in 1309. But the Cines people told her the idea was "trop beau." Duse then tried to interest a Milanese company, but again was discouraged, and came back to Rome. Camille Mallarmé, in her diary for 17 June 1917, quoted Duse as saying: "No use thinking of interesting subjects; they don't want art or soul or good work. Some trivial story with a happy ending satisfies them. . . . What they want is young and beautiful women prepared to perform any gymnastic, that's all. There's no place for Angela da Foligno, still less for me. . . ."

When nothing came of her projects, she gradually gave up hope. She was becoming increasingly involved in the war, which, for Italy, grew daily more disastrous. "Tristi giorni!" (sad days), she wrote one day on a strip of paper, which she sent to Papini.

During those war years, one of her most regular correspondents, rivaling even Enrichetta, was a young Sicilian officer named Luciano Nicastro, whom she virtually adopted. Their meeting was fortuitous, and characteristic. With a Sardinian friend, the future poet Annunzio Cervi, Nicastro was enjoying a few hours' freedom one day in Milan, on his way to report to the Bombardiers' School in Susegana. After admiring the Duomo, the two friends entered the Galleria and went into a new bookshop that had just opened at one end of it. Cervi enquired about a book by Claudel, while Nicastro looked for some Villon. As Nicastro (speaking of himself in the third person) later told it, "beside them, a lady dressed in mourning was choosing some books. Her hands took the volumes from the counter lightly. When the officers' conversation grew heated, and Cervi said that for him Claudel was a great Mediterranean, and his companion declared himself happy to take only Villon with him to the trenches, the lady's hands stopped. She turned her head and looked at the officers. She was not young. In her worn face, the beautiful and maternal eyes showed a need of comprehension and an alert sweetness. . . .

"She left her books and spoke, with a smile. . . . Learning that the two had come from Genoa and would be leaving immediately for the war zone, she asked why they were so fond of Villon and Claudel. . . ."

Finally she said to Nicastro: "Thank you, son, for telling me this and for going with such a pure spirit to the war, which is not only yours, the soldiers', but also ours . . . we who live back here. . . ."

Assuming somehow that she was a writer, Nicastro asked her name. "At first the stranger seemed reluctant to reply, then she said, simply: 'Eleonora Duse.'"

She asked Nicastro to write down his name and the address of his unit. He and Cervi wrote their addresses in her notebook and then, exchanging cries of "Viva l'Italia," Duse and the officers separated. All during the filming of *Cenere* she wrote regularly to Lieutenant Nicastro; and on Christmas Eve of 1916, on four pages of her flimsy, pale-blue paper, she wrote to him from Rome: "If I could, if only I could (dear encounter, consolatory for me, in my sad and dear Milan, on that day of sunshine), if I could be of some solace to you, in something sweet, mild, calm, in the midst of such bewildering clangor!—

"Take heart! . . . I am not writing you *because* it is Christmas, but I am so sad . . . Precisely because people *say* that it's Christmas! I went out into the streets . . . with the childish idea . . . (will you forgive me?) of sending you something.

"—What??—?—for Christmas! . . .

"I wandered the streets of Rome, amid automobiles and trams and klaxons, and lighted shop windows . . . and at a department store where, they say, you find everything that is *necessary* for soldiers . . .—Will you believe me? Forgive me—but, after all that wandering, I came home, dejected, unable to pick out anything!—This act of choosing, this anguish of tangible and material things, this pang of the soul that would like to become light and escape this earth of cruel lunatics! And among all the flannels, and gloves, and trinkets, and coffee-pots, and casseroles, and hand-warmers . . .—Stupid that I am!—I couldn't choose anything! . . ."

She asked him, instead, to tell her what he would like. "I will rob all the shops I can find. But material things—I have to be told!" Finally, when Nicastro replied that he did not need anything, she sent him books, "which are great friends and keep you company."

In January, on leave to visit his family, Nicastro stopped off in Florence to see his "war godmother." She described the encounter to Enrichetta:

"Last year he was 19, a volunteer—a year in the trenches—voilà un brave garçon. He came through Florence the day before I caught my cold. I hadn't seen him—and there he was, 19–20 ans, bien cabré—small by breed, like the people of his country (Sicilian), sensitive as a little colt, a young horse of his native race—And such a good soul! Merry, quick, laughing, tiny, and full of breeding—the good face of a *prédestiné enfant* and an admirable purity of life. He left his studies and his sisters, and a little brother of 12."

Duse then quotes him directly: "'I tell my brother.nothing about the war, because he gets hot-headed and wants to come to the trenches.'

"He had one and a half hours between trains, at the moment he was leaving I said to him, 'I'll take you to the station'—and off! he and I, in a car, as if I were the happy Maman of a child so full of spirit! Getting out of the car, at the Campo di Marte station (towards Settignano, the sky so beautiful) the boy helped me down, and we laugh, and I say: 'oh voici vos soldats! I'm coming to the front with you!' I shall never forget, ma fille, how the colt reared up! to 'attention' among the soldiers. They were waiting for him, they saluted him, army-style. 'How many minutes left?' 'Ten minutes.' And the good boy takes your Maman's hands, and kisses them—firm, calm, bold, sure of himself. Moi, I look into his good eyes, and all of a sudden—ah! the beautiful eyes, frank, calm, a bit sad, remind me of yours, ma fille—that was like a thunderbolt to the heart—then—then I remained still, too, in my place, not being able to go *into* the station, but then le petit, all of a sudden, seeing perhaps that I had almost the possibility of crying, takes my head in his hands and kisses me, saying 'Mamma!' voilà—he started running towards his coach."

On his return trip from Sicily, he stopped off again and told Eleonora about his family (his mother was dead) and his fiancée, aged seventeen. "Oh jeunesse," Eleonora wrote to Enrichetta, regretting that, since she had no advance notice, she had not been able to have a present ready for him: "a watch—cuff links—a flashlight, woollen gloves—this time I saw that he lacks these things—Voilà, he has gone back to the Carso [battlefront] and I gave him nothing! How sad that makes me! To see a child who wants something, and not give it! This time I found him even more handsome, tender, and pure-souled, even better than the first time. Je l'aime tendrement. I hope that so much sensitivity and strength will not be broken—. . ." She gave his name and address to Enrichetta, so that she too could write to him.

The letters continued, and that spring, writing from Viareggio, she called him *tu* for the first time. ". . . I call you *tu*, not because it increases a banal intimacy, but because the *tu* lifts souls, when those souls know anguish, life, and joy, and everything!—I call you *tu*, my boy, because I feel you are saint and child, soldier and man of thought, because you are of my earth, and I am Italian—Nothing else exists for me.—. . . I am not a woman of society, and I am not a patrician,—I am of *this earth*, that you love, that is yours, Italian. . . ."

Paolo Orano, on reading Nicastro's letters which Duse showed him, suggested they be made into a book. He helped her put them in order, so that they could be shown to Papini, who agreed and arranged for the small volume, entitled *La nostra salvezza*, to be published by *La voce*, the distinguished literary review of which Papini was a director and which also issued occasional books. In Duse's letters to Papini there is some suggestion that she may have underwritten, at least in part, the expenses of publication. She had also copied out some of the letters and sent them to Boito.

At a meeting with Luciano in Milan, she gave him Whitman's *Leaves of Grass* in a new Italian translation, and tried to arrange, unsuccessfully, for him and Boito to meet. When Nicastro spoke to her of philosophers, she said: "The sense of eternal poetry and the noblest revelations that you seek in philosophers, I received from Boito."

In that summer of 1917, she wrote to Enrichetta:

"Just now I delivered a little note by hand, on this same paper with this same pencil, to the Santo—I will see him tomorrow—when one has known someone for 32 years, one can easily wait till tomorrow— this evening, my heart is *hard as a stone*, a kind word would dissolve me in tears—*so* it is best to stay calmly at home—I will try to sleep (quelle trouvaille sleep is!)—

"As I came back, on foot, from the Santo's house to here . . . I know each door, each corner, each tree—I passed the house, long ago of the Giacosas, since I didn't want to pass in front of Velleda [Ferretti]'s door . . . and I thought, as I walked in this good sun, looking at this horrible Sunday crowd that eats and strolls, I thought how *many* times I have covered this short distance with my heart murdered (it's the Truth!) . . . I thought, not wanting to moan always about our separation (you and me), or mine (the Santo and I), I thought, walking along, that then, during one of those minutes, how the heart wants 'to eat'—to eat something that is its bread!—just as one is hungry to eat one's dinner— well, the heart is also hungry, que diable! It can't live on air and abstract words, at dinner time, it needs soup or meat or potatoes or carrots or cheese, so long as it has them, *has*, possesses! The heart, too, must, must have its meal! soup, choucroutte!, no matter what . . . stoicism of the heart, I have learned, finally, is also a cowardice, yes, a lack of love. . . ."

The following day she apologized and explained the tone of the letter: "Today I remain steadfast in the face of the reality of things. 1, the Santo is not at fault—he is—the Santo—2, I am wrong, basta— 3, Business men are fools." She was referring to her exhausting, fruitless cinema discussions in Milan.

"The Santo came yesterday evening, towards 9 o'clock, when he found his letter, which I had left with the concierge. She has orders not to take his letters to him. He collects them himself when he goes out. He says, that way he isn't obliged to answer immediately . . . and he came—for a moment, because he was to spend the evening at Donna Vittoria Cima's (his old friend), and seeing him again was sad and good at the same time—one *must* bestir oneself. I'm wrong, I'm wrong—Life is the present, there is neither past nor future. . . ."

Boito was the past. The present was the war. At the beginning of August she decided to go for a week to Udine, near the front. She had been invited, along with some other theatre people; but as she wrote to Enrichetta, "I criticized the invitation sharply at first, because that theatre at the front seems stupid to me—and in any case very belated; in France they set it up at the very moment of their anguish, with the Boches on their backs!—but, in the end, so it goes. I stated very clearly that I am going as *an Italian citizen*, and *not at all as an artist*. I am among the invalids, and that is where I will stay; but as citizen, my duty remains to the last day of my life—so—*I go at least to be useful*. Actors and actresses will perform some plays, and I will serve as liaison at the station, at the mouth of the trench, between them and the soldiers. I am going in my everyday dress, a warm jacket—and off! . . ."

On 8 August Nicastro received a telegram saying that the next day she would be in Udine, at the Grande Albergo d'Italia, if he could get away. At the name of Duse, his commanding officer immediately granted him permission, adding: "Tell her we all love her. . . . Tell her the 156th Battery is hers."

Nicastro traveled back as far as Cormons on his bicycle, weaving among trucks, caissons, and quartermaster horses. He described the scene in a later memoir, written in the third person: "The searchlights sought out the mountains, and those high lights, set on the peaks, recalled the glow of Etna. . . . From Cormons to Udine the officer went by train. La Duse arrived around 11, and at the Albergo d'Italia there was the anticipation that her great name always aroused, in any part of the world where she was due to arrive. . . . She wanted to reach the hotel incognito, but many already knew of her arrival, and there was a rushing and shouting on all sides—La Duse! la Duse!—as the carriage approached. The waiters could hardly restrain the crowds: la Duse got out, and she seemed a young girl."

Nicastro had remained discreetly to one side; then she saw him and he snapped to attention. Surrounded by generals and dignitaries, she excused herself, saying, "There's a soldier just come from the trenches. Allow me to greet him."

When they could talk, she repeated her reservations about performances for the troops: "There is this danger: that it degenerates into snobbery and gives the soldier in the trenches the impression that while he is living in dirt and blood, others are enjoying themselves, far from all danger."

Instead of acting (she was also suspicious of the specially commissioned patriotic texts), Duse did what she could to help, visiting the wounded, writing letters, lending a hand or an ear. To Silvio D'Amico, years later, she described the results of the acting project: "The soldiers were irritated by the country's failure to understand; they frowned on the actors and their sponsors, who claimed they had come to *entertain* them. Besides, we actors bear a curse: being separated from life, not understanding human beings beyond those we pretend to be on the stage, *acting* what other men live."

At one point, as the actors were performing Gerolamo Rovetta's old historic drama, *Romanticismo*, a character quoted Mazzini; and a soldier sitting next to Duse in the audience made "a vulgar comment." She looked at him; he caught her look and said, in Milanese: "Tomorrow you'll be going back to Milan, won't you?"

Ignoring his hostile implication, she answered: "Yes, would you like to give me some errand for your family?"

"There would be no point. In three days' time I'll be in the trenches again."

"I promise I'll be back before then."

Still suspicious, he wrote a note and his mother's address, "then he left me, cold and sullen."

Eleonora took the train at once, went to Milan, visited the boy's family and delivered the note. She immediately went back to the war zone, found the soldier, and gave him news of his family. Later she sent them money. The soldier returned to the trenches and she never saw him again.

In Milan she received a puzzling wire from Enrichetta. Years later, Enrichetta made a note about it: "On 22 August 1917 Robi Mendelssohn died in Berlin. I saw the notice of it in *The Times* of the 23rd, and tried to wire her and make her understand someone dear to her had gone, and yet I didn't want to give her a shock, so my wire named no one."

After reading the cryptic message, and not understanding it, she wrote: "I received your wire, my daughter, yesterday, coming back from the Santo's—a *warm* wire. Your heart was grieving as you telegraphed me, child, but!—I grieve too, the whole world is in anguish—" She was hurrying back to the front, but "to visit the soldiers I have had a dress made of blue cloth—I can't go there in that eternal black dress, without looking to them, like a priest in disguise. . . . In Udine, a few days before the attack, I talked with about twenty soldiers, now I will encounter others . . . I cannot speak any more, but I bestir myself, listen, understand, console—help—. . ."

A few days later, the news of Robi's death reached her. "How much happier I was yesterday, when I didn't know the sad news I am giving you—Everything that was the goodness, the tenderness, the nobility of Robi: nothing remains now except in our heart. Robi's profound goodness: nothing in the rest of our life will equal his soul. How happy I was yesterday, when I didn't know!"

At Udine, with her talent for making friends, Eleonora had met not only soldiers. From nearby Tavagnacco she wrote the next week, "Here, I entered this little house one half-hour after learning about Robi . . . The lady, whose name is Giulia, I had met in the street, in a rather difficult moment—" The difficulty was that Eleonora's hotel, in her temporary absence, had been bombed.

> And she took me with her, after I had told her my name and assured her I was "really" the Duse, for she suspected a homonym—well, we slept one night in a very calm house, while the town was going through a *very difficult* quarter-hour . . . The next day, the lady who lives in this village [Contessa Bianca di Prampero] . . . asks to see us at 5 o'clock, to patch us up a bit—so then Madame Giulia [Baronessa delle Torrazze] and I fix ourselves up as best we can to come here. It was 4 in the afternoon, of August 30—from the Albergo Italia, a maid I had sent to collect my things (my room had collapsed) brought me my letters. . . . I put on my hat—to go and pay the call—and, reluctantly, I open the letter from Gemmi [her caretaker in Florence]. He told me the news very curtly—half an hour later, I had to go and visit the new acquaintance,—and it was in making that effort that I glimpsed the real separation among human beings. It had to be done, without grumbling, keeping oneself under control—and—in fact—(a dog is whimpering as I write—)—in fact, at 5 o'clock, I entered this house—it's a very simple house—quite spacious, directly on the Tavagnacco road (you reach it by tram from Udine) and there is an enormous, lone pine, a magnificent tree! alone, mighty, already old, *green and burned* by life—Entering, my nerves on edge, my heart knotted . . . I raise my eyes and see that powerful tree—green and burned—majestic, and yet already threatened! . . . I felt the soul of Robi, I heard his voice: 'ma Chérie'—I had the feeling of his smile, of his detachment, his deliverance! What a moment!—I felt the soul of Robi, and the soul of all things—'cosmic sensation!!!'—Then I entered to call on this lady, in whose house *I have been living for a week.*

The Prampero family had suffered great losses in the war—a brother in the army and a sister in the Red Cross, both killed—and, sensing Eleonora's distress, they gave her refuge. (They were to suffer further losses, including that very house and all its contents, in the Austrian

invasion after Caporetto.) "No more tears!" Duse concluded, "understand—resist—reconstruct—know—all night the cannon—the
cannon, the cannon, flashes at the front,—from my window I can see
the Carso—but *Italy will live!*"

A week later she was in Milan again. "I came also to see the Santo—
and I saw him—to talk with him of Robi—and I talked to him—but—
have remained two days in bed without stirring, almost without
speaking—I had such need, after the jolts of Udine (and the expenses
of every sort) even of new (and charming) acquaintances I have made. I
needed 'to stretch out on the ground' or in a bed, and talk no more! . . .
The Santo?—He is so great, my child, and therefore so far from us—He
has taken as his motto the words of Marcus Aurelius, who says (I
believe he says): that we must be the most tender, and the most
impassive, among men. And so, shut up in his beautiful study; with
his little lamps, always bent over his sheets of music paper, to him our
poor earthly life seems a game of ants, who bustle about when everything, life and death, has to be fulfilled! Yes, I know, he is right; *but* the
heart mourns the departure of Robi, and I can only suffer! I know one
must die! I only wish I didn't understand that. . . . But naturally, the
Santo is the Santo—and he is right, but, an earthly consolation also
means something, when we leave one another! So then—'courage' as
the Santo says with that air of one who isn't listening to your words.
'Courage,' as one might say, 'Very well, and now let's get on with
it.' . . ."

Boito did occasionally stir from his study and the pages of the eternally unfinished *Nerone*. In May of that same 1917, he had paid a visit
with some friends to the front, to Quarin, above Cormons. At GHQ, he
was the luncheon guest of the commanding general, for whom—on
the piano of the officers' mess—he played a few pages of *Mefistofele*. On
a slow, crowded troop-train, returning from Udine to Milan, he shared
a compartment with two young convalescent officers. For their greater
comfort, he opened the window, and the gusts of cold air gave him a
severe chill. He was too polite to close it, and by the time he reached
Milan he was feverish. He was never to recover his health.

While Duse suffered Robi's loss and worried about the Santo's
decline, she had cause also to be concerned for Gabriele. He was now
in uniform, commanding a squadron of daredevil pilots and waging a
kind of personal war against the Austrians. Though he and Eleonora
had not been in touch for a decade (except for some notes and telegrams, ignored, from him to her), each was always aware of the other.
When Eleonora read of the poet's bravery—and physical courage was

a quality she had always admired—she was deeply moved and immensely proud.

In Milan, she encountered his old maidservant, Virginia, who took a word of greeting to him. And on 23 September he wrote to her:

"A little while ago I returned from the test-flight of my new plane. I was tired, and also much upset. The good Virginia came to my room, and—with a delicacy that moved me deeply—spoke to me of Ghisola.

"I needed consolation (my heart is always suffering and restless, as it was then); and consolation was given me, in an unforeseen and mysterious way.

"I leave tomorrow at dawn with my squadron. I will fly across all Italy. I will pass over Rome. Tomorrow evening I will land in a camp near the lower Adriatic. On all moonlit nights I will go to bomb an enemy port on the opposite shore. . . .

"It is sweet for me to have heard, from a poor, devoted creature, that Ghisola knows what I have done and my great love.

"But Ghisola does *not* know that in every danger I carry three talismans—always—my mother's wedding ring and the *two emeralds* (does she remember?) . . ."

Their correspondence resumed; D'Annunzio was added to the list of soldiers she wrote to. The disastrous defeat at Caporetto, at the end of October, affected her deeply, as it did Boito. But she saw the immediate effects, as the streets of Florence filled with refugees, and her new friends the Pramperos wrote to her from Rome, where they had fled. She described the crowds of refugees to Enrichetta on 22 November:

". . . And when one meets in the streets, in doorways, everywhere, everywhere, on the steps of the churches, all along the way, alone and bewildered, poor women who have never known anything but their own homes, their hearth!—all my compassion goes out to them. I have felt remorse for some days, because the first that I met, on leaving the house, towards evening—The poor woman! She had a *tiny little boy*, blond, in her arms. The baby looked at me . . . with eyes so good . . . so sad . . . my daughter . . . that so shook me, for, in the brief sight in the evening dusk, when the mother showed me the child's little legs . . . 'You see, Signora, we ran off without any stockings'—Ah, ma fille, why didn't I give her the blanket I had on my lap in that ignoble carriage where I sat!!! Why? I wept like a fool with the poor mother, but *I didn't give her the blanket!* That hurt me *so* much, I think about it all day long. I realized I *had* it, the blanket, when the carriage had already left the woman behind . . . and the woman,—I haven't encountered her again. . . ."

Though she was very short of money, she continued to give away all she had; and when she ran out, she sold her rare books to continue to help the refugees.

She grieved for strangers, and she grieved for friends. One of the sons of Liliana and Adolfo De Bosis was killed. (Another, the poet Lauro, was to die tragically years later, demonstrating against Fascism.) "Adolfo," she wrote, "how many times have you come to my aid in ephemeral sorrows, and today, when you are so stricken, I cannot come to you, to the two of you! . . . Words turn cruel, they lie. If we could hold one another by the hand, we would feel, remaining silent, that grief is eternal on this earth and escaping it is vain! . . . Your dear house, today, like this—You are all gathered around *a name*, and I cannot even speak of him to you. Anyway, the talk of outsiders, or of friends, is vain, too."

There was bad news from Nicastro, unjustly accused of insubordination during the Caporetto confusion. And bad news from Milan, where Antonietta Pisa wrote daily about the condition of the Santo. Finally, on Christmas Eve, Duse traveled to Milan, to stay with Antonietta—who had a large, heated apartment overlooking the park—from whose guest room she wrote to Enrichetta: "Velleda comes every day, between 2 and 3 o'clock—to give me the news. The Santo has regained consciousness, which actually he had never lost, except that during his fever he had some hours of delirium. But now he says himself that perhaps he is better. . . ."

It was snowing in Milan; the Pisa family, though immensely kind, were talkative and did not share Duse's intellectual interests. There was no decent table where she could write letters, and the few books in the house were in glass-fronted cases, locked up like prisoners.

On Enrichetta's birthday, 7 January 1918, her mother wrote: "Life has been good because it brought you to Edouard and your Halley—my instinct led me well in putting you on the path towards your friend and your child. Perhaps (surely) you suffered before encountering him, but . . . if I look into my heart of long ago, my suffering in living a life *far* from those I loved was as cruel as yours. That is the past; we'll speak no more of it. . . . Velleda came again yesterday—she will come today—Sometimes I look at her, or rather I listen to her talk, talk; so sl-ow-ly, and I search my heart for the love I had for her (? ! ?) = Amen. . . ."

She had tried to keep her presence in Milan a secret from Arrigo, but the meddlesome manservant Pietro saw her in the street, and a little later the Santo said to Velleda, "Tell me about Lenor." Another day he asked her to give Lenor a certain plate of his, made from a gilded fragment of the cupola of St Mark's, which Camillo had restored. After Duse left Milan, Arrigo was well enough to write her, and she answered him: "I thank and will thank again Velleda who, in the twenty-three days I stayed in Milan awaiting news of you, was faithful and dear, bringing me news almost every day. She brought me also the Venice present . . . and that seemed to me the sign that I should leave, come home, and wait."

She knitted a scarf for Enrichetta, wrote letters to little Halley, and was pleased when Japan entered the war. "Banzai!" she wrote Enrichetta, and started rereading Lafcadio Hearn. Soldiers came to the house almost daily.

Her letters to Enrichetta, usually brief during this period, contain odds and ends of her everyday life ("a hen in the garden *screams* her egg!"). She tells of the almost daily visits of Emma Garzes, her old friend from the theatre, a chatterbox but a comfortable, old-shoe sort of presence.

In March Boito was moved to a hospital, then to a nursing home, where he died on the morning of 10 June. That same evening Eleonora wrote to her daughter:

vers le soir
My child—Ma pupa—my Henriette—
You must forgive Maman, when she is sad—you, must forgive her—for she would not like to be a burden to you—and sadden you—but—that is life—that is the war—that is life—which is the war against all life!—it is raining—and the sky has something sad about it—
—came home—and I found your letter, and, the woman who delivers the evening papers, was climbing the stairs with me—I climb the stairs slowly . . . Came inside—and I settled in *my corner* to read your letter—I was reading it when, voilà, Emma—with a bright face, who says to me: 'Imagine, it's me'—'Come in, come in, Emma—just let me read Enrichetta's letter'—and I read your *dear, good* letter, which is so good! which tells of the house!—and of the children! . . .
And—afterwards, not knowing what to say, I opened the newspaper, to talk about the war with Emma, whose face was a bit sad—
—and I read—
Maman begs you to believe she is brave,—and resigned to the will of life . . . that governs us—

The Santo—is gone—yes—
—oh—for a long time I knew it—and so did he—and—he suffered so much—this morning—at 11.30, the paper says—. . .yes, yes, resignation to life—The great sorrow, was *before*, jadis jadis when I left to go about the world! and you, little—Then—yes—yes—
now—for so many years I have been . . . otherwise!
Mamma embraces you, embraces you, kisses you, ma fille, with the light of *my soul—that* was my life—and my sorrow—and my love—ah! how much love I needed to master that love—
Maman did not lie to you, ma fille—ma fille—no—
Take care of yourself—for me—that *good thing* which is the thought . . . that I have not been able to vanquish, nor do otherwise
I embrace you, my daughter, with all my soul . . .

The next day she wrote to Maria Osti, who had been expecting her at Tivoli, where rooms were being specially prepared. And she wrote again to Enrichetta:

"You see, ma pupa? It is already 11 June; already a *day* has passed, the night was calm, and I remained in silence only with the lamp burning.—I thought so much all night—towards morning the birds started singing again, as on other days, and I fell asleep. Two telegrams arrived in the night—we must think how much he was loved, and how lost Velleda and others will remain without him!—Me, I don't count—I was born, it seems, to *imitate* life, without possessing it!—It is the lot of artists—the crowd says—Ignorant people say that without suffering the artist doesn't develop—well, that happens!—because it's necessary!—I think, with a great weight on my heart, how blessed were those who were able to do something for him—My whole house is filled only with dead things. The beings who are *alive* are quite far away, for *Life* carries this condition—*separation*.

"All my thoughts, my thoughts, my wishes, my tenderness are directed to you, my child. I am sure that you *mourn*, like your Maman, and I am sure of your heart—Thank you, my child. I implore you to love *well* (without leaving)—the children—Edouard. Love *is* the sharing of the day and of the things of life. . . ."

Friends telegraphed condolences. Maria Osti came up from Rome on the 20th and took Duse back with her, to keep her for a month. The visit, from Eleonora's point of view, was not a total success, despite Maria's devotion. The house, as always, was full of people, Maria's female relatives mostly. "Il me faut ma solitude," Eleonora wrote to her daughter towards the end of July; in early August she was back in Florence.

"There was a ring at the door," she wrote to Enrichetta on 3 September, "and I was alone in the house at that moment; I went to open it . . . The visitor was a Consul from South America, who came to tell me that my husband—ill for a long time—had died a few days ago. I must go through some formalities because of some legal matter or other, for it seems, in the Consul's letter, that the person [Tebaldo] declared me his heiress. I am disconcerted by this decision, after almost 30 years of separation, and tomorrow I must see Rosadi and find out how to act. For, if by chance debts were left, I must be careful, for it is absolutely impossible for me to assume responsibility. Two people disagree— they separate—and nature follows its course—and the only law among human beings should be not to harm one another. I give you this news as I received it, ma fille, addressing myself to your intelligence and to your heart, to see in things only what is just and inevitable in human concerns—. . . God keep you, my daughter. I love you and have loved you as if I *alone* were your only support, your only resource—. . . ."

Eleonora had to make several visits to Rosadi, and there was some correspondence with Lisbon, where Tebaldo had died. And finally it turned out that the long-forgotten husband and father had left the considerable sum of 40,000 lire each for Eleonora and Enrichetta, and no debts. Though she was reluctant to accept the money, Rosadi persuaded her; it helped relieve her own debts.

In England, Enrichetta was helping her husband compile an anthology of Italian writing from the late eighteenth century to the First World War, to be published by the Cambridge University Press. She sent an outline of the scheme to her mother, for her comments. Eager always to comply with any request from her daughter, Duse sent a number of suggestions, over several letters: to leave out second-rate dramas, include moderns like Aldo Palazzeschi, Umberto Boccioni, even Ardengo Soffici—bold choices for the time—and not to forget Giuseppe Parini: "For [Giovanni] Pascoli—he is the greatest—you mustn't choose only the most familiar and the youthful, but choose rather among the more mature and less popular works." For Enrichetta's sake, Duse reread Giosuè Carducci; and in the light of a lamp bequeathed her by the Santo—the lamp that always stood on the desk in his study—she copied out some lines of Dante. In the preface to the published volume, an excellent and unconventional selection, Edward acknowledged his indebtedness to his mother-in-law. He had included several of the writers she had suggested; and the table of contents lists many of her friends: Giacosa and his brother Piero, D'Annunzio, Orvieto, Papini, Prezzolini, and Salvemini.

The war was coming to an end. "Vive l'Amérique," she wrote, "Vive Wilson!" And on 6 November, two days after Italy had signed a separate armistice with Austria and less than a week before the general cessation of hostilities, she wrote: "The light returns! Each of us knows better his own rights, his own duty! In spite of the word 'Victory', there is a great weeping in the air. The Victory is only in wanting it. But never in conquering it! Oh, how many things we are responsible for! Oh how many promises we must keep! How much self-control, boldness, and constancy. *Everything* remains to be done. . . . Oh, I wish no one would shout, no one would say useless words, and bombast would disappear from the world! . . . today a great silence, finally, is in the street; and after all these months, let each of us listen to destiny! . . ."

17
Return

During the last months of the war, the yearning for a reunion with Enrichetta filled Eleonora's thoughts. Even as the war was still raging, there had been some talk of the daughter's coming out to Italy to visit her mother. On 30 September 1918, not long before the armistice, Duse wrote a letter, which she gave to her friend Etta, about to leave for London: ". . . she will also bring you my little watch, old, worn (like me), second-hand; but it works—an object of no value but one that has lived with me and was with me in the Santo's room the last time I saw him. She will deliver it to you, living, with its tick-tock that resembles our life. Keep it, Henriette: it is the thing I love most at this moment, and I send it to you. I had nothing else alive to send you. . . ."

In mid-November Eleonora left Milan for Florence and wrote, "Maman arrived on the night of the 17th. But she traveled in an unheated train, with broken windows. No omnibus at the station. An hour's delay, which meant it was one o'clock in the morning; and a wind, a real Florence wind."

She caught a cold, and since her own house was in disorder, she lay ill in a hotel room, too tired to see friends, even Nicastro. "The war, the peace, *everything* has worn my heart—I feel in the peace only an immense, immense, terrible, empty cosmic pity."

The cold turned into dangerous influenza, but finally she was able to move back to Via della Robbia, where she had people to help her (and the nearby Trattoria Ciofini to send in hot meals). To Maria Osti, on 19 April 1919, she wrote: "Enrichetta writes just, sacrosanct things—that—given the condition of this country she cannot risk coming with the children because of the *journey* and the *food*—*milk* regime that might be hard in Italy at the present moment. Therefore, she *isn't coming!* And she's right. I find it wise and right for her *not* to come. Now, however, the fifth year since we saw each other, she and I, is nearly ended; and she begs and insists that *I* go."

Despite her health, Duse agreed to undertake the journey. "I am tired of being tired," she wrote Maria in the same letter, "and of dying drop by drop; and if the temperature were to become more mild, I'll pack myself into a compartment like a trunk, and I'll go."

First she made a brief trip to Venice, house-hunting, because she was going to have to give up Via della Robbia. But the place she had hoped to take on Murano did not work out. She returned to Florence before setting off.

A friend, the lawyer Ciani, had agreed to accompany her as far as Paris, to help her through the formalities at the frontier. Maria Osti came up from Rome to see her off.

"At the station," Maria later recalled, "we found the good Avv. Ciani. They boarded the Paris train. The big lawyer, as she called him, took his seat in the compartment, while she stood at the window, and I was on the platform below, for a last goodbye. I was deeply moved. She had said, before boarding: 'Perhaps it's farewell forever!' . . .

"The train began to move, and I followed her from the ground. I can still see her: the figure erect, index finger pointed up, the gaze almost absent and yet concentrated in promise and affirmation of secure faith. I see her as if carved, in that solemn pose, which was not theatrical but hieratic—in a certitude of soul that moved away, though remaining still present. . . ."

A friend of Enrichetta's came out from Cambridge, met Duse in Paris, and shepherded her to England. Enrichetta had been urging her to consider settling there, with the family; but, though the reunion was a happy one, it soon became clear that a permanent residence for Duse in England would be impossible. Enrichetta and her family led well-ordered lives; Duse was too fond of her own solitude. And there was also the English climate, a grave problem for one who suffered from the cold as she did. As she wrote to a friend, "May. At the fire, with a shawl around me."

Her stay lasted seven weeks, and before it was over she was homesick. A stream of letters was sent from Huntingdon Road to Italy: to Maria Osti in Tivoli, to the writer Ofelia Mazzoni, and to her friends the Casale family in Asolo, the little Veneto town where she had visited them, and where, now, she asked them to start hunting for a house that would suit her.

On 8 July she wrote to Maria: "Enrichetta and I have decided it's best for me to return; there are too many difficulties of life and climate here (as in Italy, for that matter); and since the children have to go to the sea at the end of the month, at the end of the month I will also leave for home. I will travel via the Riviera (instead of via Modane), and I will stop off in Cannes for a few days, two or three. . . ."

Camille Mallarmé had finally married Paolo Orano, and they were living in Cannes at the time. Duse's stay with them was restful; the

Oranos were consideration itself. "Their life," Eleonora wrote Maria, "is an example of how love can hold out against life!"

Maria, "taking leave from her flock," as Duse said, came all the way from Tivoli to meet her near the French border at Ventimiglia; without a passport, Maria could not go to Cannes. "I waited long hours in that dark border station where the desolate impression of the war's end still remained. The few light-bulbs were powerless to overcome the menacing darkness of that night. Now and then a rare train would arrive in silence: it would come and leave again. From a train coming from France I saw a few people descend in silence, poor families with children, bundles, poverty, coming home after God knows what painful adventures. And I stayed there waiting in that silence, in that semi-darkness, that uncertainty. . . . Midnight passed. Finally I was roused by the monotonous jangle of the signal of an incoming train, which then slowly entered the station. I saw Duse at the window, as she glimpsed me. I went to her at once. . . ."

The next morning the two friends traveled to Ponte San Pietro, a vegetarian retreat near Bergamo, run by an old friend of Duse's. Then, after a few days' rest, they went on to Asolo, where Maria left her at the Albergo Sole. The Casale family took her into their Villa Belvedere for a longer stay. There, in the province of Treviso, where some of her family had come from, she felt at home, as she had written earlier to Nicastro: "How well I know those roads of the Veneto!—sweet roads—And the soft speech of my grandmothers. . . ."

The Casales, excellent musicians, often played in the evenings, and from her room Duse could hear the music. The peace of these days was abruptly, unexpectedly destroyed by a letter, a violent and hostile letter, from Robi's widow Giulietta, her old friend, the companion of her travels. Giulietta had been silent for some time; Duse had written to ask for news, and again there had been silence. But now the reply arrived. The next day, 22 October, Eleonora wrote to tell Enrichetta about it: "Giulia's letter—very harsh—answering my, insistent and sincere, request to see her again, says that '*not even the shadow of our former friendship*' exists in her—and since I am unaware of that, she says it is useless and harmful to remember. She says that during Robi's lifetime she didn't break with me for fear of making Robi suffer, but that now nothing can keep her from refusing to continue a relationship that has no foundation any longer except bitterness—. . . ."

The attack disturbed Eleonora deeply, and the shock is evident in the second letter to Enrichetta, written later that evening: ". . . I am like a person from whom something has been *cut* inside, I don't know what

. . . But I feel a kind of *coupure* that I can't explain—Just now Pierin and Lucia played a bit of music downstairs, and that music of Beethoven brought back memory of places—and I saw again the house of Giulietta, of Robi, *their piano*, their violoncello, the little children—Berlin . . . The work of my life jadis—Voilà—vanished—Listening to that music, my heart went round my heart, and I find myself, my daughter, ma pauvre pupa, that voilà voilà voilà, a new truth revealed to my soul by G's letter = So then, ma pauvre fille, when I was going *around the world*, having no 'home', no 'foyer'—and loving the impossible—I believed, hélas, that *one, only one*, a single person, hélas, suffered through my fault: you—my child—yes, yes, yes, I knew well that I had not *wanted* that hurt,—no, but I had *caused it* inevitably, as inevitably as one is born to life, without asking, for no one asks to be born! quel cadeau!—Ma fille, voilà—not only did I cause *you* to suffer, but also another = G, who *screams* it in her letter, so fiercely. I thought this sad privilege of causing suffering, of tormenting—no, 'martyring' (as the letter says)—was limited to 'mother and daughter'—and how often I asked your forgiveness, my heart knows—But this heart is then quite deaf, blind, hard as stone, if it never sensed it was making another suffer—never!—. . . ."

In the past, apparently, Robi had felt a deep tenderness for Eleonora, who had delicately kept him at arm's length. Now, in her jealousy, Giulietta even said the two had been lovers (to the outrage of Désirée, who had been present during all Duse's Berlin visits and could testify to the contrary). "Nobody knows how to love," Duse's letter concludes, "which means forgiving oneself and forgiving others." The following summer her ache was somewhat assuaged when Giulietta's daughter, a future actress—who was named Eleonora after Duse, her godmother—escaped her mother's surveillance and paid Duse a secret, healing, affectionate visit.

In November she left Asolo—where snow already covered the surrounding mountains—and went to Tivoli, to Maria Osti's. But she was still restless, and again talked of going back to work. A severe attack of asthma and a fever kept her from taking any steps for a while; and Maria—seeing her friend's uneasiness in the country peace—found an apartment in Rome and offered to pay the rent.

In her bedroom, Duse wrote a letter to her hostess and gave it to her, declining as gently as possible the generous offer: "I myself want Peace, after the years of anguish that all of us are going through, but peace does not mean my *lying down*—and allowing myself to be carried by you!—. . . ."

In Florence, she got in touch with Countess Rucellai, cousin of her old American friends the Gilders; the Countess's family owned two houses in Asolo, and one was put at Duse's disposal. On 23 May 1920, she wrote joyously to Maria, "I am going to the Mamma's villa, which is called *La Mura*; it is a little house covered with ivy at the *entrance to the village*, where the fountain is, you remember?—This way I don't have to cross all of Asolo to arrive (convenient also for the van). . . . She is letting me have this house for the whole summer—and wants no payment. . . ."

A week later Duse was installed in La Mura, and on 30 May she wrote a letter to the Contessa, who must have read it with some dismay:

> . . . The first impression on taking over the house was that these servants of yours are very honest and rare because they are absolutely loyal to you. . . . Everything here will surely be preserved forever, under their guardianship, which can be summed up as: *Leave things where they are.*
>
> This, nowadays, is reassuring for the *owner of the house* . . . but not for—how shall I put it?
>
> Things, the objects that live with us, chosen by our spirit, *feel* our absence and our presence, and suffer if neglected. So it happens here: *everything* is in its place, obviously *left there* for years. But time is inexorable . . . and things crumble, decay, like us, day by day.
>
> The curtains are heavy with cobwebs, impregnated with accumulated dust, the picture frames . . . (and how many!) serve as nest for many *living creatures*, which enter undisturbed from the garden into the dear silence, and with security (theirs) make *nests* in the heart of the house itself . . .
>
> Piles of rugs lie moth-eaten on the ground floor, stacked like firewood . . . Enfin, if I can somehow express my gratitude it is precisely by telling you how much your presence would be necessary, here, for a few hours, to take a look at things, assess and curtail the destruction that time, absence, and the *passive fidelity* of honest servants are wreaking on your dear possessions.
>
> The wooden balcony . . . here (on the second floor, next to the lovely glassed-in study) is collapsing for want of little repairs not made in time . . . and the lovely rose bush, that entwines it, through lack of pruning has an enormous blossoming of *dead roses*, dead in May . . . what a shame!—. . . to make these beloved creatures of God suffer like this, to let them die when they ask only to live! In

short, *every thing*: nature, house, furnishing is in a state of advanced *decay*. . . .

Duse was not an easy guest, and La Mura was not the ideal house for someone in her condition. "The scant strength at my command makes it a great effort to *climb* and *descend* the stairs between the third floor and the ground floor, where there is situated that requirement of our physical health—the Water Closet [in English in the original]. . . ."

Eleonora was hoping to rent the house on an annual basis, for—in spite of its decay and discomfort—she was already in love with it. (It still stands and is still charming—and run down.) But she needed a Water Closet on the top floor, where her bedroom was, and she was willing to contribute to the expense of installation. She also wanted to eliminate a number of objects so that she could bring up some of her own things. The Contessa does not seem to have paid the requested visit, and on her own initiative Duse sought out Sor Carlo, the gardener, and had him give the roses a good pruning.

The passive resistance of the *onestissimi* domestics was less easily solved. Apologizing for what might seem ingratitude, Duse wrote to her hostess, to say that they were "*imperméable* to any exchange of *simpatia*, necessary for reciprocal toleration when people live under the same roof. . . ." And the next letter to the Contessa was written from the Albergo Sole, where Eleonora had taken refuge. Temporarily at least, the domestics had won.

From the Sole, Eleonora went for a while to Cortina. Her health was much more alarming than her generally jaunty letters suggest. While she was in Cortina she had to summon the young Bolognese doctor Gino Ravà, who had treated her on previous occasions. "I go, and I find her in a pathetic state," he recalled later. "Asthma, abundant purulent expectoration, nervous depression to a degree that did not allow her to risk traveling alone. I convince her easily to leave with me. Her strength, physical and spiritual, had to be restored; she needed a quiet place, with every comfort; I thought to escort her to the lake of Dobbiaco [Toblach, in an Alpine region newly annexed from Austria], where there was a suitable hotel. I still remember our arrival, by train, at Dobbiaco, the long—and for Duse, very painful—wait we had to bear with, to procure a carriage to take us to the lake three miles away. We were sitting outside the only hotel as yet reopened after the war's destruction, and Eleonora Duse waited, annoyed and suffering. Then I saw a de luxe open car drive up, in which there was a sturdy man and a young lady. They stop and rush, amazed, to greet the Diva. . . ."

The pair were the popular young actress Vera Vergani and the playwright-director Dario Niccodemi. After their effusive greeting, they climbed back into their expensive car and went off. Duse's wry comment to her doctor was: "These young actresses, when they see me, they are moved to tears! They should save their tears for other uses!"

Ravà pointed out that she could have asked for a lift in her admirers' smart car. "She smiled. She hadn't thought of that. She could so easily lose awareness of herself. And perhaps it was this prodigious gift that had made her the greatest actress of her time."

She spent a week at Dobbiaco, and sometimes with the doctor she talked about working. He recalled those talks: " 'How to face the stage again? This is nervous exhaustion,' she said. 'Perhaps there is no remedy.' It's old age, the vile old age she had always feared. And yet I am convinced that her only salvation lay in a return to the stage. Often I found her unwell, overcome by anguish and asthma; but if the conversation turned to a subject that interested her, her condition changed as if by magic. It was necessary to restore her faith in herself and remind her how her only consolation in life had always been *work*. . . ."

Dr Ravà had just published a little book on the treatment of nervous diseases, which Duse read and annotated. And at the end of August, she wrote to him: "To reactivate 'communications' it would be best to take action. Taking action (in my case) would be not to go *back*, now, to Asolo, but to go to the city where people work. Tomorrow morning, if you can come up to me, please bring with you a timetable for Milan. . . ."

But if she did go to Milan, the visit was short and unfruitful. The Contessa Rucellai had agreed on the renovations of La Mura, and on 9 September 1920 Duse was back there: "I found the *little room* next to the bedroom, in order, now with WC and Lavabo."

She did not enjoy her modern conveniences long, because a little later she found a house for sale, the Casa dell'Arco, at the other side of the town; and she bought it. It needed a great deal of work done at a time when workmen were still hard to find. The season was growing wintry, so she fled, first to Florence, then to Naples, where she had heard hotel rooms were easier to find. On 30 November she wired to Maria: "My address Parkers Hotel. Infinite weariness of soul and body. . . ." And to Contessa Ruccellai, the next day: "I didn't remain in Asolo for the winter, to escape my winter cough; and now I'm coughing like a dog. I didn't remain in Asolo, because the house wasn't *confortable* and in order, and here I have no house.

"And am in a Hotel . . . in one room, with twin beds, which in itself is enough to make me nervous, because I can't bear being with somebody else all day and all night. And I say this without a particle of *ingratitude* towards Désirée, who is an angel of patience with me, always ready to sympathize, but because truly this *not having had a house for six years* (of war!) has made me and is making me suffer like nothing in the world." Having sought mild weather in Naples, she found cold and a blasting wind. By the end of December, she was traveling again, back to Florence, by way of Rome.

Her plans for returning to the theatre were now serious. It was not only a matter of spiritual therapy, as Dr Ravà had sensitively divined; it was also, simply, a matter of money. Her savings, largely from the South American tour of 1907, had been deposited with Robi in the Mendelssohn Bank in Berlin. The notorious German inflation had drastically reduced those funds; and after much correspondence, mostly with Robi's less likable brother, the residue was sent to her (not, as the legends have it, with a few postage stamps, but with a banker's order). But that liquidation took time, and while she waited Duse was hard up. The Duchess of Palmelle's twin pearls—which she had pawned before—were now sold. Work was the remaining solution.

But it was not an easy solution. Assembling a company, engaging a manager, choosing a repertory, ordering sets, creating new *chiffons*, booking theatres: her uncertain health made all these tasks seem insuperable. To join a ready-made company as guest star was a more attractive prospect. An offer—among many—arrived from Holland, and she considered it seriously. "People full of fervor," she wrote to Marco Praga. But he discouraged her: the idea of her playing in Italian, surrounded by a company speaking Dutch, seemed to him "alla Tommaso Salvini, histrionic." Duse allowed herself to be dissuaded.

The dissuasion was all the easier because Praga had a counter-suggestion: Virgilio Talli, with whom she had played Gorky in 1905, was assembling a company of young people to open at the Teatro Argentina in Rome in the spring of 1921. For Duse, he suggested the parts of the mother, Rose Mamaï, in Alphonse Daudet's *L'Arlésienne*, and Lady Macbeth. When Duse showed signs of genuine interest, Talli—in his eagerness—sent her, through Praga, a draft contract. The wording irked her: Madame Duse would select her repertory, *in accord with* Commendatore Talli. She returned the document unsigned.

Actually she was out of touch with the Italian theatre, its currents and undercurrents. The figure of Talli, producer-director, was outside her experience, a new development. In the old days—in her beloved and hated *jadis*—the star was the undisputed captain of the ship. Though she could be gracious with her leading men and her company managers; though she could even allow someone else, like Andò in the early days, to take over the staging of a piece; she always had the final say about the tone, the movements, the repertory, even the props.

With Ermete Zacconi, her contemporary, she felt more at home; and when she received an offer from him she was interested. She had encountered him at the front, during the war, where he gave performances for the troops. "We found her, my wife and I," Zacconi later recalled, "in a little rustic restaurant, spirited, full of confidence. She wasn't there to perform, but to help those fine boys, and she was there in their midst, splendid and mettlesome, inspiring faith and love."

A few years later, in Florence, Zacconi's wife ran into Duse on the street. When she came home, as Zacconi recalled, she was in tears, describing the great artist: "a lady modestly dressed in black, walking along and looking around, afraid of being seen by someone." In her brief conversation with Duse, Signora Zacconi had learned of her financial situation.

"Ermete and I are yours to command," she said; and the next day both of them went to see Duse in her hotel. "All three of us were moved. I offered her everything I could, with all my heart: namely my collaboration and my company's, with no economic responsibility for her; she would receive 60 per cent of the earnings, and I, 40 per cent."

He also offered her totally free choice of her repertory. She asked him to give her some time. Repertory was the stumbling-block. She wanted to look for something new for her return to the public. She spoke with the young critic Silvio D'Amico, mentioning the living Italian writers she knew and admired: Papini, Palazzeschi, Prezzolini, Riccardo Bacchelli, Giuseppe Cardarelli. Couldn't these writers be persuaded to think of the theatre? She had read with great interest *Così è se vi pare*, the recent play by Pirandello. D'Amico gave her the even more recent *Come prima, meglio di prima*.

In early spring she went to Turin, still having made no decision, to see Zacconi and his company in Musset's *Lorenzaccio*. The next day she sent him a note: ". . . I missed not one word last night, not one emotion, one intention of yours. Alas! How can we say in words the secret anxiety that binds the spirit of one artist to another artist? For a moment, the 'soul breathed,' and all evening I was with you, dear Zacconi, devoted, admiring, and grateful. . . ."

They talked again about the prospect of collaborating, but still came to no conclusion. Duse went to Milan. Zacconi moved from Turin's

Teatro Regio, which Duse feared was too large to allow her voice to carry, into the smaller Teatro Balbo. One evening, as he was performing *Othello*, he saw her in a proscenium box. The next day, she finally told him she had chosen the two works for her rentrée: *The Lady from the Sea*, the Ibsen drama she had hoped to film, and Marco Praga's eight-year-old drama *La porta chiusa*. They would open in May with the Ibsen.

"For me, too, those were days of passion," Zacconi recalled, speaking of the rehearsal period. "La Duse was very agitated . . .; her silence of so many years, her uncertain health, everything contributed finally to keeping my heart in my mouth."

It was a nervous time. All over Italy, and especially in industrial Turin, there were strikes. A short time before, a bomb had been thrown in a theatre in Milan, with casualties. Duse, who had felt the war so intensely, felt this unrest too. Enrichetta and the children had come to Turin, and their presence was a joy, but also a preoccupation. She was often too busy, or too ill, to see them, or to see other friends, like the American Helen Mackay, who was also in Turin for the opening.

Finally it was the evening of the premiere: 5 May 1921. The little Teatro Balbo was completely sold out. In the gala audience there were many actors, including Febo Mari, her leading man in *Cenere*, and Gabriellino D'Annunzio, the poet's thirty-one-year-old son. Marco Praga was there, and the twenty-year-old Piero Gobetti, a brilliant intellectual, who wrote an acute study of her art in *La frusta teatrale*. The theatre was also filled with flowers. (Duse took them the next day to the church of San Carlo.)

The curtain rose on Dr Wangel's garden, the first scenes were played. Zacconi, playing the doctor, made his entrance. And then, from the wings, came the unmistakable voice which no audience had heard for over a decade: "Wangel, are you there?" She appeared, with her crown of silver hair, the signs of age and illness visible on her radiant face. It was an electric moment: everyone in the Balbo had a sense of being present at an historic event.

Silvio d'Amico came to see her (thus missing, in Rome, the equally historic opening night of Pirandello's *Sei personaggi in cerca d'autore*) and reviewed the performance, adding his authoritative voice to the enthusiastic chorus of critics, whose descriptions of the event are uniformly—even monotonously—favorable. In his diary d'Amico wrote, under the date of 7 May 1921: "She gave me her hands to kiss, in tears. She was happy. She feels confident again. She read my horrible article: good: she is awaiting the second. She will be happy if I defend *The Lady from the Sea*. She speaks to me at length of the drama. I say: The drama of the female spirit—! She replies:—No! The drama of everyone! . . ."

In her pleasure with her successful return, she was full of plans. First a tour of northern Italy, adding *Ghosts* to the two plays given in Turin. Then another tour of Italy in the autumn, ending in Rome. And then?

"Then, she will come back to Turin, where she plans to settle, take a little theatre, ask young writers for works, and some contemporary foreign poets. She is thinking of Yeats; she would like a translation of Synge's *Riders to the Sea* . . . De Bosis has translated *Borkman* for her. She will do the *Persians* of Aeschylus, translated by Orano. She is full of excitement and activity. Her daughter was here, left yesterday. . . ."

Next stop, for Duse and the Zacconi company, was Milan, where their emotional success was repeated. Renato Simoni wrote in the *Corriere della sera* of the acclamations during the performance and of the crowd that gathered at the stage-door afterwards. "When the pale lady with the grave and tender eyes went off in the automobile, to which some youths were clinging, more applause exploded."

As Simoni pointed out, for many members of the audience these Duse performances were a return; but for many others they were the first experience of a legend. And even for Simoni, who had seen her in the past, "the art of Eleonora Duse [has reached] an incredible expressive lightness, along with a powerful interior density. And so a bare hint of tears, a quaver in the voice, was at times more formidable than a cry would have been."

When Ibsen's somber, elusive drama was followed, a few days later, by Praga's bourgeois drama of adultery, *La porta chiusa*, the success was even greater. Praga's play had been somewhat old-fashioned even when first given in 1913, and now it was out of date. Aware of its defects, Duse still had a certain fondness for it, probably because her role—the central figure of a mother who has sinned but redeemed her past by a life of virtue and sacrifice—obviously affected her personally. The speeches of Bianca Querceta sometimes recall those anguished letters to Enrichetta asking forgiveness for the long separations of the past.

Though she was grateful to Zacconi, Duse really wanted to be on her own. "The effort with Zacconi was *passive*," she wrote Enrichetta later, "for I was working *chez lui*. This time, it will be *active*, for it will be *chez moi*. But everything, everything must be done . . . plays, actors, and actresses.—quelle affaire! . . ."

The company she put together included some of her old comrades, like Ciro Galvani and Alfredo Robert and his wife Enif; but there were also some new faces, Ruggero Lupi, and Memo Benassi, who played her son in *La porta chiusa* and the mysterious stranger in *The Lady from the Sea*. In Rome—where d'Amico again wrote enthusiastically about her—Duse received a message from D'Annunzio: a young friend of his brought her the first copy of *Notturno*. With the book, he sent a proposal to found a theatre at his villa on Lake Garda. Duse agreed to the proposal, but did not accept his invitation to come to the villa for a period of repose.

In the summer of 1922, she called on a friend in Milan, the writer and diplomat Tommaso Gallarati Scotti. "Early in July," he wrote years later, "in the summer silence of my old house, where I had remained alone . . . a maid knocked at the door of my study. . . . I was told that in the hall at the foot of the stairs a lady with gray hair, very tired-looking, asked to speak with me; she hadn't wanted to give her name. I went down. I didn't recognize her at once. Then, with amazement: la Duse."

They had known each other for a decade and had met once during the war, in Udine. Now she had come to him in her search for new plays, even though he had never written for the theatre before. "She would like to interpret a part in keeping with her age and the condition of her spirit, a play for everyone: a simple, human drama, without scenic artifices. Something religious [Gallarati Scotti was a leader of a movement of Catholic intellectuals] that could be understood and could move an audience of humble people. . . ."

He showed her a scene he had drafted, a mother's prayer. Duse began reading it, first in silence, then "she began to murmur, in a low voice, the words of the mother, clasping her fleshless hands in an attitude of prayer. . . ." When she finished, she insisted he must complete, fill out the play; for she had to perform it. It was to be called *Così sia* ("So Be It").

While she was still in Milan, D'Annunzio arrived, invited to make an important speech from the balcony of Palazzo Marino, the city hall, opposite La Scala. It was occupied by the Fascists, on the eve of assuming power. They had sent an ultimatum to Prime Minister Facta after the wave of strikes called by the harassed workers. D'Annunzio improvised an address on the (for that moment) unlikely theme of goodness. "I see sparkling in you the effective, militant goodness, affirmative and creative goodness, the goodness of fighters and builders: victorious goodness." The crowd had trouble hearing him, but he was given an ovation all the same. Mussolini was disappointed.

That same day, at the Hotel Cavour where both Gabriele and Eleonora were staying, the two met. Not, as some romantic biographers have suggested, by accident, but by appointment. Duse had business to talk over with him: she had decided to add *La città morta* to her repertory, and she wanted the author's sanction for some necessary cuts.

No one else was present during their meeting, though D'Annunzio's aide Italo Rossignoli had accompanied the Comandante—as the poet was now called—as far as Duse's door. When he was shut outside, he peered through the keyhole, but could hear none of the talk. The encounter—after eighteen years of separation—was moving. D'Annunzio could not resist a dramatic statement: "How much you loved me!" he is supposed to have said. Duse's comment, afterwards, to Olga Signorelli, was: "And inside myself, I thought: here's a man with yet another illusion. If I had really loved him the way he believes, then when we separated, I should have died of it. Instead, I was able to live." Actually, Duse had thought of dying, in that terrible March of 1904, but by 1922 she had revised her own history.

Italian unrest was reported abroad, and Duse was worried about how the news might affect Enrichetta. Two days after the meeting with Gabriele, Eleonora wrote to her daughter: "The papers will speak perforce of blood and conflict (and fraternal blood was spilled) But—But— for one who listens to the beating of the heart, (and sees the *cause*) (and not only the *effect*), I can assure you, yes, with sorrow—that our country *will not perish. It is no longer hatred* that animates this youth of soldiers, but the *search for faith*, and the search to *love one another*, and to be united. . . . From Asolo, when I am home, I will get my bearings and tell you, faithful to the spirit, the things seen and felt between *the soldier*, the *Poet*, and me—

"I *obeyed* your advice, my child, and I kept *my soul* listening to that force (him, G. D'A.) . . . For the moment, I will only say that, though there remains in me, limpid, this *complete absence of joy*, I recognize clearly a *great benefit* from that contact—and I thank God, who ordained it."

Just over a week later, a mysterious accident occurred. Gabriele fell—or was pushed—from a window of his villa, and was rumored to be close to death. Distressed, Duse actually made the trip to the Vittoriale, to see for herself that he was all right. This was their farewell. From that time on, the poet emerged more and more rarely from his eyrie, part hermitage and part stronghold. Duse was soon to leave for her last tour.

Her return to the theatre was not all ovations. She still had battles to fight. And when she was not in the big cities, she did not always play to full houses. On one occasion, in despair, she had to borrow 30,000 lire from a Genoa impresario. Towards the end of the summer, she wrote to Enrichetta again: "No use suffering—I must *obey*. There is the only, great word. I try to '*tune myself*,' my daughter, like a violoncellist who *tunes* his instrument. Alone, I adjust, *tune* the strings, to draw sound from them, and not break them. . . ."

In December she opened a brief season at the Teatro Costanzi in Rome, the opera house where two decades earlier she had presented the memorable production of *Francesca da Rimini*. Here she now presented *Così sia*. The house was "too big and unsuitable," according to Gallarati Scotti, and the play was a failure. Olga Signorelli, who was in the audience, recalled: "After the first speeches, despite the moving simplicity with which Eleonora Duse, at the side of the dying child, said the prayer to the Madonna of Miracles, whistles resounded in the house."

Duse reacted as if wounded. She stood erect, and—as Signorelli said—seemed to become taller. She continued the prayer in a soft voice. Afterwards, coming to her dressing room, she found the author. She held out both hands to him and said: "All the same, I feel I am right. If it wasn't understood today, it will be tomorrow . . . I will put it on the stage everywhere, in Italy and in the world."

Her great Roman success was *Ghosts*. Her Mrs Alving, as d'Amico wrote in the *Idea nazionale*, "is not the sorrowing bourgeois mother of *La porta chiusa*, and she is not the pathetic peasant mother of *Così sia*. She is the woman who, through the ghastly experience of her torment, through long introspection, long meditation, has come to achieve the terrible awareness of the error in which her existence has taken place, in which the life of all men and all women, the universal drama, has taken and is taking place. Look at her worn face, crowned by the sanctity of her beautiful gray hair. Or her proud, erect person, cloaked in the abundant Norwegian dress. And her regal walk, those gestures and attitudes in each of which, despite the apparent and almost naked spontaneity, there is a total, ineffable harmony. . . . We remained stunned, intoxicated by her beauty. . . ."

Mussolini was, after the March on Rome, the Prime Minister. He was staying temporarily at the Grand Hotel, not far from the more modest Albergo Reale in Via XX Settembre, where Duse was lodged. He sent word that he wished to see her and asked her to set a time for his visit. Surprised, she agreed to receive him next day.

At first the visit was not a success. Like many other Italians, including a number of future anti-Fascists, Eleonora had hopes that Mussolini would bring Italy inner peace, as she had written to Enrichetta; but she did not take a liking to the new head of government. After the visit, she gave a full account to Olga, who recorded it:

"At three o'clock sharp I hear a knock at the door. 'I have come as Prime Minister,' Mussolini says, the moment he enters the room. 'Your Excellency, I am at your feet,' I answer him, concealing behind the jest the uneasiness I felt at his gaze, that hard face with jutting jaw. But when he clasped my hand in his, a small, sensitive hand, and said in a tone almost of anxious expectation: 'Tell me, tell me what can be done for the Italian theatre?' I felt myself won over. We spoke of art, of what must be done for art. We spoke at length. He told me he will never forget this conversation. And I will not forget it, either. When he was about to leave, we said goodbye three times: at the table, in the middle of the room, at the door. He told me to submit a plan."

Duse submitted nothing, and Mussolini was too busy to think of the theatre for a while. Later D'Annunzio told the dictator about Duse's grave financial difficulties (which were common knowledge and newspaper fodder, in any case), and he offered her a pension. But, as she said to Olga, "No, my dear, I cannot accept. There are other misfortunes, more serious ones, to be relieved now. The mother of Cesare Battisti must have a pension: an artist, no, never. An artist *must* work. I can still work and I *want* to work."

But she couldn't work, not for a while. The Rome season, and the fiasco of *Così sia*, had worn her out. She had to break off the season. On 29 January she appealed to her rich English friend Katherine Onslow, who lent her the needed money to pay off the troupe. D'Annunzio also managed to arrange an advance on hypothetical future performances, in an equally hypothetical State Theatre. Later, when Duse was better, Katherine organized a series of performances in London.

At this period, as Olga Signorelli relates, Eleonora was looking for a play to replace *La porta chiusa*, whose faults were becoming more and more apparent to her. "Nowadays," she said, "when so many mothers have suffered the anxiety of having their sons in the war, it seems to me puerile and exaggerated for that mother [Bianca, in the play] to worry so much about a son who is leaving for Africa, perhaps in comfort, in a Wagon-Lits."

Pirandello, who had heard of her search for new works and perhaps also of her admiration of his plays, sent her *La vita che ti diedi* (The Life I Gave You), the story of a mother written with her in mind.

The Sicilian dramatist was now at the height of his powers, on the brink of international recognition. But the play he sent Duse cannot be ranked among his best; the intellectual game, the play of irony and paradox, is too bare; the characters are too puppet-like. Though attracted by the role of the mother who refuses to believe her son's death, Duse did not feel the play was right. Taking great pains (several drafts of the letter are in the Cini Foundation), she asked Pirandello to give her some time to ponder the work. He asked her to set an outside limit, after which he would be free to send the play to others.

"You are right–" she answered, "the word *wait* is absurd in the 'running existence' that life imposes on us."

She tried to resume work that spring, and on 9 May she gave *Così sia* in Florence. "My soul helped me," she wrote Olga a week later, "but the effort, the alienation of *having* to work, in order to leave the so-called 'take' of the evening in the manager's hands . . . and the next day, the same difficulties, the same urgency of things to carry it all *one step further*. . . ."

She gave only that performance, then paused again. "So as not to starve to death," she accepted the performances in London. On 7 May 1923 *The Times* of London reported: "Mr C.B. Cochran announces that arrangements were made on Saturday night as a result of which Signora Eleonora Duse will appear under his direction for a series of six matinées. The first performance is to take place on June 6, and it is probable that at this Signora Duse will appear either in Ibsen's *Ghosts* or *The Lady of the Sea* [sic]. She has not acted in this country since 1906, when she appeared at Miss Ellen Terry's 'Jubilee' performance."

On 28 May, *The Times* announced Duse's arrival in the city: "Miss Ellen Terry was unable to be present herself at Victoria last night, but she was represented by Miss St John, and in this way the greatest living British actress paid her tribute to her great comrade." Though the train did not get in until after midnight, a "representative gathering" was on the platform to greet her before she was whisked off to Claridge's. "Signora Duse bore the voyage well, although she is now in her 63rd year, and her only complaint was at the density of the tobacco smoke in the Pullman carriage on the way from Folkestone to Victoria." Besides the Italian Consul and other representatives of the London Italian colony, among those at Victoria was the actress Pauline Lord, starring in Eugene O'Neill's *Anna Christie*, which was about to achieve its fiftieth performance in London.

Duse was appearing at a former music-hall, the New Oxford Theatre, where Cochran was also presenting the Lucien Guitry company and an American farce, *Little Nellie Kelly*. Each of Duse's six performances drew capacity audiences; in one of them was the nineteen-year-old John Gielgud, who has recalled the experience and the times: "Perhaps the most legendary theatrical figures of the time were the international star actresses, those great creatures whose names alone could fill a theatre. I saw Eleonora Duse in *Ghosts* at the New Oxford Theatre in Tottenham Court Road, long since demolished. I stood at the back of the packed theatre at a matinée. Every actor in London was there, and the feeling in the audience was unforgettable, a mixture of respect and awe, a sense that we would never see this great woman again. When Duse came on, the atmosphere was already electric, and she could hardly fail to make the most wonderful impression. I did not know the play very well, but Duse looked infinitely sad and distinguished with her white hair, and wearing a plain black dress with a shawl draped over her shoulders. I remember that her acting seemed very, very simple. She had marvellous hands and all her movements were weary and poetic. Here was a legendary figure whose career had spanned fifty or sixty years of the nineteenth-century theatre, and she succeeded, to my mind, in living up to her legend, although she was evidently old and tired."

The critic of *The Times* felt that Duse was "above the part." He said:

"Her grief is august. She helplessly waves her arms and wrings her hands in arabesques of suave beauty. Beauty! that is the key-note of the performance: beauty of line, of sound, of gesture, of every kind of emotional expression. . . . Ibsen himself, we think, would have marvelled to see what poetic splendour the genius of this Italian lady could evoke from his own already great, but prosaically great, conception. . . ."

The white hair disturbed some spectators, including the critic of *The Stage*, who wrote of her as Ellida that she "dared to play the part without any attempt at make-up, simply as the Duse. This could not but disturb one's feelings regarding any sexual influence that might have been exerted over Ellida by the mysterious Stranger."

Curiously enough, *Così sia*, such a fiasco in Italy, was a great success; *The Times* critic compared it to a Giotto fresco. The young Armenian director Rouben Mamoulian, about to leave for the United States and a successful career on Broadway and in Hollywood, was at a matinée. He has described how she appeared from the back of the stage, "a small, fragile form . . ., in a peasant's dress, a colored kerchief around her head. It would be wrong to say she made an entrance: she appeared, as if materializing from the air of the stage. I didn't even know who she was, until a belated wave of applause engulfed the audience. The figure stopped in the middle of the stage, completely immobile, until the applause calmed down. This was la Duse! My God! An old, old woman. And so light and frail that you could blow her off the stage as easily as blowing out a match. A pale, almost transparent face. Beautiful. Oh yes! really beautiful, with immense black eyes. . . ."

The spectator's first reaction was dismay, almost embarrassment. "In a few minutes I realized how wrong and how cowardly I had been. A miracle took place—one of those miracles you can never forget. . . . Through the white magic of genius, only a few minutes later, the same Duse—wrinkles, white hair, and all the rest—became a young woman, vibrant, beautiful, strong."

Later, in the last act, when the part required the protagonist to age, "I had rather the impression that Duse, young, had to play a character role. . . . she was a different woman. She seemed really to have lived thirty years. And yet no change had taken place in her external appearance. . . ."

The London matinées had given her enough confidence—and enough money—to face an American tour. She signed a contract with the colorful New York impresario Morris Gest, son-in-law of Belasco. But in the meanwhile she accepted a brief engagement in Vienna. For the last performance there–La porta chiusa–Olga Signorelli was able to join her and witness her success.

"Eleonora was very gay that evening. We dined in her sitting room. She ordered champagne. Someone had sent her some beautiful fruit, which was very welcome. She read the donor's letter; he was a critic, asking for an interview. Laughing, she said it was just as well she had found this out only after the end of the meal. Otherwise the pleasure of the gift would have been spoiled by the remorse of her refusal. It was already midnight. The next morning at ten she was leaving for Cherbourg, where she would sail for America."

18
The closed door

Enrichetta, who had joined her for a few days in Paris, accompanied her on the train to Cherbourg, where mother and daughter said good-bye for the last time. Duse boarded the *Olympic* on 10 October, accompanied by her maid Maria Avogadro, by the faithful Désirée, and by her English friend and patron Katherine Onslow.

The news of her coming had kindled unusual excitement, and the astute Gest fanned the flames. There were the customary articles of advance publicity, quoting her as being "tired of Europe" and eager to breathe the "invigorating atmosphere" of America. More seriously, the critic Stark Young wrote an "open letter" to her, emphasizing the significance of her forthcoming journey:

"Madame, we need you in America to remind us that for every man there is only his kind of truth to make in the end any sense for him. . . . Your art is your own personal dilation of reality. You have no false purposes, you never conclude, you never solve, you only create and reveal. Most of all, madame, our young actors need you."

The American theatre, Young felt, was currently in a troubled, confused state. He spoke of the country's young actors: "They see promiscuous advertising and press comment that seems to assure them that they may follow as great artists actors who have nothing to go on but personality, insolence, ignorance, or superficial charm or good luck. These young actors have few good models of anything except success. They hear on all sides that acting copies nature, that their business is to reproduce what they see in life. And so they try, the better of them, to copy nature before they have eyes to see it with . . . they need to lean on life, not expedients. They need to see that in you always there is something that the great artists must always have, something that baffles, something withheld. What we get in you, madame, is only the echo of all you are. . . . You are the artist and the performance is yours; but behind all that, as the world of nature is behind a flower, is you. . . ."

Once again she had to defend herself against the press. On 17 October, the day after the *Olympic* landed, the *New York Times* published a statement (drafted by Gest's office): "I hope the strict rule of silence and retirement which for so many years I have been obliged to impose upon myself will be accepted and understood. . . ."

She stayed at the new Majestic Hotel, on the upper West Side, at 72nd Street and Broadway; a special police escort accompanied her there from the pier. After eighteen years, she glimpsed a different New York, a city that had rapidly expanded uptown. The neighborhood of her hotel and of the sumptuous, brand-new Century Theater, the "theatre of millionaires" as it was called, was quite new to her. The *Times* also mentioned her admiration for New York's Finest, who stopped traffic for her at the intersections. "Fine looking soldiers," she was quoted as saying; and since she often referred to herself as a *soldato*, it was a high compliment to the police.

Gest had been reluctant for her to open with *The Lady from the Sea*, a drama unfamiliar to New York audiences (it had had only one production, in 1911, at the Lyric); but Duse had insisted, wiring him several times from Paris, insisting he must have *confiance* in her. He did, and on 29 October, at the old Metropolitan Opera House—scene of the exceptional gala premiere—thousands of people had to be turned away at the box-office. Scalpers were getting as much as $200 a seat. According to Gest that night's take was over $30,000. The audience included writers, like the penniless young poet Langston Hughes, and superstars like the reigning Hollywood queen, Gloria Swanson ("I made my escort take me backstage, but she could receive no visitors").

The critics were respectful, enthusiastic, but not without complaints. With some of the other papers, the *New York Times* disliked the "plaintive" drama. In the *Herald Tribune*, Percy Hammond recalled Duse's farewell on her last visit, also at the Met, when "we were one of twenty-eight persons who saw her play Francesca," and he called her current play "third-rate Ibsen." His hostility to Duse continued throughout her American stay.

On the other hand, Stark Young in *The New Republic* and Ludwig Lewisohn in *The Nation* were ecstatic. As on previous visits, readers wrote Letters to the Editor debating Duse's worth, criticizing her for not covering her white hair with a wig. After her repetition of the Ibsen drama at the Century, John Corbin explained the critics' problem in the *Times*: "Those who are doomed to write about her emerge with sprained vocabularies. In point of fact we do not ourselves know what it is we admire in her."

Not only Gloria Swanson, but actors of every generation and at every level of talent made sure to see her. Among the youngest and brightest was Eva Le Gallienne, twenty-four years old, already a promising artist. As she was playing in Ferenc Molnár's *The Swan*, she could not come to the Met gala, but she did not miss a single matinée at the Century and many years later recorded her impressions of those Tuesdays and Fridays, when she could see and study Duse.

"The first play I saw her in was *Così sia*. She was on the stage at the rise of the curtain. The moment I heard her voice and saw the frail, yet curiously strong, ageless body—imbued with such intense inner vitality that it seemed to shine with light—I knew I was in the presence of a master who had achieved absolute perfection.

"The voice was not an actor's voice, though it carried, as though by magic, and without the slightest trace of 'projection,' to the very last rows of the vast theatre. It was the voice of a human being. Like everything else about Duse it was completely natural; not the kind of pseudo-naturalness acquired in classroom or studio, but true naturalness, which can come only from an acute awareness of nature itself. . . . Duse, on the stage, seemed oblivious of being watched; this was one of the secrets of her naturalness. . . ."

Duse's repertory for this tour comprised five plays—*The Lady from the Sea*, *Ghosts*, *Così sia*, *La porta chiusa*, and *La città morta*—and in New York she gave them in succession, two performances of each weekly for five weeks. Though this schedule was devised to allow her time to rest—and was one of the many conditions in her contract—she still had her days of weariness. As Le Gallienne said: "I attended the matinee of *La Città morta*. It was Duse's second performance of the play, the first had been on the preceding Tuesday. This was the only time that I noticed a distinct difference in her playing. On Tuesday she had seemed tired, drained, remote. The flame was burning low, though the architecture of her performance was impeccable and harmonious as always. But on the Friday she played with such fervour, such incomparable beauty, that it was like a miracle. The externals had not changed, but they were filled with an extraordinary radiance of spirit, which had been missing in the previous performance. . . ."

Duse was able to fulfil all her obligations in New York, but her health troubled her, and she was particularly afraid of drafts backstage. Morris Gest, who was not only her impresario and admirer but by now also a warm, considerate friend, designed a portable dressing room to shield her from the dread *courants d'air*. "IDÉE MAGNIFIQUE," she wired him on 3 November. Part of Gest's consideration was, no doubt, enlightened self-interest: he was eager to persuade her to extend her tour and go to California. On 10 December he wired Mary Pickford: "Eight weeks ago when Duse arrived in America I asked her would she not love to go to California stop. She answered I would love to, especially to see the little angel Mary Pickford these were exactly her words stop confidentially her dream might come true. . . ." And at the same time he wired Charlie Chaplin: "When you were in New York you said Gest if you will bring Madame Duse to California I will pay her fare stop you won't have to there is hope stop please keep this confidential. . . ." Duse, after all, was a movie fan; and in those darkened cinemas of Rome, where she had spent so many afternoons, she had surely seen Chaplin and Pickford any number of times.

After ten performances in New York, according to the contract, Duse was to play ten more, divided among other Eastern cities: Baltimore, Philadelphia, Washington, and Boston. Gest continued urging her to stay longer, though it would mean cancelling some Vienna appearances and paying the penalty. Actually, though she was being paid $2,500 a performance, she was not making huge sums, as the expenses of the whole troupe were her responsibility. She managed to repay her debt to Katherine Onslow, but she was saving little or nothing.

Other impresarios were also approaching her. As she wrote to Gest from Washington on 27 December 1923:

"I have insisted on giving you the preference in extending my contract, without taking into consideration *any other* plan for work outside *New York*. . . .

"This morning after so many discussions I find you insist on your terms—Despite my friendly feeling towards you—*I am forced*, I repeat (les affaires sont les affaires) to listen to other proposals. . . ."

She sent the letter to New York by hand, carried by her tour manager Guido Carrera, but Gest could not increase his offer. At this same time, he had imported the Moscow Arts Theatre and was producing Max Reinhardt's *The Miracle*, so he may not have had much ready cash. The result was that she signed with another management, the Selwyns, in collaboration with Fortune Gallo. The prospective earnings looked good, but the tour was to be wearing, with long train journeys and— far more insidious—violent changes of climate. Already in Washington Duse had had to cancel a performance because of indisposition.

She wrote to Enrichetta whenever she could. The morning after the gala opening, she had Désirée send a telegram: "Happy happy happy to tell you that the evening at the Metropolitan was marvelous. . . . Thank God she [Duse] was not too tired. She is well, eats, sleeps. . . ."

From New York they went to Boston, where she wrote to Enrichetta, in ink ("always a good sign," Enrichetta once commented in the notebooks). "Your mother is working and doing *everything in her power* to keep the ship afloat—yes, the 'success,' as they say, is *enormous*. Perhaps God will permit me to tell you about it one day—, but I am in it, and must go on. . . ." In the same letter she is already mentioning California, or rather—as she calls it—San Francesco.

In the papers, gossip occupied as much space as serious criticism. Duse's health was as newsworthy as her art. A *Tribune* article is typical: "Eleonora Duse will be borne in a sedan chair when she leaves New York for Boston. . . . Two sturdy chair bearers, who will be taken along with her company, will carry the tragedienne from her motor car to the train in the Grand Central Terminal and from train to automobile and into hotels and theatres in the cities she will visit. . . . The sedan chair for the elderly actress is being remodeled now on Mr Gest's orders from one in the studio of his father-in-law, David Belasco. It was used in the latter's production of 'Madame Dubarry' several seasons ago. Gilt and scarlet decorations will be removed so the equipage will be as inconspicuous as possible. . . ."

The story sounds more *ben trovato* than *vero*, and it would not be the only piece of fiction printed as fact during the tour. The last stop under Gest's solicitous management was Chicago, where Eleonora played four performances at the Chicago Auditorium, a building designed by the pioneer architects Dankmar Adler and Louis Sullivan. Enjoying a period of good health, she not only gave her performances but actually went to the opera. One of the stars, Galli-Curci, was staying in Duse's hotel, and she formed another of her immediate, intense friendships with the soprano. The reviews were critical of the repertory ("ghastly" was the *Daily News*'s adjective for *Ghosts*). In 1902, D'Annunzio's *Francesca da Rimini* had failed in Chicago; his *Città morta*, which she performed on 3 January 1924, fared no better. "Fourth-rate drama," it was called.

Gallo and the Selwyns took over the tour and transported the company to New Orleans. As Gallo wrote in his autobiography: "She had no business making the tour. To ensure that she kept each engagement it required the services of a diplomat, strategist, page, nurse and physician. Throughout the major part of her tour I was the first three and sometimes the fourth. It was necessary to have oxygen tanks present at all times in her hotel suite and at the theatre. Doctors constantly hovered in attendance. One almost needed a wind gauge to measure the air currents, for even the slightest draft affected her. Lengthy jumps were made in hermetically sealed railway drawing rooms, with cooking utensils for her personal use."

The undercurrent of irritation is evident. Never an easy charge, Eleonora—perhaps frightened by her own responsibilities and her scant strength—became more demanding than ever. The new management was less sympathetic than the intelligent Gest. But she was followed everywhere by the solicitude of friends. One of these was the poet Amy Lowell, who had seen Duse on previous tours, had met her, and had developed virtually an obsession with her. On their meeting again in 1923, Lowell wrote a series of poems to the actress, and invited her with Katherine to the Lowell estate, Sevenels, in Brookline, Massachusetts. There, the hostess discovered that, though Duse ate little and drank less, she did enjoy an occasional glass of champagne. America was in the grip of Prohibition, but Amy cheerfully despoiled the family cellar to supply the actress with vintage champagne for the tour. She also wrote to her wide network of friends across the country, to make sure her adored actress would be able to drink her modest fill wherever she went.

The trip from Chicago to New Orleans was tiring, but the warm air of the Gulf revived Duse after the icy January on Lake Michigan. She went out a bit in society and attended a piano recital by Ernst von Dohnányi at the Jerusalem Temple, where she was to give *La porta chiusa*, her only performance in the city. In New Orleans she received a wire from Enrichetta: "Malaise past am convalescing." It was "a bolt from the blue," Duse wrote her at once; "I believe some letters or wires must have been lost." Then Duse remembered that in Paris Enrichetta had said something about an appendectomy. Another wire, reassuring, came from Edward.

Duse wrote on 28 January 1924 from Havana, where the company had gone from New Orleans, after great difficulties with U.S. Customs, who did not want to let them take sets out of the country only to bring them back. In Havana, too, there was the boon of good weather. "We are giving four soirées," she told Enrichetta, meaning evening performances, not parties. "The crossing to arrive here was a bit rough. Habana is a very pretty place, actually the first place I like." She stayed there two weeks, then returned to New Orleans and entrained for California at last.

There was an unusual heat wave in Los Angeles, where she opened on 19 February. Duse would not grant an interview; but Katherine did, and commented on American weather with British tartness. "Yes, all America suffers from unusual weather," she said, "unusual frost in New Orleans. An unusual stew in Houston. An unusual snow blizzard in Chicago!"

The audience at the Philharmonic Auditorium included an exceptional critic, Charles Chaplin, who wrote a long review in the *Los Angeles Daily Times* of 20 February, the day after Duse opened in *La porta chiusa*.

"She is obviously and frankly a very old woman; yet there is something about her that suggests a pitiful child. I suppose this is the simplicity of her art. . . . behind the child is a great heart that is fed upon experience. . . . Of course the sum of these is the perfect artist: the simple, direct child soul; the experienced craftsman in technique; the heart that has been taught the lesson of human sympathy, and the incisive analytical brain of the psychologist. Bernhardt was always studied and more or less artificial. Duse is direct and terrible. . . ."

With an actor's eye, Chaplin then described the second-act climax of the Praga play, the scene when the mother learns that her son knows he is illegitimate: "An actress of lesser genius would have torn this emotion absolutely to tatters. Duse sank into a chair and curled up her body almost like a little child in pain. You did not see her face; there was no heaving of the shoulders. She lay quietly almost without moving. Only once through her body ran a sort of shudder of pain like a paroxysm. That and the instinctive shrinking of her body from her son's outstretched hand were almost the only visible movement. Yet so great is her dramatic power, so tremendous is her knowledge of dramatic technique, that this scene fairly wrung your heart. I confess it drew tears from me. . . . When she turned at last, both hands flung out in one gesture of utter despair, resignation—surrender—it was the finest thing I have seen on the stage. Through all her grief, her self-abasement, her contrition, ran terrible irony. It was all in that one gesture. . . ."

Chaplin also praised—and in this he was unique among American reviewers of this tour—the stage direction. "If we could only direct pictures as this play was directed," he wrote. ". . . Some of the most remarkable effects are gained in ways that violate every rule. . . . Actors entering at doors are covered and hidden by other actors; the lighting is against all rules that we know anything about. . . . I can't clearly understand by just what arts and devices he [the director] brings into focus the actor who is next to occupy the attention of the audience. . . ."

The director, naturally, was Duse herself, who cared little about doors and positions, but a great deal about the *concerto*, the interplay of performers.

Hollywood's little angel was unfortunately out of town, but Morris Gest sent Eleonora a bright telegram: "Have just seen Mary Pickford, who will come especially to your Detroit performance." Meanwhile, there was San Francisco. From there, Duse wired Maria Osti: ". . . Continue working till mid May wild broom blossoming here like Tivoli Eleonora Fairmont Hotel."

The thought of Detroit—a trip that Gest had tried to spare her—now filled her with dread. On 7 March, three days after the usual triumphant opening in San Francisco, she wrote to Enrichetta—it was the last letter from mother to daughter—in a tone of mixed weariness and courage.

"Ma fille. *Perhaps* there has been suffering enough to dare say that I hope to see you again.

"Que Dieu donne!

"From January, all through February, life has been hard. Now, here, a bit of pause is granted. Dieu donne! That's all I can say.—Yes, *prière et confiance*. It is impossible for me to tell the material things or those of the soul in a letter. Let us hope—hope to speak to each other!—from here there will be a long way to go towards N. York. . . . The debt to Katherine *is entirely paid*. I hope to find the strength to do everything—and find you again. I hope you will come to meet me in France, and let us go to Asolo together!! Dieu donne! Mamma"

The train set off on the long journey across the desert, then northwards. In her diary, one of the company, Enif Robert, noted:

"For kilometers, as far as the eye can see, gigantic cactus with violent-colored flowers, almost monstrous, as a yellow, impalpable sand is at the mercy of a strong wind that hurls it against the speeding train. The windows are double-glazed, but you breathe in some of that sand. For us it is only tiresome, but for the poor tired lungs of the Duse it is real suffering. I go to see her every now and then in her private car. It is hot: she holds to her mouth either the oxygen tube or a handkerchief soaked in ice. She asks anxiously: 'Is it finished . . . this terrible desert?'

"She has drawn the curtains, it horrifies her to look out. Meanwhile the train eats up the kilometers. A few hours later I can rush to her, because the cactuses have disappeared and I have glimpsed traces of snow, announcing the nearness of the northern cities awaiting us. 'Signora, the sand, the dust are finished . . . there's snow!' 'Snow? . . .

Dio mio.' How that expressive face of hers betrayed the new anguish! 'Snow . . . already!' . . ."

The snow was worse in Detroit, after rain and wind. Unhappy with her managers, she wired Gest, asking him to come to see her, and he did. On 24 March, she gave an inspired performance of La porta chiusa, her only appearance in the city. Mary Pickford was, as promised, in the audience, with Douglas Fairbanks.

"Never a pause," Enif Robert continued, in her diary. "Grand hotels, immense and filled theatres; we perform only twice a week and miraculously, every evening she plays, Duse manages to find the purest of tones, the limpid voice, the attitudes—always new and always complex—of her great art. One city follows another, and on 3 April we will be in Pittsburgh."

In Indianapolis, one of the cities on the way east, the News was enthusiastic about La porta chiusa, but noticed the artist's weariness; and the next day, before leaving for Pittsburgh, she wired Gest: "Yesterday was a difficult day, but am better this morning. Am collecting all my strength, to leave tonight. Afraid to stay here alone so far away. Hope in Pittsburgh to feel nearer New York or at least on my way back. Thanks for your kindness. Counting the hours till I am back in New York."

On 1 April they reached Pittsburgh. "La plus hideuse ville du monde," Duse had called it; but the local paper—with characteristic inventiveness—quoted her as saying the city was "an ideal vacation spot."

Duse stayed at the Hotel Schenley, then somewhat remote from the center of the city, but in sight of the vast Syria Mosque, where she was to perform. On the evening of 5 April, her opening, she actually walked from the hotel, despite a driving rain, with Désirée, who had tried to make her take a taxi.

"How well one knows those vast, cold buildings," Eva Le Gallienne wrote, having heard an account of the tragic evening from Désirée herself, "a solid block of closed doors, all alike, all firmly locked but one—which one searches for in vain."

"La Duse remained a good five minutes under the lash of the rain," Enif Robert recorded, "ill-protected by the great fur that Désirée tried to hold tight around her. It seems that the secretary rushed to the main entrance and, accompanied by the doorman, finally succeeded in getting the wretched closed door open. But by then la Duse was chilled and soaked with rain. She went into her over-heated dressing room, trembling, and apparently felt very ill."

Ironically, the play that Duse was to give was *La porta chiusa*, the closed door. She insisted on giving the performance. Enif records: "A frenzied house applauded, on its feet, Bianca Querceta, the sweet and despairing mother of the play, at every act. But we see that Duse is at the end of her strength and only a will power such as she has allows her to continue. Every now and then, in a low voice, she begs those on stage with her: 'Hurry . . . hurry . . .' The public calls her out ten times, never sated with admiring the gentle figure who bows her white head, thanking them, and they have no idea of the effort they are imposing on her. Poor Duse! How tired she is! Where does she get that inexhaustible capacity for going forward?"

Except for those with her, no one was aware of her condition. The review in the next morning's *Gazette Times* was the familiar rave: "Mme Duse's art may be measured in feet and inches. Syria Mosque is a vast place and a figure less imposing easily could be lost in its extensive reaches of space. No ordinary player could conquer it."

Maria Avogadro—described by Enrichetta as a "superior sort" of maid—also wrote a description of the last performance: "She had an intense desire to get it over with. And in the last act, at the moment when she had to utter the word *sola* ["alone," the final word in Duse's cut version of the play], she said it in such a striking tone—as one had never heard her say it before—that her close associates who were present felt their hearts rent. The moment she was back in the Hotel Schenley, she takes to her bed with a high fever."

The impresarios wanted to keep the seriousness of her illness a secret. When the tour's next stop, a performance of *Ghosts* in Cleveland on 8 April, was canceled, the Pittsburgh *Sun* made a joke of it: "Ze tour? Ze performance? Ze peepul? Pouf! Pouf-pouf! Ze temperament? Ah, zat ees ze only ting. Madame Eleonora Duse is still in Pittsburgh. . . . Madame Duse likes not the snow, the crisp air, the ice. She likes them so little she will not venture outside her room at the Schenley Hotel. She longs for her sunny southern [*sic*] Italy. . . . No instructions have emanated from the madame's suite of rooms regarding baggage, and there seems to be no intention of leaving until madame gets entirely in the frame of mind to leave. . . ."

The next day, the worst rumors were confirmed. Enif Robert's diary reports: "Yes. It's pneumonia! But we trust she will overcome the crisis."

She was not yet delirious, and she spoke of leaving, of reaching New York at least, then embarking for Italy. According to Maria Avogadro, she said, "I do not want to die here," when she realized she was seriously ill. "She guessed and read my sadness in my eyes, and it frightened her. She didn't want to be left alone, and Mlle Désirée and I never left her. The following week, which was Holy Week, her strength abandoned her completely."

On 12 April, Enif Robert wrote: "We actors go every morning and evening to her hotel for news. But we can rarely go up to her room. The doctors have forbidden visiting her and speaking to her." Two days later: "Mademoiselle Désirée invites me to enter the room, but without speaking to her. My heart is pounding as I look in at the door: I see the beautiful head sunk into the pillows, immobile. An immobility that makes me shudder and start. Désirée comforts me, taking my hand: 'She's dozed off . . . she'll get well . . . the crisis seems to be past.'"

Hearing of Duse's illness, Amy Lowell immediately got in touch with some Pittsburgh friends, the Binghams, who sent her reassuring news: the doctors reported improvement. It was no more than a bronchial cold. The troupe also seemed reassured. On Holy Saturday, 19 April, Enif Robert wrote: "Duse sent for me. She wants to see me. She is better. I hurry to the hotel. My husband accompanies me. In a little street we pass along, I see a playing card, face down, on the ground. With my foot I try to turn it over. Alfredo, not in time to stop me, says: 'No, no . . . don't look . . . let's go on!' My foot has already turned it over: it is the ace of spades. Alfredo can hardly stifle a curse: 'I told you not to touch it. Don't look at it!' and he walks on, irritated. I'm not superstitious. I catch him up and say: 'What difference does a card make? It can't change anything. Let's go.' But I am distressed."

The visit, at about 6 in the afternoon, distressed her further. "Saw Duse. Went in and she was dozing, but I wait because she said she wanted to speak to me. Mademoiselle Désirée tells me that last night she read the Easter greeting I sent her, then leaves me alone. She opens her eyes: 'Come close and speak loud: I'm dazed and half-deaf after all the quinine they've given me. I don't like taking such heavy doses. Oh, if I had my Italian doctors here, Professor Ravà . . . or Signorelli . . . who knows my organism . . .' She dozes off again. I try to arrange a lock of hair that has fallen over her forehead. She reopens her eyes, smiles at me as if to thank me. Then, suddenly, with an energy that seems impossible in a body so tired, she raises herself from the pillows and, clear, strong, her voice recites the verses of a dear Roman-dialect poet:

"'E doppo er serra serra/riecchece pe' terra.' [And after all the commotion, here we are flat on the ground again.]

"She puts her head back on the pillows and is silent for a long time, with her eyes closed. I tiptoe towards the door to find Désirée. Her voice stops me at the door, saying: 'What are all of you doing . . . all alone and lost? . . . And it's Easter, tomorrow! Keep together . . . be patient. I'll get well . . . (she seems to want to apologize for her illness) and we'll leave at once for Italy. As soon as I'm on my feet . . . immediately . . . away, away . . . to Asolo! You will accompany me to Asolo . . .' I went back to the side of the bed. I bend over, moved, to kiss her hand lying on the blanket. 'Yes . . . yes, Signora! I'll come to Asolo!' She looks hard at me, as if to scrutinize my secret thoughts. Do I believe it possible? She repeats: 'Yes, you will accompany me to Asolo.' I was not to see her again alive."

On that Holy Saturday the papers carried the first stories about the real gravity of her illness. "Little hope for recovery", was the headline in the Pittsburgh *Post*. But a rival paper, the *Gazette Times*, on the following day, ran a story about the "reckless reports" and described Duse as "much annoyed" by the exaggerated accounts of her illness. It is unlikely that she saw them or that Katherine translated them for her. It is unlikely, too, that she saw the telegrams arriving from all over the world.

On Easter Sunday she saw some of the artists and announced that the whole company would be leaving, with her, the next day. Maria and Désirée pretended to pack the trunks as they had done so many dozens of times before; and they answered her repeated questions about the time, as she seemed eager to hasten the moment of departure.

Maria wrote afterwards to Duse's friend and biographer Edouard Schneider: "At eight o'clock, the evening of that same day, the doctor told us the end was near. She was turning in her bed, but without suffering, and at two-twenty a.m. on 21 April she pulled herself up in bed with an extraordinary strength, resting on her fists, supporting her poor body. Then, looking hard at us, Mademoiselle Désirée and me, she asked us what we were doing there immobile and said: 'We must move! We must leave! Do something! Do something!' [*agir*—the word means "to act," but not in the theatrical sense]. Her voice was still beautiful. But, suddenly, she was seized with a horrible chill and trembling. 'Cover me!' she asked. Ten minutes later she died."

In less than an hour Duse's body was taken from the hotel, down a service elevator, and removed to a mortuary, where the company visited her that afternoon. "They filed into the somber chamber," the *Pittsburgh Post* wrote on 22 April 1924, "their eyes steeled on the cold form of their Duse, her face paled by the ravages of pneumonia that ebbed the last particle of her strength when death came." They all knelt and said prayers in Latin. It was their last moment with her alone. Soon they too were caught up in the drama, the spectacle of the long funeral.

Though both Katherine and Désirée tried to insist that Duse had wanted a quiet, private interment, the authorities would allow nothing of the kind. The moment D'Annunzio heard of her death, he wired, then wrote to Mussolini, who despatched the Italian ambassador in Washington to Pittsburgh. A simple service was held there on 23 April, and Ambassador Caetani laid an official wreath on the casket. Three days later the body was taken by train to New York.

With its escort of actors and officials, the body arrived in New York on Sunday evening, 27 April, and was taken from Pennsylvania Station to the church of St Vincent Ferrer on Lexington Avenue and 66th Street, where it was placed in the chapel of St Joseph. More than 3,000 people had been waiting in silence for hours outside the church to show their devotion.

Four days later there was a formal funeral service. The demand to attend was so great that tickets had to be issued. Among those present was Amy—Amie, Duse used to call her—Lowell, who wrote later to her friend Millicent Bingham:

"Katherine Onslow told me that their train was quite late, that they stopped in Philadelphia for some little time and a band of Fascisti with black shirts came into the car and saluted Madame's coffin, which was very impressive. They were met at the train by the Consular Committee, and went at once to the church . . . where some sort of short receiving service was performed. From this point on, the body was in the charge of the Dominican Fathers, and the company seem to have given up their vigil of watching, which I suppose they will resume on the ship.

"I went down to the church the next day and again two days later; it was a most impressive sight. It is a beautiful church, one of Goodhue's . . . The windows . . . are simply diamonds and squares in patterns with an occasional pane of slightly tinted red or blue glass. The colours are very faint, but they do pick out a sort of pattern, which, however, does not tinge the daylight at all, so that the whole inside is full of daylight. . . ."

Then, after mentioning the little "vigil lights" which flickered in the church, Amy Lowell described the flowers and the steady stream of people, from six in the morning till nine at night: "Mrs Belmont had got consular tickets for Ada and me, which meant that we could go to the funeral and be in one of the first fifteen rows—as a matter of fact, we were in the fourth row. The church part was rather badly managed, for they did not let in even the stamped ticket holders for a long time, and, by some mistake, there had not been enough unstamped tickets given out, so that the back pews of the church and the side far back were empty, while ten thousand people stood outside longing to get in and were refused admittance. . . .

"The solemn high requiem mass was given, which I had never heard before. They had something like seventy-five choir boys, I believe, and the choir was exceedingly fine. [Giovanni] Martinelli, of the Metropolitan Opera House, sang the Benedictus. Ten or eleven Dominican Fathers officiated, with superb silver and black velvet copes and some entirely white . . ."

The *Herald Tribune*'s description, published on 2 May, included a touching incident: "As the tall provincial (Rev. Raymond Meagher) moved solemnly toward the casket and the following procession of priests began to chant . . . the clouds in the southeast sky beyond the church walls were pushed aside and the sun broke brilliantly through: A broad ray of light suddenly poured through a window and the flag-covered, flower-bedecked casket was flooded with its radiance. The kneeling congregation caught its breath."

"At the end of the service," Amy Lowell wrote, "the coffin was wheeled out of the door of one of the transepts, followed immediately by the Ambassador and Katherine Onslow, and after them the members of the company and the Consular Committee. We went out with the crowd afterwards and had some difficulty in finding our motor, and when we did find it we pursued the funeral, but only reached Central Park after demonstrations by the Fascisti and the Berserglieri [*sic*] and other organizations of the sort had finished. . . ."

From the church the procession went to Fifth Avenue, up to 72nd Street, across Central Park, down to 57th Street and then west to Pier 97, where the Italian liner, the *Duilio*, was waiting. The casket was not stowed in the hold, but in a little compartment on the second deck, which had been converted into a shrine.

In a curious editorial, published the day after Duse's death, the *New York Times* said: "The last to linger of the great histrionic group of the 1890s, Eleonora Duse has left the least legible character on the page of theatric history, and the record that will soonest fade. That is part and parcel of her distinction, of the quality in which she transcended them all. Bernhardt and Coquelin, Irving, Mansfield, and von Sonnenthal wrought primarily with the concrete materials of their art. Their stature and bearing, gesture and facial expression, were such as could be definitely put into words, caught by the camera . . . but the major part of Duse's art lay in a thing which no one could definitely see or adequately describe—the thing for which we have only the poor, hackneyed word 'spirit.'"

In Naples, where the *Duilio* docked, an immense crowd—including a royal duchess—was waiting to receive Duse's remains. In the throng was her old friend Matilde Serao, who had come out despite a fever to give Eleonora—Nennella—a last greeting.

In Rome, at Santa Maria degli Angeli, there was another funeral ceremony, with pomp and officialdom. And as the train moved northwards, through Florence, Bologna, Padua, there were more demonstrations by immense crowds that gathered at the stations. Finally, from Padua—where several companies of actors had collected, along with a host of other mourners—the body journeyed to Asolo, to the cemetery of Sant'Anna. Yet another procession, another ceremony, more crowds. Then finally the crowds dispersed, and Duse was left, at last, in her beloved solitude.

Acknowledgments
Bibliographical Note
Notes to the Text
Bibliography
Sources of illustrations
Index

Acknowledgments

My greatest debt and most profound gratitude are to Sister Mary Mark, Duse's granddaughter, who has generously deposited her collection of family papers, including hundreds of letters to and from Duse, in the Fondazione Giorgio Cini in Venice, where they are available to qualified scholars. Sister Mary Mark has also encouraged me and assisted me in other ways. She did not see this book before publication and is therefore in no way responsible for its contents, but it could not have been written without her.

In the half-dozen years I have worked on the book, I have received help from many friends and strangers (some of whom have become friends), as well as from libraries, archives, foundations, and other institutions. I hope I have listed all of them below. If there are omissions, they are due to oversight, not ingratitude.

In 1978 I received a fellowship from the John Simon Guggenheim Memorial Foundation. It supported a large part of my research, and I am extremely grateful. I am grateful also to the Gladys Krieble Delmas Foundation, which underwrote a stay in Venice.

I wish to thank the Library of the Performing Arts, New York, and Monte Arnold; the New York Public Library; the library of the Century Association and Andrew Zaremba; the Hoblitzelle Theater Arts Library of the Humanities Research Center, Austin, Texas, and the late Mrs Jane Combs; the Film Library of the Museum of Modern Art and Adrienne Mancia. In Italy, I am indebted to the Museo Teatrale alla Scala, Milan, and Giampiero Tintori, Adriana Corbella, and Lorenzo Siliotti; the Biblioteca Civica, Verona; the Fondazione Primoli, Rome, and Carlo Pietrangeli and Eugenia Cianfanelli; the Biblioteca Classense, Ravenna, and Dante Bolognesi; the Berenson Library at the Harvard Institute for the Study of Italian Renaissance Art, Villa I Tatti, Settignano, and Craig Smyth, Nelda Feraci, Anna Terni, Fiorella Superbi; the Bilbioteca Universitaria and the Biblioteca Nazionale, Naples; the Museo Civico Teatrale, Trieste, and F. Rasman; the Biblioteca Teatrale del Burcardo, Rome, and Cesare Branchini, Patrizia Frisoli, Maria Rosaria Galerano, and Grazia Antonelli; Istituto Gramsci, Rome, and Bruna Conti; Museo Civico, Asolo, and Corrado Fabris, Gabriele Farronato, Flora Franceschini; Il Vittoriale degli italiani, Gardone, and Emilio Mariano and Margherita Ragusini. I owe a special debt to the Biblioteca Consortile città di Arezzo and Gianfranco Peluzzi, who patiently procured books for me from libraries all over Italy, enabling me to work in the peace of my study.

In Paris, the Conservateur of the Bibliothèque de l'Arsenal kindly allowed Duse's letters to Lugné-Poe to be photographed for me.

The assistance of the Fondazione Giorgi Cini in Venice was essential to my work. I thank Vittore Branca, Anna Conte, Carla Barbantini, and Luisa Corsa.

In New York, my thanks are due to Rosamond Gilder, Margery Gori-Montanelli, Eric Gordon, Shirley Hazzard, Norman MacAfee, John Pope-Hennessy, Andrew Porter, Robin Prising, Gordon Rogoff, Dorle Soria, Francis Steegmuller, Elliott Stein, Martin Waldron, Christiane Zimmer; in Hartford, Michael Campo; in Amherst, Richard Tedeschi; in Los Angeles, Bernice Anfuso and John D. Weaver; in Austin, Robert Hill, Millicent Marcus, Maria Wells; in London, John Black, Gertrude Buckman, Richard Jeffree, Nicholas John, Patrick O'Connor, John Sandoe; in Manchester, Giovanni Pontiero; in Paris, Jan Barnes, David Stevens, Liliane Ziegel; in Frankfurt, Leonhard Fiedler; in Oslo, Charles Darden, Pôl Christian Moe; in Venice, Elsie Gozzi, Kazuo Nakajima, Monica Radaelli; in Asolo, Annelise Seidenfaden; in Padua, Giuliano Bersani; in Viareggio, Massimo Pistelli; in Genoa, Alessandra Cenni; in Florence, Harold Acton, Thekla and John Clark, Hanna Kiel, Laura Meconcelli, Leonardo Pinzauti; in Pisa, Martha King; in Turin, Adriana Prolo, Giorgio Rampone, Eileen Romano; in Lucca, John Fleming, Hugh Honour; in Rome, Ginevra Bompiani, Bice Brichetto, Gaetano Cafiero, Luisa Chiarelli, Elena Croce, Sandro d'Amico, Gerardo Guerrieri, Ilaria Occhini, Walter Talevi; in Naples, Gianni Infusino, Carlo Knight. I am grateful also to my Tuscan neighbors Luisa Clerici, Licia and Pippo Greghi, and Floriano Vecchi.

William Weaver
Monte San Savino, August 1983

Bibliographical Note

Much of this book is based on material previously unpublished. Sources are indicated in the Notes for the individual chapters; but to complete the Bibliography, I will list here the most important collections: Duse's correspondence with her daughter Enrichetta and a number of other surviving letters to and from Duse are in the Fondazione Giorgio Cini, where the papers of Olga Signorelli are also deposited; Duse's letters to D'Annunzio are in Il Vittoriale degli Italiani; the papers of impresario Morris Gest and Duse's correspondence with him about her last American tour are in the Humanities Research Center, Austin, Texas; Mary Berenson's diaries are in the Berenson Archive, Villa I Tatti, Settignano; the diaries of Noccioli and Galvani, Duse's letters to Alberta Alberti, to Ettore Mazzanti, and others, are in the Biblioteca Teatrale del Burcardo, Rome; Duse's letters to Primoli, his journal and other documents are in the Fondazione Primoli, Rome; Duse's letters to Yvette Guilbert, Laura Groppallo, and others are in the Museo Teatrale alla Scala, Milan; Duse's letters to Sibilla Aleramo (or rather, copies made by Aleramo before she sold them) are in the Istituto Gramsci, Rome; Duse's letters to Lugné-Poe and his wife are in the Bibliothèque de l'Arsenal, Paris. I am indebted to the direction and staff of these institutions for their assistance.

I am also indebted to private owners of Duse's letters, and in particular to Ilaria Occhini, granddaughter of the Giovanni Papini; Luisa Chiarelli, daughter of Maria Osti; and Rosamond Gilder and her sister Francesca Palmer, daughters of Richard Watson Gilder and Helena Gilder.

An unpublished Master of Arts thesis for the University of California, Los Angeles, by Bernice Sciorra Anfuso, deals with Duse's American tours and includes many reviews of her performances and other hard-to-find articles; the thesis, as will be clear from the Notes, was of invaluable help.

Newspaper archives were essential in the writing of this work. I have consulted old theatrical magazines and newspapers in the Biblioteca del Burcardo in Rome, the Biblioteca Nazionale and the Biblioteca Universitaria in Naples; the Biblioteca Civica, Verona; the Biblioteca Nazionale, Florence; and the London Library. I have also worked in the archives of *La nazione* in Florence and the *International Herald-Tribune* in Paris. I am grateful to my colleagues on these papers, and to the librarians who assisted my research.

Duse's letters, as the reader can see from the sample in the illustrations section, were a visual as well as verbal form of communication. Her underlinings, use of upper case, even the placing of the words on the paper were idiosyncratic and expressive and are impossible to reproduce in cold type. I have tried, here and there, to give some idea of their special quality; but only a facsimile could truly convey their charm and their impact. Her letters in Italian are sprinkled with French phrases, as her letters in French often contain some Italian words. Most of her letters to her daughter are, nominally, in French. Again, I have tried to give some of their flavor, while translating—in the interest of comprehensibility—both Italian and French into English.

W.W.

Notes

Rather than impede the flow of the narration, I have reluctantly decided to forego footnotes. I believe that, in many cases, the source of a given piece of information is clear from the context. But for further clarity I have compiled the notes below, chapter by chapter.

NB. I have included precise page numbers only when the reader might encounter some difficulty in tracing the reference.

Chapter One

For the legends concerning Duse's birth and her early days, see Antona Traversi 1926. For information about Vigevano and its theatres I am grateful to Luigi Casoni; the archivists of the Comune di Vigevano were also helpful. For the life of strolling players in the late nineteenth century, see Zacconi 1946. Enrichetta's notes on her grandfather's diary are in the Fondazione Cini. Morelli's *Prontuario* is quoted at length in Siro Ferroni 1979, vol. II. The appendices to this series of publications by Einaudi are rich in information about the period. For the question of "roles," see Possenti and Tofano (chapter VI). Duse's letter to Papini—like her other letters to him, quoted later—is in the collection of his granddaughter, Ilaria Occhini, Rome. The Zara poster is reproduced in Ferruggia.

Chapter Two

Much of this chapter is based on original research in Neapolitan libraries. For the Teatro de' Fiorentini see De Flavis, Scalera. I am grateful to Carlo Knight for sending me the obituaries of Cafiero in the Naples newspapers, enabling me to give a somewhat more rounded picture of Cafiero than has been given in the past; Carlo Knight also found the engraved portrait of Cafiero reproduced among the illustrations. For Giacinta Pezzana see Ciotti Cavaletto. An idea of the Naples of the time can be found in Ghirelli. I am grateful to Martha King for her exhaustive research in the civil and archdiocesan archives in Pisa.

Chapter Three

The description of Turin is by the pseudonymous Acrofilo and is quoted in Fusero, pp. 63 ff. For the Compagnia reale sarda see Costetti 1893. Giacosa's letter to Boito about *Il conte Rosso* is in Nardi's biography of Giacosa, p. 395. Alessandro's letters to his brother Enrico Duse are in the Fondazione Cini; Dumas's letters to Primoli are quoted in *La Revue de Paris*; the originals are in the Fondazione Primoli, which also preserves Duse's letters to Primoli, almost all of them hitherto unpublished. Tebaldo's letter to d'Arcais is quoted in Ridenti, pp. 9 ff. Tebaldo's birthday letter to Enrichetta is in the Fondazione Cini. Serao on Tebaldo, in Serao 1977. Duse's conversation with Huret about Bernhardt in Antona Traversi 1926, pp. 36 ff. (also Schurmann's description of Duse at the time). Duse's letter to Somigli, Fusero, p. 92. Letters of Giacosa and Verga to Primoli are in the Fondazione Primoli (some are quoted in Spaziani). Primoli's journal is published in Primoli 1959. Descriptions of the premiere of *Cavalleria rusticana* in Alexander, pp. 109 ff. Also in Alexander, Duse's measurements, letters of Giacosa and Torelli-Viollier. Giacosa's letters to his mother are in Nardi's biography of him. Boito's letters to Duse and hers to him are in the Fondazione Cini; they are published in Radice. Giacosa's letters to Fogazzaro are in Nardi's *Giacosa*, pp. 509 ff. Duse to Fiacchi, in Nardi's *Boito*, p. 523.

Chapter Four

A colorful picture of South America a century ago and its large Italian colony emerges from Michele Puccini's letters, in Marchetti (some, translated by William Weaver, were published in *Opera News*, New York, 5 December 1981 and 16 January 1982). Cesare Rossi's letters were published, at the time, in the *Gazzetta piemontese*; I am grateful to Giorgio Rampone for transcribing them. Duse's letters to Serao are in Antona Traversi 1926 and Signorelli 1955. For the relations between Duse and Ristori, see Guerrieri 1974. I am grateful to F. Rasman of the Museo Civico

Teatrale of Trieste for telling me about the theatre's ledgers and for allowing me to examine them.

Chapter Five

Duse's and Boito's letters are in Radice. The reviews of *Tristi amori* by Pozza and Depanis are quoted in Nardi's *Giacosa*, pp. 593–94. I am grateful to Sir Harold Acton for giving me information about his Neapolitan cousins and Matilde Acton. For a thoroughly researched and well-written account of the *Antony and Cleopatra* production see Vazzoler, who quotes numerous reviews.

Chapter Six

Boito's letters to Verdi (and some to Bellaigue) are in Medici-Conati. For Marco Praga's account of *La moglie ideale*, see Praga. For Bahr, see Bahr and Signorelli 1962. Russian reviews of Duse are in Signorelli 1962. Also Chekhov's letter. The letter announcing the death of Alessandro Duse is in the Fondazione Cini.

Chapter Seven

For Duse's first performances in Vienna see Maddalena and Antona Traversi 1926. Duse's letter to Sudermann in Antona Traversi 1926, p. 83. Duse on Ibsen and the Germans *ibid.*, p. 84. Duse to Corrado Ricci, Fusero, p. 173. Duse's letters to Helena Gilder, collection Rosamond Gilder, New York (most are published in Gilder). Duse's letters to Cesare Rossi, preserved in the Biblioteca Federiciana in Fano, are partly published in Guerrieri 1962.

Chapter Eight

For a description of Duse's Venice see Damerini. Queen Victoria's journal entry is in Buckle, G. E. (ed.), *The Letters of Queen Victoria, Third Series, a selection of Her Majesty's Correspondence and Journal between the years 1886 and 1901* (3 vols.), London, 1931. II, 400. I am grateful to John Black for transcribing the passage for me.

Chapter Nine

Duse and D'Annunzio in Venice, in Damerini. Hohenlohe in Ojetti. For D'Annunzio at this time, see also Chiara and

Mariano. Mariano publishes a few of Duse's letters to D'Annunzio, but most have not been published. All are in the archives of the Vittoriale. I am grateful to Professor Mariano for permission to study them and to the librarian, Margherita Ragusini, for her cordial assistance. Shaw's comparison of Duse and Bernhardt is in Shaw, I, 144 ff. It is quoted with the kind permission of the Society of Authors.

Chapter Ten

There is a complete run of *Il Convito* in the library of the Vittoriale, where I was able to consult it. For the voyage of the *Fantasia*, see Chiara; D'Annunzio to Treves quoted in Chiara, p. 103. Duse's American reviews, again, in Anfuso. Duse's letter to De Bosis, in Signorelli 1955, p. 144.

Chapter Eleven

For Duse in Paris, see Mapes, Primoli 1897, Antona Traversi 1926, Montesquiou, Guerrieri 1974. Huret's description of Duse's hotel room in Signorelli 1955. Bernhardt's letter to Montesquiou, in Montesquiou.

Chapter Twelve

Mary Berenson's diaries are in the Berenson Library, Villa I Tatti, Settignano. I am grateful to her granddaughter, Barbara Halpern, for permission to quote them. I am also grateful to Professor Craig Smyth and his wife Barbara for their help and hospitality. Ojetti's description of Duse at Palazzo Primoli is in Signorelli 1955, pp. 181 ff. For descriptions and anecdotes of La Capponcina, see Palmerio. The Morasso–D'Annunzio interview is quoted in Damerini. Duse's letters to the Marchesa Groppallo are in the Museo teatrale alla Scala; they are published in Setti 1978. Boito's letter to a friend (Camille Bellaigue) is in Medici-Conati. The Egyptian episodes are in Jandolo. D'Annunzio's letter to Treves from Corfu, Signorelli 1955. D'Annunzio's letters to Zacconi and the actor's recollections, in Zacconi.

In *D'Annunzio romano* there is a long article on the projected Albano theatre by Cesare Pascarella, jr.

Duse's letters to Adolfo and Liliana De Bosis, in Signorelli 1955 (a number of typescripts, made by Signorelli, are in the Fondazione Cini). Duse's letters to Zacconi, in Zacconi. Scarfoglio's story about D'Annunzio's misbehaving during *La gloria* in Naples, in Chiara, p. 126. D'Annunzio's letter to Conti, in Damerini, pp. 60–61. Duse to Calvé in Signorelli 1955, pp. 204–5. For the Zurich episode, see Simone, Chiara, Rolland. I am grateful to Mme Romain Rolland for providing me with a typescript of her husband's journal for the period. D'Annunzio's notes in Vienna, in *Taccuini*, pp. 380–81. Beerbohm, in Beerbohm. Joyce, in Ellmann, who erroneously says the writer saw Duse in *La città morta*, not given in London that season. The Vicenza visit is described in Damerini. For the premiere of *Francesca da Rimini*, see Frajese, I, 190 ff. and also *D'Annunzio romano*, Antongini. Duse's letter to *Le Gaulois*, in facsimile, in Antona Traversi 1926.

Chapter Thirteen

Newspapers quoted from Anfuso. For Huneker's study, see Huneker, chapter X, "Duse and D'Annunzio." Talli's reminiscences of *La figlia di Jorio*, in Talli. Ruggeri's description of the opening, in Pandolfi. D'Annunzio's letter to Duse, 17 July 1904, in Nardi 1975.

Chapter Fourteen

Letter from Duse to De Bosis about *Monna Vanna*, in Signorelli 1959. The *Illustrazione italiana* quoted in Signorelli 1962. Letter to Emma Garzes reproduced in Signorelli 1959. Ojetti quoted in Signorelli 1962. For further information about the Duse version of Hofmannsthal's *Elektra*, see the bilingual edition (Fr.-It.) published by Mondadori in 1978 (Taglioni, A., ed.). For meeting of Duse and Gordon Craig, see Steegmuller. Duse's letter to Bernhardt is reproduced in Signorelli 1959. For Duse and L'Oeuvre, see Lugné-Poe 1933. Duse at this time is described by her supporting actor Ciro Galvani in an unpublished diary in the Biblioteca del Burcardo. The largely unpublished letters of Duse to Lugné-Poe and his wife are in the Bibliothèque de l'Arsenal, Paris (Correspondance Duse/Lugné-Poe, côte: Manuscrits 14777). The stay in Kristiania described in Lugné-Poe 1933; for additional information about the season I am grateful to Pôl Christian Moe, Oslo. Ellen Terry's jubilee described in Prideaux and in Terry. The Florence *Rosmersholm*, in Duncan, Noccioli, Steegmuller, as well as in all the biographies of Duse. Duse's telegrams to Craig,

Humanities Research Center, Austin. Tony Lamberg, in Lugné-Poe 1933. Letter from Russia to Angiolo Orvieto in Signorelli 1955. For information concerning her last performances in Berlin, I am indebted to Giovanni Pontiero.

Chapter Fifteen

For Sibilla Aleramo and Lina Poletti, see A. Cenni. Duse and Lina at the Villa Curonia, in Luhan, chapter 17. For Rilke and *The White Princess*, see Butler and Rilke. Maria Osti's unpublished reminiscences and her letters from Duse were generously put at my disposal by Maria Osti's daughter, Luisa Chiarelli, who also shared personal recollections with me. Sofia Bisi Albini's letter and Duse's reply are quoted in Fusero, p. 348, and in other biographies. There is some mystery about Duse's communication to the feminists. It is quoted in Signorelli 1955, in Fusero, and in Setti 1978. I have been unable to find the original. Signorelli and Fusero are vague about the date; Setti says 1914 and suggests that this was when Duse thought of establishing the Libreria delle Attrici (but, as we learn from Osti, the idea dated from at least 1911). In any case, I have included the document—quoting from the above sources—since it has the undeniable ring of authenticity. Boito's letter to Bellaigue about the war, in Nardi's *Boito*, p. 702.

Chapter Sixteen

For Claudel and Duse, see Courtault-Deslandes 1978. In Courtault-Deslandes 1977–79 there is a thorough examination of *Cenere* and other Duse film projects. I am grateful to Liliane Ziegel for photocopying the Colette article in Paris. For Ambrosio and the Italian film world of the period, see Prolo. For the meeting with Nicastro, see Nicastro vol. I. D'Annunzio's letters to Duse in Nardi 1975. Edward Bullough's *Cambridge Readings in Italian Literature* was published in 1920.

Chapter Seventeen

A copy by Enrichetta of Désirée's letter to her about Robi, Giulietta, and Duse is in the Fondazione Cini. Duse's letters to Contessa Rucellai are in Guerrieri 1974. Letters from the Mendelssohn Bank, written after Robi's death, are in the Fondazione Cini. For Duse's failure to agree with Talli, see Guerrieri 1974.

Also d'Amico in Guerrieri 1962. Helen Mackay's unpublished reminiscences are in the Cini Foundation. For Duse's performances in 1921 see d'Amico 1963 and Simoni 1951. The genesis of *Così sia* is described in Gallarati Scotti. For Duse's post-war meeting with D'Annunzio see Signorelli 1955, pp. 361–62, and Winwar, pp. 312–13. The Duse–Mussolini encounter is described in Signorelli 1955, p. 369. Gielgud's description of Duse in *Ghosts* in Gielgud pp. 38–40. Mamoulian is in Signorelli 1962 (unable to find the original, presumably in English, I have had to translate Signorelli's Italian version).

Chapter Eighteen

Stark Young's open letter to Duse in Young, *The Flower in Drama*, pp. 155–62. Duse's telegrams and letters to Morris Gest and many other documents associated with the last tour are in the Humanities Research Center, Austin. Reviews and articles from Anfuso. Eva Le Gallienne in Le Gallienne. Fortune Gallo's comments on the last tour, in Gallo. Galli-Curci and Duse, in Moore. For Amy Lowell and Duse, see Damon and Gould. Enif Roberts' diary in Ridenti, pp. 89–90, and in Fusero, p. 406. Maria Avogadro's letter to Schneider, in Schneider p. 143.

Bibliography

The following list is not meant to be a definitive Duse Bibliography. The amount of writing about Duse is enormous—there is hardly a memoir or a collection of letters of the period in which she is not mentioned—and I have listed chiefly the books and articles that I have read and, in most cases, found useful. Here I would like to express my admiration for my predecessors, especially the invaluable Olga Signorelli, whose affectionate and pioneering work on Duse was of inestimable value. I have relied on it often, as the notes will make clear. For information about other actors of Duse's time, about theatres, and about dramatists, I have made considerable use of the Enciclopedia dello spettacolo.

I *Books on Duse*

Antona Traversi, Camillo, *Eleonora Duse, sua vita, sua gloria, suo martirio*. succ. Nistri-Lischi, Pisa, 1926

Benassi, Memo, *L'ultimo viaggio di Eleonora*. Neri Pozza, Vicenza, 1967

Boglione, Giuseppe, *L'arte della Duse*. Boglione, Roma, 1960

Bolla, Nino, *Eleonora Duse nell'amore e nell'arte*. Edizioni Italia, Milano, 1954

Bordeaux, Jeanne, *Eleonora Duse: The Story of Her Life*. Doran, New York, n.d. (but 1925)

Bullo, C., *Eleonora Duse e suo nonno*. Venezia, 1897

Cimoroni, Oreste, *Eleonora Duse*. Garzanti, Milano, 1940

Ferruggia, Gemma, *La nostra vera Duse*. Sonzogno, Milano, 1924

Fried, Alfred, *Führer durch das Gastspiel der Eleonora Duse*. Fried, Berlin und Leipzig, 1892

Fusero, Clemente, *Eleonora Duse*. dall'Oglio, Milano, 1971

Guerrieri Gerardo, (ed.), *Eleonora Duse nel suo tempo* (texts by Silvio d'Amico, Guido Noccioli, Olga Signorelli). Quaderni del Piccolo teatro 3, Milano, 1962

Guerrieri, Gerardo, *Eleonora Duse e il suo tempo* (catalogue). Canova, Treviso, 1974

Harding, Bertita, *Age Cannot Wither*. Lippincott, Philadelphia and New York, 1947

Le Gallienne, Eva, *The Mystic in the Theatre, Eleonora Duse*. Southern Illinois University Press, Carbondale and Edwardsville, 1965

Mapes, Victor, *Duse and the French*. The Dunlap Society, New York, 1898

Mazzoni, Ofelia, *Con la Duse*. Alpes, Milano, 1927

Nicastro, Luciano, *Confessioni di Eleonora Duse*. Gentile, Milano, 1945

Pontiero, Giovanni (ed.), *Duse on Tour* (Guido Noccioli's Diaries 1906–07). Manchester University Press, Manchester, 1982

Rasi, Luigi, *La Duse*. Bemporad, Firenze, 1901
Ravà, Gino, *Eleonora Duse, note di un suo medico*. Zanetti, Venezia, n.d.
Rheinhardt, E. A., *The Life of Eleonora Duse*. Martin Secker, London, 1930 (English translation of *Das Leben der Eleonora Duse*, Fischer, Berlin, 1928)
Ridenti, Lucio, *La Duse minore*. Casini, Roma, 1966
Schneider, Edouard, *Eleonora Duse*. Grasset, Paris, 1925
Signorelli, Olga, *Eleonora Duse*. Casini, Roma, 1955 (revised version of *Eleonora Duse*, originally published by Angelo Signorelli editore, Roma, 1938)
Signorelli, Olga, *Eleonora Duse*. Silvana, Milano, 1959
Signorelli, Olga, *Vita di Eleonora Duse*. Cappelli, Bologna, 1962
Stubbs, Jean, *Eleanora* [sic] *Duse*. Stein and Day, New York, 1970
Symons, Arthur, *Eleonora Duse*. Duffield, New York, 1927
Vergani, Leonardo, *Eleonora Duse*. Martello, Milano, 1958
Winwar, Frances, *Wingless Victory*. Harper & Bros., New York, 1956

II *Correspondence*

Medici, Mario and Conati, Marcello (eds.), *Carteggio Verdi-Boito*. Istituto di studi verdiani, Parma, 1978
Nardi, Piero (ed.), *Carteggio D'Annunzio–Duse*. Le Monnier, Firenze, 1975
Radice, Raul (ed.), *Eleonora Duse Arrigo Boito Lettere d'amore*. Il saggiatore, Milano, 1979
Rolland, Romain; Lugné-Poe. Aurélien. *Correspondance 1894–1901*. L'Arche, Paris, 1957
Setti, Dora (ed.), *Eleonora Duse ad Antonietta Pisa*. Ceschina, Milano, 1972
Setti, Dora (ed.), *La Duse com'era*. Pan editrice. Milano, 1978
Sieber-Rilke, and Sieber, C. (eds.), *Rainer Maria Rilke: Briefe aus den Jahren 1907 bis 1914*. Insel-Verlag, Leipzig, 1933
Spaziani, Marcello, *Con Gégé Primoli nella Roma bizantina*. Edizioni di Storia e letteratura. Roma, 1962
Tosi, Guy (ed.). *Gabriele D'Annunzio à Georges Hérelle*. Denoël, Paris, 1946

III *Books in which Duse or people connected with her appear prominently*

Alexander, Alfred, *Giovanni Verga*. Grant & Cutler. London, 1972

Antona Traversi, Camillo, *Ricordi parigini*. La Lucerna, Ancona, 1929
Antonigini, Tom, *Vita segreta di Gabriele D'Annunzio*. Mondadori, Milano, 1938
Butler, E. M., *Rainer Maria Rilke*. Cambridge University Press, Cambridge, 1941
Calvé, Emma, *Sous tous les ciels j'ai chanté*. Plon, Paris, 1940
Cattaneo, G., *Verga*. UTET. Torino, 1963
Ceccuti, C. and Vannucci, M. (eds.), *Immagini nelle parole: Ugo Ojetti*. Longanesi, Milano, 1978
Cenni, Alessandra (ed.), *Sibilla Aleramo, Lettere d'amore a Lina*. Savelli, Roma, 1982
Cenni, G. V., *Arte e vita prodigiosa di Ermete Zacconi*. Ceschina, Milano, 1945
Chiara, Piero. *Vita di Gabriele D'Annunzio*. Mondadori, Milano, 1978
Damerini, Gino. *D'Annunzio a Venezia*, Mondadori, Milano, 1943
Damon, S. Foster, *Amy Lowell, a chronicle*. Archon, Hamden CT, 1966
D'Annunzio, Gabriele, *Libro segreto* (in *Prose di ricerca II*). Mondadori, Milano, 1950
D'Annunzio, *Taccuini*. Mondadori, Milano, 1965 (a cura di Enrica Bianchetti e Roberto Forcella)
D'Annunzio, *Altri taccuini*. Mondadori, Milano, 1976 (a cura di Enrica Bianchetti)
D'Annunzio romano (various authors). Palombi, Roma, 1963
Duncan, Isadora, *My Life*. Boni & Liveright, New York, 1927
Ellmann, Richard, *James Joyce*. Oxford University Press, London, 1959
Gallarati Scotti, Tommaso, *Due drammi e la Duse*. Mondadori, Milano, 1963
Gallo, Fortune, *Lucky Rooster*. Exposition Press, New York, 1967
Gielgud, John, *An Actor and His Time*. Sidgwick & Jackson, London, 1979
Gould, Jean, *Amy*. Dodd Mead, New York, 1975
Guilbert, Yvette, *La Passante Emerveillé*. Grasset, Paris, 1929
Infusino, Gianni (ed.), *Matilde Serao tra giornalismo e letteratura*. Guida, Napoli, 1981
Jandolo, Augusto, *Le memorie di un antiquario*. Ceschina, Milano, 1935
Lugné-Poe, Aurélien, *Sous les Etoiles*. Gallimard, Paris, 1933
Luhan, Mabel Dodge, *European Experiences* (volume two of *Intimate Memories*). Harcourt Brace, New York, 1933 (reissued 1971)
Marchetti, Arnaldo (ed.), *Puccini com'era*. Curci, Milano, 1973
Mariano, Emilio, *Sentimento del vivere ovvero*

Gabriele D'Annunzio. Mondadori, Milano, 1962

Montesquiou, Robert de, *Mémoires*, Tome II, Emile-Paul Frères, Paris, 1923

Moore, Edward C., *Forty Years of Opera in Chicago.* Horace Liveright, New York, 1930

Nardi, Piero, *Vita di Arrigo Boito.* Mondadori, Milano, 1942

Nardi, Piero, *Vita e tempo di Giuseppe Giacosa.* Mondadori, Milano, 1949

Nicastro, Luciano, *La nostra salvezza (Lettere di guerra 1915–1918).* Libreria della Voce, Firenze, 1918

Ojetti, Ugo, *Cose viste* (vols: I–V). Treves, Milano, 1923–31

Pardieri, Giuseppe, *Ermete Zacconi.* Cappelli, Bologna, 1960

Parmiero, Benigno, *Con D'Annunzio alla Capponcina.* Vallecchi, Firenze, 1938

Paskowski Papini, Viola, *La bambina guardava.* Mondadori, Milano, 1956

Prideaux, Tom, *Love or Nothing* (The Life and Times of Ellen Terry). Scribner's, New York, 1975

Primoli, Joseph-Napoléon, *Pages inédites* (Spaziani, M., ed.). Edizioni di storia e letteratura, Roma, 1959

Pullini, Giorgio, *Marco Praga.* Cappelli, Bologna, 1960

Rolland, Romain, *Mémoires* (introduction by A. Wormser). Cercle du Bibliophile, Paris, 1971

Rhodes, Anthony, *The Poet as Superman: D'Annunzio.* Weidenfeld and Nicolson, London, 1959

Scarfoglio, Edoardo, *Il libro di Don Chisciotte,* La Rinascita del libro, Firenze, 1911 (nuova edizione)

Seroff, Victor, *The Real Isadora.* Dial, New York, 1971

Simone (Benda), *Sous de nouveaux soleils.* Gallimard, Paris, 1957

Skinner, Cornelia Otis, *Madame Sarah.* Houghton Mifflin, Boston, 1967

Sorel, Cécile, *Les belles heures de ma Vie.* Editions du Rocher, Monaco, 1946

Steegmuller, Francis, *Your Isadora.* Macmillan, New York, 1974

Swanson, Gloria, *Swanson on Swanson.* Random House, New York, 1980

Talli, Virgilio, *La mia vita di teatro I.* Treves, Milano, 1927

Terry, Ellen, *The Story of My Life.* McClure, New York, 1908

Zacconi, Ermete, *Ricordi e battaglie.* Garzanti, Milano, 1946

IV   *Volumes of criticism with discussion of Duse*

Bahr, Hermann, *Studien zur Kritik der Moderne.* Ruiten & Loening, Frankfurt a.M., 1894

Beerbohm, Max, *Around Theatres.* Greenwood Press, New York, 1968 (reissue of 1930 edition)

Bracco, Roberto, *Tra le arti e gli artisti.* Giannini, Napoli, 1919

d'Amico, Silvio, *Cronache del teatro 1914–1928.* Laterza, Bari, 1963

Huneker, James, *Iconoclasts.* Scribner's, New York, 1905

Shaw, G. B., *Our Theatres in the Nineties,* vol. III. Constable, London, 1932

Simoni, Renato, *Trent'anni di cronaca drammatica.* Società editrice torinese, Torino, 1951

Young, Stark, *Glamour.* Scribner's, New York, 1925

Young, Stark, *The Flower in Drama.* Scribner's, New York, 1925

V   *Books on the Italian theatre and on the period*

Boccardi, Alberto, *Teatro e vita.* Balestra, Trieste, 1905

Casoni, Luigi, *Il Cagnoni ha cento anni.* Teatro comunale, Vigevano, 1973

Cauda, Giuseppe, *Chiaroscuro di palcoscenico.* Galimberti, Savigliano, 1910

Ciotti Cavaletto, Giovanna, *Attrici e società nell'Ottocento italiano.* Mursia, Milano, 1978

Costetti, Giuseppe, *Il teatro italiano nel 1800.* Cappelli, Rocca San Casciano, 1901

Costetti, Giuseppe, *La compagnia reale sarda e il teatro italiano dal 1821 al 1855.* Kantorowicz, Milano, 1893

Doglio, Federico, *Teatro e Risorgimento.* Cappelli, Bologna, 1961

Faccioli, Emilio (ed.) *Il teatro italiano: La tragedia dell'Ottocento,* 3 vols. Einaudi, Torino, 1981

Ferrone, Siro (ed.), *Teatro dell'Italia unita.* Il Saggiatore, Milano, 1980

Ferrone, Siro (ed.), *Il teatro italiano: La commedia e il drama borghese dell'Ottocento,* 3 vols. Einaudi, Torino, 1979

Frajese, Vittorio, *Dal Costanzi all 'Opera,* 4 vols. Capitolium, Roma, 1977

Ghirelli, Antonio, *Napoli italiana,* Einaudi, Torino, 1977

Lenotti, Tullio, *L'arena di Verona.* Edizioni di "Vita veronese," Verona, 1972

Monaco, Vanda, *La repubblica del teatro (momenti italiani 1796–1860).* LeMonnier, Firenze, 1968

Pandolfi, Vito, *Antologia del grande attore*. Laterza, Bari, 1954

Possenti, Eligio, *Vita segreta del teatro*. Garzanti, Milano, 1948

Scalera, Erminio, *Dal Fiorentini all'Eldorado*. Fausto Fiorentino editore, Napoli, 1971

Tofano, Sergio, *Il teatro all'antica italiana*. Rizzoli, Milano, 1965

VI *Articles*

Chiara, Piero, "Le grida e i sussurri nelle lettere inedite della Duse tradita" in *Il Corriere della sera*, Milano, 18 April 1976

Courtault-Deslandes, "Paul Claudel et Eleonora Duse" in *Bulletin de la Société Paul Claudel*, No. 72, Paris, 1978

Courtault-Deslandes, "Eleonora Duse attrice cinematografica" in *Notiziario* del Museo nazionale del cinema, Torino, nn. 34–5–6, Anni XVI, XVII, XVIII, gennaio 1977–dicembre 1979

Craig, Gordon, "On Signora Eleonora Duse" in *The Dial*, New York, May 1928

D'Annunzio, Renata, "A Nettuno con la Signora" in *Il tempo*, Roma, 8 January 1950

D'Annunzio, Renata, "Addio alla 'Signora'" in *Il tempo*, Roma, 9 January 1950

de Cesco, Bruno, "Contrattempi, entusiasmi e quasi drammi nei rapporti d'arte fra la Duse e Verona" in *Verona fedele*, Verona, 28 February 1982

De Flavis, C., 'Il Teatro dei Fiorentini nei secoli XVIII e XIX" in *La lettura*, Milano, ottobre 1921

Gilder, Rosamond, "La Nostalgilder: Some letters of Eleonora Duse" in *Theatre Arts Monthly*, New York, January 1926

Gramatica, Emma, "Per la mia signora" in *La lettura*, Milano, 1 April 1931

Hofmannsthal, Hugo von, "Eleonora Duse: Eine Wiener Theaterwoche" in *Gesammelte Werke*, Prosa I (Steiner, H. ed.). S. Fischer, Frankfurt a.M., 1956

Infusino, Gianni, "Napoli e la Serao: La Duse" in *Napoli in terza pagina*, Guida, Napoli, 1980

Leblanc, Georgette, "Mes conversations avec Eléonora Duse" in *Oeuvres libres*, Paris (n.d.)

Lugné-Poe, Aurélien, "Avec Eléonora Duse au Brésil" in *Revue bleue*, 70e année, No. 24, Paris, 17 December 1932

Maddalena, Edgardo, "La Duse a Vienna" in *Rivista teatrale italiana*, V. 9, 3, pp. 72–83, Napoli, March 1905

Pirandello, Luigi, "The Art of Duse" in *The Columbian Monthly*, Vol. I, no. 7, New York, July 1928

Praga, Marco, "Malinconie" in *La Lettura*, Milano, February 1920 (reprinted in *Ricordi di Marco Praga*, Roma, 1959)

Primoli, Joseph-Napoléon, "La Duse" in *La Revue de Paris*, Paris, 1 juin 1897

Serao, Matilde, "La famiglia della Duse" in *Matilde Serao, vita opere testimonianze* (Infusino, G., ed.) Quarto potere, Napoli, marzo 1977

Vazzoler, Laura, "Eleonora Duse e Arrigo Boito: lo spettacolo sull' 'Antonio e Cleopatra' di Shakespeare" in *Biblioteca teatrale*, 6/7, Bulzoni, Roma, 1973

VII *Cinema*

Lindsay, Vachel, *The Art of the Moving Picture*. Liveright, New York, 1915

Prolo, Maria Adriana, *Storia del cinema muto italiano*. Poligono, Milano, 1951

Sources of illustrations

Milan, Museo Teatrale alla Scala: 13, 14, 16, 17, 48
Naples, Collection Carlo Knight: 5
New York, Museum of Modern Art Film Stills Archive: 41, 42, 43
Rome, Biblioteca Teatrale del Burcardo: 1, 6, 7, 8, 11, 15, 18, 19, 20, 21, 22, 33, 34, 35, 36, 37, 38

Rome, Collection Luisa Chiarelli: 45
Rome, Fondazione Primoli: 23, 24, 25, 39
Venice, Instituto di Storia dell'Arte, Fondazione Giorgio Cini: 2, 3, 4, 9, 10, 12, 26, 27, 29, 30, 31, 32, 40, 44, 46, 47, 49, 50, 51, 52, 53

Index

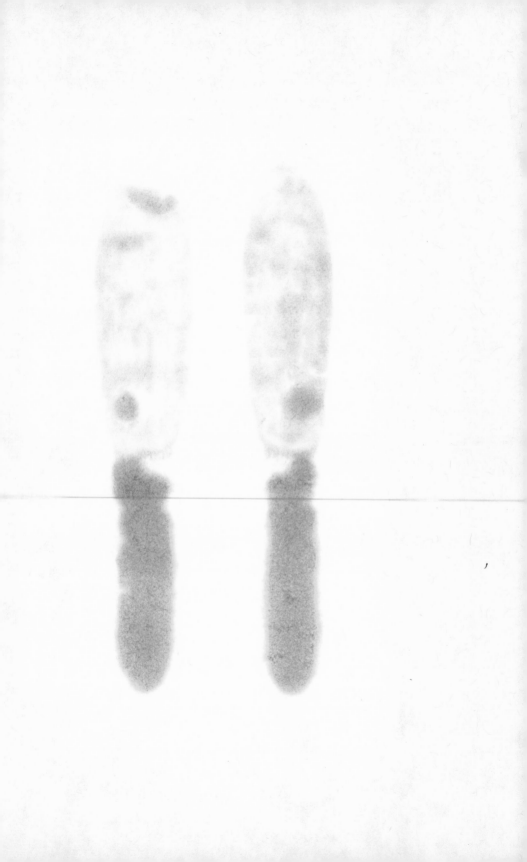